History of Dogma

ADOLPH HARNACK

History of Dogma

VOLUME THREE

New York

RUSSELL AND RUSSELL

The Library of Congress has cataloged
this book as follows:

Harnack, Adolf von, 1851–1930.
　　History of dogma. Translated from the 3d German ed.,
by Neil Buchanan. ₍New York, Russell & Russell, 1958₎

　　　　7 v. 23 cm. (Theological translation library, v. 2, 7–12)

　　　　Vols. 3, 5 translated by J. Millar; v. 4, by E. B. Speirs and J. Millar;
v. 6–7, by W. M'Gilchrist.
　　　　Translation of Lehrbuch der Dogmengeschichte.

　　　　1. Theology, Doctrinal—Hist.　　(Series: Theological translation
library, v. 2 ₍etc.₎)
　　　　　　　　　　　　　　Full name: Carl Gustav Adolf von Harnack.

BT21.H33　1958　　　　　　230　　　　　　　58–12862

Library of Congress

Printed in the United States of America by

NOBLE OFFSET PRINTERS, INC.

EDITOR'S PREFACE.

THE first chapter in this volume forms the concluding chapter of the First Volume of the German Work. It answers to the Seventh Chapter of the Second Book of the first great division of the subject, which has for its aim to shew the *origin of Ecclesiastical Dogma*. The First Book treats of the Preparation for Dogma; the Second of the Laying of the Foundation. This Second Book begins with the second volume of the English Translation, and closes with the first chapter of the third volume now published. Thereafter commences the Second Part of the Work, which deals with the *Development of Dogma*. The numbering of the chapters here begins anew, running on from I. to VI.

The Second Volume of the German Work commences with the Second Part, and tells the story of the Development of Dogma till the time of Augustine. Only a portion of it appears in this volume. The remainder will form the contents of the Fourth Volume. The author has prefixed to the volume two prefaces, one to the first, the other to the third Edition. These are here given.

The Appendix on Manichæism is the last of four which appear at the end of the first volume of the German Edition. The first three of these will be found at the end of the first volume of the English Edition.

A. B. BRUCE.

Glasgow, August, 1897.

AUTHOR'S PREFACE TO FIRST EDITION OF VOLUME II. OF THE GERMAN WORK.

The first half of the second part of the History of Dogma is here given apart and as the second volume, because it is complete in itself, and I shall be prevented from completing the work at once by other tasks.

The account contained in the following pages would have been shorter, if I could have persuaded myself of the correctness of the opinion, that a single, all-determining thought obtained its true development in the History of Dogma from the fourth to the eighth century. This opinion dominates, apart from a few monographs, all writings on the History of Dogma, and gives a uniform impress to the accounts of Protestants and Catholics. I share it within certain limits; but these very limits, which I have endeavoured to define, [1] have not yet received due attention. In the fourth century the formula that was correct, when judged by the conception of redemption of the ancient Church, prevailed; but the Fathers, who finally secured its triumph, did not give it the exposition which it originally demanded. In the fifth century, or the seventh, on the contrary, a formula that, measured by the same standard, was incorrect, prevailed; yet it was associated with an exposition that to some extent compensated for the incorrectness. In both cases, however, the imperfections of the conclusion, which are explained from various circumstances, became of the highest importance. For in them we find the reason why the phantom Christ did not wholly oust the historical; and, in order to overcome them, men turned anew to Philosophy, especially to Aristotle. The orthodox Church owes two things to the incorrect form in which the Trinitarian and Christological Dogma was finally stated: (1) contact with the Gospel, and (2) renewed contact with ancient science, *i.e.*, scholasticism.

[1] *Vide* pp. 167 ff. of this volume.

The account of these conditions demanded a more minute discussion of the process of the History of Dogma, than is usual in the ordinary text-books. Dogma developed slowly and amid great obstacles. No single step should be overlooked in the description, and, in particular, the period between the fourth and fifth Councils is not less important than any other. Political relationships, at no point decisive by themselves, yet everywhere required, as well as western influences, careful attention. I should have discussed them still more thoroughly, if I had not been restrained by considerations of the extent of the book. I have included the state of affairs and developments in the West, so far as they were related to, and acted upon, those in the East. In the following Book I shall begin with Augustine. The scientific theological expositions of the Fathers have only been brought under review, where they appeared indispensable for the understanding of Dogma. In any case I was not afraid of doing too much here. I am convinced that a shorter description ought not to be offered to students of Theology, unless it were to be a mere guide. The history of Christian Dogma—perhaps the most complicated history of development which we can completely review—presents the investigator with the greatest difficulties; and yet it is, along with the study of the New Testament, and in the present position of Protestantism, the most important discipline for every one who seeks really to study Theology. The theologian who leaves the University without being thoroughly familiar with it, is, in the most critical questions, helplessly at the mercy of the authorities of the day. But the royal way to the understanding of the History of Dogma, opened up by F. Chr. Baur, and pursued by Thomasius, does not lead to the goal; for by it we become acquainted with the historical matter only in the abbreviated form required for the defence of the completed Dogma.

The history of the *development* of Dogma does not offer the lofty interest, which attaches to that of its *genesis*. When we return from the most complicated and elaborate doctrinal formulas, from the mysticism of the Cultus and Christian Neoplatonism, from the worship of saints and ceremonial ritual of the seventh and eighth centuries, back to Origen and the third century, we are astonished to find that all we have mentioned was really in existence at the earlier date. Only it existed then amid a mass of different material, and its footing was insecure. In many respects the whole historical development of Dogma from the fourth century to John of Damascus and Theodore of Studion was simply a vast process of reduction, selection, and definition. In the

East we are no longer called upon to deal in any quarter with new and original matter, but always rather with what is traditional, derivative, and, to an increasing extent, superstitious. Yet that to which centuries devoted earnest reflection, holding it to be sacred, will never lose its importance, as long as there still exists among us a remnant of the same conditions which belonged to those times. But who could deny that those conditions—in the Church and in learning —are still powerful among us? Therefore even the religious formulas are still in force which were created in the Byzantine age; nay, they are the dogmas κατ ἐξοχήν in all Churches, so that the popular idiom is nowise wrong which with the word "dogma" primarily designates the doctrines of the Trinity and the divine humanity of Christ. The inquirer who follows the development of these dogmas after the fourth century, and who, owing to the want of originality and freshness in his material, loses pleasure in his work, is ever and again reanimated, when he considers that he has to deal with matters which have gained, and still exercise, an immense power over the feelings and minds of men. And how much it is still possible for us to learn, as free Evangelical Christians, especially after generations of scholars have dedicated to this history the most devoted industry, so that no one can enter into their labours without becoming their disciples!

I know very well that it would be possible to treat the material reviewed in this book more universally than I have done. My chief purpose was to show how matters arose and were *in their concrete manifestation*. But the task of making dogma really intelligible in all its aspects within the limits of a History of Dogma, is after all as insoluble as any similar problem which isolates a single object from Universal History, and requires its investigation in and by itself. This limitation I need only recall. But something further has to be said. Dogmas, undoubtedly, admit of a process of refinement, which would bring them closer to our understanding and our feeling. But my powers are not equal to this lofty task, and even if I possessed the uncommon qualities of the psychologist and the religious philosopher, I should have hesitated about employing them in this book; for I did not wish to endanger the reliability of what I had to present by reflections, which must always remain more or less subjective. Thus I have limited myself to a few hints; these will only be found where the nature of the material itself induced me to seek for the far remote thought underlying the expression.

I have throughout striven in this volume, to give such an account as

would demand to be read connectedly; for a work on the history of
dogma, which is used only for reference, has missed its highest aim.
I have believed that I could not dispense with the addition of numerous
notes, but the text of the book is so written that the reader, if he
prefers it, may disregard them.

Marburg, 14 June, 1887.

PREFACE TO THE THIRD EDITION.

I HAVE subjected this volume to a thorough revision, and have
sought to improve and strengthen it in not a few places. May this new
edition also promote the study of a historical period whose products
are still held by many among us to be incapable of reform.

Berlin, 28 May, 1894.   ADOLF HARNACK.

CONTENTS.

FIRST PART: SECOND BOOK CONTINUED. [1]

[1] *Vide* Editor's Preface to this volume.

SECOND PART.

THE DEVELOPMENT OF ECCLESIASTICAL DOGMA.

FIRST BOOK.

*The History of the Development of Dogma as the Doctrine of
the God-man on the basis of Natural Theology.*

A.—*Presuppositions of Doctrine of Redemption or Natural Theology.*

B.— *The doctrine of Redemption in the Person of the God-man, in its
historical development.*

CHAPTER I.

THE DECISIVE SUCCESS OF THEOLOGICAL SPECULATION IN THE SPHERE OF THE RULE OF FAITH, OR, THE DEFINING OF THE NORM OF THE DOCTRINE OF THE CHURCH DUE TO THE ADOPTION OF THE LOGOS CHRISTOLOGY. [1]

1. *Introduction.*

FROM the great work of Irenæus and the anti-gnostic writings of Tertullian, it would seem as if the doctrine of the Logos, or, the doctrine of the pre-existence of Christ as a distinct person, was at the end of the second century an undisputed tenet of Church orthodoxy, and formed a universally recognised portion of the baptismal confession interpreted anti-gnostically, *i.e.*, of the rule of faith. [2] But certain as it is that the Logos Christology was in the second century not merely the property of a few Christian philosophers, [3] it is, on the other hand, as clear that it did not belong to the solid structure of the Catholic faith. It was not on the same footing as, *e.g.*, the doctrines of God the Creator, the real body of Christ, the resurrection of the body, etc. The great conflicts which, after c. A.D. 170,

---

[1] See Dorner, Entw.-Gesch. d. Lehre v. d. Person Christi, 1 Thl. 1845; Lange, Gesch. u. Entw. der Systeme der Unitarier vor der nic. Synode, 1831; Hagemann, Die römische Kirche und ihr Einfluss auf Disciplin und Dogma in den ersten drei Jahrh. 1864, (the most important and most stimulating monograph on the subject); and my art. 'Monarchianismus' in Herzog's R. E., 2nd ed., vol. X., pp. 178—213, on which the following arguments are based.

[2] See Vol. II., pp. 20—38 and Iren. I. 10, 1; Tertull. De præscr. 13; Adv. Prax. 2. In the rule of faith, De virg., vel. 1, there is no statement as to the pre-existence of the Son of God.

[3] See Vol. I., p. 192, Note (John's Gospel, Revelation, Κήρυγμα Πέτρου, Ignatius, and esp. Celsus in Orig. II. 31, etc.).

were waged for more than a century *within* the Catholic Church rather show, that the doctrine only gradually found its way into the creed of the Church. [1] But a higher than merely Christological interest attaches to the gradual incorporation of the Logos doctrine in the rule of faith. *The formula of the Logos, as it was almost universally understood, legitimised speculation, i.e., Neo-platonic philosophy, within the creed of the Church.* [2] When Christ was designated the incarnate Logos of God, and when this was set up as His supreme characterisation, men were directed to think of the divine in Christ as the reason of God realised in the structure of the world and the history of mankind. This implied a definite philosophical view of God, of creation, and of the world, and the baptismal confession became a compendium of scientific dogmatics, *i.e.*, of a system of doctrine entwined with the Metaphysics of Plato and the Stoics. But at the same time an urgent impulse necessarily made itself felt to define the contents and value of the Redeemer's life and work, not, primarily, from the point of view of the proclamation of the Gospel, and the hopes of a future state, but from that of the cosmic significance attaching to his divine nature concealed in the flesh. Insomuch, however, as such a view could only really reach and be intelligible to those who had been trained in philosophical speculations, the establishing of the Logos Christology within the rule of faith was equivalent for the great mass of Christians to the setting up of a mystery, which in the first place could only make an impression through its high-pitched formulas and the glamour of the incomprehensible. But as soon as a religion expresses the

[1] The observation that Irenæus and Tertullian treat it as a fixed portion of the rule of faith is very instructive; for it shows that these theologians were ahead of the Church of their time. Here we have a point given, at which we can estimate the relation of what Irenæus maintained to be the creed of the Church, to the doctrine which was, as a matter of fact, generally held at the time in the Church. We may turn this insight to account for the history of the Canon and the constitution, where, unfortunately, an estimate of the statements of Irenæus is rendered difficult.

[2] By Neo-platonic philosophy we, of course, do not here mean Neo-platonism, but the philosophy (in method and also in part, in results), developed before Neo-platonism by Philo, Valentinus, Numenius, and others.

loftiest contents of its creed in formulas which must remain
mysterious and unintelligible to the great mass of its adherents,
those adherents come under guardians. In other words, the
multitude must believe in the creed; at the same time they no
longer derive from it directly the motives of their religious and
moral life; and they are dependent on the theologians, who,
as professors of the mysterious, alone understand and are capable of interpreting and practically applying the creed. The
necessary consequence of this development was that the mysterious creed, being no longer in a position practically to control
life, was superseded by *the authority of the Church, the cultus,
and prescribed duties,* in determining the religious life of the
laity; while the theologians, or the priests, appeared alone as
the possessors of an independent faith and knowledge. But as
soon as the laity were actuated by a desire for religious independence, which produced a reaction, and yet was not powerful enough to correct the conditions out of which this state of
matters arose, there made its appearance only an expedient of
a conservative sort, viz., the order of the monks. As this order
did not tamper with the prevailing system of the Church, the
Church could tolerate it, and could even use it as a valve, by
which to provide an outlet for all religious subjectivity, and
for the energies of a piety that renounced the world. The history of the Church shows us, or, at any rate, lets us divine,
this situation at the transition from the 3rd to the 4th century.
On the one hand, we see—at least in the East—that the
Christian faith had become a theology, which was regarded, to
all intents without question, as the revealed faith, and only
capable of being represented and expounded by "teachers".
On the other hand, we find a lay Christendom tied to the priest,
the cultus, the sacraments, and a ceremonial penitence, and
revering the creed as a mystery. Between these arose with
elemental force the order of the monks, which—apart from a
few phenomena—did not attack the ecclesiastical system, and
which could not be suppressed by priests and theologians, because it strove to realise on earth the object to which they
themselves had subordinated the whole of theology, because it,
as it were, sought to soar on wings to the same height, to

which the steps of the long ladders constructed by theology were meant to conduct. [1]

Now the incorporation in the creed of philosophic (Platonic) speculation, *i.e.*, the Hellenising of the traditional doctrines, was not the only condition, but it was certainly one of the most important of the conditions, that led to the rise of this three-fold Christendom of clergy, laity, and monks, in the Church. That the Catholic Church was capable of accommodating these three orders in its midst is a proof of its power. That the combination forms up to the present day the signature of Catholic Churches is evidence, moreover, of the practical value attached by the Church to this unified differentiation. It, in fact, could not but best correspond to the different wants of men united to form a universal Church. So far as it was a consequence of the general conditions under which the Church existed in the third century, we must here leave its origin untouched, [2] but so far as it was due to the reception of philosophical speculation into the Church, its prior history must be presented. Yet it may not be superfluous to begin by noticing expressly, that the confidence with which first the Apologists identified the Logos of the philosophers and the Christ of faith, and the zeal with which the anti-gnostic Fathers then incorporated the Logos-Christ in the creed of believers, are also to be explained from a Christian interest. In their scientific conception of the world the Logos had a fixed place, and was held to be the "alter ego" of God, though at the same time he was also regarded as the representative of the Reason that operated in the Cosmos. Their conception of Christ as the appearance of the Logos in a personal form only proves that they sought to make the highest possible assertion concerning him, to justify worship being rendered him, and to demonstrate the absolute and unique nature of the contents of the Christian religion. The Christian religion was only in a position to gain the cultured, to conquer Gnosticism, and to thrust aside Polytheism in the Roman empire, because it had concluded an alliance with that intellectual potentate which already swayed the minds and hearts of the

[1] See my lecture on Monachism, 3rd ed. 1886.
[2] Yet see Vol. II., pp. 122—127.

best men, the philosophic-religious ethics of the age. This alliance found expression in the formula: Christ *is* word and law (Χριστὸς λόγος καὶ νόμος). The philosophic Christology arose, so to speak, at the circumference of the Church, and thence moved gradually to the centre of the Christian faith. The same is true of theology generally; its most concise description is philosophic Christology. A complete fusion of the old faith and theology, one that tranquillised the minds of the devout, was not consummated till the fourth, strictly speaking, indeed, till the fifth century (Cyril of Alexandria). Valentinus, Origen, the Cappadocians mark the stages of the process. Valentinus was very speedily ejected as a heretic. Origen, in spite of the immense influence which he exerted, was in the end unable to retain his footing in the Church. The Cappadocians almost perfected the complete fusion of the traditional faith of the Church conceived as mystery and philosophy, by removing Origen's distinction between those who knew and those who believed (Gnostics and Pistics); meanwhile they retained much that was comparatively free and looked on with suspicion by the traditionalists. Cyril's theology first marked the complete agreement between faith and philosophy, authority and speculation, an agreement which finally, in the sixth century, suppressed every independent theology. But from the end of the second century up to the closing years of the third, the fundamental principle of philosophic theology had naturalised itself, in the very faith of the Church. This process in which, on the one hand, certain results of speculative theology became legitimised within the Church as revelations and mysteries, and on the other—as a sort of antidote—the freedom of theology was limited, is to be described in what follows.

It has been shown above (Vol. I., p. 190 ff.) that about the middle of the second century there existed side by side in the Churches chiefly two conceptions of the person of Christ. In the *Adoptian* view Jesus was regarded as the man in whom divinity or the spirit of God dwelt, and who was finally exalted to godlike honour. In the *Pneumatic* conception, Jesus was looked upon as a heavenly spirit who assumed an earthly body. The latter was adopted in their speculations by the Apologists.

The fixing of the apostolic tradition, which took place in opposition to the Gnostics, as also to the so-called Montanists, in the course of the second half of the second century, did not yet decide in favour of either view.[1] The Holy Scriptures could be appealed to in support of both. But those had decidedly the best of it, in the circumstances of the time, who recognised the incarnation of a special divine nature in Christ; and as certainly were the others in the right, in view of the Synoptic gospels, who saw in Jesus the man chosen to be his Son by God, and possessed of the Spirit. The former conception corresponded to the interpretation of the O. T. theophanies which had been accepted by the Alexandrians, and had proved so convincing in apologetic arguments;[2] it could be supported by the testimony of a series of Apostolic writings, whose authority was absolute;[3] it protected the O. T. against Gnostic criticism. It, further, reduced the highest conception of the value of Christianity to a brief and convincing formula: "*God became man in order that men might become gods;*" and, finally,—which was not least—it could be brought, with little trouble, into line with

[1] The points, which, as regards Christ, belonged in the second half of the second century to ecclesiastical orthodoxy, are given in the clauses of the Roman baptismal confession to which ἀληθῶς is added, in the precise elaboration of the idea of creation, in the εἷς placed alongside Χριστὸς Ἰησοῦς, and in the identification of the Catholic institution of the Church with the Holy Church.

[2] The Christian doctrine of the Son of God could be most easily rendered acceptable to cultured heathens by means of the Logos doctrine; see the memorable confession of Celsus placed by him in the lips of his "Jew" (II. 31): ὡς εἴγε ὁ λόγος ἐστὶν ὑμῖν υἱὸς τοῦ Θεοῦ, καὶ ἡμεῖς ἐπαινοῦμεν; see also the preceding: σοφίζονται οἱ Χριστιανοὶ ἐν τῷ λέγειν τὸν υἱὸν τοῦ Θεοῦ εἶναι αὐτολόγον.

[3] The conviction of the harmony of the Apostles, or, of all Apostolic writings, could not but result in the Christology of the Synoptics and the Acts being interpreted in the light of John and Paul, or more accurately, in that of the philosophic Christology held to be attested by John and Paul. It has been up to the present day the usual fate of the Synoptics, and with them of the sayings of Jesus, to be understood, on account of their place in the Canon, in accordance with the caprices of the dogmatics prevalent at the time, Pauline and Johannine theology having assigned to it the role of mediator. The "lower" had to be explained by the "higher" (see even Clemens Alex. with his criticism of the "pneumatic", the spiritual, Fourth Gospel, as compared with the first three). In older times men transformed the sense right off; nowadays they speak of *steps* which lead to the *higher* teaching, and they dress the old illusion with a new *scientific* mantle.

the cosmological and theological tenets which had been borrowed from the religious philosophy of the age to serve as a foundation for a rational Christian theology. The adoption of the belief in the divine Logos to explain the genesis and history of the world at once decided the means by which also the divine dignity and sonship of the Redeemer were alone to be defined. [1] In this procedure the theologians themselves had no danger to fear to their monotheism, even if they made the Logos more than a product of the creative will of God. Neither Justin, Tatian, nor any of the Apologists or Fathers show the slightest anxiety on this point. For the infinite substance, resting behind the world,—and as such the deity was conceived— could display and unfold itself in different subjects. It could impart its own inexhaustible being to a variety of bearers, without thereby being emptied, or its unity being dissolved (μοναρχία κατ' οἰκονομίαν, as the technical expression has it). [2] But, lastly, the theologians had no reason to fear for the "deity' of the Christ in whom the incarnation of that Logos was to be viewed. For the conception of the Logos was capable of the most manifold contents, and its dexterous treatment could be already supported by the most instructive precedents. This conception could be adapted to every change and accentuation of the religious interest, every deepening of speculation, as

1 But the substitution of the Logos for the, otherwise undefined, spiritual being (πνεῦμα) in Christ presented another very great advantage. It brought to an end, though not at once (see Clemens Alex.), the speculations which reckoned the heavenly personality of Christ in some way or other in the number of the higher angels or conceived it as one Æon among many. Through the definition of this " Spiritual Being " as Logos his transcendent and unique dignity was firmly outlined and assured. For the Logos was universally accepted as the Prius logically and temporally, and the causa not only of the world, but also of all powers, ideas, æons, and angels. He, therefore, did not belong—at least in every respect—to their order.

2 Augustine first wrought to end this questionable monotheism, and endeavoured to treat seriously the monotheism of the living God. But his efforts only produced an impression in the West, and even there the attempt was weakened from the start by a faulty respect for the prevalent Christology, and was forced to entangle itself in absurd formulas. In the East the accommodating Substance-Monotheism of philosophy remained with its permission of a plurality of divine persons; and this doctrine was taught with such naïvety and simplicity, that the Cappadocians, e.g., proclaimed the Christian conception of God to be the just mean between the polytheism of the heathens and the monotheism of the Jews.

well as to all the needs of the Cultus, nay, even to new results of Biblical exegesis. It revealed itself gradually to be a variable quantity of the most accommodating kind, capable of being at once determined by any new factor received into the theological ferment. It even admitted contents which stood in the most abrupt contradiction to the processes of thought out of which the conception itself had sprung, *i.e.*, contents which almost completely concealed the cosmological genesis of the conception. But it was long before this point was reached. And as long as it was not, as long as the Logos was still employed as the formula under which was comprehended either the original idea of the world, or the rational law of the world, many did not entirely cease to mistrust the fitness of the conception to establish the divinity of Christ. For those, finally, could not but seek to perceive the full deity in the Redeemer, who reckoned on a deification of man. Athanasius first made this possible to them by his explanation of the Logos, but he at the same time began to empty the conception of its original cosmological contents. And the history of Christology from Athanasius to Augustine is the history of the displacing of the Logos conception by the other, destitute of all cosmical contents, of the Son,—the history of the substitution of the immanent and absolute trinity for the economic and relative. The complete divinity of the Son was thereby secured, but in the form of a complicated and artificial speculation, which neither could be maintained without reservation before the tribunal of the science of the day, nor could claim the support of an ancient tradition.

But the first formulated opposition to the Logos Christology did not spring from anxiety for the complete divinity of Christ, or even from solicitude for monotheism; it was rather called forth by interest in the evangelical, the Synoptic, idea of Christ. With this was combined the attack on the use of Platonic philosophy in Christian doctrine. The first public and literary opponents of the Christian Logos-speculations, therefore, did not escape the reproach of depreciating, if not of destroying, the dignity of the Redeemer. It was only in the subsequent period, in a second phase of the controversy, that these opponents of the Logos Christology were able to fling back the reproach at

its defenders. With the Monarchians the first subject of interest
was the man Jesus; then came monotheism and the divine
dignity of Christ. From this point, however, the whole theological interpretation of the two first articles of the rule of faith,
was again gradually involved in controversy. In so far as they
were understood to refute a crude docetism and the severance
of Jesus and Christ they were confirmed. But did not the doctrine of a heavenly æon, rendered incarnate in the Redeemer,
contain another remnant of the old Gnostic leaven? Did not
the sending forth of the Logos (προβολὴ τοῦ λόγου) to create
the world recall the emanation of the æons? Was not ditheism
set up, if two divine beings were to be worshipped? Not only
were the uncultured Christian laity driven to such criticisms,—
for what did they understand by the "economic mode of the
existence of God"?—but also all those theologians who refused
to give any place to Platonic philosophy in Christian dogmatics.
A conflict began which lasted for more than a century, in
certain branches of it for almost two centuries. Who opened
it, or first assumed the aggressive, we know not. The contest
engages our deepest interest in different respects, and can be
described from different points of view. We cannot regard it,
indeed, directly as a fight waged by theology against a still
enthusiastic conception of religion; for the literary opponents
of the Logos Christology were no longer enthusiasts, but, rather,
from the very beginning their declared enemies. Nor was it
directly a war of the theologians against the laity, for it
was not laymen, but only theologians who had adopted the
creed of the laity, who opposed their brethren. [1] We must

---

[1] The Alogi opposed the Montanists and all prophecy; conversely the western
representatives of the Logos Christology, Irenæus, Tertullian and Hippolytus were
Chiliasts. But this feature makes no change in the fact that the incorporation of
the Logos Christology and the fading away of eschatological apocalyptic hopes
went hand in hand. Theologians were able to combine inconsistent beliefs for a
time; but for the great mass of the laity in the East the mystery of the person of
Christ took the place of the Christ who was to have set up his visible Kingdom
of glory upon earth. See especially the refutation of the Chiliasts by Origen
(περὶ ἀρχ. II. 11) and Dionysius Alex. (Euseb. H. E. VII. 24, 25). The continued
embodiment in new visions of those eschatological hopes and apocalyptic fancies
by the monks and laymen of later times, proved that the latter could not make
the received mystery of dogma fruitful for their practical religion.

describe it as the strenuous effort of Stoic Platonism to obtain supremacy in the theology of the Church; the victory of Plato over Zeno and Aristotle in Christian science; the history of the displacement of the historical by the pre-existent Christ, of the Christ of reality by the Christ of thought, in dogmatics; finally, as the victorious attempt to substitute the mystery of the person of Christ for the person Himself, and, by means of a theological formula unintelligible to them, to put the laity with their Christian faith under guardians—a state desired and indeed required by them to an increasing extent. When the Logos Christology obtained a complete victory, the traditional view of the Supreme deity as one person, and, along with this, every thought of the real and complete human personality of the Redeemer was in fact condemned as being intolerable in the Church. Its place was taken by "the nature" [of Christ], which without "the person" is simply a cipher. The defeated party had right on its side, but had not succeeded in making its Christology agree with its conception of the object and result of the Christian religion. This was the very reason of its defeat. A religion which promised its adherents that their nature would be rendered divine, could only be satisfied by a redeemer who in his own person had deified human nature. If, after the gradual fading away of eschatological hopes, the above prospect was held valid, then those were right who worked out this view of the Redeemer.

In accordance with an expression coined by Tertullian, we understand by Monarchians the representatives of strict, not economic, monotheism in the ancient Church. In other words, they were theologians who held firmly by the dignity of Jesus as Redeemer, but at the same time would not give up the personal, the numerical, unity of God; and who therefore opposed the speculations which had led to the adoption of the duality or trinity of the godhead. [1] In order rightly to under-

---

[1] This definition is, in truth, too narrow; for at least a section, if not all, of the so-called Dynamistic Monarchians recognised, besides God, the Spirit as eternal Son of God, and accordingly assumed two Hypostases. But they did not see in Jesus an incarnation of this Holy Spirit, and they were therefore monarchian in their doctrine of Christ. Besides, so far as I know, the name of Monarchians was

stand their position in the history of the genesis of the dogmatics of the Church, it is decisive, as will have been already
clear from the above, that they only came to the front,
after the anti-gnostic understanding of the baptismal confession
had been substantially assured in the Church. It results from
this that they are, generally speaking, to be criticised as men
who appeared on the soil of Catholicism, and that therefore,
apart from the points clearly in dispute, we must suppose agreement between them and their opponents. It is not superfluous
to recall this expressly. The confusion to which the failure to
note this presupposition has led and still continually leads may
be seen, *e.g.,* in the relative section in Dorner's History of the
development of the doctrine of the Person of Christ, or in

not applied in the ancient Church to these, but only to the theologians who taught
that there was in Christ an incarnation of God the Father Himself. It was not
extended to the earlier Dynamistic Monarchians, because, so far as we know, the
question whether God consisted of one or more persons did not enter into the
dispute with them. In a wider sense, the Monarchians could be taken also to
include the Arians, and all those theologians, who, while they recognised the personal
independence of a divine nature in Christ, yet held this nature to have been one
created by God; in any case, the Arians were undoubtedly connected with Paul of
Samosata through Lucian. However, it is not advisable to extend the conception
so widely; for, firstly, we would thus get too far away from the old classification, and,
secondly, it is not to be overlooked that, even in the case of the most thorough-
going Arians, their Christology reacted on their doctrine of God, and their strict
Monotheism was to some extent modified. Hence, both on historical and logical
grounds, it is best for our purpose to understand by Monarchians those theologians
exclusively who perceived in Jesus either a man filled, in a unique way, with the
Spirit, or an incarnation of God the Father; with the reservation, that the former
in certain of their groups regarded the Holy Spirit as a divine Hypostasis, and were
accordingly no longer really Monarchians in the strict sense of the term. For the
rest, the expression "Monarchians" is in so far inappropriate as their opponents
would also have certainly maintained the "monarchia" of God. See Tertulli., Adv.
Prax. 3 f.; Epiphan. H. 62. 3: οὐ πολυθεΐαν εἰσηγούμεθα, ἀλλὰ μοναρχίαν κηρύττομεν.
They would even have cast back at the Monarchians the reproach that they were destroying the monarchy. "Ἡ μοναρχία τοῦ Θεοῦ" was in the second century a standing
title in the polemics of the theologians against polytheists and Gnostics—see the
passages collected from Justin, Tatian, Irenæus etc. by Coustant in his Ep. Dionysii
adv. Sabell. (Routh, Reliq. Sacræ III., p. 385 f.). Tertullian has therefore by no
means used the term "Monarchians" as if he were thus directly branding his
opponents as heretical; he rather names them by their favourite catch-word in a
spirit of irony (Adv. Prax 10; "vanissimi Monarchiani"). The name was therefore
not really synonymous with a form of heresy in the ancient Church, even if here
and there it was applied to the opponents of the doctrine of the Trinity.

Krawutzcky's study on the origin of the Didache.[1] The so-called Dynamistic Monarchians have had especially to suffer from this criticism, their teaching being comfortably disposed of as "Ebionitic". However, imperative as it certainly is, in general, to describe the history of Monarchianism without reference to the ancient pre-Catholic controversies, and only to bring in the history of Montanism with great caution, still many facts observed in reference to the earliest bodies of Monarchians that come clearly before us, seem to prove that they bore features which must be characterised as pre-Catholic, but not un-Catholic. This is especially true of their attitude to certain books of the New Testament. Undoubtedly we have reason even here to complain of the scantiness and uncertainty of our historical material. The Church historians have attempted to bury or distort the true history of Monarchianism to as great an extent as they passed over and obscured that of the so-called Montanism. At a very early date, if not in the first stages of the controversy, they read Ebionitism and Gnosticism into the theses of their opponents; they attempted to discredit their theological works as products of a specific secularisation, or as travesties, of Christianity, and they sought to portray the Monarchians themselves as renegades who had abandoned the rule of faith and the Canon. By this kind of polemics they have made it difficult for after ages to decide, among other things, whether certain peculiarities of Monarchian bodies in dealing with the Canon of the N. T. writings spring from a period when there was as yet no N. T. Canon in the strict Catholic sense, or whether these characteristics are to be regarded as deviations from an already settled authority, and therefore innovations. Meanwhile, looking to the Catholicity of the whole character of Monarchian movements, and, further, to the fact that no opposition is recorded as having been made by them to the N. T. Canon after its essential contents and authority appear to have been established; considering, finally, that the Montanists, and even the Marcionites and Gnostics, were very early charged with attempts on the Catholic Canon, we need no longer

[1] See Theol. Quartalschr. 1884, p. 547 ff. Krawutzcky holds the Didache to be at once Ebionitic and Theodotian.

doubt that the Monarchian deviations point exclusively to a time when no such Canon existed; and that other "heresies", to be met with in the older groups, are to be criticised on the understanding that the Church was becoming, but not yet become, Catholic. [1]

The history of Monarchianism is no clearer than its rise in the form of particular theological tendencies. Here also we have before us, at the present day, only scanty fragments. We cannot always trace completely even the settled distinction between Dynamistic—better, Adoptian—and Modalistic Monarchianism; [2] between the theory that made the power or Spirit of God dwell in the man Jesus, and the view that sees in Him the incarnation of the deity Himself. [3]

Certainly the common element, so far as there was one, of the Monarchian movements, lay in the form of the conception of God, the distinguishing feature, in the idea of revelation. But all the phenomena under this head cannot be classified with certainty, apart from the fact that the most numerous and important "systems" exist in a very shaky tradition. A really reliable division of the Monarchianism that in all its forms rejected the idea of a physical fatherhood of God, and only saw the Son of God in the *historical* Jesus, is impossible on the strength of the authorities up till now known to us. Apart from a fragment or two we only possess accounts by opponents. The chronology, again, causes a special difficulty. Much labour has been spent upon it since the discovery of the Philosophumena; but most of the details have remained very uncertain. The dates of the Alogi, Artemas, Praxeas, Sabellius, the Antiochian Synods against Paul of Samosata, etc., have not yet been firmly settled. The concise remarks on the subject in what follows rest on independent labours. Finally, we

---

[1] It is very remarkable that Irenæus has given us no hint in his great work of a Monarchian controversy in the Church.

[2] It was pointed out above, (Vol. I., p. 193) and will be argued more fully later on, that the different Christologies could pass into one another.

[3] We have already noticed, Vol. I., p. 195, that we can only speak of a naïve Modalism in the earlier periods; Modalism first appeared as an exclusive doctrine at the close of the second century; see under.

are badly informed even as to the geographical range of the controversies. We may, however, suppose, with great probability, that at one time or other a conflict took place in all centres of Christianity in the Empire. But a connected history cannot be given.

2. *The Secession of Dynamistic Monarchianism or Adoptianism.*

(a). The so-called Alogi in Asia Minor. [1]

Epiphanius [2] and Philastrius (H. 60) know, from the Syntagma of Hippolytus, of a party to which the latter had given the nickname of "Alogi". Hippolytus had recorded that its members rejected the Gospel and the Apocalypse of John, [3] attributing these books to Cerinthus, and had not recognised the Logos of God to whom the Holy Spirit had borne witness in the Gospel. Hippolytus, the most prolific of the opponents of the heretics, wrote, besides his Syntagma, a special work against these men in defence of the Johannine writings; [4] and he per-

---

[1] Merkel, Aufklärung der Streitigkeiten der Aloger, 1782; Heinichen, De Alogis, 1829; Olshausen, Echtheit der vier Kanonischen Evangelien, p. 241 f.; Schwegler, Montanismus, p. 265 ff. etc.; Volkmar, Hippolytus, p. 112 f.; Döllinger, Hippolytus u. Kallistus, p. 229 f.; Lipsius, Quellenkritik des Epiphanius, p. 23 f., 233 f.; Harnack in d. Ztschr. f. d. histor. Theol. 1874, p. 166 f.; Lipsius, Quellen der ältesten Ketzergeschichte, p. 93 f., 214 f.; Zahn in d. Ztschr. für die histor. Theol., 1875, p. 72 f.; Caspari, Quellen III., p. 377 f., 398 f., Soyres, Montanism, p. 49 f.; Bonwetsch, Montanismus vv. ll.; Iwanzov-Platonov, Häresien und Schismen der drei ersten Jahr. 1, p. 233 f.; Zahn, Gesch. d. N. T. Kanons I., p. 220 ff.; Harnack, das N. T. um d. J. 200, p. 38 ff.; Jülicher, Theol. Lit. Ztg., 1889, No. 7; Salmon i. Hermathena, 1892, p. 161 ff.

[2] Hær. 51; after him Augustine H. 30, Prædest. H. 30 etc. The statement of the Prædest. that a Bishop named Philo refuted the Alogi is worthless. Whether the choice of the name was due to the Alexandrian Jew is unknown.

[3] Nothing is reported as to the Letters. Epiphanius is perhaps right in representing that they were also rejected (l.c. ch. 34); but perhaps they were not involved in the discussion.

[4] See the list of writings on the statue of Hippolytus: υπερ του κατα ιωαν[ν]ην ευαγγελιου και αποκαλυψεως; and Ebed Jesu, catal. 7 (Assemani, Bibl. Orient. III. 1, 15): "Apologia pro apocalypsi et evangelio Johannis apostoli et evangelistæ." Besides this . Hippolytus wrote: "Capita adversus Caium," a Roman sympathiser with the Alogi. Of this writing a few fragments have been preserved (Gwynn, Hermathena VI., p. 397 f.; Harnack, Texte und Unters. VI. 3, p. 121 ff.; Zahn, Gesch. des N. T. Kanons, II., p. 973 ff.

haps also attacked them in another work aimed at all Monarchians.[1] The character of the party can still be defined, in its
main features, from the passages taken by Epiphanius from
these writings, due regard being given to Irenæus III. 11, 9.
The Christological problem seems not to have occupied a fore-
most place in the discussion, but rather, the elimination of all
docetic leaven, and the attitude to prophecy. The non-descript,
the Alogi, were a party of the radical, anti-montanist, opposition in Asia Minor, existing within the Church—so radical that
they refused to recognise the Montanist communities as Christian.
They wished to have all prophecy kept out of the Church; in
this sense they were decided contemners of the Spirit (Iren. l.c.;
Epiph. 51, ch. 35). This attitude led them to an historical
criticism of the two Johannine books, the one of which contained Christ's announcement of the Paraclete, a passage which
Montanus had made the most of for his own ends, while the
other imparted prophetic revelations. They came to the conclusion, on internal grounds, that these books could not be
genuine, that they were composed "in the name of John"
(εἰς ὄνομα Ἰωάννου ch. 3, 18), and that by Cerinthus
(ch. 3, 4,); the books ought not therefore to be received in the

[1] It is certain that Epiphanius, besides the relative section of the Syntagma, also
copied at least a second writing against the "Alogi", and it is probable that this
likewise came from Hippolytus. The date of its composition can still be pretty
accurately determined from Epiphan. H. 31, ch. 33. It was written about A.D. 234;
for Epiphanius' authority closes the period of the Apostles 93 years after the
Ascension, and remarks that since that date 112 years had elapsed. Lipsius has
obtained another result, but only by an emendation of the text which is unnecessary
(see Quellen der ältesten Ketzergeschichte, p. 109 f.). Hippolytus treats his unnamed opponents as contemporaries; but a closer examination shows that he only
knew them from their writings—of which there were several (see ch. 33), and therefore knew nothing by personal observation of the conditions under which they
appeared. A certain criterion of the age of these writings, and therefore of the
party itself, is given by the fact that, at the time when the latter flourished, the
only Church at Thyatira was, from their own testimony, Montanist, while the
above-mentioned authority was already able to tell of a rising catholic Church, and
of other Christian communities in that place. A Christian of Thyatira, by name
Papylus, appears in the Martyrium Carpi et Papyli (see Harnack, Texte u. Unters.
III. 3, 4). The date when this movement in Asia Minor flourished can be discovered more definitely, however, by a combination, proved by Zahn to be justified,
of the statements of Hippolytus and Irenæus III. 11. 9. According to this, the
party existed in Asia Minor, A.D. 170—180.

Cnurch (ch. 3: οὐκ ἄξια αὐτά φασιν εἶναι ἐν ἐκκλησίᾳ). The Gospel was charged with containing what was untrue; it contradicted the other Gospels, [1] and gave a quite different and, indeed, a notoriously false order of events; it was devoid of any sort of arrangement; it omitted important facts and inserted new ones which were inconsistent with the Synoptic Gospels; and it was docetic. [2] Against the Apocalypse it was alleged, above all, that its contents were often unintelligible, nay, absurd and untrue (ch. 32—34). They ridiculed the seven angels and seven trumpets, and the four angels by the Euphrates; and on Rev. II. 18, they supposed that there was no Christian community in Thyatira at the time, and that accordingly the Epistle was fictitious. Moreover, the objections to the Gospel must also have included the charge (ch. 18) that it favoured Docetism, seeing that it passed at once from the incarnation of the Logos to the work of the ministry of Christ. In this connection they attacked the expression "Logos" for the Son of God; [3] indeed, they scented Gnosticism in it, contrasted John I. with the beginning of Mark's Gospel, [4] and arrived at the result, that writings whose contents were partly docetic, partly sensuously Jewish and unworthy of God, must have been composed by Cerinthus, the gnosticising Judaist. In view of this fact it is extremely surprising to notice how mildly the party was criticised and treated by Irenæus as well as by Hippolytus. The former distinguishes them sharply from the declared heretics. He places them on a line with the Schismatics, who gave up communion with the Church on account of the hypo-

---

[1] Epiph. LI., ch. 4: φάσκουσι ὅτι οὐ συμφωνεῖ τὰ βιβλία τοῦ Ἰωάννου τοῖς λοιποῖς ἀποστόλοις, ch. 18: τὸ εὐαγγέλιον τὸ εἰς ὄνομα Ἰωάννου ψεύδεται ... λέγουσι τὸ κατὰ Ἰωάννην εὐαγγέλιον, ἐπειδὴ μὴ τὰ αὐτὰ τοῖς ἀποστόλοις ἔφη, ἀδιάθετον εἶναι.

[2] Epiphanius has preserved for us in part the criticism of the Alogi on John I. II., and on the Johannine chronology (ch. 3, 4, 15, 18, 22, 26, 28, 29). In their conception the Gospel of John precluded the human birth and development of Jesus.

[3] Epiph. LI. 3, 28: τὸν λόγον τοῦ Θεοῦ ἀποβάλλονται τὸν διὰ Ἰωάννην κηρυχθέντα.

[4] Epiph. LI., ch. 6: λέγουσιν Ἰδοὺ δεύτερον εὐαγγέλιον περὶ Χριστοῦ σημαῖνον καὶ οὐδαμοῦ ἄνωθεν λέγον τὴν γέννησιν· ἀλλά, φησίν, Ἐν τῷ Ἰορδάνῃ κατῆλθε τὸ πνεῦμα 'επ' αὐτὸν καὶ φωνή· Οὗτός ἐστιν ὁ υἱὸς ὁ ἀγαπητός, Ἐφ' ὃν ηὐδόκησα.

crites to be found in it. He approves of their decided opposition to all pseudo-prophetic nonsense, and he only complains that in their zeal against the bad they had also fought against the good, and had sought to eject all prophecy. In short, he feels that between them and the Montanists, whom likewise he did not look on as heretics,[1] he held the middle position maintained by the Church. And so with Hippolytus. The latter, apart from features which he could not but blame, confirms the conformity to the Church, claimed by the party itself (ch. 3), and conspicuous in their insistence on the harmony of the Scriptures συμφωνία τῶν βιβλῶν).[2] He nowhere sets them on a line with Cerinthus, Ebion, etc., and he has undoubtedly treated even their Christological views, on which Irenæus had communicated no information, more mildly, because he found so much in them of an anti-docetic, anti-montanistic nature, with which he could agree. But what was their teaching as to Christ? If Lipsius[3] were correct in his opinion that the Alogi only saw in Jesus a man naturally procreated, that they only pretended to hold by the current doctrine, then the attitude to them of Irenæus and Hippolytus would be incomprehensible. But our authority gives no support to such a view. It rather shows plainly that the Alogi recognised the first three Gospels, and consequently *the miraculous birth* from the Holy Ghost and the virgin. They placed, however, the chief emphasis on the human life of Jesus, on his birth, baptism, and temptation as told by the Synoptics, and for this very reason rejected the formula of the Logos, as well as the "birth from above", *i.e.*, the eternal generation of Christ. The equipment of Christ at his baptism was to them, in view of Mark, ch. I., of crucial importance (see p. 16, Note 4) and thus they would assume, without themselves making use of the phrase "a mere man" (ψιλὸς ἄνθρωπος), an advancement

---

[1] This milder criticism—and neither Montanists nor Alogi stand in Irenæus' catalogue of heretics—naturally did not prevent the view that those "unhappy people" had got into an extremely bad position by their opposition to the prophetic activity of the Spirit in the Church, and had fallen into the unforgivable sin against the Holy Ghost.

[2] In Epiph. LI., ch. 4: δοκοῦσι καὶ αὐτοὶ τὰ ἴσα ἡμῖν πιστεύειν.

[3] Quellen, p. 102 f., 112.

(προκοπή) of the Christ, ordained at his baptism to be Son
of God. [1]

The earliest opponents known to us of the Logos Christology were men whose adherence to the position of the
Church in Asia Minor was strongly marked. This attitude of
theirs was exhibited in a decided antagonism both to the Gnosticism, say, of Cerinthus, and to "Kataphrygian" prophecy. In
their hostility to the latter they anticipated the development of
the Church by about a generation; while rejecting all prophecy
and "gifts of the Spirit" (ch. 35), they, in doing so, gave the
clearest revelation of their Catholic character. Since they did
not believe in an age of the Paraclete, nor entertain materialistic hopes about the future state, they could not reconcile
themselves to the Johannine writings; and their attachment to
the conception of Christ in the Synoptics led them to reject
the Gospel of the Logos. An explicitly Church party could
not have ventured to promulgate such views, if they had been
confronted by a Canon already closed, and giving a fixed place
to these Johannine books. The uncompromising criticism, both
internal and external—as in the hypothesis of the Cerinthian
authorship—to which these were subjected, proves that, when
the party arose, no Catholic Canon existed as yet in Asia Minor,
and that, accordingly, the movement was almost as ancient as
that of the Montanists, which it followed very closely. [2] On this

[1] It is not quite certain whether we may appeal to the words in Epiph. LI.
ch. 18 (20): νομίζοντες ἀπὸ Μαρίας καὶ δεῦρο Χριστὸν αὐτὸν καλεῖσθαι καὶ υἱὸν Θεοῦ
καὶ εἶναι μὲν πρότερον ψιλὸν ἄνθρωπον, κατὰ προκοπὴν δὲ εἰληφέναι τὴν τοῦ Θεοῦ
προσηγορίαν.

[2] As regards the problem of the origin and gradual reception of the Johannine
writings, and especially of the Gospel, their use by Montanus, and their abrupt rejection
by the Alogi, are of the greatest significance, especially when we bear in mind the
Churchly character of the latter. The rise of such an opposition in the very region in
which the Gospel undoubtedly first came to light; the application to the fourth of a
standard derived from the Synoptic Gospels; the denial without scruple, of its apostolic
origin; are facts which it seems to me have, at the present day, not been duly
appreciated. We must not weaken their force by an appeal to the dogmatic character
of the criticism practised by the Alogi; the attestation of the Gospel canno
have been convincing, if such a criticism was ventured on in the Church. Bu
the Alogi distinctly denied to John and ascribed to Cerinthus the Apocalypse as

understanding, the party had a legitimate place within the developing Catholic Church, and only so can we explain the criticism which their writings encountered in the period immediately succeeding. Meanwhile, the first express opposition with which we are acquainted to the Logos Christology was raised within the Church, by a party which, yet, must be conceived by us to have been in many respects specifically secularised. For the radical opposition to Montanism, and the open, and at the same time jesting, criticism on the Apocalypse,[1] can only be so regarded. Yet the preference of the Logos Christology to others is itself indeed, as Celsus teaches, a symptom of secularisation and innovation in the creed. The Alogi attacked it on this ground when they took it as promoting Gnosticism (Docetism). But they also tried to refute the Logos Doctrine and the Logos Gospel on historical grounds, by a reference to the Synoptic Gospels. *The representatives of this movement were, as far as we know, the first to undertake within the Church a historical criticism, worthy of the name, of the Christian Scriptures and the Church tradition.* They first confronted John's Gospel with the Synoptics, and found numerous contradictions; Epiphanius,— and probably, before him, Hippolytus,—called them, therefore, word-hunters (λεξιθηροῦντες H. 51, ch. 34). They and their opponents could retort on each other the charge of introducing innovations; but we cannot mistake the fact that the larger proportion of innovations is to be looked for on the side of the Alogi. How long the latter held their ground; how, when, and by whom they were expelled from the Church in Asia Minor, we do not know.

well as the Gospel. Of Cerinthus we know far too little to be justified in sharing in the holy horror of the Church Fathers. But even if the above hypothesis is false, and it is in fact very probable that it is, yet the very fact that it could be set up by Churchmen is instructive enough; for it shows us, what we do not know from any other source, that the Johannine writings met with, and had to overcome, opposition in their birth-place.

[1] The Roman Caius took over this criticism from them, as is shown by Hippolytus' Cap. adv. Caium. But, like Theodotus, to be mentioned presently, he rejected the view of the Alogi as regards John's Gospel.

(b). The Roman Adoptians.—Theodotus the leather-worker
and his party: Asclepiodotus, Hermophilus, Apollonides,
Theodotus the money-changer, and also the
Artemonites. [1]

Towards the end of the episcopate of Eleutherus, or at the
beginning of that of Victor ($\pm$ 190) there came from Byzantium
to Rome the leather-worker Theodotus, who afterwards was

[1] See Kapp, Hist. Artemonis, 1737; Hagemann, Die römische Kirche in den drei
ersten Jahrh., 1864; Lipsius, Quellenkritik, p. 235 f.; Lipsius, Chronologie der
römischen Bischöfe, p. 173 f.; Harnack, in the Ztschr. f. d. hist. Theol., 1874,
p. 200; Caspari, Quellen III., pp. 318—321, 404 f.; Langen, Geschichte der römischen Kirche I., p. 192 f.; Caspari, Om Melchizedekiternes eller Theodotianernes
eller Athinganernes Laerdomme og om hvad de herve at sige, naar de skulle bline
optagne i. den kristelige Kirke, in the Tidsskr f. d. evang. luth. Kirke. Ny Raekke,
Bd. VIII., part 3, pp. 307—337. Authorities for the older Theodotus are; (1) the
Syntagma of Hippolytus according to Epiph. H. 54, Philaster H. 50. and Pseudo-
Tertull. H. 28; (2) the Philosophumena VII. 35, X. 23, IX. 3, 12, X. 27; (3) the
fragment of Hippolytus against Noëtus, ch. 3. 4) the fragments from the so-called
Little Labyrinth (in Euseb. H. E. V. 28), which was perhaps by Hippolytus, and
was written in the fourth decade of the third century, and after the Philosophumena.
This work was directed against Roman Dynamistic Monarchians under the leader-
ship of a certain Artemas, who are to be distinguished from the Theodotians.
(For the age and author of the Little Labyrinth, and for its connection with the
writings against the Alogi and against Noëtus; also for the appearance of Artemas,
which is not to be dated before $\pm$ 235: see Caspari, Quellen l.c., and my art.
"Monarchianismus", p. 186). Eusebius has confined his extracts from the Little
Labyrinth to such as deal with the Theodotians. These extracts and Philos. Lib. X.
are used by Theodoret (H. F. II. 4. 5); it is not probable that the latter had himself examined the Little Labyrinth. A writing of Theodotus seems to have been
made use of in the Syntagma of Hippolytus. As regards the younger Theodotus, his
name has been handed down by the Little Labyrinth, the Philosoph. (VII. 36) and
Pseudo-Tertull. H. 29 (Theodoret H. F. II. 6). The Syntagma tells of a party of
Melchizedekians, which is traced in the Philosoph. and by the Pseudo-Tertullian to
the younger Theodotus, but neither the party nor its founder is named. Very
mysterious in contents and origin is the piece, edited for the first time from Parisian
MSS. by Caspari (see above): περὶ Μελχισεδεκιανῶν καὶ Θεοδοτιανῶν καὶ 'Αθιγ-
γανῶν. The only controversial writing known to us against Artemas (Artemon) is
the Little Labyrinth. Unfortunately Eusebius has not excerpted the passages aimed
at him. Artemas is, again, omitted in the Syntagma and in the Philosoph. For this
reason Epiphanius, Pseudo-Tertull. and Philaster have no articles expressly dealing
with him. He is, however, mentioned prominently in the edict of the last Synod
of Antioch held to oppose Paul of Samosata (so also in the Ep. Alexandri in
Theodoret H. E. I. 3 and in Pamphilus' Apology Pro Orig. in Routh, Reliq. S. IV.
p. 367); therefore many later writers against the heretics have named him (Epiph.
H. 65. 1, esp. Theodoret H. F. II. 6. etc.). Finally, let it be noticed that the state-

characterised as the "founder, leader, and father of the God-denying revolt", *i.e.*, of Adoptianism. Hippolytus calls him a "rag" (ἀπόσπασμα) of the Alogi, and it is in fact not improbable that he came from the circle of those theologians of Asia Minor. Stress is laid on his unusual culture; "he was supreme in Greek culture, very learned in science" (ἐν παιδείᾳ Ἑλληνικῇ ἀκρός, πολυμαθὴς τοῦ λόγου); and he was, therefore, highly respected in his native city. All we know for certain of his history is that he was excommunicated by the Roman Bishop, Victor, on account of the Christology which he taught in Rome (Euseb. V. 28. 6: ἀπεκήρυξε τῆς κοινωνίας); *his is, therefore, the first case of which we are certain, where a Christian who took his stand on the rule of faith was yet treated as a heretic.*[1] As regards his teaching, the Philosophumena expressly testify to the orthodoxy of Theodotus in his theology and cosmology.[2] In reference to the Person of Christ he taught: that Jesus was a man, who, by a special decree of God, was born of a virgin through the operation of the Holy Spirit; but that we were not to see in him a heavenly being, who had assumed flesh in the virgin. After the piety of his life had been thoroughly tested, the Holy Ghost descended upon him in baptism; by this means he became Christ and received his equipment (δυνάμεις) for his special vocation; and he demonstrated the righteousness, in virtue of which he excelled all men, and was, of necessity, their authority. Yet the descent of the Spirit upon Jesus was not sufficient to justify the contention that he was now "God". Some of the followers of Theodotus represented

ments in the Synodicon Pappi, and in the Prædestinatus are worthless, and that the identification of the younger Theodotus with the Gnostic of the same name, extracts from whose works we possess, is inadmissable, not less so than the identification with Theodotus, the Montanist, of whom we are informed by Eusebius. In this we agree with Zahn (Forschungen III., p. 123) against Neander and Dorner. As an authority for the Roman Monarchians, Novatian, De Trinitate, also falls to be considered.

1 It is significant that this took place in Rome. The Syntagma is further able to tell that Theodotus had denied Christ during the persecution in his native city before he came to Rome. See on this point my article on Monarchianism, p. 187.

2 VII. 35: φάσκων τὰ περὶ μὲν τῆς τοῦ παντὸς ἀρχῆς σύμφωνα ἐκ μέρους τοῖς τῆς ἀληθοῦς ἐκκλησίας, ὑπὸ τοῦ Θεοῦ πάντα ὁμολογῶν γεγονέναι.

Jesus as having become God through the resurrection; others disputed even this. [1] This Christology, Theodotus and his party sought to prove from Scripture. Philaster says in general terms: "they use the chapters of Scripture which tell of Christ as man, but they avoid those which speak of him as God, reading and by no means understanding" (Utuntur capitulis scripturarum quæ de Christo veluti de homine edocent, quæ autem ut deo dicunt ea vero non accipiunt, legentes et nullo modo intellegentes). Epiphanius has, fortunately, preserved for us fragments of the biblical theological investigations of Theodotus, by the help of the Syntagma. These show that there was no longer any dispute as to the extent of the N. T. Canon; the Gospel of John is recognised, and in this respect also Theodotus is Catholic. The investigations are interesting, however, because they are worked out by the same prosaic methods of exegesis, adopted in the above discussed works of the Alogi. [2]

---

[1] Philos. VII. 35: Θεὸν δὲ οὐδέποτε τοῦτον γεγονέναι θέλουσιν ἐπὶ τῇ καθόδῳ τοῦ πνεύματος, ἕτεροι δὲ μετὰ τὴν ἐκ νεκρῶν ἀνάστασιν. The description in the text is substantially taken from the Philos., with whose account the contents of the Syntagma are not inconsistent. The statement that Theodotus denied the birth by the virgin is simply a calumny, first alleged by Epiphanius. The account of the Philos. seems unreliable, at most, on a single point, viz., where, interpreting Theodotus, it calls the Spirit which descended at the baptism "Christ" But possibly this too is correct, seeing that Hermas, and, later, the author of the Acta Archelai have also identified the Holy Spirit with the Son of God. (Compare also what Origen [περὶ ἀρχ. pref.] has reported as Church tradition on the Holy Spirit.) In that case we would only have to substitute the "Son of God" for " Christ", and to suppose that Hippolytus chose the latter term in order to be able to characterise the teaching of Theodotus as Gnostic (Cerinthian). On the possibility that the Theodotians, however, really named the Holy Spirit " Christ", see later on.

[2] Epiphanius mentions the appeal of the Theodotians to Deut. XVIII. 15; Jer. XVII. 9; Isa. LIII. 2 f.; Mat. XII. 31; Luke I. 35; John VIII. 40; Acts II. 22; 1 Tim. II. 5. They deduced from Mat. XII. 31, that the Holy Spirit held a higher place than the Son of Man. The treatment of the verses in Deut. and Luke is especially instructive. In the former Theodotus emphasised, not only the "προφήτην ὡς ἐμέ", and the "ἐκ τῶν ἀδελφῶν", but also the "ἐγερεῖ", and concluded referring the passage to the Resurrection: ὁ ἐκ Θεοῦ ἐγειρόμενος Χριστὸς οὗτος οὐκ ἦν Θεὸς ἀλλὰ ἄνθρωπος, ἐπειδὴ ἐξ αὐτῶν ἦν, ὡς καὶ Μωϋσῆς ἄνθρωπος ἦν—accordingly the resuscitated Christ was not God. On Luke I. 35 he argued thus: "The Gospel itself says in reference to Mary: 'the Spirit of the Lord will come upon thee'; but it does not say: 'the Spirit of the Lord will be in thy body', or,'will enter into thee.'"— Further, if we may trust Epiphanius, Theodotus sought to divide the sentence— διὸ καὶ τὸ γεννώμενον ἐκ σοῦ ἅγιον κληθήσεται υἱὸς Θεοῦ—, from the first half of

Theodotus' form of teaching was, even in the life-time of its author, held in Rome to be intolerable, and that by men disposed to Modalism—*e.g.*, the Bishop himself, see under—as well as by the representatives of the Logos Christology. It is certain that he was excommunicated by Victor, accordingly before A.D. 199, on the charge of teaching that Christ was "mere man" (ψιλὸς ἄνθρωπος). We do not know how large his following was in the city. We cannot put it at a high figure, since in that case the Bishop would not have ventured on excommunication. It must, however, have been large enough to allow of the experiment of forming an independent Church. This was attempted in the time of the Roman Bishop Zephyrine (199—218) by the most important of the disciples of Theodotus, viz., Theodotus the money-changer, and a certain Asclepiodotus. It is extremely probable that both of these men were also Greeks. A native, Natalius the confessor, was induced, so we are told by the Little Labyrinth, to become Bishop of the party, at a salary of 150 denarii a month. The attempt failed. The oppressed Bishop soon deserted and returned into the bosom of the great Church. It was told that he had been persuaded by visions and finally by blows with which "holy angels" pursued him during the night. The above undertaking is interesting in itself, since it proves how great had already become the gulf between the Church and these Monarchians in Rome, about A.D. 210; but still more instructive is the sketch given of the leaders of the party by the Little Labyrinth, a sketch that agrees excellently with the accounts given of the 'λεξιθηροῦντες' in Asia, and of the exegetic labours of the older Theodotus. [1]

the verse, as if the words "διὸ καὶ" did not exist, so that he obtained the meaning that the Sonship of Christ would only begin later,—subsequent to the test. Perhaps, however, Theodotus entirely deleted "διὸ καὶ", just as he also read "πνεῦμα κυρίου" for "πνεῦμα ἅγιον" in order to avoid all ambiguity. And since Hippolytus urges against him that John I. 14 did not contain "τὸ πνεῦμα σὰρξ ἐγένετο", Theodotus must at least have interpreted the word "λόγος" in the sense of "πνεῦμα"; and an ancient formula really ran: "Χριστὸς ὢν μὲν τὸ πρῶτον πνεῦμα ἐγένετο σάρξ" (2 Clem. IX. 5), where later "λόγος" was, indeed, inserted in place of "πνεῦμα". See the Cod. Constantinop.

[1] Euseb. (H. E. V. 28): "They falsified the Holy Scriptures without scruple, rejected the standards of the ancient faith, and misunderstood Christ. For they did not examine what the Scriptures said, but carefully considered what logical

The offence charged against the Theodotians was three-fold: the grammatical and formal exegesis of Holy Scripture, the trenchant textual criticism, and the thorough-going study of Logic, Mathematics, and the empirical sciences. It would seem at a first glance as if these men were no longer as a rule inter-ested in theology. But the opposite was the case. Their oppo-nent had himself to testify that they pursued grammatical exe-gesis "in order to prove their godless tenets," textual criticism in order to correct the manuscripts of the Holy Scriptures, and philosophy "in order by the science of unbelievers to support their heretical conception." He had also to bear witness to the fact that these scholars had not tampered with the inspiration of the Holy Scriptures, or the extent of the Canon (V. 28. 18). [1] Their whole work, therefore, was in the service of their theology. But the method of this work,—and we can infer it to have been also that of the Alogi and the older Theodotus—conflicted with the dominant theological method. Instead of Plato and

figure they could obtain from it that would prove their godless teaching. And if any one brought before them a passage from Holy Scripture, they asked whether a conjunctive or disjunctive figure could be made of it. They set aside the Holy Scriptures of God, and employ themselves, instead, with geometry, being men who are earthly, and talk of what is earthly, and know not what comes from above. Some of them, therefore, study the geometry of Euclid with the greatest devotion ; Aristotle and Theophrastus are admired; Galen is even worshipped by some. But what need is there of words to show that men who misuse the sciences of the unbelievers to prove their heretical views, and falsify with their own godless cunning the plain faith of Scripture, do not even stand on the borders of the faith ? They have therefore laid their hands so unscrupulously on the Holy Scriptures under the pretext that they had only amended it critically (διωρθωκέναι). He who will can convince himself that this is no calumny. For, if one should collect the manuscripts of any one of them and compare them, he would find them differ in many passages. At least, the manuscripts of Asclepiodotus do not agree with those of Theodotus. But we can have examples of this to excess; for their scholars have noted with ambitious zeal all that any one of them has, as they say, critically amended, *i.e.*, distorted (effaced?). Again, with these the manuscripts of Hermo-philus do not agree; and those of Apollonides even differ from each other. For if we compare the manuscripts first restored by them (him ?) with the later re-corrected copies, variations are found in many places. But some of them have not even found it worth the trouble to falsify the Holy Scriptures, but have simply rejected the Law and the Prophets, and have by this lawless and godless doctrine hurled themselves, under the pretext of grace, into the deepest abyss of perdition.

[1] See under.

Zeno, the Adoptians revered the Empiricists; instead of the allegorical interpretation of Scripture, the grammatical was alone
held to be valid; instead of simply accepting or capriciously
trimming the traditional text, an attempt was made to discover
the original. How unique and valuable is this information!
How instructive it is to observe that this method struck the disciple of the Apologists and Irenæus [1] as strange, nay, even as
heretical, that while he would have seen nothing to object to
in the study of Plato, he was seized with horror at the idea of
Aristotle, Euclid, and Galen, being put in the place of Plato!
The difference was, indeed, not merely one of method. In the
condition of the theology of the Church at that time, it could
not be supposed that religious conviction was especially strong
or ardent in men who depreciated the religious philosophy of
the Greeks. For whence, if not from this source, or from
Apocalyptics, did men then derive a distinctively pious enthusiasm? [2] It is also little to be wondered at that the attempt
made by these scholars to found a Church in Rome, was so
quickly wrecked. They were fated to remain officers without
an army; for with grammar, textual criticism, and logic one
could only throw discredit, in the communities, on the form of
Christological doctrine which held the highest place and had
been rendered venerable by long tradition. These scholars,
therefore, although they regarded themselves as Catholic, stood
outside the Church. [3] Of the works of these, the earliest exegetical scholars, nothing has come down to us. [4] They have gor

[1]   See V. 28. 4, 5.

[2]   The triumph of Neo-platonic philosophy and of the Logos Christology in
Christian theology is, in this sense, to be considered an advance. That philosophy,
indeed, in the third century, triumphed throughout the empire over its rivals, and
therefore the exclusive alliance concluded with it by Christian tradition was one
which, when it took place, could be said to have been inevitable. Suppose, however, that the theology of Sabellius or of Paul had established itself in the Church
in the 3rd century, then a gulf would have been created between the Church and
Hellenism that would have made it impossible for the religion of the Church to
become that of the empire. Neo-platonic tradition was the final product of antiquity;
it disposed, but as a living force, of the intellectual and moral capital of the past.

[3]   As "genuine" scholars—and this is a very characteristic feature—they took very
great care that each should have the credit of his own amendments on the text.

[4]   The Syntagma knows of these; Epiph. H. 55. c. 1: πλάττουσιν ἑαυτοῖς καὶ
βίβλους ἐπιπλάστους,

without leaving any appreciable effect on the Church. Contrast
the significance gained by the schools of Alexandria and Antioch! The latter, which rose about 60 years later, took up again
the work of this Roman school. It, too, came to stand outside
the great Church; but it brought about one of the most important crises in the dogmatics of the Church, because in its philoso-
phico-theological starting-point it was at one with orthodoxy.

The methodical and exegetical examination of the Holy
Scriptures confirmed the Theodotians in their conception of
Christ as the man in whom in an especial manner the Spirit
of God had operated, and had made them opponents of the
Logos Christology. The author of the Little Labyrinth does
not state wherein the doctrine of the younger Theodotus differed
from that of the older. When he says that some of the Theodotians rejected the law and the prophets προφάσει χάριτος, we
may well suppose that they simply emphasised—in a Pauline
sense, or because of considerations drawn from a historical
study of religion—the relativity of the authority of the O. T.; [1]
for there is as little known of any rejection of the Catholic
Canon on the part of the Theodotians, as of a departure from
the rule of faith. Now Hippolytus has extracted from the exegetical works of the younger Theodotus one passage, the discussion of Hebr. V. 6, 10; VI. 20f; VII. 3, 17; and out of
this he has made an important heresy. Later historians eagerly
seized on this; they ascribed to the younger Theodotus, as
distinguished from the older, a cultus of Melchizedek and invented a sect of Melchizedekians (= Theodotians). The money-
changer taught, it was said (Epiph. H. 55), that Melchizedek
was a very great power, and more exalted than Christ, the
latter being merely related to the former as the copy to the
original. Melchizedek was the advocate of the heavenly powers
before God, and the High Priest among men, [2] while Jesus as

---

[1] Even the great anti-gnostic teachers had come to this view (see Vol. II., p. 304)
without indeed drawing the consequences which the Theodotians may have deduced
more certainly.

[2] L.c. Δεῖ ἡμᾶς τῷ Μελχισεδὲκ προσφέρειν, φασίν, ἵνα δι' αὐτοῦ προσενεχθῇ ὑπὲρ
ἡμῶν, καὶ εὕρωμεν δι' αὐτοῦ ζωήν.

priest stood a degree lower. The origin of the former was completely concealed, because it was heavenly, but Jesus was born of Mary. To this Epiphanius adds that the party presented its oblations in the name of M. (εἰς ὄνομα τοῦ Μελχισεδέκ); for he was the guide to God, the prince of righteousness, the true Son of God. It is apparent that the Theodotians cannot have taught this simply as it stands. The explanation is not far to seek. There was a wide-spread opinion in the whole ancient Church, that Melchizedek was a manifestation of the true Son of God; and to this view many speculations attached themselves, here and there in connection with a subordinationist Christology. [1] The Theodotians shared this conception. Immediately after the sentence given above Epiphanius has (55, c. 8): And Christ, they say, was chosen that he might call us from many ways to this one knowledge, having been anointed by God, and chosen, when he turned us from idols and showed us the way. And the Apostle having been sent by him revealed to us that Melchizedek is great and remains a priest for ever, and behold how great he is; and because the less is blessed by the greater, therefore he says that he as being greater blessed Abraham the patriarch; of whom we are initiated that we may obtain from him the blessing. [2]

Now the Christological conception, formulated in the first half

---

[1] See Clem. Alex. Strom. IV. 25. 161; Hierakas in Epiph. H. 55, c. 5, H. 67, c. 3; Philast. H. 148. Epiph. has himself to confess (H. 55, c. 7), that even in his time the view to be taken of Melchizedek was still a subject of dispute among Catholic Christians: οἱ μὲν γὰρ αὐτὸν νομίζουσι φύσει τὸν υἱὸν τοῦ Θεοῦ ἐν ἰδέᾳ ἀνθρώπου τότε τῷ Ἀβραὰμ πεφηνέναι. Jerome Ep. 73 is important. The Egyptian hermit, Marcus, wrote, about A.D. 400, an independent work εἰς τὸν Μελχισεδὲκ κατὰ Μελχισεδεκειῶν, i.e., against those who saw in Melchizedek a manifestation of the true Son of God (see Photius, Biblioth. 200; Dict. of Christ. Biog. III. p. 827; Herzog's R. E., 2 Aufl. IX. p. 290); cf. the above described fragment, edited for the first time by Caspari; further Theodoret H. F. II. 6, Timotheus Presb. in Cotelier, Monum. Eccl. Græcæ III. p. 392 etc.

[2] Καὶ Χριστὸς μὲν, φάσιν, ἐξελέγη, ἵνα ἡμᾶς καλέσῃ ἐκ πολλῶν ὁδῶν εἰς μίαν ταύτην τὴν γνῶσιν, ὑπὸ Θεοῦ κεχρισμένος καὶ ἐκλεκτὸς γενόμενος, ἐπειδὴ ἀπέστρεψεν ἡμᾶς ἀπὸ εἰδώλων καὶ ὑπέδειξεν ἡμῖν τὴν ὁδόν. Ἐξ οὗπερ ὁ ἀπόστολος ἀποσταλεὶς ἀπεκάλυψεν ἡμῖν, ὅτι μέγας ἐστὶν ὁ Μελχισεδέκ, καὶ ἱερεὺς μένει εἰς τὸν αἰῶνα, καὶ, Θεωρεῖτε πηλίκος οὗτος· καὶ ὅτι τὸ ἔλασσον ἐκ τοῦ μείζονος εὐλογεῖται, διὰ τοῦτο, φησί, καὶ τὸν Ἀβραὰμ τὸν πατριάρχην εὐλόγησεν ὡς μείζων ὤν· οὗ ἡμεῖς ἐσμὲν μύσται, ὅπως τύχωμεν παρ' αὐτοῦ τῆς εὐλογίας.

of this paragraph, was certainly not reported from an opponent.
It is precisely that of the Shepherd, [1] and accordingly very ancient in the Roman Church. [2] From this, and by a reference
to the controversial writing of Hippolytus (Epiph. l.c. ch. 9),
the "heretical" cultus of Melchizedek is explained. These Theodotians maintained, as is also shown by their exegesis on 1 Cor.
VIII. 6, [3] three points: First, that besides the Father the only
divine being was the Holy Spirit, who was identical with
the Son—again simply the position of Hermas; secondly, that
this Holy Spirit appeared to Abraham in the form of the King
of Righteousness—and this, as has been shown above, was no
novel contention; thirdly, that Jesus was a man anointed with
the power of the Holy Ghost. But, in that case, it was only
logical, and in itself not uncatholic, to teach that offerings and
worship were due, as to the true, eternal Son of God, to this
King of Righteousness who had appeared to Abraham, and
had blessed him and his real descendants, i.e., the Christians.
And if, in comparison with this Son of God, the chosen and
anointed servant of God, Jesus, appears inferior at first, precisely in so far as he is man, yet their position was no more
unfavourable in this respect than that of Hermas. For Hermas
also taught that Jesus, being only the adopted Son of God,
was really not to be compared to the Holy Spirit, the Eternal
Son; or, rather, he is related to the latter, to use a Theodotian
expression, as the copy to the original. Yet there is undoubtedly a great distinction between the Theodotians and Hermas.
They unmistakably used their speculations as to the eternal

---

[1] Cf. the striking agreement with Sim. V., especially ch. VI. 3 : αὐτὸς καθαρίσας
τὰς ἁμαρτίας τοῦ λαοῦ ἔδειξεν αὐτοῖς τὰς τρίβους τῆς ζωῆς.

[2] The theologico-philosophical impress which, as distinguished from Sim. V.,
marks the whole passage, is of course unmistakable. Notice what is said as to
Paul, and the expression "μύσται".

[3] The Theodotians seem to have taken Christ in this verse to mean not Jesus,
but the Holy Spirit, the eternal Son of God, deleting the name Jesus (Epiph.
H. 55, ch. 9). If that is so then the Philosophumena is right when it relates that
the Theodotians had also given the name of Christ to the pre-existent Son of God,
the Holy Ghost. Yet it is not certain whether we should regard the above
quoted chapter of Epiphanius at all as reporting the Theodotian interpretation
of 1 Cor. VIII. 6.

Son of God in order to rise to that Son from the man Jesus
of history, and to transcend the historical in general as something subordinate.[1] There is not a word of this to be found
in Hermas. Thus, the Theodotians sought, in a similar way to
Origen, to rid themselves by speculation of what was merely
historical, setting, like him, the eternal Son of God above the
Crucified One. We have evidence of the correctness of this
opinion in the observation that these speculations on Melchizedek were continued precisely in the school of Origen. We
find them, and that with the same tendency to depreciate the
historical Son of God, in Hieracas and the confederacy of
Hieracite monks;[2] as also in the monks who held the views of
Origen in Egypt in the fourth and fifth centuries.

We have accordingly found that these theologians retained
the ancient Roman Christology represented by Hermas; but
that they edited it theologically and consequently changed its
intention. If, at that time, the "Pastor" was still read in the
Roman Church, while the Theodotian Christology was condemned, then its Christology must have been differently interpreted. In view of the peculiar character of the book, this
would not be difficult. We may ask, however, whether the teaching of the Theodotians is really to be characterised as Monarchian,
seeing that they assigned a special, and as it seems, an independent role to the Holy Spirit apart from God. Meanwhile,
we can no longer determine how these theologians reconciled
the separate substance (hypostasis) of the Holy Ghost, with
the unity of the Person of God. But so much is certain, that
in their Christology the Spirit was considered by them only as
a power, and that, on the other hand, their rejection of the
Logos Christology was not due to any repugnance to the idea
of a second divine being. This is proved by their teaching as
to the Holy Spirit and His appearance in the Old Testament.

---

[1] Epiph. H. 55, ch. 8: εἰς ὄνομα δὲ τούτου τοῦ Μελχισεδὲκ ἡ προειρημένη
αἵρεσις καὶ τὰς προσφορὰς ἀναφέρει, καὶ αὐτὸν εἶναι εἰσαγωγέα πρὸς τὸν Θεὸν καὶ
δι᾿ αὐτοῦ, φησί, δεῖ τῷ Θεῷ προσφέρειν, ὅτι ἄρχων ἐστὶ δικαιοσύνης, ἐπ᾿ αὐτῷ τούτῳ
κατασταθεὶς ὑπὸ τοῦ Θεοῦ ἐν οὐρανῷ, πνευματικός τις ὢν, καὶ υἱὸς Θεοῦ τεταγμένος
.... c. 1: Χριστός, φησίν, ἐστὶν ἔτι ὑποδεέστερος τοῦ Μελχισεδέκ.

[2] See my art. in Herzog R. E., 2 Aufl. VI. p. 100 (Epiph. LV. 5; LXVII. 3).

But then the difference between them and their opponents does not belong to the sphere of the doctrine of God; they are rather substantially at one on this subject with a theologian like Hippolytus. If that is so, however, their opponents were undoubtedly superior to them, while they themselves fell short of the traditional estimate of Christ. In other words, if there was an eternal Son of God, or any one of that nature, and if He appeared under the old covenant, then the traditional estimate of Jesus could not be maintained, once he was separated from that Son. [1] The formula of the man anointed with the Spirit was no longer sufficient to establish the transcendent greatness of the revelation of God in Christ, and it is only a natural consequence that the O. T. theophanies should appear in a brighter light. We see here why the old Christological conceptions passed away so quickly, comparatively speaking, and gave place so soon in the Churches to the complete and essential elevation of Jesus to the rank of deity, whenever theological reflection awoke to life. It was, above all, the distinctive method of viewing the Old Testament and its theophanies that led to this.

In certain respects the attempt of the Theodotians presents itself as an innovation. They sought to raise a once accepted, but, so to speak, enthusiastic form of faith to the stage of theology and to defend it as the only right one; they expressly refused, or, at least, declared to be matter of controversy, the use of the title "God" ($\Theta\epsilon\acute{o}\varsigma$) as applied to Jesus; they advanced beyond Jesus to an eternal, unchangeable Being (beside God). In this sense, in consequence of the new interest which the representatives of the above doctrine took in the old formula, it is to be regarded as novel. For we can hardly attribute to pre-catholic Christians like Hermas, a special interest in the essential humanity of Jesus. They certainly believed that they gave full expression in their formulas to the highest possible estimate of the Redeemer; they had no other idea. These theologians, on the other hand, defended a lower conception of Christ against a higher. Thus we may judge them on their own ground; for they let the idea of a heavenly Son of God

---

[1] Hermas did not do this, in so far as in the language of religion he speaks only of _a_ Son of God (Simil. IX.).

stand, and did not carry out the complete revision of the prevailing doctrine that would have justified them in proving their
Christological conception to be the one really legitimate and
satisfactory. They indeed supported it by Scriptural proof, and
in this certainly surpassed their opponents, but the proof did
not cover the gaps in their dogmatic procedure. Since they
took their stand on the *regula fidei*, it is unjust and at the
same time unhistorical to call their form of doctrine " Ebionitic ",
or to dispose of them with the phrase that Christ was to them
exclusively a mere man (ψιλὸς ἄνθρωπος). But if we consider the
circumstances in which they appeared, and the excessive ex-
pectations that were pretty generally attached to the possession
of faith—above all, the prospect of the future deification of
every believer—we cannot avoid the impression, that a doctrine
could not but be held to be destructive, which did not even
elevate Christ to divine honours, or, at most, assigned him
an apotheosis, like that imagined by the heathens for their
emperors or an Antinous. Apocalyptic enthusiasm passed gradually into Neo-platonic mysticism. In this transition these scholars took no share. They rather sought to separate a part of
the old conceptions, and to defend that with the scientific means
of their opponents.

Once more, 20 to 30 years later, the attempt was
made in Rome by a certain Artemas to rejuvenate the old
Christology. We are extremely ill informed as to this last phase
of Roman Adoptianism; for the extracts taken by Eusebius
from the Little Labyrinth, the work written against Artemas and
his party, apply almost exclusively to the Theodotians. We
learn, however, that the party appealed to the historical justification of their teaching in Rome, maintaining that Bishop
Zephyrine had first falsified the true doctrine which they defended. [1] The relative correctness of this contention is indisput-
able, especially if we consider that Zephyrine had not dis-

---

[1] Euseb. H. E. V. 28. 3: φασὶ γὰρ τοὺς μὲν προτέρους ἅπαντας καὶ αὐτοὺς τοὺς
ἀποστόλους, παρειληφέναι τε καὶ δεδιδαχέναι ταῦτα, ἅ νῦν οὗτοι λέγουσι, καὶ τετη-
ρῆσθαι τὴν ἀλήθειαν τοῦ κηρύγματος μέχρι τῶν χρόνων τοῦ Βίκτορος ... ἀπὸ δὲ τοῦ
διαδόχου αὐτοῦ Ζεφυρίνου παρακεχαράχθαι τὴν ἀλήθειαν.

approved of the formula, certainly novel, that "the Father had
suffered". The author of the Little Labyrinth reminds them that
Theodotus had been already excommunicated by Victor, and
of this fact they themselves cannot have been ignorant. When,
moreover, we observe the evident anxiety of the writer to impose Theodotus upon them as their spiritual father, we come
to the conclusion that the party did *not* identify themselves
with the Theodotians. What they regarded as the point of
difference we do not know. It is alone certain that they also
refused to call Christ "God"; for the writer feels it necessary to justify the use of the title from tradition. [1] Artemas was
still alive in Rome at the close of the 7th decade of the 3rd century,
but he was completely severed from the great Church, and
without any real influence. No notice is taken of him even in
the letters of Cyprian. [2] Since Artemas was characterised as the
"father" of Paul in the controversy with that Bishop (Euseb.
H. E. VII. 30. 16), he had afterwards attained a certain cele-
brity in the East, and had supplanted even Theodotus in the
recollection of the Church. In the subsequent age, the phrase:
"Ebion, Artemas, Paulus (or Photinus)" was stereotyped; this
was afterwards supplemented with the name of Nestorius, and
in that form the phrase became a constant feature in Byzantine
dogmatics and polemics.

(c). Traces of Adoptian Christology in the West after Artemas.

Adoptian Christology—Dynamistic Monarchianism—apparently
passed rapidly and almost entirely away in the West. The
striking formula, settled by the Symbol, "Christus, homo et
deus", and, above all, the conviction that Christ had appeared
in the O. T., brought about the destruction of the party. Yet,

[1] Euseb. H. E. V. 28. 4, 5.

[2] We know that he still lived about 270 from the document of the Synod of
Antioch in the case of Paul of Samosata. We read there (Euseb. H. E. VII. 30. 17):
"Paul may write letters to Artemas and the followers of A. are said to hold
communion with him." We have probably to regard as Artemonites those unnamed
persons, mentioned in Novatian De Trinitate, who explained Jesus to be a mere
man (homo nudus et solitarius). Artemas is also named in Methodius Conviv.
VIII. 10, Ed. Jahn, p. 37.

here and there—in connection, doubtless, with the reading of Hermas [1]—the old faith, or the old formula, that the Holy Spirit is the
eternal Son of God and at the same time the Christ-Spirit, held its
ground, and, with it, conceptions which bordered on Adoptianism.
Thus we read in the writing " De montibus Sina et Sion " [2] composed
in vulgar Latin and attributed wrongly to Cyprian, ch. IV: "The
body of the Lord was called Jesus by God the Father; the
Holy Spirit that descended from heaven was called Christ
by God the Father, *i.e.*, anointed of the living God, the Spirit
joined to the body Jesus Christ" (Caro dominica a deo patre
Jesu vocita est; spiritus sanctus, qui de cælo descendit, Christus,
id est unctus dei vivi, a deo vocitus est, spiritus carni mixtus
Jesus Christus). Compare ch. XIII.: the H. S., Son of God, sees
Himself double, the Father sees Himself in the Son, the Son
in the Father, each in each (Sanctus spiritus, *dei filius*, gemi-
natum se videt, pater in filio et filius in patre utrosque se in se
vident). There were accordingly only two hypostases, and the
Redeemer is the flesh (caro), to which the pre-existent Holy
Spirit, the eternal Son of God, the Christ, descended. Whether
the author understood Christ as "forming a person" or as a
power cannot be decided; probably, being no theologian, the
question did not occur to him. [3] We do not hear that the
doctrine of Photinus, who was himself a Greek, gained any
considerable approval in the West. But we learn casually that
even in the beginning of the 5th century a certain Marcus was
expelled from Rome for holding the heresy of Photinus, and
that he obtained a following in Dalmatia. Incomparably more
instructive, however, is the account given by Augustine (Confess. VII. 19. [25]) of his own and his friend Alypius' Christological belief, at a time when both stood quite near the Catho-

---

[1] Even Tertullian used the Christological formula of Hermas when he was not
engaged in Apologetics or in polemics against the Gnostics.

[2] Hartel, Opp. Cypr. III., p. 104 sq.

[3] Hilary's work "De trinitate" also shows (esp. X. 18 ff., 50 ff.) what different
Christologies still existed in the West in the middle of the 4th century. There
were some who maintained: "quod in eo ex virgine creando efficax dei sapientia
et virtus exstiterit, et in nativitate eius divinæ prudentiæ et potestatis opus intelle-
gatur, sitque in eo efficientia potius quam natura sapientiæ.

lic Church, and had been preparing to enter it. At that time
Augustine's view of Christ was practically that of Photinus;
and Alypius denied that Christ had a human soul; *yet both had
held their Christology to be Catholic*, and only afterwards learned
better.[1] Now let us remember that Augustine had enjoyed a
Catholic education, and had been in constant intercourse with
Catholics, and we see clearly that among the laity of the West
very little was known of the Christological formulas, and very
different doctrines of Christ were in fact current even at the
close of the 4th century.[2]

(d). The Ejection of the Adoptian Christology in the East,— Beryll of Bostra, Paul of Samosata, etc.

We can see from the writings of Origen that there were also
many in the East who rejected the Logos Christology. Those
were undoubtedly most numerous who identified the Father and
the Son; but there were not wanting such as, while they made a
distinction, attributed to the Son a human nature only,[3] and

[1] Augustine, l.c. ... Quia itaque vera scripta sunt (sc. the Holy Scriptures) totum
hominem in Christo agnoscebam; non corpus tantum hominis, aut cum corpore sine
mente animam, sed ipsum hominem, non persona veritatis, sed magna quadam naturæ
humanæ excellentia et perfectiore participatione sapientiæ præferri cæteris arbitrabar.
Alypius autem deum carne indutum ita putabat credi a Catholicis, ut præter deum
et carnem non esset in Christo anima, mentemque hominis non existimabat in eo
prædicari ... Sed postea hæreticorum Apollinaristarum hunc errorem esse cognos-
cens, catholicæ fidei collætatus et contemperatus est. Ego autem aliquanto posterius
didicisse me fateor, in eo quod "verbum caro factum est" quomodo catholica veritas
a Photini falsitate dirimatur.

[2] In the Fragment, only preserved in Arabic, of a letter of Pope Innocent I.
to Severianus, Bishop of Gabala (Mai, Spicileg. Rom. III., p. 702) we still read
the warning: "Let no one believe that it was only at the time when the divine
Word on earth came to receive baptism from John that this divine nature originated,
when, *i.e.*, John heard the voice of the Father from heaven. It was certainly
not so, etc."

[3] Orig. on John II. 2, Lomm. I., p. 92: Καὶ τὸ πολλοὺς φιλοθέους εἶναι εὐχο-
μένους ταράσσον, εὐλαβουμένους δύο ἀναγορεῦσαι θεούς, καὶ παρὰ τοῦτο περιπίπτοντας
ψευδέσι καὶ ἀσεβέσι δόγμασιν, ἤτοι ἀρνουμένους ἰδιότητα υἱοῦ ἑτέραν παρὰ τὴν τοῦ
πατρός, ὁμολογοῦντας Θεὸν εἶναι τὸν μέχρι ὀνόματος παρ᾽ αὐτοῖς υἱὸν προσαγορευ-
όμενον, ἢ ἀρνουμένους·τὴν θεότητα τοῦ υἱοῦ, τιθέντας δὲ αὐτοῦ τὴν ἰδιότητα καὶ τὴν
οὐσίαν κατὰ περιγραφὴν τυγχάνουσαν ἑτέραν τοῦ πατρός, ἐντεῦθεν λύεσθαι δύναται,
see also what follows. Pseudo-Gregor. (Apollinaris) in Mai (Nov. Coll. VII. 1,

accordingly taught like the Theodotians. Origen by no means
treated them, as a rule, as declared heretics, but as misled, or
"simple", Christian brethren who required friendly teaching.
He himself, besides, had also inserted the Adoptian Christology
into his complicated doctrine of Christ; for he had attached the
greatest value to the tenet that Jesus should be held a real man
who had been chosen by God, who in virtue of his free will,
had steadfastly attested his excellence, and who, at last, had
become perfectly fused with the Logos in disposition, will,
and finally also in nature (see Vol. II., p. 369 f.). Origen laid
such decided emphasis on this that his opponents afterwards
classed him with Paul of Samosata and Artemas, [1] and Pamphilus required to point out "that Origen said that the Son of
God was born of the very substance of God, *i.e.*, was ὁμοούσιος,
which means, of the same substance with the Father, but that
he was not a creature who became a son by adoption, but a
true son by nature, generated by the Father Himself" (quod
Origines filium dei de ipsa dei substantia natum dixerit, id est,
ὁμοούσιον, quod est, eiusdem cum patre substantiæ, et non esse
creaturam *per adoptionem* sed *natura* filium verum, ex ipso patre
generatum).[2] So Origen in fact taught, and he was very far
from seeing more in the Adoptian doctrine than a fragment of
the complete Christology. He attempted to convince the Adoptians of their error, more correctly, of their questionable one-
sidedness, [3] but he had seldom any other occasion to contend
with them.

p. 171) speaks of men who conceived Christ as being 'filled with divinity', but
made no specific distinction between Him and the prophets, and worshipped a man
with divine power after the manner of the heathens.

  [1] Pamphili Apolog. in Routh, IV., p. 367; Schultz in the Jahrbb. f. protest.
Theol. 1875, p. 193 f. On Origen and the Monarchians, see Hagemann, l.c., p. 300 f.
  [2] See l.c., p, 368.
  [3] Orig. in Ep. ad Titum, Lomm. V., p. 287 "Sed et eos, qui hominem dicunt
dominum Iesum præcognitum et prædestinatum, qui ante adventum carnalem sub-
stantialiter et proprie non exstiterit, sed quod homo natus patris solam in se habuerit
deitatem, ne illos quidem sine periculo est ecclesiæ numero sociari." This passage,
undoubtedly, need not necessarily be applied to Dynamistic Monarchians, any more
than the description about to be quoted of the doctrine of Beryll. There may have
existed a middle type between Dynamistic and Modalistic Monarchianism, according
to which the humanity as well as the *deitas patris* in Jesus Christ was held to
be personal.

Perhaps we should here include the action against Beryll of Bostra. This Arabian Bishop taught Monarchianism. His doctrine aroused a violent opposition. The Bishops of the province were deeply agitated and instituted many examinations and discussions. But they appear not to have come to any result. Origen was called in, and, as we are informed by Eusebius, who had himself examined the acts of the Synods, he succeeded in a disputation in amicably convincing the Bishop of his error.[1] This happened, according to the common view, in A.D. 244. We have to depend, for the teaching of Beryll, on one sentence in Eusebius, which has received very different interpretations.[2] Nitzsch says rightly,[3] that Eusebius missed in Beryll the recognition of the separate divine personality (hypostasis) in Christ and of his pre-existence, but not the recognition of his deity. However, this is not enough to class the Bishop with certainty among the Patripassians, since Eusebius' own Christological view, by which that of Beryll was here gauged, was very vague. Even the circumstance, that at the Synod of Bostra (according to Socrates) Christ was expressly decreed to have a human soul, is not decisive; for Origen might have carried the recognition of this dogma, which was

[1] Euseb. H. E. VI. 33. See also Socrates H. E. III. 7.

[2] L.c.: τὸν σωτῆρα καὶ κύριον ἡμῶν μὴ προϋφεστάναι κατ᾽ ἰδίαν οὐσίας περιγραφὴν πρὸ τῆς εἰς ἀνθρώπους ἐπιδημίας, μηδὲ θεότητα ἰδίαν ἔχειν, ἀλλ᾽ ἐμπολιτευομένην αὐτῷ μόνην τὴν πατρικήν. The word περιγραφή is first found in the Excerpta Theodoti 19, where κατὰ περιγραφήν is contrasted in the sense of personality with the κατ᾽ οὐσίαν (τοῦ Θεοῦ). The latter was accordingly felt to be Modalistic: καὶ ὁ λόγος σὰρξ ἐγένετο, οὐ κατὰ τὴν παρουσίαν μόνον ἄνθρωπος γενόμενος, ἀλλὰ καὶ ἐν ἀρχῇ ὁ ἐν ταυτότητι λόγος κατὰ περιγραφὴν καὶ οὐ κατ᾽ οὐσίαν γενόμενος, ὁ υἱός; cf., ch. 10, where περιγράφεσθαι also expresses the personal existence, i.e., what was afterwards termed ὑπόστασις. This word was not yet so used, so far as I know, in the 3rd century. In Origen περιγραφή is likewise the expression for the strictly self-contained personality; see Comm. on John I. 42, Lomm. I. 88: ὥσπερ οὖν δυνάμεις Θεοῦ πλείονές εἰσιν, ὧν ἑκάστη κατὰ περιγραφήν, ὧν διαφέρει ὁ σωτήρ, οὕτως ὁ λόγος—εἰ καὶ παρ᾽ ἡμῖν οὐκ ἔστι κατὰ περιγραφὴν ἐκτὸς ἡμῶν—νοηθήσεται ὁ Χριστὸς κ.τ.λ. In our passage and Pseudo-Hippol. c. Beron. I, 4, it means simply "configuration".

[3] Dogmengesch. I., p. 202. See on Beryll, who has become a favourite of the historians of dogma, apart from the extended historical works, Ullmann, de Beryllo, 1835; Theod. Stud. u. Krit., 1836; Fock Diss. de Christologia B. 1843; Rossel in the Berliner Jahrbb., 1844, No. 41 f.; Kober in the Theol. Quartalschr., 1848, I.

of the highest importance to him, whatever the doctrine of
Beryll had been. That the Bishop rather taught Dynamistic
Monarchianism is supported, first, by the circumstance that
this form of doctrine had, as we can prove, long persisted in
Arabia and Syria; and, secondly, by the observation that Origen,
in the fragment of his commentary on the Ep. of Titus (see
above), has *contrasted* with the Patripassian belief [1] a kind of
teaching which seems to coincide with that of Beryll. Primitive
Dynamistic Monarchian conceptions must, however, be imputed also to those Egyptian Millenarians whom Dionysius of
Alexandria opposed, and whom he considered it necessary to
instruct "in the glorious and truly divine appearing of our
Lord" (περὶ τῆς ἐνδόξου καὶ ἀληθῶς ἐνθέου τοῦ κυρίου ἡμῶν
ἐπιφανείας. [2]

These were all, indeed, isolated and relatively unimportant
phenomena; but they prove that even about the middle of the
3rd century the Logos Christology was not universally recognised in the East, and that the Monarchians were still treated
indulgently. [3] Decisive action was first taken and Adoptianism was
ranked in the East with Ebionitism as a heresy, in the case of
the incumbent of the most exalted Bishopric in the East, Paul
of Samosata, Bishop of Antioch from 260, but perhaps a little
earlier. He opposed the already dominant doctrine of the
essential natural deity of Christ, and set up once more the old
view of the human Person of the Redeemer. [4] That happened

---

[1] It is contained in the words of Origen given above, p. 35, note 3.

[2] Euseb. H. E. VII. 24, 5. By the Epiphany we have to understand the future
appearing; but thorough-going Millenarians in the East, in the country districts,
hardly recognised the doctrine of the Logos.

[3] The uncertainty which still prevailed in the 3rd century in reference to
Christology is seen whenever we take up works not written by learned theologians.
Especially the circumstance that, according to the Creed and the Gospel, the Holy
Ghost took part in the conception of Jesus, constantly prompted the most curious
phrases regarding the personal divinity of Christ, and the *assumptio carnis* of the
Logos, see, *e.g.*, Orac. Sibyll. VI. V. 6, where Christ is called "Sweet God whom
the Spirit, in the white plumage of the dove, begot."

[4] Feuerlein, De hæresi Pauli Samosat., 1741; Ehrlich, De erroribus P.S., 1745;
Schwab, Diss. de P.S. vita atque doctrina, 1839; Hefele, Conciliengesch. 2 Aufl. I.,
p. 135; Routh, Reliq. S. III., pp. 286—367; Frohschammer, Ueber die Verwerfung
des ὁμοούσιος, in the Theol. Quartalschr. 1850, I.

at a time when, through Alexandrian theology, the use of the
categories λόγος (word), οὐσία (being), ὑπόστασις (substance),
ἐνυπόστατος (subsisting), πρόσωπον (person), περιγραφὴ οὐσίας (configuration of essence), etc., had almost already become legitimised, and when in the widest circles the idea had taken root
that the Person of Jesus Christ must be accorded a background
peculiar to itself, and essentially divine.

We do not know the circumstances in which Paul felt himself impelled to attack the form of doctrine taught by Alexandrian philosophy. Yet it is noticeable that it was not a
province of the Roman Empire, but Antioch, then belonging
to Palmyra, which was the scene of this movement. When we
observe that Paul held a high political office in the kingdom
of Zenobia, that close relations are said to have existed
between him and the Queen, and that his fall implied the
triumph of the Roman party in Antioch, then we may assume
that a political conflict lay behind the theological, and that
Paul's opponents belonged to the Roman party in Syria. It
was not easy to get at the distinguished Metropolitan and experienced theologian, who was indeed portrayed by his enemies
as an unspiritual ecclesiastical prince, vain preacher, ambitious
man of the world, and wily Sophist. The provincial Synod,
over which he presided, did not serve the purpose. But already,
in the affair of Novatian, which had threatened to split up the
East, the experiment had been tried A.D. 252 (253) of holding
an Oriental general-council, and that with success. It was repeated. A great Synod—we do not know who called it—met
in Antioch A.D. 264; Bishops from various parts of the East
attended it, and, especially, Firmilian of Cæsarea. The aged
Dionysius, Bishop of Alexandria, excused his absence in a letter
in which he did not take Paul's side. The first Synod came
to an end without result, because, it is alleged, the accused
had cunningly concealed his false doctrines.[1] A second was
also unsuccessful. Firmilian himself gave up the idea of a condemnation "because Paul promised to change his opinions."
It was only at a third Synod, between 266 and 269, probably

---

[1] Eusebius speaks (H. E. VII. 28. 2) of a whole party (οἱ ἀμφὶ τὸν Σαμοσατέα)
having been able to conceal their heterodoxy at the time.

268, at Antioch, Firmilian having died at Tarsus on his way thither, that excommunication was pronounced on the Bishop, and his successor Domnus was appointed. The number of the members of Synod is stated differently at 70, 80, and 180; and the argument against Paul was led by Malchion, a sophist of Antioch and head of a high school, as also a presbyter of the Church. He alone among them all was in a position to unmask that "wily and deceitful man." The Acts of the discussion together with a detailed epistle, were sent by the Synod to Rome, Alexandria, and all Catholic Churches. Paul, protected by Zenobia, remained four years longer in his office; the Church in Antioch split up: "there took place schisms among the people, revolts among the priests, confusion among the pastors" (ἐγένοντο σχίσματα λαῶν, ἀκαταστασίαι ἱερέων, ταραχὴ ποιμένων).[1] In the year A.D. 272 Antioch was at last taken by Aurelian, and the Emperor, to whom an appeal was brought, pronounced on the spot the famous judgment, that the Church building was to be handed to him with whom the Christian Bishops of Italy and of Rome corresponded by letter. This decision was of course founded on political grounds.[2]

[1] Basilius Diac., Acta Concilii Ephes., p. 427, Labb.

[2] The most important authorities for Paul's history and doctrine are the Acts of the Synod of Antioch held against him, *i.e.*, the shorthand report of the discussion between Paul and Malchion, and the Synodal epistle. These still existed in the 6th century, but we now possess them only in a fragmentary form: in Euseb. H. E. VII. 27—30 (Jerome de vir. inl. 71); in Justinian's Tract. c. Monophys.; in the Contestatio ad Clerum C P.; in the Acts of the Ephesian Council; in the writing against Nestor. and Eutych. by Leontius of Byzant.; and in the book of Petrus Diaconus, "De incarnat. ad Fulgentium": all in Routh l.c. where the places in which they are found are also stated. Not certainly genuine is the Synodal epistle of six Bishops to Paul, published by Turrianus (Routh, l.c., p. 289 sq.); yet its authenticity is supported by overwhelming reasons. Decidedly inauthentic is a letter of Dionysius of Alex. to Paul (Mansi, I., p. 1039 sq.), also a pretended Nicene Creed against him (Caspari, Quellen IV., p. 161 f.), and another found in the libel against Nestorius (Mansi, IV., p. 1010). Mai has published (Vet. Script. Nova Coll. VII., p. 68 sq.) five fragments of Paul's speeches: οἱ πρός Σαβῖνον λόγοι (not quite correctly printed in Routh, l.c., p. 328 sq.) which are of the highest value, and may be considered genuine, in spite of their standing in the very worst company, and of many doubts being roused by them which do not admit of being completely silenced. Vincentius mentions writings by Paul (Commonit. 35). In the second grade we have the testimony of the great Church Fathers of the 4th century, which rested partly on the Acts, partly on oral tradition : see, Athanas c.

The teaching of Paul was characterised by the Fathers as a renewal of that of Artemas, but sometimes also as Neo-Jewish, Ebionitic, afterwards as Nestorian Monothelite, etc. It was as follows. God was simply to be regarded as one person. Father, Son, and Spirit were the One God (ἐν πρόσωπον). In God a Logos (Son) or a Sophia (Spirit) can be distinguished—both can again according to Paul become identified—but they are *qualities*.[1] God puts forth of Himself the Logos from Eternity, nay, He begets him, so that he can be called Son and can have being ascribed to him, but he remains an impersonal power.[2] Therefore it was absolutely impossible for him to assume a visible form.[3] This Logos operated in the prophets, to a still higher degree in Moses, then in many others, and most of all (μᾶλλον καὶ διαφερόντως) in the Son of David, born of the virgin by the Holy Ghost. The Redeemer was by the constitution of his nature a man, who arose in time by birth; he was accordingly "from beneath", but the Logos of God inspired him from above.[4] The union of the Logos

Apoll. II. 3, IX. 3; de Synod. Arim. et Seleuc. 26, 43—45, 51, 93; Orat. c. Arian. II., No. 43; Hilarius, De synod. §§ 81, 86, pp. 1196, 1200; Ephræm Junior in Photius, Cod. 229; Gregor Nyss, Antirrhet. adv. Apoll., § 9, p. 141; Basilius, ep. 52 (formerly 300); Epiphan. H. 65 and Anaceph.; cf. also the 3 Antiochian formulas and the Form. Macrostich. (Hahn Biblioth. der Symbole, 2 Aufl. §§ 85, 89), as also the 19 Canon of the Council of Nicæa, according to which Paul's followers were to be re-baptised before reception into the Catholic Church. One or two notes also in Cramer's Catena on S. John, pp. 235, 259 sq. Useful details are given by Innocentius I., ep. 22; by Marius Mercator, in the Suppl. Imp. Theodos. et Valentinian adv. Nestor. of the Deacon Basilius; by Theodorus of Raithu (see Routh, l.c., pp. 327 sq. 357); Fulgentius, etc. In the later opponentsof the heretics from Philaster, and in resolutions of Synods from the 5th century, we find nothing new. Sozom. H. E. IV. 15 and Theodoret H. F. II. 8 are still of importance. The Libellus Synodicus we must leave out of account.

1 Μὴ εἶναι τὸν υἱὸν τοῦ Θεοῦ ἐνυπόστατον, ἀλλὰ ἐν αὐτῷ τῷ Θεῷ—ἐν Θεῷ ἐπιστήμη ἐνυπόστατος—εἷς Θεὸς ὁ πατὴρ καὶ ὁ υἱὸς αὐτοῦ ἐν αὐτῷ ὡς λόγος ἐν ἀνθρώπῳ.

2 Λόγος προφορικός—ὁ πρὸ αἰώνων υἱός—τὸν λόγον ἐγέννησεν ὁ Θεὸς ἄνευ παρθένου καὶ ἄνευ τινὸς οὐδενὸς ὄντος πλὴν τοῦ Θεοῦ· καὶ οὕτως ὑπέστη ὁ λόγος.

3 Σοφία οὐκ ἦν δυνατὸς ἐν σχήματι εὑρίσκεσθαι, οὐδὲ ἐν θέᾳ ἀνδρός· μείζων γὰρ τῶν ὁρωμένων ἐστίν.

4 'Λόγος μὲν ἄνωθεν, 'Ιησοῦς δὲ Χριστὸς ἄνθρωπος ἐντεῦθεν—Χριστὸς ἀπο Μαρίας καὶ δεῦρό ἐστιν—ἄνθρωπος ἦν ὁ 'Ιησοῦς, καὶ ἐν αὐτῷ ἐνέπνευσεν ἄνωθεν ὁ λόγος· ὁ πατὴρ γὰρ ἅμα τῷ υἱῷ (scil. τῷ λόγῳ) εἷς Θεός, ὁ δὲ ἄνθρωπος κάτωθεν τὸ ἴδιον πρόσωπον ὑποφαίνει, καὶ οὕτως τὰ δύο πρόσωπα πληροῦνται—Χριστὸς ἐντεῦθεν τῆς ὑπάρξεως τὴν ἀρχὴν ἐσχηκώς—λέγει 'Ιησοῦν Χριστὸν κάτωθεν.

with the man Jesus is to be represented as an indwelling[1] by means of an inspiration acting from without,[2] so that the Logos becomes that in Jesus which in the Christian is called by the Apostle "the inner man"; but the union which is thus originated is a contact in knowledge and communion (συνάφεια κατὰ μάθησιν καὶ μετουσίαν) a coming together (συνέλευσις); there does not arise a being existent in a body (οὐσία οὐσιωμένη ἐν σώματι), i.e., the Logos dwelt in Jesus not "in substance but in quality" (οὐσιωδῶς, ἀλλὰ κατὰ ποιότητα).[3] Therefore the Logos is to be steadily distinguished from Jesus;[4] he is greater than the latter.[5] Mary did not bear the Logos, but a man like us in his nature, and in his baptism it was not the Logos, but the man, who was anointed with the Spirit.[6] However, Jesus was, on the other hand, vouchsafed the divine grace in a special degree,[7] and his position was unique.[8] Moreover, the proof he gave of his moral perfection corresponded to his peculiar equipment.[9] The only unity between two persons, accordingly between God and Jesus, is that of the disposition and the will.[10]

---

[1] Ὡς ἐν ναῷ—ἐλθόντα τὸν λόγον καὶ ἐνοικήσαντα ἐν Ἰησοῦ ἀνθρώπῳ ὄντι; in support of this Paul appealed to John XIV. 10: "sapientia habitavit in eo, sicut et habitamus et nos in domibus"—

[2] Λόγον ἐνεργὸν ἐξ οὐρανοῦ ἐν αὐτῷ—σοφίας ἐμπνεούσης ἔξωθεν.

[3] Οὐ δίδως, says Malchion, οὐσιῶσθαι ἐν τῷ ὅλῳ σωτῆρι τὸν μονογενῆ.

[4] Ἄλλος γάρ ἐστιν Ἰησοῦς Χριστὸς καὶ ἄλλος ὁ λόγος.

[5] Ὁ λόγος μείζων ἦν τοῦ Χριστοῦ· Χριστὸς γὰρ διὰ σοφίας μέγας ἐγένετο.

[6] Μαρία τὸν λόγον οὐκ ἔτεκεν οὐδὲ γὰρ ἦν πρὸ αἰώνων ἡ Μαρία, ἀλλὰ ἄνθρωπον ἡμῖν ἴσον ἔτεκεν—ἄνθρωπος χρίεται, ὁ λόγος οὐ χρίεται· ὁ Ναζωραῖος χρίεται, ὁ κύριος ἡμῶν,

[7] Οὐκ ἐστιν ὁ ἐκ Δαβὶδ χρισθεὶς ἀλλότριος τῆς σοφίας.

[8] Ἡ σοφία ἐν ἄλλῳ οὐχ οὕτως οἰκεῖ—κρείττων κατὰ πάντα, ἐπειδὴ ἐκ πνεύματος ἁγίου καὶ ἐξ ἐπαγγελιῶν καὶ ἐκ τῶν γεγραμμένων ἡ ἐπ' αὐτῷ χάρις.

[9] Paul has even spoken of a διαφορὰ τῆς κατασκευῆς (συστάσεως) τοῦ Χριστοῦ.

[10] From this point we refer to the Λόγοι πρὸς Σαβῖνον of Paul. We give them here on account of their unique importance: (1) Τῷ ἁγίῳ πνεύματι χρισθεὶς προσηγορεύθη Χριστός, πάσχων κατὰ φύσιν, θαυματουργῶν κατὰ χάριν· τῷ γὰρ ἀτρέπτῳ τῆς γνώμης ὁμοιωθεὶς τῷ Θεῷ, καὶ μείνας καθαρὸς ἁμαρτίας ἠνώθη αὐτῷ, καὶ ἐνηργήθη που ἐλέσθαι τὴν τῶν θαυμάτων δυναστείαν, ἐξ ὧν μίαν αὐτὸς καὶ τὴν αὐτὴν πρὸς τῇ θελήσει ἐνέργειαν ἔχειν δειχθείς, λυτρωτὴς τοῦ γένους καὶ σωτὴρ ἐχρημάτισεν.—(2) Αἱ διάφοροι φύσεις καὶ τὰ διάφορα πρόσωπα ἕνα καὶ μόνον ἑνώσεως ἔχουσι τρόπον τὴν κατὰ θέλησιν σύμβασιν, ἐξ ἧς ἡ κατὰ ἐνέργειαν ἐπὶ τῶν οὕτως συμβιβασθέντων ἀλλήλοις ἀναφαίνεται μονάς.—(3) "Ἅγιος καὶ δίκαιος γεγενημένος ὁ σωτήρ, ἀγῶνι καὶ πόνῳ τὰς τοῦ προπάτορας ἡμῶν κρατήσας ἁμαρτίας· οἷς κατορθώσας τῇ ἀρετῇ συνήφθη τῷ Θεῷ, μίαν καὶ τὴν αὐτὴν πρὸς αὐτὸν βούλησιν καὶ ἐνέργειαν ταῖς τῶν ἀγαθῶν

Such unity springs from love alone; but love can certainly
produce a complete unity, and only that which is due to love
—not that attained by "nature"—is of worth. Jesus was like
God in the unchangeableness of his love and his will, and became one with God, being not only without sin himself, but
vanquishing, in conflict and labour, the sins of our ancestor.
As he himself, however, advanced in the manifestation of
goodness and continued in it, the Father furnished him with
power and miracles, in which he made known his steadfast
conformity to the will of God. So he became the Redeemer
and Saviour of the human race, and at the same time entered
into an eternally indissoluble union with God, because his love
can never cease. Now he has obtained from God, as the reward of his love, the name which is above every name; God
has committed to him the judgment, [1] and invested him with
divine dignity, so that now we can call him "God [born] of
the virgin". [2] So also we are entitled to speak of a pre-existence of Christ in the prior decree [3] and prophecy [4] of God, and

προκοπαῖς ἐσχηκώς· ἣν ἀδιαίρετον φυλάξας τὸ ὄνομα κληροῦται τὸ ὑπὲρ πᾶν ὄνομα,
στοργῆς ἔπαθλον αὐτῷ χαρισθέν.—(4) Τὰ κρατούμενα τῷ λόγῳ τῆς φύσεως οὐκ ἔχει
ἔπαινον· τὰ δὲ σχέσει φιλίας κρατούμενα ὑπεραινεῖται, μιᾷ καὶ τῇ αὐτῇ γνώμῃ κρατούμενα, διὰ μιᾶς καὶ τῆς αὐτῆς ἐνεργείας βεβαιούμενα, καὶ τῆς κατ᾽ ἐπαύξησιν οὐδέποτε παυομένης κινήσεως· καθ᾽ ἣν τῷ Θεῷ συναφθεὶς ὁ σωτὴρ οὐδέποτε δέχεται
μερισμὸν εἰς τοὺς αἰῶνας μίαν αὐτὸς καὶ τὴν αὐτὴν ἔχων θέλησιν καὶ ἐνέργειαν, ἀεὶ
κινουμένην τῇ φανερώσει τῶν ἀγαθῶν.—(5) Μὴ θαυμάσῃς ὅτι μίαν μετὰ τοῦ Θεοῦ
τὴν θέλησιν εἶχεν ὁ σωτήρ· ὥσπερ γὰρ ἡ φύσις μίαν τῶν πολλῶν καὶ τὴν αὐτὴν
ὑπάρχουσαν φανεροῖ τὴν οὐσίαν, οὕτως ἡ σχέσις τῆς ἀγάπης μίαν τῶν πολλῶν καὶ
τὴν αὐτὴν ἐργάζεται θέλησιν διὰ μιᾶς καὶ τῆς αὐτῆς φανερουμένην εὐαρεστήσεως.
Similar details are to be found in Theodorus of Mops.; but the genuineness of
what is given here seems to me to be guaranteed by the fact that there is absolutely
not a word of an ethical unification of the eternal Son of God (the Logos) with
Jesus. It is God Himself who is thus united with the latter.

[1] Χρὴ δὲ γιγνώσκειν, we read in the Catena S. Joh., ὅτι ὁ μὲν Παῦλος ὁ Σαμ.
οὕτω φησίν· ἔδωκεν αὐτῷ κρίσιν ποιεῖν, ὅτι υἱὸς ἀνθρώπου ἐστὶν.

[2] Athanas.: Παῦλος ὁ Σαμ. Θεὸν ἐκ τῆς παρθένου ὁμολογεῖ, Θεὸν ἐκ Ναζαρὲτ
ὀφθέντα.

[3] Athanas.: Ὁμολογεῖ Θεὸν ἐκ Ναζαρὲτ ὀφθέντα, καὶ ἐντεῦθεν τῆς ὑπάρξεως τὴν
ἀρχὴν ἐσχηκότα, καὶ ἀρχὴν βασιλείας παρειληφότα, Λόγον δὲ ἐνεργὸν ἐξ οὐρανοῦ, καὶ
σοφίαν ἐν αὐτῷ ὁμολογεῖ, τῷ μὲν προορισμῷ πρὸ αἰώνων ὄντα, τῇ δὲ ὑπάρξει ἐκ
Ναζαρὲτ ἀναδειχθέντα, ἵνα εἷς εἴη, φησίν, ὁ ἐπὶ πάντα Θεὸς ὁ πατήρ. Therefore it
is said in the letter of the six Bishops that Christ is God from eternity, οὐ προγνώσει,
ἀλλ᾽ οὐσίᾳ καὶ ὑποστάσει.

[4] Προκαταγγελτικῶς. See p. 41, note 8.

to say that he became God through divine grace and his constant manifestation of goodness. [1] Paul undoubtedly perceived
in the imparting of the Spirit at the baptism a special stage
of the indwelling of the Logos in the man Jesus; indeed Jesus
seems only to have been Christ from his baptism: "having
been anointed with the Holy Spirit he was named Christ—the
anointed son of David is not different from wisdom" (τῷ ἁγίῳ
πνεύματι χρισθεὶς προσηγορεύθη Χριστός—ὁ ἐκ Δαβὶδ χρισθεὶς οὐκ
ἀλλότριός ἐστι τῆς σοφίας). The Bishop supported his doctrine
by copious proofs from Scripture, [2] and he also attacked the
opposite views. He sought to prove that the assumption that
Jesus was by nature (φύσει) Son of God, led to having two
gods, [3] to the destruction of Monotheism; [4] he fought openly,
with great energy, against the old expositors, i.e., the Alexandrians, [5] and he banished from divine service all Church psalms
in which the essential divinity of Christ was expressed. [6]

The teaching of Paul was certainly a development of
the old doctrine of Hermas and Theodotus, and the Church
Fathers had a right to judge it accordingly; but on the other
hand we must not overlook the fact that Paul not only, as
regards form, adapted himself more closely to the accepted
terminology, but that he also gave to the ancient type of doctrine, already heterodox, a philosophical, an Aristotelian, basis,
and treated it ethically and biblically. He undoubtedly learned
much from Origen; but he recognised the worthlessness of the
double personality construed by Origen, for he has deepened

[1] Κάτωθεν ἀποτεθεῶσθαι τὸν κύριον—ἐξ ἀνθρώπου γεγονέναι τὸν Χριστὸν Θεόν—
ὕστερον αὐτὸν ἐκ προκοπῆς τεθεοποιῆσθαι.

[2] Vincentius, Commonit. 35—Athanasius (c. Ariam IV. 30) relates that the disciples of Paul appealed to Acts X. 36 in support of their distinction between the
Logos and Jesus: τὸν λόγον ἀπέστειλεν τοῖς υἱοῖς Ἰσραὴλ εὐαγγελιζόμενος εἰρήνην
διὰ Ἰησοῦ Χριστοῦ. They said that there was a distinction here like that in the
O. T. between the word of the Lord and of the prophets.

[3] Epiphan. l.c., c. 3; see also the letter of the six Bishops in Routh, l.c., p. 291.

[4] On the supreme interest taken by Paul in the unity of God see p. 42, note 3,
Epiph. l.c., ch. I.

[5] Euseb. H. E. VII. 30. 9.

[6] Euseb. l.c., § 10.

the exposition given by the latter of the personality of Christ, and seen that "what is attained by nature is void of merit" (τὰ κρατούμενα τῷ λόγῳ τῆς φύσεως οὐκ ἔχει ἔπαινον). Paul's expositions of nature and will in the Persons, of the essence and power of love, of the divinity of Christ, only to be perceived in the work of His ministry, because exclusively contained in unity of will with God, are almost unparalleled in the whole dogmatic literature of the Oriental Churches in the first three centuries. For, when such passages do occur in Origen, they at once disappear again in metaphysics, and we do not know the arguments of the Alogi and the Theodotians.[1] It is, above all, the deliberate rejection of metaphysical speculation which distinguishes Paul; he substituted for it the study of history and the determination of worth on moral grounds alone, thus reversing Origen's maxim: ὁ σωτὴρ οὐ κατ' μετουσίαν, ἀλλὰ κατ' οὐσίαν ἐστὶ θεός (the Saviour is God not by communion, but in essence). As he kept his dogmatic theology free from Platonism, his difference with his opponents began in his conception of God. The latter described the controversy very correctly, when they said that Paul "had betrayed the mystery of the Christian faith,"[2] i.e., the mystic conception of God and Christ due to natural philosophy; or[3] when they complained of Paul's denial that the difficulty of maintaining the unity of deity, side by side with a plurality of persons, was got

---

[1] The three fragments of "Ebion" given by Mai, l.c., p. 68, and strangely held by Hilgenfeld to be genuine (Ketzergeschichte, p. 437 f.), seem to me likewise to belong to Paul: at any rate they correspond to his doctrine: Ἐκ τῆς περὶ προφητῶν ἐξηγήσεως (1) Κατ' ἐπαγγελείαν μέγας καὶ ἐκλεκτὸς προφήτης ἐστίν, ἴσως μεσίτης καὶ νομοθέτης τῆς κοείττονος διαθήκης γενόμενος· ὅστις ἑαυτὸν ἱερουργήσας ὑπὲρ πάντων μίαν ἐφάνη καὶ θέλησιν καὶ ἐνέργειαν ἔχων πρὸς τὸν Θεόν, θέλων ὥσπερ Θεὸς πάντας ἀνθρώπους σωθῆναι καὶ εἰς ἐπίγνωσιν ἀληθείας ἐλθεῖν τῆς δι' αὐτοῦ τῷ κόσμῳ δι' ὧν εἰργάσατο φανερωθείσης.—(2) Σχέσει γὰρ τῇ κατὰ δικαιοσύνην καὶ πόθῳ τῷ κατὰ φιλανθρωπίαν συναφθεὶς τῷ Θεῷ, οὐδὲν ἔσχεν μεμερισμένον πρὸς τὸν Θεόν, διὰ τὸ μίαν αὐτοῦ καὶ τοῦ Θεοῦ γενέσθαι τὴν θέλησιν καὶ τὴν ἐνέργειαν τῶν ἐπὶ τῇ σωτηρίᾳ τῶν ἀνθρώπων ἀγαθῶν.—(3) Εἰ γὰρ ἐθέλησεν αὐτὸν Θεὸς σταυρωθῆναι, καὶ κατεδέξατο λέγων. Μὴ τὸ ἐμόν, ἀλλὰ τὸ σὸν γενέσθω θέλημα, δῆλον ὅτι μίαν ἔσχεν μετὰ τοῦ Θεοῦ τὴν θέλησιν καὶ τὴν πρᾶξιν, ἐκεῖνο θελήσας καὶ πράξας, ὑπερ ἔδοξε τῷ Θεῷ. The second and third fragments may be by Theodorus of Mops., but hardly the first.

[2] In Euseb. H. E. VII. 30. 10.

[3] Epiph. l. c., ch. III.: Παῦλος οὐ λέγει μόνον Θεὸν διὰ τὸ πηγὴν εἶναι τὸν πατέρα.

over simply by making the Father their source. What is that
but to admit that Paul started in his idea of God, not from
the *substance*, but from the *person?* He here represented the
interests of theism as against the chaotic naturalism of Platonism. And in appreciating the character of Jesus he refused
to recognise its uniqueness and divinity in his "nature"; these
he found only in his disposition and the direction of his will.
Therefore while Christ as a person was never to him "mere
man" (ψιλὸς ἄνθρωπος), yet Christ's natural endowment he would
not recognise as exceptional. But as Christ had been predestinated by God in a unique manner, so in conformity to the promises the Spirit and the grace of God rested on him exceptionally; and thus his work in his vocation and his life, with and
in God, had been unique. This view left room for a human
life, and if Paul has, ultimately, used the formula, that Christ
had become God, his appeal to Philipp. II. 9 shows in what
sense he understood the words.

His opponents, indeed, charged him with sophistically and
deceitfully concealing his true opinion behind phrases with an
orthodox sound. It is possible, in view of the fact, *e.g.*, that
he called the impersonal Logos "Son", that there is some
truth in this; but it is not probable. He was not understood,
or rather he was misunderstood. Many theologians at the present
day regard the theology of Hermas as positively Nicene, although it is hardly a whit more orthodox than that of Paul. If
such a misunderstanding is possible to the scholars of to-day—
and Hermas was certainly no dissembler,—why can Firmilian
not have looked on Paul as orthodox for a time? He taught
that there was an eternal Son of God, and that he dwelt in
Jesus; he proclaimed the divinity of Christ, held there were
two persons (God and Jesus), and with the Alexandrians rejected
Sabellianism. On this very point, indeed, a sort of concession
seems to have been made to him at the Synod. We know that
the Synod expressly censured the term "ὁμοούσιος",[1] and this

---

[1] This was a well-known matter at the time of the Arian controversy, and the Semi-
Arians, *e.g.*, appealed expressly to the decision at Ancyra. See Sozomen H. E. IV. 15;
Athanas., De Synod. 43 sq.; Basilius, Ep. 52; Hilarius de synodis 81, 86; Routh, l.c.,
pp. 360—365, Hefele, Conciliengesch. I., 2, p. 140 f. : Caspari, Quellen IV., p. 170 f.

was done, Athanasius conjectures, to meet an objection of Paul.
He is said to have argued as follows:—If Christ is not, as he
taught, essentially human, then he is ὁμοούσιος with the Father.
But if that be true then the Father is not the ultimate source
of the deity, but Being (the οὐσία), and thus we have three
οὐσίαι;[1] in other words the divinity of the Father is itself derivative, and the Father is of identical origin with the Son,—
"they become brothers". This can have been an objection
made by Paul. The Aristotelian conception of the οὐσία
would correspond to his turn of thought, and so would the
circumstance, that the possibility of a subordinate, natural,
divinity on the part of the Son is left out of the question. The
Synod again can very well have rejected ὁμοούσιος in the interests of anti-sabellianism.[2] Yet it is just as possible that, as
Hilarius says, the Synod condemned the term because Paul
himself had declared God and the impersonal Logos (the Son)
to be ὁμοούσιος, i.e., "of the same substance, of one substance".[3]
However that may be, whenever Paul's view was seen through,
it was at once felt by the majority to be in the highest degree
heretical. No one was yet quite clear as to what sort of thing
this "naturally—divine" element in Christ was. Even Origen
had taught that he possessed a divinity to which prayer might
not be offered.[4] But to deny the divine nature (physis) to the
Redeemer, was universally held to be an attack on the Rule
of Faith.[5] They correctly perceived the really weak point in
Paul's Christology, his teaching, namely, that there were actually
two Sons of God;[6] Hermas, however, had already preached

---

[1] Athanas. l.c.; ἀνάγκη τρεῖς οὐσίας εἶναι, μίαν μὲν προηγουμένην, τὰς δὲ δύο ἐξ ἐκείνης.

[2] This is also the opinion of Basilius (l.c.): ἔφασαν γὰρ ἐκεῖνοι (the Bishops assembled against Paul) τὴν τοῦ ὁμοουσίου φωνὴν παριστᾶν ἔννοιαν οὐσίας τε καὶ τῶν ἀπ᾽ αὐτῆς, ὥστε καταμερισθεῖσαν τὴν οὐσίαν παρέχειν τοῦ ὁμοουσίου τὴν προσηγορίαν τοῖς εἰς ἃ διῃρέθη.

[3] Dorner's view (l.c. I. p. 513) is impossible because resting on a false interpretation of the word ὁμοούσιος; Paul held the Father and Jesus to be ὁμοούσιοι in
so far as they were *persons*, and therefore the Synod condemned the term.

[4] See De orat. 15, 16.

[5] Euseb. H. E. VII. 30. 6, 16.

[6] See Malchion in Leontius (Routh, l.c., p. 312): Παῦλος φησίν, μὴ δύο ἐπίστασ-
θαι υἱούς· εἰ δὲ υἱὸς ὁ ᾽Ι, Χρ. τοῦ Θεοῦ, υἱὸς δὲ καὶ ἡ σοφία, καὶ ἄλλο μὲν ἡ σοφία,

this, and Paul was not in earnest about the "eternal Son".
Yet this was only a secondary matter. The crucial difference
had its root in the question as to the divine nature (physis) of
the Redeemer.

Now here it is of the highest interest to notice how far, in
the minds of many Bishops in Palestine and Syria, the speculative interpretation of the Rule of Faith had taken the place
of that rule itself. If we compare the letter of Hymenæus of
Jerusalem and his five colleagues to Paul with the *regula fidei*
—not, say, that of Tertullian and Irenæus—but the Rule of
Faith with which Origen has headed his great work: περὶ ἀρχῶν,
then we are astonished at the advance in the times. The
Bishops explain at the opening of their letter, [1] that they desired
to expound, "in writing, the faith which we received from the
beginning, and possess, having been transmitted and kept in
the Catholic Church, proclaimed up to our day by the successors
of the blessed Apostles, who were both eye-witnesses and assistants
of the Logos, from the law and prophets and the New Testament."
(ἔγγραφον τὴν πίστιν ἣν ἐξ ἀρχῆς παρελάβομεν καὶ ἔχομεν παρα-
δοθεῖσαν καὶ τηρουμένην ἐν τῇ καθολικῇ καὶ ἁγίᾳ ἐκκλησίᾳ, μέχρι
τῆς σήμερον ἡμέρας ἐκ διαδοχῆς ἀπὸ τῶν μακαρίων ἀποστόλων, οἳ
καὶ αὐτόπται καὶ ὑπηρέται γεγόνασι τοῦ λόγου, καταγγελλομένην,
ἐκ νόμου καὶ προφητῶν καὶ τῆς καινῆς διαθήκης.) *But what they
presented as "the faith" and furnished with proofs from Scripture, was the speculative theology,* [2] In no other writing can

---

ἄλλο δὲ 'I. Χρ., δύο ὑφίστανται υἱοί. See also Ephraem in Photius, Biblioth. cod.
229. Farther the Ep. II. Felicis II. papæ ad Petrum Fullonem.

[1] See Routh, l.c., p. 289 sq.

[2] The πίστις ἐξ ἀρχῆς παραληφθεῖσα reads (l.c.): ῞Οτι ὁ Θεὸς ἀγέννητος, εἷς ἄναρ-
χος, ἀόρατος, ἀναλλοίωτος, ὃν εἶδεν οὐδεὶς ἀνθρώπων, οὐδὲ ἰδεῖν δύναται· οὗ τὴν δόξαν
ἢ τὸ μέγεθος νοῆσαι ἢ ἐξηγήσασθαι καθώς ἐστιν ἀξίως τῆς ἀληθείας, ἀνθρωπίνῃ φύσει
ἀνέφικτον· ἔννοιαν δὲ καὶ ὁπωσοῦν μετρίαν περὶ αὐτοῦ λαβεῖν, ἀγαπητόν, ἀποκαλυπ-
τοντος τοῦ υἱοῦ αὐτοῦ... τοῦτον δὲ τὸν υἱὸν γεννητόν, μονογενῆ υἱόν, εἰκόνα τοῦ
ἀοράτου Θεοῦ τυγχάνοντα, πρωτότοκον πάσης κτίσεως σοφίαν καὶ λόγον καὶ δύναμιν
Θεοῦ, πρὸ αἰώνων ὄντα, οὐ προγνώσει, ἀλλ' οὐσίᾳ καὶ ὑποστάσει Θεὸν Θεοῦ υἱόν, ἕν
τε παλαιᾷ καὶ νέᾳ διαθήκῃ ἐγνωκότες ὁμολογοῦμεν καὶ κηρύσσομεν. ὃς δ' ἂν ἀντιμά-
χηται τὸν υἱὸν τοῦ Θεοῦ Θεὸν μὴ εἶναι πρὸ καταβολῆς κόσμου (δεῖν) πιστεύειν καὶ
ὁμολογεῖν, φάσκων δύο θεοὺς καταγγέλλεσθαι, ἐὰν ὁ υἱὸς τοῦ Θεοῦ Θεὸς κηρύσσηται
τοῦτον ἀλλότριον τοῦ ἐκκλησιαστικοῦ κανόνος ἡγούμεθα, καὶ πᾶσαι αἱ καθολικαὶ
ἐκκλησίαι συμφωνοῦσιν ἡμῖν. The prehistoric history of the Son is now expounded,

we see the triumph in the sphere of religion of the theology of philosophy or of Origen, *i.e.*, of Hellenism, so clearly, as in this letter, in which philosophical dogmatics are put forward as the faith itself. But further. *At the end of the third century even the baptismal confessions were expanded in the East by the adoption of propositions borrowed from philosophical theology;*[1] *or, to put it in another way,—baptismal confessions apparently now first formulated, were introduced in many Oriental communities, which also now contained the doctrine of the Logos.* Since these statements were directed against Sabellianism as well as against "Ebionitism"; they will be discussed later on.

With the deposition and removal of Paul the historian's interest in his case is at an end. It was henceforth no longer possible to gain a hearing, in the great forum of Church life, for a Christology which did not include the personal pre-existence of the Redeemer: no one was permitted henceforth to content himself with the elucidation of the divinely-human life of Jesus in his work. It was necessary to believe in the divine nature (physis) of the Redeemer.[2] The smaller and remote communities were compelled to imitate the attitude of the larger. Yet we know from the circular letter of Alexander of Alexandria, A.D. 321,[3] that the doctrine of Paul did not by any means pass away without leaving a trace. Lucian and his

---

and then it goes on: τὸν δὲ υἱὸν παρὰ τῷ πατρὶ ὄντα Θεὸν μὲν καὶ κύριον τῶν γενητῶν ἁπάντων, ὑπὸ δὲ τοῦ πατρὸς ἀποσταλέντα ἐξ οὐρανῶν καὶ σαρκωθέντα ἐνηνθρωπηκέναι. διόπερ καὶ τὸ ἐκ τῆς παρθένου σῶμα χωρῆσαν πᾶν τὸ πλήρωμα τῆς θεότητος σωματικῶς, τῇ θεότητι ἀτρέπτως ἥνωται καὶ τεθεοποίηται and at the close: εἰ δὲ Χριστὸς Θεοῦ δύναμις καὶ Θεοῦ σοφία πρὸ αἰώνων ἐστίν· οὕτω καὶ καθὸ Χριστὸς ἓν καὶ τὸ αὐτὸ ὢν τῇ οὐσίᾳ· εἰ καὶ τὰ μάλιστα πολλαῖς ἐπινοίαις ἐπινοεῖται. See also Hahn, Bibl. d. Symbol. 2 Aufl. § 82.

[1] The propositions are undoubtedly as a rule phrased biblically, and they are biblical; but they are propositions preferred and edited by the learned exegesis of the Alexandrian which certainly was extremely closely allied with philosophical speculation.

[2] The followers of Paul were no longer looked upon as Christians even at the beginning of the fourth century, and therefore they were re-baptised. See the 19 Canon of Nicæa: Περὶ τῶν Παυλιανισάντων, εἶτα προσφυγόντων τῇ καθολικῇ ἐκκλησίᾳ, ὅρος ἐκτέθειται ἀναβαπτίζεσθαι αὐτοὺς ἐξάπαντος.

[3] Theodoret H. E. I. 4.

famous academy, the alma mater of Arianism, were inspired by
the genius of Paul. [1] Lucian—himself perhaps, a native of Samosata—had, during the incumbency of three Bishops of Antioch,
remained, like Theodotus and his party in Rome, at the head
of a school outside of the great Catholic Church. [2] In his
teaching, and in that of Arius, the foundation laid by Paul is
unmistakable. [3] But Lucian has falsified the fundamental thought
of Paul in yielding to the assumption of a Logos, though a
very subordinate and created Logos, and in putting this in the
place of the man Jesus, while his disciples, the Arians, have,
in the view sketched by them of the person of Christ, been
unable to retain the features Paul ascribed to it; though they
also have emphasised the importance of the will in Christ. We
must conclude, however, that Arianism, as a whole, is nothing
but a compromise between the Adoptian and the Logos Christology, which proves that after the close of the 3rd century,
no Christology was possible in the Church which failed to recognise the personal pre-existence of Christ.

Photinus approximated to Paul of Samosata in the fourth
century. Above all, however, the great theologians of Antioch
occupied a position by no means remote from him; for the
presupposition of the personal Logos Homousios in Christ,
which they as Church theologians had to accept simply, could
be combined much better with the thought of Paul, than the

---

1 See my article "Lucian" in Herzog's R.E. 2 Aufl., Bd. VIII., p. 767 ff.

2 See Theodoret l.c.: αὐτοὶ γὰρ Θεοδίδακτοι ἐστέ, οὐκ ἀγνοοῦντες ὅτι ἡ ἔναγχος
ἐπαναστᾶσα τῇ ἐκκλησιαστικῇ εὐσεβείᾳ διδασκαλία Ἐβίωνός ἐστι καὶ Ἀρτεμᾶ, καὶ
ζῆλος τοῦ κατ᾽ Ἀντιόχειαν Παύλου τοῦ Σαμοσατέως, συνόδῳ καὶ κρίσει τῶν ἁπαν-
ταχοῦ ἐπισκόπων ἀποκηρυχθέντος τῆς ἐκκλησίας—ὃν διαδεξάμενος Λουκιανὸς ἀποσυ-
νάγωγος ἔμεινε τριῶν ἐπισκόπων πολυετεῖς χρόνους—ὧν τῆς ἀσεβείας τὴν τρύγα
ἐρροφηκότες (scil. Arian and his companions) νῦν ἡμῖν τὸ Ἐξ οὐκ ὄντων ἐπεφύησαν,
τὰ ἐκείνων κεκρυμμένα μοσχεύματα.

3 See esp. Athanas. c. Arian I. 5. "Arius says that there are two wisdoms, one
which is the true one and at the same time exists in God; through this the Son arose
and by participation in it he was simply named Word and Wisdom; for wisdom, he
says, originated through wisdom according to the will of the wise God. Then he also
says that there is another Word apart from the Son in God, and through participation
therein the Son himself has been again named graciously Word and Son." This
is the doctrine of Paul of Samos., taken over by Arius from Lucian. On the
distinction see above.

Arian assumption of a subordinate god, with attributes half-human, half-divine. So also the arguments of Theodore of Mop-suestia as to the relation of the Logos and the man Jesus, as to nature, will, disposition, etc., are here and there verbally iden-tical with those of Paul; and his opponents, especially Leontius, [1] were not so far wrong in charging Theodore with teaching like Paul. [2] Paul was in fact condemned a second time in the great scholars of Antioch, and—strangely—his name was once more mentioned, and for the third time, in the Monothelite contro-versy. In this case his statements as to the one will ($\mu i\alpha$ $\theta\epsilon\lambda\eta\sigma\iota\varsigma$ sc. of God and Jesus) were shamefully misused, in order to show to the opposition that their doctrine had been already condemned in the person of the arch-heretic.

We possess, however, another ancient source of information, of the beginning of the 4th century, the Acta Archelai. [3] This shows us that at the extreme eastern boundary of Christendom there persisted even among Catholic clerics, if we may use here the word Catholic, Christological conceptions which had remained unaffected by Alexandrian theology, and must be classed with Adoptianism. The author's exposition of Christ consists, so far as we can judge, in the doctrine of Paul of Samosata. [4] Here we are shown clearly that the Logos Christology had, at the beginning of the 4th century, not yet passed beyond the borders of the Christendom comprehended in the Roman Empire.

[1] See in Routh, l.c., p. 347 sq.

[2] See the careful and comprehensive collection of the arguments of Theodore in reference to christology, in Swete, Theodori Episcopi Mopsuesteni in epp. B. Pauli Commentarii, Vol. II. (1882), pp. 289—339.

[3] We have to compare also the treatises of Aphraates, written shortly before the middle of the 4th century. He adheres to the designation of Christ as Logos according to John I. 1; but it is very striking that in our Persian author there is not even the slightest allusion in which one could perceive an echo of the Arian controversies (Bickell, Ausgewählte Schriften der syr. Kirchenväter 1874, p. 15). See tract 1, "On faith", and 17, "Proof that Christ is the Son of God."

[4] On the origin of the Acta Archelai see my Texte und Unters. I. 3, 137 ff. The principal passages are to be found in ch. 49 and 50. In these the Churchman disputes the view of Mani, that Jesus was a spirit, the eternal Son of God, perfect by nature. "Dic mihi, super quem spiritus sanctus sicut columba descendit? Si perfectus erat, si filius erat, si virtus erat, non poterat spiritus ingredi, sicut nec

3. Expulsion of Modalistic Monarchianism.

(a). The Modalistic Monarchians in Asia Minor and in the West: Noëtus, Epigonus, Cleomenes, Aeschines, Praxeas, Victorinus (Victor), Zephyrinus, Sabellius, Callistus. [1]

The really dangerous opponent of the Logos Christology in the period between A.D. 180 and 300 was not Adoptianism, but the doctrine which saw the deity himself incarnate in Christ, and conceived Christ to be God in a human body, the Father

regnum potest ingredi intra regnum. Cuius autem ei cælitus emissa vox testimonium detulit dicens: Hic est filius meus dilectus, in quo bene complacui? Dic age nihil remoreris, quis ille est, qui parat hæc omnia, qui agit universa? Responde itane blasphemiam pro ratione impudenter allegas, et inferre conaris?" The following Christology is put in the lips of Mani: "Mihi pium videtur dicere, quod nihil eguerit filius dei in eo quod adventus eius procuratur ad terras, neque opus habuerit columba, neque baptismate, neque matre, neque fratribus." On the other hand Mani says in reference to the Church views: "Si enim hominem eum tantummodo ex Maria esse dicis et in baptismate spiritum percepisse, ergo per profectum filius videbitur et non per naturam. Si tamen tibi concedam dicere, secundum profectum esse filium quasi hominem factum, hominem vere esse opinaris, id est, qui caro et sanguis sit?" In what follows Archelaus says: "Quomodo poterit vera columba verum hominem ingredi atque in eo permanere, caro enim carnem ingredi non potest? sed magis si Iesum hominem verum confiteamur, eum vero, qui dicitur, sicut columba, Spiritum Sanctum, salva est nobis ratio in utraque. Spiritus enim secundum rectam rationem habitat in homine, et descendit et permanet et competenter hoc et factum est et fit semper... *Descendit spiritus super hominem dignum se*... Poterat dominus in cælo positus facere quæ voluerat, si spiritum eum esse et non hominem dices. Sed non ita est, quoniam exinanivit semetipsum formam servi accipiens. *Dico autem de eo, qui ex Maria factus est homo.* Quid enim? non poteramus et nos multo facilius et lautius ista narrare? sed absit, ut a veritate declinemus iota unum aut unum apicem. Est enim qui de Maria natus est filius, qui totum hoc quod magnum est, voluit perferre certamen Iesus. *Hic est Christus dei, qui descendit super eum, qui de Maria est*... Statim (post baptismum) in desertum a *Spiritu* ductus est *Iesus, quem cum diabolus ignoraret, dicebat ei: Si filius est dei. Ignorabat autem propter quid genuisset filium dei* (scil. *Spiritus*), *qui prædicabat regnum cælorum, quod erat habitaculum magnum,* nec ab ullo alio parari potuisset; unde et affixus cruci cum resurrexisset ab inferis, *assumptus est illuc, ubi Christus filius dei regnabat*... Sicut enim Paracleti pondus nullus alius valuit sustinere nisi soli discipuli et Paulus beatus, *ita etiam spiritum,* qui de cælis descenderat, per quem vox paterna testatur dicens: Hic est filius meus dilectus, *nullus alius portare prævaluit, nisi qui ex Maria natus est super omnes sanctos Iesus.*" It is noteworthy that the author (in ch. 37) ranks Sabellius as a heretic with Valentinus, Marcion, and Tatian.

[1] Döllinger, Hippolytus und Kallistus, 1853. Volkmar, Hippolyt. und die röm. Zeitgenossen, 1855. Hagemann, Die römische Kirche, 1864. Langen, Gesch. d. römischen Kirche I., p. 192 ff. Numerous monographs on Hippolytus and the

become flesh. Against this view the great Doctors of the Church—Tertullian, Origen, Novatian, but above all, Hippolytus—had principally to fight. Its defenders were called by Tertullian "Monarchiani", and, not altogether correctly, "Patripassiani", which afterwards became the usual names in the West (see *e.g.*, Cypr., Ep. 73: 4). In the East they were all designated, after the famous head of the school, "Sabelliani" from the second half of the third century; yet the name of "Patripassiani" was not quite unknown there also. [1] Hippolytus tells us in

origin of the Philosophumena, as also on the authorities for the history of the early heretics, come in here. See also Caspari, Quellen III., vv. *ll.* The authorites are for Noëtus, the Syntagma of Hippolytus (Epiph., Philaster, Pseudo-Tertull.), and his great work against Monarchianism, of which the so-called Ὁμιλία Ἱππολύτου εἰς τὴν αἵρεσιν Νοήτου τινός (Lagarde, Hippol. quæ feruntur, p. 43 sq.) may with extreme probability be held to be the conclusion. Both these works have been made use of by Epiph. H. 57. [When Epiph. (l.c. ch. 1) remarks that "Noëtus appeared ± 130 years ago", it is to be inferred that he fixed the date from his authority, the anti-monarchian work of Hippolytus. For the latter he must have had a date, which he believed he could simply transfer to the period of Noëtus, since Noëtus is described in the book as οὐ πρὸ πολλοῦ χρόνου γενόμενος. But in that case his source was written about A.D. 230—240, *i.e.*, almost at the same time as the so-called Little Labyrinth. It is also possible, however, that the above date refers to the excommunication of Noëtus. In that case the work which has recorded this event, can have been written at the earliest in the fourth decade of the fourth century]. Most of the later accounts refer to that of Epiph. An independent one is the section Philos. IX. 7 sq. (X. 27; on this Theodoret is dependent H. F. III. 3). For Epigonus and Cleomenes we have Philos. IX. 7, 10, 11, X. 27; Theodoret H. F. III. 3. For Æschines: Pseudo-Tertull. 26; Philos. VIII. 19, X. 26; for Praxeas: Tertull. adv. Prax., Pseudo-Tertull. 30. The later Latin writers against heretics are at this point all dependent on Tertullian; yet see Optat., de schism. I. 9. Lipsius has tried to prove that Tertullian has used "Hippolytus against Noëtus" in his work adv. Prax. (Quellen-kritik, p. 43; Ketzergeschichte, p. 183 f.; Jahrbuch für deutsche Theologie, 1868, p. 704); but the attempt is not successful (see Ztschr. f. d. hist. Theol., 1874, p. 200 f.). For Victorinus we have Pseudo-Tertull. 30. For Zephyrinus and Callistus: Philos. IX. 11 sq. Origen has also had Roman Monarchians in view in many of the arguments in his commentaries. On Origen's residence in Rome and his relations with Hippolytus, see Euseb. H. E. VI. 14; Jerome, De vir. inl. 61; Photius Cod. 121; on his condemnation at Rome, see Jerome Ep. 33, ch. 4.

[1] Orig. in Titum, Lomm. V., p. 287 "... sicut et illos, qui superstitiose magis quam religiose, uti ne videantur duos deos dicere, neque rursum negare salvatoris deitatem, unam eandemque substantiam patris ac filii asseverant, id est, duo quidem nomina secundum diversitatem causarum recipientes, unam tamen ὑπόστασιν subsistere, id est, unam personam duobus nominibus subiacentem, qui latine Patripassiani appellantur." Athanas., de synod. 7 after the formula Antioch. macrostich.

the Philosophumena, that at that time the Monarchian controversy agitated the whole Church, [1] and Tertullian and Origen testified, that in their day the "economic" trinity, and the technical application of the conception of the Logos to Christ, were regarded by the mass of Christians with suspicion. [2] Modalism, as we now know from the Philosoph., was for almost a generation the official theory in Rome. That it was not an absolute novelty can be proved; [3] but it is very probable, on

[1] IX. 6: μέγιστον τάραχον κατὰ πάντα τὸν κόσμον ἐν πᾶσιν τοῖς πιστοῖς ἐμβάλλουσιν.

[2] Ad. Prax. 3: Simplices quique, ne dixerim imprudentes et idiotæ, quæ maior semper pars credentium est, quoniam et ipsa regula fidei a pluribus diis sæculi ad unicum et verum deum transfert, non intelligentes unicum quidem, sed cum sua οἰκονομία esse credendum, expavescunt ad οἰκονομίαν... Itaque duos et tres iam iactitant a nobis prædicari, se vero unius dei cultores præsumunt,.. monarchiam inquiunt tenemus." Orig., in Joh. II 3. Lomm. I. p. 95: "Ετεροι δὲ οἱ μηδὲν εἰδότες, εἰ μὴ Ἰησοῦν Χριστὸν καὶ τοῦτον ἐσταυρωμένον, τὸν γενόμενον σάρκα λόγον τὸ πᾶν νομίσαντες εἶναι τοῦ λόγου, Χριστὸν κατὰ σάρκα μόνον γιγνώσκουσι τοιοῦτου δέ ἐστι τὸ πλῆθος τῶν πεπιστευκέναι νομιζόμενων. Origen has elsewhere distinguished four grades in religion: (1) those who worship idols, (2) those who worship angelic powers, (3) *those to whom Christ is the entire God*, (4) those whose thoughts rise to the unchangeable deity. Clement (Strom. VI. 10) had already related that there were Christians who, in their dread of heresy, demanded that everything should be abandoned as superfluous and alien, which did not tend directly to blessedness.

[3] See above (Vol. I., p. 195) where reference is made, on the one hand, to the Modalism reflected in Gnostic and Enkratitic circles (Gosp. of the Egypt., and Acta Lenc., Simonians in Iren. I. 231); on the other, to the Church formulas phrased, or capable of being interpreted, modalistically (see II. Ep. of Clement, Ign. ad Ephes., Melito [Syr. Fragments]; and in addition, passages which speak of God having suffered, died, etc.). It is instructive to notice that the development in Marcionite Churches and Montanist communities moved parallel to that in the great Church. Marcion himself, being no dogmatist, did not take any interest in the question of the relation of Christ to the higher God. Therefore it is not right to reckon him among the Modalists, as Neander has done (Gnost. Syxteme, p. 294, Kirchengesch. I. 2, p. 796). But it is certain that later Marcionites in the West taught Patripassianism (Ambros. de fide V. 13. 162, T. II., p. 579; Ambrosiaster ad I. Cor. II. 2, T. II., App. p. 117). Marcionites and Sabellians were therefore at a later date not seldom classed together. Among the Montanists at Rome there were, about A.D. 200, a Modalistic party and one that taught like Hippolytus; at the head of the former stood Æschines, at the head of the latter Proculus. Of the followers of Æschines, Hippolytus says (Philos. X. 26) that their doctrine was that of Noëtus: αὐτὸν εἶναι υἱὸν καὶ πατέρα, ὁρατὸν καὶ ἀόρατον; γεννητὸν καὶ ἀγέννητον, θνητὸν καὶ ἀθάνατον. It is rather an idle question whether Montanus himself and the prophetic women taught Modalism. They certainly used formulas which had a Modalistic sound; but they had also others which could afterwards be

the other hand, that a Modalistic doctrine, which sought to exclude every other, only existed from the end of the second century. It was in opposition to Gnosticism that the first effort was made to fix theologically the formulas of a naïve Modalism, and that these were used to confront the Logos Christology in order (1) to avert Ditheism, (2) to maintain the complete divinity of Christ, and (3) to prevent the attacks of Gnosticism. An attempt was also made, however, to prove Modalism by exegesis. That is equivalent to saying that this form of doctrine, which was embraced by the great majority of Christians, [1] was supported by *scientific* authorities, from the end of the second century. But it can be shown without difficulty, how hurtful any contact with theology could not fail to be to the naïve conception of the incarnation of the deity in Christ, and we may say that it was all over with it—though of course the death-struggle lasted long—when it found itself compelled to attack others or to defend itself. When it required to clothe itself in a cloak manufactured by a scientific theology, and to reflect on the idea of God, it belied its own nature, and lost its *raison d'être*. What it still retained was completely distorted by its opponents. Hippolytus has in the Philosophumena represented the doctrine of Noëtus to have been borrowed from Heraclitus. That

nterpreted and could not but be interpreted "economically". In the Test. of the XII. Patriarchs many passages that, in the Jewish original, spoke of Jehovah's appearance among his people must now have received a Christian impress from their Christian editor. It is remarkable that, living in the third century, he did not scruple to do this, see Simeon 6: ὅτι ὁ κύριος ὁ Θεὸς μέγας τοῦ Ἰσραήλ, φαινόμενος ἐπὶ γῆς ὡς ἄνθρωπος καὶ σώζων ἐν αὐτῷ τὸν Ἀδάμ ... ὅτι ὁ Θεὸς σῶμα λαβὼν καὶ συνεσθίων ἀνθρώποις ἔσωσεν ἀνθρώπους; Levi 5, Jud. 22, Issachar. 7: ἔχοντες μεθ' ἑαυτῶν τὸν Θεὸν τοῦ οὐρανοῦ, συμπορευόμενον τοῖς ἀνθρώποις: Zebul. 9: ὄψεσθε Θεὸν ἐν σχήματι ἀνθρώπου; Dan. 5; Naphth. 8: ὀφθήσεται Θεὸς κατοικῶν ἐν ἀνθρώποις ἐπὶ τῆς γῆς: Asher 7: ἕως οὗ ὁ ὕψιστος ἐπισκέψηται τὴν γῆν, καὶ αὐτὸς ἐλθὼν ὡς ἄνθρωπος μετὰ ἀνθρώπων ἐσθίων καὶ πίνων; Benjamin 10. Very different Christologies, however, can be exemplified from the Testaments. It is not certain what sort of party Philaster (H. 51) meant (Lipsius Ketzergesch., p. 99 f.). In the third century Modalism assumed various forms, among which the conception of a formal transformation of God into man, and a real transition of the one into the other, is noteworthy. An exclusive Modalistic doctrine first existed in the Church after the fight with Gnosticism.

[1] Tertull. l.c. and ch. I.: "simplicitas doctrinæ", ch. 9, Epiphan. H. 62. 2 ἀφελέστατοι ἢ ἀκέραιοι. Philos. IX. 7, 11: Ζεφυρῖνος ἰδιώτης καί ἀγράμματος, l.c. ch. 6: ἀμαθεῖς.

is, of course, an exaggeration. But once we grasp the whole problem "philosophically and scientifically"—and it was so understood even by some scientific defenders of Monarchianism—then it undoubtedly resembles strikingly the controversy regarding the idea of God between the genuine Stoics and the Platonists. As the latter set the transcendent, apathetic God of Plato above the λόγος-θεός of Heraclitus and the Stoics, so Origen, e.g., has charged the Monarchians especially with stopping short at the God manifest, and at work, in the world, instead of advancing to the "ultimate" God, and thus apprehending the deity "economically". Nor can it surprise us that Modalistic Monarchianism, after some of its representatives had actually summoned science, i.e., the Stoa, to their assistance, moved in the direction of a pantheistic conception of God. But this does not seem to have happened at the outset, or to the extent assumed by the opponents of the school. Not to speak of its uncultured adherents, the earliest literary defenders of Modalism were markedly monotheistic, and had a real interest in Biblical Christianity. It marks the character of the opposition, however, that they at once scented the God of Heraclitus and Zeno—a proof of how deeply they themselves were involved in Neo-platonic theology.[1] As it was in Asia

---

[1] That the scientific defenders of Modalism adopted the Stoic method—just as the Theodotians had the Aristotelian (see above)—is evident, and Hippolytus was therefore so far correct in connecting Noëtus with Heraclitus, i.e., with the father of the Stoa. To Hagemann belongs the merit (Röm. Kirche, pp. 354—371) of having demonstrated the traces of Stoic Logic and Metaphysics in the few and imperfectly transmitted tenets of the Modalists. (See here Hatch, The influence etc., p. 19 f. on the συμπάσχειν and the substantial unity of ψυχή and σῶμα). We can still recognise, especially from Novatian's refutation, the syllogistic method of the Modalists, which rested on nominalist, i.e., Stoic, logic. See, e.g., the proposition: Si unus deus Christus, Christus autem deus, pater est Christus, quia unus deus; si non pater sit Christus, dum et deus filius Christus, duo dii contra scripturas introducti videantur." But those utterances in which contradictory attributes, such as visible—invisible etc., are ascribed to God, could be excellently supported by the Stoic system of categories. That system distinguished ἴδια (οὐσία, ὑποκείμενον) from συμβεβηκότα, or more accurately (1) ὑποκείμενα (substrata, subjects of judgment); (2) ποιά (qualitatives); (3) πὼς ἔχοντα (definite modifications) and (4) πρὸς τι πὼς ἔχοντα (relative modifications). Nos. 2—4 form the qualities of the idea as a συγκεχυομένον; but 2 and 3 belong to the conceptual sphere of the subject itself, while 4 embraces the variable relation of the subject to other subjects. The designations

Minor that Adoptianism first entered into conflict with the
Logos Christology, so the Church of Asia Minor seems to
have been the scene of the first Modalistic controversy, while in
both cases natives of that country transferred the dispute to Rome.

Father and Son, visible and invisible etc., must be conceived as such relative,
accidental, attributes. The same subject can in one relation be Father, in another
Son, or, according to circumstances, be visible or invisible. One sees that this
logical method could be utilised excellently to prove the simple unreasoned propositions of the old Modalism. There are many traces to show that the system was
applied in the schools of Epigonus and Cleomenes, and it is with schools we have
here to deal. Thus, e.g., we have the accusation which, time and again, Origen
made against the Monarchians, that they only assnme one ὑποκειμένον, and combine
Father and Son indiscriminately as modes in which it is manifested. (Hagemann
refers to Orig. on Matt. XVI. 14: οἱ συγχέοντες πατρὸς καὶ υἱοῦ ἔννοιαν; and on
John X. 21: συγχεόμενοι ἐν τῷ περὶ πατρὸς καὶ υἱοῦ τόπῳ—but συγχέειν is the
Stoic term). The proposition is also Stoic that while the one ὑποκειμένον is capable
of being divided (διαιρεῖν), it is only subjectively, in our conceptions of it (τῇ
ἐπινοίᾳ μόνῃ), so that merely ὀνόματα not differences καθ' ὑπόστασιν, result. Further,
the conception of the Logos as a mere sound is verbally that of the Stoics, who
defined the φωνή (λόγος) as ἀὴρ πεπληγμένος ἢ τὸ ἴδιον αἰσθητὸν ἀκοῆς. Tertullian
adv. Prax. 7; "quid est enim, dices, sermo nisi vox et sonus oris et sicut gram-
matici tradunt, aër offensus, intelligibilis auditu, ceterum vacuum nescio quid et
inane et incorporale?" Hippolyt., Philos. X. 33: Θεὸς λόγον ἀπογεννᾷ, οὐ λόγον
ὡς φωνήν. Novatian, de trinit. 31: "sermo filius natus est, qui non in sono per-
cussi aëris aut tono coactæ de visceribus vocis accipitur." The application of
Nominalist Logic and Stoic Methaphysics to theology was discredited in the
controversy with the Modalists under the names of "godless science", or "the
science of the unbelievers", just as much as Aristotelian philosophy had been in
the fight with the Adoptians. Therefore, even as early as about A.D. 250, one of
the most rancorous charges levelled at Novatian by his enemies was that he was
a follower of another, i.e., of the Stoic, philosophy (Cornelius ap. Euseb. H. E. VI.
43. 16; Cypr. Ep. 55. 24, 60. 3). Novatian incurred this reproach because he opposed
the Monarchians with their own, i.e., the syllogistic, method, and because he had
maintained, as was alleged, imitating the Stoics, "omnia peccata paria esse."
Now if the philosophy of Adoptian scholars was Aristotelian, and that of
Modalistic scholars was Stoic, so the philosophy of Tatian, Tertullian, Hippolytus, and Origen, in reference to the One and Many, and the real evolutions
(μερισμός) of the one to the many is unmistakably Platonic. Hagemann (l.c. pp.
182—206) has shown the extent to which the expositions of Plotinus (or Porphyry)
coincide in contents and form, method and expression—see especially the conception
of Hypostasis (substance) in Plotinus—with those of the Christian theologians mentioned,
among whom we have to include Valentinus. (See also Hipler in the östr. Vierteljahrsschr.
f. Kath. Theol. 1869, p. 161 ff., quoted after Lösche, Ztschr. f. wiss. Theol. 1884, p. 259).
When the Logos Christology triumphed completely in the Church at the end of
the third century, Neoplatonism also triumphed over Aristotelianism and Stoicism in
ecclesiastical science, and it was only in the West that theologians, like Arnobius,
were tolerated who in their pursuit of Christian knowledge rejected Platonism.

It is possible that Noëtus was not excommunicated till about A.D. 230, and, even if we cannot now discover his date more accurately, it seems to be certain that he first excited attention as a Monarchian, and probably in the last twenty years of the second century. This was perhaps in Smyrna,[1] his native place, perhaps in Ephesus.[2] He was excommunicated in Asia Minor, only after the whole controversy had, comparatively speaking, come to a close in Rome.[3] This explains why Hippolytus has mentioned him last in his great work against the Monarchians, while in the Philosoph. he describes him as the originator (IX. 6: ἀρχηγόν) of the heresy.[4] A disciple of his, Epigonus, came to Rome in the time of Zephyrinus, or shortly before (+ 200), and is said to have there diffused the teaching of his master, and to have formed a separate party of Patripassians. At first Cleomenes, the disciple of Epigonus, was regarded as the head of the sect, and then, from c. A.D. 215, Sabellius. Against these there appeared, in the Roman Church, especially the presbyter Hippolytus, who sought to prove that the doctrine promulgated by them was a revolutionary error. But the sympathies of the vast majority of the Roman Christians, so far as they could take any part in the dispute, were on the side of the Monarchians, and even among the clergy only a minority supported Hippolytus. The "uneducated" Bishop Zephyrine, advised by the prudent Callistus, was himself disposed, like Victor, his predecessor (see under), to the Modalistic views; but his main effort seems to have been to calm the contending parties, and at any cost to avoid a new

---

[1] Hippol. c. Noët. I., Philos. IX. 7.

[2] Epiph. l.c., ch. I.

[3] According to Hippol. c. Noët. I., he was not condemned after the first trial, but only at the close of a second,—a proof of the uncertainty that still prevailed. It is impossible now to discover what ground there was for the statement that Noëtus gave himself out to be Moses, and his brother to be Aaron.

[4] The fact that Noëtus was able to live for years in Asia Minor undisturbed, has evidently led Theodoret into the mistake that he was a later Monarchian who only appeared after Epigonus and Cleomenes. For the rest, Hippolytus used the name of Noëtus in his attack on him, simply as a symbol under which to oppose later Monarchians (see Ztschr. f. d. hist. Theol. 1874, p. 201); this is at once clear from ch. 2.

schism in the Roman Church, already sadly split up. After his
death the same policy was continued by Callistus (217—222),
now raised to the Bishopric. But as the schools now attacked
each other more violently, and an agreement was past hoping
for, the Bishop determined to excommunicate both Sabellius and
Hippolytus, the two heads of the contending factions.[1] The
Christological formula, which Callistus himself composed, was
meant to satisfy the less passionate adherents of both parties,
and this it did, so far as we may conjecture. The small party
of Hippolytus "the true Catholic Church", held its ground in
Rome for only about fifteen years, that of Sabellius probably
longer. The formula of Callistus was the bridge, on which the
Roman Christians, who were originally favourable to Monarchianism, passed over to the recognition of the Logos Christology,
following the trend of the times, and the science of the Church.
This doctrine must have already been the dominant theory in
Rome when Novatian wrote his work *De Trinitate,* and from
that date it was never ousted thence. It had been established in
the Capital by a politician, who, for his own part, and so far

---

[1] Philos. IX. 12: Οὕτως ὁ Κάλλιστος μετὰ τὴν τοῦ Ζεφυρίνου τελευτὴν νομίζων
τετυχηκέναι οὗ ἐθηρᾶτο, τὸν Σαβέλλιον ἀπέωσεν ὡς μὴ φρονοῦντα ὀρθῶς, δεδοικὼς ἐμὲ
καὶ νομίζων οὕτω δύνασθαι ἀποτρίψασθαι τὴν πρὸς τὰς ἐκκλησίας κατηγορίαν, ὡς μὴ
ἀλλοτρίως φρονῶν. Hippolytus, whose treatment of Sabellius is respectful, compared
with his attitude to Callistus, says nothing of his own excommunication; it is therefore possible that he and his small faction had already separated from Callistus,
and for their part had put him under the ban. This cannot have happened under
Zephyrine, as is shown directly by Philos. IX. 11, and all we can infer from ch. 7
is that the party of Hippolytus had ceased to recognise even Zephyrine as Bishop;
so correctly Döllinger, l.c., p. 101 f., 223 f.; a different view in Lipsius, Ketzergeschichte, p. 150. The situation was doubtless this: Epigonus and Cleomenes had
founded a real school (διδασκαλεῖον) in the Roman Church, perhaps in opposition
to that of the Theodotians, and this school was protected by the Roman bishops.
(s. Philos. IX. 7: Ζεφυρῖνος [τῷ κέρδει προσφερομένῳ πειθόμενος] συνεχώρει τοῖς
προσιοῦσι τῷ Κλεομένει μαθητεύεσθαι ... Τούτων κατὰ διαδοχὴν διέμεινε τὸ διδασκαλεῖον κρατυνόμενον καὶ ἐπαῦξον διὰ τὸ συναίρεσθαι αὐτοῖς τὸν Σεφυρῖνον καὶ τὸν
Κάλλιστον). Hippolytus attacked the orthodoxy and Church character of the school,
which possessed the sympathy of the Roman community, and he succeeded, after
Sabellius had become its head, in getting Callistus to expel the new leader from
the Church. But he himself was likewise excommunicated on account of his Christology, his "rigourism" and his passionate agitations. At the moment the community of Callistus was no longer to him a Catholic Church, but a διδασκαλεῖον
(see Philos. IX. 12, p 458, 1; p. 462, 42).

as he took any interest at all in dogmatics, had been more inclined to the Modalistic theory. [1]

The scantiness of our sources for the history of Monarchianism in Rome,—not to speak of other cities—in spite of the discovery of the Philosophumena, is shown most clearly by the circumstance that Tertullian has not mentioned the names of Noëtus, Epigonus, Cleomenes, or Callistus; on the other hand, he has introduced a Roman Monarchian, Praxeas, whose name is not mentioned by Hippolytus in any of his numerous controversial writings. This fact has seemed so remarkable that very hazardous hypotheses have been set up to explain it. It has been thought that "Praxeas" is a nickname (= tradesman), and that by it we ought really to understand Noëtus, [2] Epigonus, [3] or Callistus. [4] The correct view is to be found in Döllinger [5] and Lipsius. [6] Praxeas [7] had come to Rome before Epigonus, at a date anterior to the earliest of Hippolytus' personal recollections, accordingly about contemporaneously with Theodotus, or a little earlier, while Victor was Bishop; according to Lipsius, and this is probable, even during the episcopate of Eleutherus. [8] He probably resided only a short time in Rome,

---

[1] The attempt has been made in the above to separate the historical kernel from the biassed description of Hippolytus in the Philos. His account is reproduced most correctly by Caspari (Quellen III., p. 325 ff.). Hippolytus has not disguised the fact that the Bishops had the great mass of the Roman community on their side (IX. 11), but he has everywhere scented hypocrisy, intrigues and subserviency, where it is evident to the present day that the Bishops desired to protect the Church from the *rabies theologorum*. In so doing, they only did what their office demanded, and acted in the spirit of their predecessors, in whose days the acceptance of the brief and broad Church confession was alone decisive, while beyond that freedom ruled. It is also evident that Hippolytus considered Zephyrine and the rest a set of ignorant beings (*idiotes*), because they would not accede to the new science and the "economic" conception of God.

[2] According to Pseudo-Tertull. 30, where in fact the name of Praxeas is substituted for Noëtus.

[3] De Rossi, Bullet. 1866, p. 170.

[4] So, *e g*., Hagemann, l.c., p. 234 f., and similarly at an earlier date, Semler.

[5] L.c., p. 198.

[6] Jahrb. f. deutsche Theologie, 1868, H. 4.

[7] The name has undoubtedly not been shown elsewhere up till now.

[8] Chronol. d. röm. Bischöfe, p. 173 f.

where he met with no opposition; and he founded no school
in the city. When, twenty years afterwards, the controversy was
at its height in Rome and Carthage, and Tertullian found himself compelled to enter the lists against Patripassianism, the
name of Praxeas was almost forgotten. Tertullian, however,
laid hold of him because Praxeas had been the first to raise a
discussion in Carthage also, and because he had an antipathy
to Praxeas who was a decided anti-montanist. In his attack,
Tertullian has, however, reviewed the historical circumstances of
about the year A.D. 210, when his work Adv. Prax. was
written; nay, he manifestly alludes to the Roman Monarchians,
i.e., to Zephyrinus and those protected by him. This observation contains what truth there is in the hypothesis that Praxeas
is only a name for another well-known Roman Monarchian.

Praxeas was a confessor of Asia Minor, and the first to bring
the dispute as to the Logos Christology to Rome. [1] At the
same time he brought from his birth-place a resolute zeal against
the new prophecy. We are here, again, reminded of the faction
of Alogi of Asia Minor who combined with the rejection of the
Logos Christology an aversion from Montanism; cf. also the
Roman presbyter Caius. Not only did his efforts meet with no
opposition in Rome, but Praxeas induced the Bishop, by giving
him information as to the new prophets and their communities
in Asia, to recall the *litteræ pacis*, which he had already sent
them, and to aid in expelling the Paraclete. [2] If this Bishop was
Eleutherus, and that is probable from Euseb. H. E. V. 4, then
we have four Roman Bishops in succession who declared themselves in favour of the Modalistic Christology, viz., Eleutherus,
Victor, Zephyrine, and Callistus; for we learn from Pseudo-
Tertullian that Victor took the part of Praxeas. [3] But it is also

---

[1] Adv. Prax.: Iste primus ex Asia hoc genus perversitatis intulit Romam, homo
et alias inquietus, insuper de iactatione martyrii inflatus ob solum et simplex et
breve carceris tædium.

[2] L.c.: Ita duo negotia diaboli Praxeas Romæ procuravit, prophetiam expulit et
hæresim intulit, paracletum fugavit et patrem crucifixit.

[3] Pseudo-Tertull.: Praxeas quidem hæresim introduxit quam Victorinus corrobo-
rare curavit. This Victorinus is rightly held by most scholars to be Bishop Victor;
(1) there is the name (on Victor = Victorinus, see Langen l.c., p. 196; Caspari,
Quellen III., p. 323, n. 102); (2) the date; (3) the expression "curavit" which

possible that Victor was the Bishop whom Tertullian (Adv. Prax.) was thinking of, and in that case Eleutherus has no place here. It is at all events certain that when Dynamistic Monarchianism was proscribed by Victor, it was expelled not by a defender of the Logos Christology, but in the interests of a Modalistic Christology. The labours of Praxeas did not yet bring about a controversy in Rome with the Logos Doctrine; he was merely the forerunner of Epigonus and Cleomenes there. From Rome he betook himself to Carthage, [1] and strove against the assumption of any distinction between God and Christ. But he was resisted by Tertullian, who, at that time, still belonged to the Catholic Church, and he was silenced, and even compelled to make a written recantation. With this ended the first phase of the dispute. [2] The name of Praxeas does not again occur. But it was only several years afterwards that the controversy became really acute in Rome and Carthage, and caused Tertullian to write his polemical work. [3] Of the final stages of Monarchianism in Carthage and Africa we know nothing certain. Yet see under.

It is not possible, from the state of our sources, to give a complete and homogeneous description of the doctrine of the older Modalistic Monarchianism. But the sources are not alone to blame for this. As soon as the thought that God Himself

points to a high position, and is exactly paralleled by the συναίρεσθαι used by Hippolytus in referring to Zephyrine and Callistus (see p. 58, note 1); lastly, the fact that Victor's successors, as we know definitely, held Monarchian views. The excommunication of Theodotus by Victor proves nothing, of course, to the contrary; for the Monarchianism of this man was of quite a different type from that of Praxeas.

[1] This is definitely to be inferred from the words of Tertullian (l.c.): "Fructicaverant avenæ Praxeanæ hic quoque superseminatæ dormientibus multis in simplicitate doctrinæ"; see Caspari, l.c.; Hauck, Tertullian, p. 368; Langen, l.c., p. 199; on the other side Hesselberg, Tertullian's Lehre, p. 24, and Hagemann, l.c.

[2] Tertullian, l.c.: Avenæ Praxeanæ traductæ dehinc per quem deus voluit (scil. per me), etiam evulsæ videbantur. Denique caverat pristinum doctor de emendatione sua, et manet chirographum apud psychicos, apud quos tunc gesta res est; exinde silentium.

[3] Tertull., l.c. Avenæ vero illæ ubique tunc semen excusserant. Ita altquamdiu per hypocrisin subdola vivacitate latitavit, et nunc denuo erupit. Sed et denuo eradicabitur, si voluerit dominus.

was incarnate in Christ had to be construed theologically, very various attempts could not fail to result. These could lead, and so far did lead, on the one hand, to hazardous conceptions involving transformation, and, on the other, almost to the border of Adoptianism; for, as soon as the indwelling of the deity of the Father (*deitas patris*) in Jesus was not grasped in the strict sense as an incarnation, as soon as the element that in Jesus consti- tuted his personality was not exclusively perceived in the deity of the Father, these Christians were treading the ground of the Artemonite heresy. Hippolytus also charged Callistus with wavering between Sabellius and Theodotus,[1] and in his work against Noëtus he alludes (ch. III.) to a certain affinity between the latter and the leather-worker. In the writings of Origen, more- over, several passages occur, regarding which it will always be uncertain whether they refer to Modalists or Adoptians. Nor can this astonish us, for Monarchians of all shades had a com- mon interest in opposition to the Logos Christology: *they re- presented the conception of the Person of Christ founded on the history of salvation, as against one based on the history of his nature.*

Among the different expositions of the doctrine of the older Modalists that of Hippolytus in his work against Noëtus shows us it in its simplest form. The Monarchians there described are introduced to us as those who taught that Christ is the Father himself, and that the Father was born, suffered and died.[2] If Christ is God, then he is certainly the Father, or he would not be God. If Christ, accordingly, truly suffered, then the God, who is God alone, suffered.[3] But they were not only influenced by a decided interest in Monotheism,[4] a cause which they held to have been injured by their opponents,[5] whom

---

[1]   Philos. IX. 12, X. 27.   Epiph. H. 57. 2.

[2]   C. 1: ἔφη τὸν Χριστὸν αὐτὸν εἶναι τὸν πατέρα καὶ αὐτὸν τὸν πατέρα γεγεννῆσθαι καὶ πεπονθέναι καὶ ἀποτεθνηκέναι.

[3]   C. 2: Εἰ οὖν Χριστὸν ὁμολογῶ Θεόν, αὐτὸς ἄρα ἐστιν ὁ πατήρ, εἴ γε ἔστιν ὁ Θεός. ἔπαθεν δὲ Χριστὸς, αὐτὸς ὢν Θεός, ἄρα οὖν ἔπαθεν πατήρ, πατὴρ γὰρ αὐτὸς ἦν

[4]   Φάσκουσιν συνιστᾶν ἕνα Θεόν (c. 2).

[5]   Hippolytus defends himself, c. 11. 14: οὐ δύο θεοὺς λέγω, s. Philos. IX. 11, fin. 12: δημοσίᾳ ὁ Κάλλιστος ἡμῖν ὀνειδίζει εἰπεῖν· δίθεοί ἐστε. From c. Noët. 11 it

they called ditheists (δίθεοι), but they fought in behalf of the
complete deity of Jesus, which, in their opinion, could only be
upheld by their doctrine. [1] In support of the latter they appealed,
like the Theodotians, chiefly to the Holy Scriptures, and, indeed,
to the Catholic Canon; thus they quoted Exod. III. 6, XX. 2f.;
Isa. XLIV. 6, XLV. 5, 14 f.; Baruch. III. 36; John. X. 30,
XIV. 8f.; Rom. IX. 5. Even John's Gospel is recognised; but
this is qualified by the most important piece of information
which Hippolytus has given about their exposition of the Scriptures. They did not regard that book as justifying the introduction of a Logos, and the bestowal on him of the title Son
of God. The prologue of the Gospel, as well as, in general,
so many passages in the book, was to be understood allegoric-
ally. [2] The use of the category of the Logos was accordingly
emphatically rejected in their theology. We do not learn any
more about the Noëtians here. But in the Philosoph. Hippolytus has discussed their conception of God, and has presented
it as follows: [3] "They say that one and the same God was
creator and Father of all things; that he in his goodness
appeared to the righteous of olden times, although he is invisible; in other words, when he is not seen, he is invisible,
but when he permits himself to be seen, he is visible; he is
incomprehensible, when he wills not to be apprehended, comprehensible when he permits himself to be apprehended. So in
the same way he is invincible and to be overcome, unbegotten
and begotten, immortal and mortal." Hippolytus continues:

appears that the Monarchians opposed the doctrine of the Logos, because it led to
the Gnostic doctrine of Æons. Hippolytus had to reply: τὶς ἀποφαίνεται πλήθυν
Θεῶν παραβαλλομένην κατὰ καιρούς. He sought to show (ch. 14 sq.) that the μυστήριον οἰκονομίας of the Trinity taught by him was something different from the
doctrine of the Æons.

[1] Hippol. (c. Noët. I.) makes his opponent say, τὶ οὖν κακὸν ποιῶ δοξάζων τὸν
Χριστόν; see also ch. II. sq: Χριστὸς ἦν Θεὸς καὶ ἔπασχεν δι᾽ ἡμᾶς αὐτὸς ὢν πατήρ,
ἵνα καὶ σῶσαι ἡμᾶς δυνηθῇ, ἄλλο οὐ δυνάμεθα λέγειν; see again ch. IX. where Hippolytus says to his opponents that the Son must be revered in the way defined by
God in Holy Scriptures.

[2] S. c. 15: ἀλλ᾽ ἐρεῖ μοι τὶς· Ξένον φέρεις λόγον λέγων υἱόν. Ἰωάννης μὲν γὰρ
λέγει λόγον, ἀλλ᾽ ἄλλως ἀλληγορεῖ.

[3] L. IX. 10. See also Theodoret.

"Noëtus says, 'So far, therefore, as the Father was not made, he is appropriately called Father; but in so far as he passively submitted to be born, he is by birth the Son, not of another, but of himself.'" In this way he meant to establish the *Monarchia*, and to say that he who was called Father and Son, was one and the same, not one proceeding from the other, but he himself from himself; he is distinguished in name as Father and Son, according to the change of dispensations; but it is one and the same who appeared in former times, and submitted to be born of the virgin, and walked as man among men. He confessed himself, on account of his birth, to be the Son to those who saw him, but he did not conceal the truth that he was the Father from those who were able to apprehend it. [1] Cleomenes and his party maintain that "he who was nailed to the cross, who committed his spirit to himself, who died and did not die, who raised himself on the third day and rested in the grave, who was pierced with the lance and fastened with nails, was the God and Father of all." The distinction between Father and Son was accordingly nominal; yet it was to this extent more than nominal, that the one God, in being born man, *appeared* as Son; it was real, so far, from the point of view of the history of salvation. In support of the identity of the "manifested" and the invisible, these Monarchians referred to the O. T. theophanies, with as good a right as, nay, with a better than, the defenders of the Logos Christology. Now as regards the idea of God, it has been said that "the element of finitude was here potentially placed in God himself," and that these Monarchians were influenced by Stoicism, etc. While the former statement is probably unwarranted, the Stoic influence, on the contrary, is not to be denied. [2] But the foundation to which we have to refer them consists of two ancient liturgical

---

[1] We perceive very clearly here that we have before us not an unstudied, but a thought-out, and theological Modalism. As it was evident, in the speculations about Melchisedec of the Theodotians, that they, like Origen, desired to rise from the crucified Jesus to the eternal, godlike Son, so these Modalists held the conception, that the Father himself was to be perceived in Jesus, to be one which was only meant for those-who could grasp it.

[2] See above (p. 55, note 1). In addition Philos. X. 27: τοῦτον τὸν πατέρα αὐτὸν υἱὸν νομίζουσι κατὰ καιροὺς καλούμενον πρὸς τὰ συμβαίνοντα.

formulas, used by Ignatius, the author of the II. Ep. of Clement, and Melito, [1] whom we include, although he wrote a work "Concerning the creation and genesis of Christ" (περὶ κτίσεως καὶ γενέσεως Χριστοῦ). Further, even Ignatius, although he held Christ to have been pre-existent, knew only of one birth of the Son, namely, that of God from the virgin. [2] We have here to recognise the conception, according to which, God, in virtue of his own resolve to become finite, capable of suffering etc., can and did decide to be man, without giving up his divinity. It is the old, religious, and artless Modalism, which has here been raised, with means furnished by the Stoa, to a theological doctrine, and has become exclusive. But in the use of the formula "the Father has suffered," we have undoubtedly an element of novelty; for it cannot be indicated in the post-apostolic age. It is very questionable, however, whether it was ever roundly uttered by the theological defenders of Modalism. They probably merely said that "the Son, who suffered, is the same with the Father."

We do not learn what conception these Monarchians formed of the human σάρξ (flesh) of Jesus, or what significance they attached to it. Even the Monarchian formulas, opposed by Tertullian in "Adv. Prax", and attributed to Callistus by Hippolytus, are already more complicated. We easily perceive that they were coined in a controversy in which the theological difficulties inherent in the Modalistic doctrine had become notorious. Tertullian's Monarchians still cling strongly to the perfect identity of the Father and Son; [3] they refuse to admit the Logos into their Christology; for the "word" is no substance, but

---

[1] See Ignat. ad Ephes. VII. 2: εἷς ἰατρός ἐστιν σαρκικός τε καὶ πνευματικός, γεννητὸς καὶ ἀγέννητος, ἐν σαρκὶ γενόμενος Θεός, ἐν θανάτῳ ζωὴ ἀληθινή, καὶ ἐκ Μαρίας καὶ ἐκ Θεοῦ, πρῶτον παθητὸς καὶ τότε ἀπαθής, Ἰησοῦς Χριστός; and see for Clement Vol. I., p. 186 ff.

[2] It is interesting to notice that in the Abyssinian Church of to-day there is a theological school which teaches a threefold birth of Christ, from the Father in eternity, from the virgin, and from *the Holy Ghost at the Baptism;* see Herzog, R. E., 2 Aufl., Bd. I., p. 70.

[3] C. 1: "Ipsum dicit patrem descendisse in virginem, ipsum ex ea natum, ipsum passum ipsum denique esse Iesum Christum." c. 2: "post tempus pater natus et pater passus, ipse deus, dominus omnipotens, Iesus Christus prædicatur"; see also c. 13.

merely a "sound";[1] they are equally interested with the Noëtians in monotheism,[2] though not so evidently in the full divinity of Christ; like them they dread the return of Gnosticism;[3]
they hold the same view as to the invisibility and visibility of
God;[4] they appeal to the Holy Scriptures, sometimes to the
same passages as the opponents of Hippolytus;[5] but they find
themselves compelled to adapt their teaching to those proof-
texts in which the Son is contrasted, as a distinctive subject,
with the Father. This they did, not only by saying that
God made himself Son by assuming a body,[6] or that the Son
proceeded from himself[7]—for with God nothing is impossible;[8]
but they distinctly declared that the flesh changed the Father
into the Son; or even that in the person of the Redeemer the

---

[1] C. 7: "Quid est enim, dices, sermo nisi vox et sonus oris, et sicut gramma-
tici tradunt, aër offensus, intellegibilis auditu, ceterum vanum nescio quid."

[2] C. 2: "Unicum deum non alias putat credendum, quem si ipsum eundemque
et patrem et filium et spiritum s. dicat." c. 3: "Duos et tres iam iactitant a nobis
prædicari, se vero unius dei cultores præsumunt ... monarchiam, inquiunt, tenemus."
c. 13: "inquis, duo dii prædicuntur." c. 19: "igitur si propterea eundem et patrem
et filium credendum putaverunt, ut unum deum vindicent etc." c. 23: "ut sic duos
divisos diceremus, quomodo iactitatis etc."

[3] C. 8: "Hoc si qui putaverit me προβολὴν aliquam introducere," says Tertullian
"qnod facit Valentinus, etc."

[4] See c. 14. 15: "Hic ex diverso volet aliquis etiam filium invisibilem contendere, ut sermonem, ut spiritum ... Nam et illud adiiciunt ad argumentationem, quod
si filius tunc (Exod. 33) ad Moysen loquebatur, ipse faciem suam nemini visibilem
pronuntiaret, quia scil. ipse invisibilis pater fuerit in filii nomine. Ac per hoc si
eundem volunt accipi et visibilem et invisibilem, quomodo eundem patrem et filium ...
Ergo visibilis et invisibilis idem, et quia utrumque, ideo et ipse pater invisibilis, qua
et filius, visibilis ... Argumentantur, recte utrumque dictum, visibilem quidem
in carne, invisibilem vero ante carnem, ut idem sit pater invisibilis ante carnem,
qui et filius visibilis in carne."

[5] Thus to Exod. XXXIII. (ch. 14), Rev. I. 18 (ch. 17), Isa. XXIV. 24 (ch. 19),
esp. John X. 30; XIV. 9, 10 (ch. 20), Isa. XLV. 5 (ch. 20). They admit that in
the Scriptures sometimes two, sometimes one, are spoken of; but they argued
(ch. 18): "Ergo quia duos et unum invenimus, ideo ambo unus atque idem et
filius et pater."

Ch. 10: "Ipse se sibi filium fecit."

[7] Ch. 11: "Porro qui eundem patrem dicis et filium, eundem et protulisse ex
semetipso facis."

[8] To this verse the Monarchians, according to ch. 10, appealed, and they quoted
as a parallel the birth from the virgin.

body (the man, Jesus) was the Son, but that the Spirit (God, Christ) was the Father.[1] For this they appealed to Luke I. 35. They conceived the Holy Spirit to be identical with the power of the Almighty, *i.e.*, with the Father himself, and they emphasised the fact that that which was *born*, accordingly the flesh, not the Spirit, was to be called Son of God.[2] The Spirit (God) was not capable of suffering, but since he entered into the flesh, he sympathised in the suffering. The Son suffered,[3] but the Father "sympathised"[4]—this being a Stoic expression. Therefore Tertullian says (ch. 23), "Granting that we would thus say, as you assert, that there were two separate (gods), it was more tolerable to affirm two separate (gods) than one dissembling (turn-coat) god" [Ut sic divisos diceremus, quomodo iactitatis, tolerabilius erat, duos divisos quam unum deum versipellem prædicare].

It is very evident that whenever the distinction between *caro* (filius) and *spiritus* (pater), between the flesh or Son and the Spirit or Father, is taken seriously, the doctrine approximates to the Artemonite idea. It is in fact changing its coat (versipellis). But it is obvious that even in this form it could not satisfy the defenders of the Logos Christology, for the personal identity between the Father and the Spirit or Christ is still retained. On the whole, every attempt made by Modalism to meet the demands of the Logos doctrine could not fail logically to lead to Dynamistic Monarchianism. We know definitely that the formulas of Zephyrine and Callistus arose out of attempts

---

[1] Ch. 27: "Æque in una persona utrumque distinguunt, patrem et filium, discentes filium carnem esse, id est hominem, id est Iesum, patrem autem spiritum, id est deum, id est Christum." On this Tertullian remarks : " et qui unum eundemque contendunt patrem et filium, iam incipiunt dividere illos potius quam unare; talem monarchiam apud Valentinum fortasse didicerunt, duos facere Iesum et Christum." Tertullian, accordingly, tries to retort on his opponents the charge of dissolving the Monarchia; see even ch. 4. The attack on the assumption of a transformation of the divine into the human does not, for the rest, affect these Monarchians (ch. 27 ff.).

[2] See ch. 26, 27: "propterea quod nascetur sanctum, vocabitur filius dei ; caro itaque nata est, caro itaque erit filius dei."

[3] Ch. 29: "mortuus est non ex divina, sed ex humana substantia."

[4] L. c.: "Compassus est pater filio."

at a compromise, [1] though the charge of having two gods was raised against Hippolytus and his party. Zephyrine's thesis (IX. 11), "I know one God, Christ Jesus, and besides him no other born and suffering," which he announced with the limiting clause, "the Father did not die, but the Son," [2] agrees with the doctrines of "Praxeas", but, as is clear from the Philos., is also to be understood as a formula of compromise. Callistus went still further. He found it advisable after the excommunication of Sabellius and Hippolytus, to receive the category of the Logos into the Christological formula meant to harmonise all parties, an act for which he was especially abused by Hippolytus, while Sabellius also accused him of apostasy. [3] According to Zephyrine: God is in himself an indivisible Pneuma, which fills all things, or, in other words, the Logos; as Logos he is nominally two, Father and Son. The Pneuma, become flesh in the virgin, is thus in essence not different from, but identical with, the Father (John XIV. 11). He who became manifest, i.e., the man, is the Son, but the Spirit, which entered into the Son, is the Father. "For the Father, who is in the Son, deified the flesh, after he had assumed it, and united it with himself, and established a unity of such a nature that now Father and Son are called one God, and that henceforth it is impossible that this single person can be divided into two; rather the thesis holds true that the Father suffered in sympathy with the Son" — not the Father suffered. [4]

---

[1] Philos. IX. 7, p. 440. 35 sq.; 11, p. 450. 72 sq.

[2] Ἐγὼ οἶδα ἕνα Θεὸν Χριστὸν Ἰησοῦν καὶ πλὴν αὐτοῦ ἕτερον οὐδένα γεννητὸν καὶ παθητόν—οὐχ ὁ πατὴρ ἀπέθανεν, ἀλλὰ ὁ υἱός.

[3] L.c. IX. 12, p. 458, 78 : ἀλλὰ καὶ διὰ τὸ ὑπὸ τοῦ Σαβελλίου συχνῶς κατηγορεῖσθαι ὡς παραβάντα τὴν πρώτην πίστιν. It is apparently the very formula "Compassus est pater filio" that appeared unacceptable to the strict Monarchians.

[4] Philos. IX. 12, p. 458, 80 : Κάλλιστος λέγει τὸν λόγον αὐτὸν εἶναι υἱόν, αὐτὸν καὶ πατέρα ὀνόματι μὲν καλούμενον, ἓν δὲ ὂν τὸ πνεῦμα ἀδιαίρετον. οὐκ ἄλλο εἶναι πατέρα, ἄλλο δὲ υἱόν, ἓν δὲ καὶ τὸ αὐτὸ ὑπάρχειν, καὶ τὰ πάντα γέμειν τοῦ θείου πνεύματος τά τε ἄνω καὶ κάτω· καὶ εἶναι τὸ ἐν τῇ παρθένῳ σαρκωθὲν πνεῦμα οὐχ ἕτερον παρὰ τὸν πατέρα, ἀλλὰ ἓν καὶ τὸ αὐτό. Καὶ τοῦτο εἶναι τὸ εἰρημένον. John. 14. 11. Τὸ μὲν γὰρ βλεπόμενον, ὅπερ ἐστὶν ἄνθρωπος, τοῦτο εἶναι τὸν υἱόν, τὸ δὲ ἐν τῷ υἱῷ χωρηθὲν πνεῦμα τοῦτο εἶναι τὸν πατέρα· οὐ γὰρ, φησίν, ἐρῶ δύο θεοὺς πατέρα καὶ υἱόν, ἀλλ' ἕνα. Ὁ γὰρ ἐν αὐτῷ γενόμενος πατὴρ προσλαβόμενος τὴν σάρκα ἐθεο-

Hippolytus discovered in this formula a mixture of Sabellian and Theodotian ideas, and he was right. [1] The approximation to the Christology founded on the doctrine of substances (hypostases), and the departure from the older Monarchianism, are, in fact, only brought about by Callistus having also made use of a Theodotian idea. [2] He still kept aloof from the Platonic conception of God; nay, it sounds like a reminiscence of Stoicism, when, in order to obtain a rational basis for the incarnation, he refers to the Pneuma (Spirit) which fills the universe, the upper and under world. But the fact that his formulas, in spite of this, could render valuable service in Rome in harmonising different views, was not only due to their admission of the Logos conception. It was rather a result of the thought expressed in them, that God in becoming incarnate had deified the flesh, and that the Son, in so far as he represented the essentially deified σάρξ, was to be conceived as a second person, and yet as one really united with God. [3] At this point the ultimate Catholic interest in the Christology comes correctly to light, and this is an interest not clearly perceptible elsewhere in Monarchian theories. It was thus that men were gradually tranquillised in Rome, and only the few extremists of the Left and Right parties offered any resistance. Moreover, the formula was extraordinarily adapted, by its very vagueness, to set up among the believing people the religious Mystery, under whose pro-tection the Logos Christology gradually made good its entrance.

The latter was elaborated in opposition to Modalism by Ter-

πσίησεν ἐνώσας ἑαυτῷ, καὶ ἐποίησεν ἕν, ὡς καλεῖσθαι πατέρα καὶ υἱὸν ἕνα Θεόν. καὶ τοῦτο ἓν ὂν πρόσωπον μὴ δύνασθαι εἶναι δύο, καὶ οὕτως τὸν πατέρα συμπεπονθέναι τῷ υἱῷ· οὐ γὰρ θέλει λέγειν τὸν πατέρα πεπονθέναι καὶ ἓν εἶναι πρόσωπον...
Here something is wanting in the text.

[1] Catholic theologians endeavour to give a Nicene interpretation to the theses of Callistus, and to make Hippolytus a ditheist; see Hagemann, l.c.; Kuhn, Theol. Quartalschrift, 1885, II.; Lehir, Études bibliques, II., p. 383; de Rossi and various others.

[2] This is also Zahn's view, Marcell., p. 214. The doctrine of Callistus is for the rest so obscure,—and for this our informant does not seem to be alone to blame—that, when we pass from it to the Logos Christology, we actually breathe freely, and we can understand how the latter simpler and compact doctrine finally triumphed over the laboured and tortuous theses of Callistus.

[3] See the Christology of Origen.

tullian, Hippolytus, and Novatian in the West.[1] While Adop
tianism apparently played a very small part in the developmen
of the Logos Christology in the Church, the Christological these
of Tertullian and the rest were completely dependent on th
opposition to the Modalists.[2] This reveals itself especially i
the strict subordination of the Son to the Father. It was onl
by such a subordination that it was possible to repel the charge
made by opponents, of teaching that there were two Gods
The philosophical conception of God implied in the Logo
theory was now set up definitely as the doctrine of the Church
and was construed to mean that the unity of God was simpl
to be understood as a "unicum imperium", which God coul
cause to be administered by his chosen officials. Further, th
attempt was made to prove that Monotheism was satisfactoril
guarded by the Father remaining the sole First Cause.[3] Bu
while the reproach was thus repelled of making Father and So
"brothers", an approach was made to the Gnostic doctrine o
Æons, and Tertullian himself felt, and was unable to avert, th
danger of falling into the channel of the Gnostics.[4] His argu
ments in his writing *Adv. Praxeas* are not free from half con
cessions and uncertainties, while the whole tenor of the worl
contrasts strikingly with that of the anti-gnostic tractates. Ter
tullian finds himself time and again compelled in his work to
pass from the offensive to the defensive, and the admission
that he makes show his uncertainty. Thus he concedes tha
we may not speak of two Lords or two Gods, that in certair
circumstances the Son also can be called Almighty, or ever
Father, that the Son will in the end restore all things to the
Father, and, as it would seem, will merge in the Father; finally
and especially, that the Son is not only not *aliud a patre*
(different in substance from the Father), but even in some way

[1] See Vol. II., p. 256.

[2] This can be clearly perceived by comparing the Christology of Tertullian and
Hippolytus with that of Irenæus.

[3] See Tertullian adv. Prax. 3; Hippol. c. Noët. 11.

[4] Adv. Prax. 8, 13. It is the same with Hippolytus; both have in their attacks
on the Modalists taken Valentine, comparatively speaking, under their protection
This is once more a sign that the doctrine of the Church was modified Gnosticism.

not *alius a patre* [1] (different in person etc). Yet Tertullian and
his comrades were by no means at a disadvantage in comparison with the Monarchians. They could appeal (1) to the Rule
of Faith in which the personal distinction between the Father
and Son was recognised; [2] (2) to the Holy Scriptures from
which it was, in fact, easy to reduce the arguments of the
Monarchians *ad absurdum;* [3] (3) to the distinction between
Christians and Jews which consisted, of course, in the belief of
the former in the Son; [4] and lastly, and this was the most important point, they could cite the Johannine writings, especially
in support of the doctrine of the Logos. It was of the highest
importance in the controversy that Christ could be shown to
have been called the Logos in John's Gospel and the Apoca-
ypse. [5] In view of the way in which the Scriptures were then
used in the Church, these passages were fatal to Monarchianism.
The attempts to interpret them symbolically [6] could not but
fail in the end, as completely as those, *e.g.,* of Callistus and
Paul of Samasota, to combine the use of the expression "Logos"
with a rejection of the apologetic conception of it based on
Philo. Meanwhile Tertullian and Hippolytus did not, to all
appearance, yet succeed in getting their form of doctrine approved
in the Churches. The God of mystery of whom they taught
was viewed as an unknown God, and their Christology did not
correspond to the wants of men. The Logos was, indeed, to
be held one in essence with God; but yet he was, by his being
made the organ of the creation of the world, an inferior

---

[1] Ch. 18, in other passages otherwise.

[2] Tertull. adv. Prax. 2. Hippol. c. Noët. I.

[3] The Monarchian dispute was conducted on both sides by the aid of proofs
drawn from exegesis. Tertullian, besides, in *Adv. Prax.*, appealed in support of the
"economic" trinity to utterances of the Paraclete.

[4] See ad. Prax. 21: "Ceterum Iudaicæ fidei ista res, sic unum deum credere, ut
filium adnumerare ei nolis, et post filium spiritum. Quid enim erit inter nos et
illos nisi differentia ista? Quod opus evangelii, si non exinde pater et filius et
spiritus, tres crediti, unum deum sistunt?"

[5] Πιστεύσωμεν, says Hippolyt. c. Noët. 17—κατὰ τὴν παράδοσιν τῶν ἀποστόλων
ὅτι Θεὸς λόγος ἀπ' οὐρανῶν κατῆλθεν,—see already Tatian, Orat. 5 following Joh. I. 1 :
Θεὸς ἦν ἐν ἀρχῇ, τὴν δὲ ἀρχὴν λόγου δύναμιν παρειλήφαμεν.

[6] See above, p. 63.

divine being, or rather at once inferior and not inferior. This conception, however, conflicted with tradition as embodied in worship, which taught men to see God Himself in Christ, quite as much as the attempt was opposed by doctrinal tradition, to derive the use of the name "Son of God" for Christ, not from His miraculous birth, but from a decree dating before the world. [1] For the rest, the older enemies of Monarchianism still maintained common ground with their opponents, in so far as God's evolving of Himself in several substances (Hypostases) was throughout affected by the history of the world (cosmos), and in this sense by the history of revelation. The difference between them and at least the later Monarchians was here only one of degree. The latter began at the incarnation (or at the theophanies of the O. T.), and from it dated a nominal plurality, the former made the "economic" self-unfolding of God originate immediately before the creation of the world. Here we have the cosmological interest coming once more to the front in the Church Fathers and displacing the historical, while it ostensibly raised the latter to a higher plane.

Wherever the doctrine of the Logos planted itself in the third century the question, whether the divine being who appeared on earth was identical with the Deity, was answered in the negative. [2] In opposition to this Gnostic view, which was first to be corrected in the fourth century, the Monarchians maintained a very ancient and valuable position in clinging to the identity of the eternal Deity, with the Deity revealed on earth. But does not the dilemma that arises show that the speculation on both sides was as untenable as unevangelical? Either we preserve the identity, and in that case defend the thesis, at once absurd and inconsistent with the Gospel, that Christ was the Father himself; or with the Gospel we retain the distinction between Father and Son, but then announce a subordinate God after the fashion of a Gnostic polytheism. Certainly, as regards religion, a very great advance was arrived at, when Athanasius, by his exclusive formula of Λόγος ὁμο-

---

[1] In the Symbolum the "γεννηθέντα ἐκ πνεύματος ἁγίου" is to be understood as explaining τὸν υἱὸν τοῦ Θεοῦ.

[2] See *Adv. Prax.* 16.

οὐσίος (consubstantial Logos), negatived both Modalism and sub-ordinationist Gnosticism, but the Hellenic foundation of the whole speculation was preserved, and for the rational observer a second rock of offence was merely piled upon a first. How-ever, under the conditions of scientific speculation at the time, the formula was the saving clause by which men were once for all turned from Adoptianism, whose doctrine of a deification of Jesus could not fail, undoubtedly, to awaken the most question-able recollections.

(b) The last stages of Modalism in the West, and the State of Theology.

Our information is very defective concerning the destinies of Monarchianism in Rome and the West, after the close of the first thirty years of the third century; nor are we any better off in respect to the gradual acceptance of the Logos Christ-ology. The excommunication of Sabellius by Callistus in Rome resulted at once in the Monarchians ceasing to find any follow-ers in the West, and in the complete withdrawal soon after-wards of strict and aggressive Modalism. [1] Callistus himself has, besides, not left to posterity an altogether clean reputation as regards his Christology, although he had covered himself in the main point by his compromise formula. [2] Hippolytus' sect had ceased to exist about A.D. 250; nay, it is not altogether improbable that he himself made his peace with the great Church shortly before his death. [3] We can infer from Novatian's im-portant work " De trinitate ", that the following tenets were recog-

---

[1] On these grounds the doctrine of Sabellius will be described under, in the history of Eastern Modalism.

[2] In forged Acts of Synod of the 6th century we read (Mansi, Concil. II., p. 621): "qui se Callistus ita docuit Sabellianum, ut arbitrio suo sumat unam per-sonam esse trinitatis." The words which follow later, "in sua extollentia separabat trinitatem" have without reason seemed particularly difficult to Döllinger (l.c., p. 247) and Langen (l.c., p. 215). Sabellianism was often blamed with dismembering the Monas (see Zahn, Marcell. p. 211.)

[3] See Döllinger, l.c., Hippolytus was under Maximinus banished along with the Roman Bishop Pontian to Sardinia. See the Catal. Liber. sub "Pontianus" (Lip-sius, Chronologic, pp. 194, 275).

nised in Rome about 250:[1] (1) Christ did not first *become* God. (2) The Father did not suffer. (3) Christ pre-existed and is true God and man.[2] But it was not only in Rome that these tenets were established, but also in many provinces. If the Roman Bishop Dionysius could write in a work of his own against the Sabellians, that "Sabellius blasphemed, saying that the Son was himself Father",[3] then we must conclude that this doctrine was then held inadmissible in the West. Cyprian again has expressed himself as follows (Ep. 73. 4): "Patripassiani, Valentiniani, Appelletiani, Ophitæ, Marcionitæ et ceteræ hæreticorum pestes" (—the other plagues of heretics), and we must decide that the strict Modalistic form of doctrine was then almost universally condemned in the West. Of the difficulties met with in the ejection of the heresy, or the means employed, we have no information. Nothing was changed in the traditional Creed——a noteworthy and momentous difference from the oriental Churches! But we know of one case in which an important alteration was proposed. The Creed of the Church of Aquileia began, in the fourth century, with the words "I believe in God the Father omnipotent, invisible, and impassible" (Credo in deo patre omnipotente, *invisibili et impassibili*), and Rufinus, who

---

[1] This writing shows, on the one hand, that Adoptians and Modalists still existed and were dangerous in Rome, and on the other, that they were not found within the Roman Church. On the significance of the writing see Vol. II., p. 313 f.

[2] The Roman doctrine of Christ was then as follows: He has always been with the Father (sermo dei), but he first proceeded before the world from the substance of the Father (ex patre) for the purpose of creating the world. He was born into the flesh, and thus as *filius dei* and *deus* adopted a *homo*; thus he is also *filius hominis*. "Filius dei" and "filius hominis" are thus to be distinguished as two substances (substantia divina—homo), but he is one person; for he has completely combined, united, and fused the two substances in himself. At the end of things, when he shall have subjected all to himself, he will subject himself again to the Father, and will return to and be merged in him. Of the Holy Spirit it is also true, that he is a person (Paraclete), and that he proceeds from the substance of the Father; but he receives from the Son his power and sphere of work, he is therefore less than the Son, as the latter is less than the Father. But all three persons are combined as indwellers in the same substance, and united by love and harmony. Thus there is only one God, from whom the two other persons proceed.

[3] Σαβέλλιος βλασφημεῖ, αὐτὸν τὸν υἱὸν εἶναι λέγων τὸν πάτερα. See Routh, Reliq. S. III., p. 373.

has preserved it for us, tells [1] that the addition was made, at any rate as early as the third century, in order to exclude the Patripassians.

But the exclusion of the strict Modalists involved neither their immediate end, nor the wholesale adoption of the teaching of Tertullian and Hippolytus, of the philosophical doctrine of the Logos. As regards the latter, the recognition of the name of Logos for Christ, side by side with other titles, did not at once involve the reception of the Logos doctrine, and the very fact, that no change was made in the Creed, shows how reluctant men were to give more than a necessary minimum of space to philosophical speculations. They were content with the formula, extracted from the Creed, "Jesus Christus, deus et homo", and with the combination of the Biblical predicates applied to Christ, predicates which also governed their conception of the Logos. In this respect the second Book of the Testimonies of Cyprian is of great importance. In the first six chapters the divinity of Christ is discussed, in terms of Holy Scripture, under the following headings. (1) Christum primogenitum esse et ipsum esse sapientiam dei, per quem omnia facta sunt; (2) quod sapientia dei Christus; (3) quod Christus idem sit et sermo dei; (4) quod Christus idem manus et brachium dei; (5) quod idem angelus et deus; (6) quod deus Christus. Then follows, after some sections on the appearing of Christ: (10) quod et homo et deus Christus. The later Nicene and Chalcedonian doctrine was the property of the Western Church from the third century, not in the form of a philosophically technical speculation, but in that of a categorical Creed-like expression of faith—see Novatian's "De trinitate", in which the doctrine of the Logos falls into the background. Accordingly the statement of Socrates (H. E. III. 7)

---

[1] Expos. Symboli Apost. ch. 19. The changes which can be shown to have ɔeen made on the first article of the Creed elsewhere in the West—see especially he African additions—belong probably at the earliest to the fourth century. Should :hey be older, however, they are all, it would seem, to be understood antignostically; in other words, they contain nothing but explanations and comfirmatory additions. It is in itself incredible and incapable of proof that the Roman and after it the Western Churches should, at the beginning of the third century, have leleted, as Zahn holds, a ἕνα which originally stood in the first article of the ꓡreed, in order to confute the Monarchians.

is not incredible, that the Western Churchman Hosius had already declared the distinction between οὐσία and ὑπόστασις (substantia and persona) before the Council of Nicæa. [1] The West welcomed in the fourth century all statements which contained the complete divinity of Christ, without troubling itself much about arguments and proofs, and the controversy between the two Dionysii in the middle of the third century (see under), proves that a declared interest was kept up in the complete divinity of Christ, as an inheritance from the Monarchian period in Rome. [2] Nay, a latent Monarchian element really continued to exist in the Western Church; this we can still study in the poems of Commodian. [3] Commodian, again, was not yet acquainted with speculations regarding the "complete" humanity of Jesus; he is satisfied with the flesh of Christ being represented as a sheath, (V. 224, "And suffers, as he willed, in our likeness"; [4] on the other hand, V. 280, "now the flesh was God, in which the virtue of God acted.") [5] But these are only symptoms

[1] See Vol. IV.

[2] We, unfortunately, do not know on what grounds the Roman Bishop approved of the excommunication of Origen, or whether Origen's doctrine of subordination was regarded in Rome as heretical.

[3] Here follow in the original illustrations which we relegate to this footnote. Compare Instruct. II. 1 (Heading): "De populo absconso sancto omnipotentis Christi dei vivi;" II. 1, p. 28. 22, ed. Ludwig): "omnipotens Christus descendit ad suos electos;" II. 23, p. 43, 11 sq.: "Unde deus clamat: Stulte, hac nocte vocaris." II. 39. 1, p. 52. Carmen apolog. 91 sq.: "Est deus omnipotens, unus, a semetipso creatus, quem infra reperies magnum et humilem ipsum. Is erat in verbo positus, sibi solo notatus, Qui pater et filius dicitur et spiritus sanctus;" 276: "Hic pater in filio venit, deus unus ubique." (See also the following verses according to the edition of Dombart): 285: "hic erat Omnipotens;" "334: "(ligno) deus pependit dominus;" 353: "deum talia passum, Ut enuntietur crucifixus conditor orbis;" 359 sq.: "Idcirco nec voluit se manifestare, quid esset, Sed filium dixit se missum fuisse a patre;" 398: "Prædictus est deus carnaliter nasci pro nobis;" 455: "quis deus est ille, quem nos crucifiximus;" 610: "ipsa spes tota, deo credere, qui ligno pependit;" 612: "*Quod filius dixit, cum sit deus pristinus ipse;*" 625: "hic erat venturus, commixtus sanguine nostro, ut videretur homo, sed deus in carne latebat ... dominus ipse veniet." 630, 764: "Unus est in cælo deus dei, terræ marisque, Quem Moyses docuit ligno pependisse pro nobis;" etc. etc. Commodian is usually assigned to the second half of the third century, but doubts have recently been expressed as to this date. Jacobi, Commodian u. d. alt Kirchlich. Trinitätslehre, in der deutschen Ztschr. f. Christl. Wissensch., 1853, p, 203 ff.

[4] Et patitur, quomodo voluit sub imagine nostra.

[5] Iam caro deus erat, in qua dei virtus agebat.

of a Christian standpoint which was fundamentally different from that of oriental theologians, and which Commodian was by no means the only one to occupy. He, Lactantius, and Arnobius [1] are very different from each other. Commodian was a practical Churchman; Arnobius was an empiricist and in some form also a sceptic and decided opponent of Platonism; [2] while Lactantius was a disciple of Cicero and well acquainted besides with the speculations of Greek Christian theology. But they are all three closely connected in the contrast they present to the Greek theologians of the school of Origen; *there is nothing mystical about them, they are not Neoplatonists.* Lactantius has, indeed, expounded the doctrine of Christ, the incarnate Logos, as well as any Greek; as a professional teacher it was all known and familiar to him; [3] but as he nowhere encounters any problems in his Christology, as he discusses doctrines with very few theological or philosophical formulas, almost in a light tone, as if they were mere matters of course, we see that he had no interest of his own in them. He was rather interested in exactly the same questions as Arnobius and Commodian, who again showed no anxiety to go beyond the simplest Christological formulas—that Christ was God, that he had, however, also assumed flesh, or united himself with a man, since otherwise we could not have borne the deity: "And God was man, that he might possess us in the future" (Et fuit homo deus, ut nos in futuro haberet). [4] [5] The Christianity and theology which these

---

[1] See Francke's fine discussion, Die Psychologie und Erkentnisslehre des Arnobius (Leipzig, 1878).

[2] We recall the Theodotians of Rome.

[3] See Instit. IV. 6—30. The doctrine of the Logos is naturally worked out in a subordinationist sense. Besides this, many other things occur which must have seemed very questionable to the Latin Fathers 60 years afterwards: " Utinam," says Jerome, "tam nostra confirmare potuisset quam facile aliena destruxit."

[4] Commod., Carmen apolog. 761.

[5] See the Christological expositions, in part extremely questionable, of Arnobius I. 39, 42, 53, 60, 62, and elsewhere. A. demands that complete divinity should be predicated of Christ on account of the divine teaching of Christ (II. 60). In his own theology many other antique features crop up; he even defends the view that the supreme God need not be conceived as creator of this world and of men (see the remarkable chap. 46 of the second book, which recalls Marcion and Celsus). Many Church doctrines Arnobius cannot understand, and he admits them to be

Latins energetically supported against polytheism, were summed
up in Monotheism, a powerfully elaborated morality, the hope
of the Resurrection which was secured by the work of the God
Christ who had crushed the demons, and in unadulterated Chiliasm.[1] Monotheism—in the sense of Cicero's "De natura deo-
rum"—Moralism, and Chiliasm: these are the clearly perceived
and firmly held points, and not only for Apologetic purposes,
but also, as is proved especially by the second book of Commodian's "Instructiones", in independent and positive expositions.
These Instructions are, along with the *Carmen Apolog.*, of the
highest importance for our estimate of Western Christianity in
the period A.D. 250—315. We discover here, 100 years after
the Gnostic fight, a Christianity that was affected, neither by
the theology of the anti-gnostic Church Fathers, nor specially
by that of the Alexandrians, one which the dogmatic contentions
and conquests of the years 150—250 have passed over, hardly
leaving a trace. Almost all that is required to explain it by the
historian who starts with the period of Justin is to be found in
the slightly altered conditions of the Roman world of culture,
and in *the development of the Church system* as a practical
power, a political and social quantity.[2] Even in the use of
Scripture this Christianity of the West reveals its conservatism.
The Books of the O. T. and the Apocalypse are those still
most in vogue.[3] Commodian does not stand alone, nor are the
features to be observed in his "Instructiones" accidental. And

---

puzzles whose solution is known to God alone (see *e.g.*, B. II. 74). Even in the
doctrine of the soul, which to him is mortal and only has its life prolonged by
receiving the doctrine brought by Christ, there is a curious mixture of antique
empiricism and Christianity. If we measure him by the theology of the fourth century,
Arnobius is heterodox on almost every page.

[1] See the Carmen apolog. with its detailed discussions of the final Drama, Antichrist (Nero) etc.; Lactant IV. 12, VII. 21 sq.; Victorinus, Comm. on Revelation.

[2] We can notice throughout in Commodian the influence of the institution of
penance, that measuring-tape of the extent to which Church and World are
entwined.

[3] The oldest commentary preserved, in part, to us is that of Victorinus of Pettan
on the Apocalypse.

we are not limited to the Apologists Arnobius and Lactantius for purposes of comparison. We learn much the same thing as to African Christianity from the works of Cyprian, or, even from the theological attitude of the Bishop himself, as we infer from Commodian's poems. And, on the other hand, Latin Church Fathers of the fourth century, *e.g.*, Zeno and Hilary, show in their writings that we must not look for the theological interests of the West in the same quarter as those of the East. *In fact the West did not, strictly speaking, possess a specifically Church "theology" at all.*[1] It was only from the second half of the fourth century that the West was invaded by the Platonic theology which Hippolytus, Tertullian, and Novatian had cultivated, to all appearance without any thorough success. Some of its results were accepted, but the theology itself was not. Nor, in some ways, was it later on, when the Western structure of Monotheism, energetic practical morality, and conservative Chiliasm fell a prey to destruction. The mystical tendencies, or the perceptions that led to them, were themselves awanting. Yet there is no mistake, on the other hand, as we are taught by the Institutiones of Lactantius as well as the Tractates of Cyprian, that the rejection of Modalism and the recognition of Christ as the Logos forced upon the West the necessity of rising from faith to a philosophical and, in fact, a distinctively Neoplatonic dogmatic. It was simply a question of time when this departure should take place. The recognition of the Logos could not fail ultimately to produce everywhere a ferment which transformed the Rule of Faith into the compendium of a scientific religion. It is hardly possible to conjecture how long and where Monarchians maintained their ground as independent sects in the West. It is yet most probable that there were Patripassians in Rome in the fourth century. The Western Fathers and opponents of heretics from the middle of the fourth century speak not infrequently of Monarchians— Sabellians; but they, as a rule, have simply copied Greek sources,

---

[1] The work of Arnobius is, in this respect, very instructive. This theologian did not incline as a theologian to Neoplatonism, at a time when, in the East, the use of any other philosophy in Christian dogmatics was *ipso facto* forbidden as heretical.

from which they have transferred the confusion that prevailed among the Greek representatives of Sabellianism, and to a still greater extent, we must admit, among the historians who were hostile to it. [1]

[1] Epiphanius (H. 62. 1) tells us that there were Sabellians in Rome in his time. Since he was acquainted with no other province or community in the West we may perhaps believe him. This information seems to be confirmed by a discovery made in A.D. 1742 by Marangoni. "He found at the Marancia gate on the road leading to S. Paolo a stair closed in his time which, as the discoverer believed, led to a cubiculum of S. Callisto, and in which were painted Constantine's monogram in very large letters, and, secondly, Christ sitting on a globe, between Peter and Paul. On the cover, in a mosaic of green stones, stood the inscription "Qui et filius diceris et pater inveniris" (Kraus, Rom. sott. 2 Aufl., p. 550). De Rossi, Kraus, and Schultze (Katakomben, p. 34) suppose that we have here the discovery of a burial place of Modalistic Monarchians, and that, as the monogram proves, of the fourth century. The sepulchre has again disappeared, and we have to depend entirely on Marangoni's account, which contains no facsimile. It is not probable that a Sabellian burial-place lay in immediate proximity to Domitilla's catacomb in the fourth century, or that the grave-yard of any sect was preserved. If we can come to any decision at all, in view of the uncertainty of the whole information, it seems more credible that the inscription belongs to the third century, and that the monogram was added to deprive it of its heretical character.

Whether Ambrosius and Ambrosiaster refer in the following quotations to Roman or say Western Monarchians living in their time is at least questionable. (Ambrosius, de fide V. 13. 162, Ed. Bened. II. p. 579 "Sabelliani et Marcionitæ dicunt, quod hæc futura sit Christi ad deum patrem subjectio, ut in patrem filius refundatur"; Ambrosiaster in Ep. ad Cor. II. 2, Ed. Bened. App. II., p. 117, "quia ipsum patrem sibi filium appellatum dicebant, ex quibus Marcion traxit errorem ").

Optatus (I. 9) relates that in the African provinces not only the errors, but even the names, of Praxeas and Sabellius had passed away; in I. 10, IV. 5, V. 1 he discusses the Patripassians briefly, but without giving anything new. Nor can we infer from Hilary (de trinitate VII. 39; ad Constant. II. 9) that there were still Monarchians in his time in the West. Augustine says (Ep. 118 c. II. [12] ed. Bened. II., p. 498) dissensiones quæstionesque Sabellianorum silentur." Second-hand information regarding them is to be found in Augustine, Tract. in Joh. (passim) and Hær. 41. (The remarks here on the relation of Sabellius to Noëtus are interesting. Augustine cannot see why orientals count Sabellianism a separate heresy from Monarchianism).

Again we have similar notices in Aug. Prædest. H. 41—in H. 70 Priscillians and Sabellians are classed together; as already in Leo I—, in Isidor, H. 43, Gennadius, Eccl. Dogm. I. 4 ("Pentapolitana hæresis") Pseudo-hieron. H. 26 ("Unionita" etc., etc. In the Consult. Zacch. et Appollon. l. II. 11 sq. (Gallandi T. IX., p. 231 sq.)—a book written about 430—a distinction is made between the Patripassians and Sabellians. The former are correctly described, the latter confounded with the Macedonians. Vigilius Dial. adv. Arian. (Bibl. Lugd. T. VIII.).

(c) The Modalistic Monarchians in the East: Sabellianism and the History of Philosophical Christology and Theology after Origen. [1]

After the close of the third century the name of "Sabellians" became the common title of Modalistic Monarchians in the East. In the West also the term was used here and there, in the same way, in the fourth and fifth centuries. In consequence of this the traditional account of the doctrines taught by Sabellius and his immediate disciples is very confused. Zahn has the credit of having shown that the propositions, especially, which were first published by Marcellus of Ancyra, were characterised by opponents as Sabellian because Monarchian, and in later times they have been imputed to the older theologian. But not only does the work of Marcellus pass under the name of Sabellius up to the present day, Monarchianism undoubtedly assumed very different forms in the East in the period between Hippolytus and Athanasius. It was steeped in philosophical speculation. Doctrines based on *kenosis* and transformation were developed.

[1] S. Schleiermacher in the Theol. Zeitschr. 1822, part 3; Lange in the Zeitschr. f. d. histor. Theol. 1832, II. 2. S. 17—46; Zahn, Marcell. 1867. Quellen: Orig., περὶ ἀρχ. I. 2; in Joh. I. 23, II. 2. 3, X. 21; in ep. ad Titum fragm. II; in Mt. XVI. 8, XVII. 14; c. Cels. VIII. 12, etc. For Sabellius, Philosoph. IX. is, in spite of its meagreness, of fundamental importance. Hippolytus introduces him in a way that shows plainly he was sufficiently well known at the time in the Roman Church not to need any more precise characterisation (see Caspari, Quellen III., p. 327). Epiphanius (H. 62) has borrowed from good sources. If we still possessed them, the letters of Dionysius of Alex. would have been our most important original authorities on S. and his Libyan party. But we have only fragments, partly in Athanasius (de sententia Dionysii), partly in later writers—the collection in Routh is not complete, Reliq. S. III., pp. 371—403. All that Athanasius imparts, though fragmentary, is indispensable (espec. in the writings De synod.; de decret. synod. Nic. and c. Arian. IV. This discourse has from its careless use led to a misrepresentation of Sabellian teaching; yet see Rettberg, Marcell. Præf.; Kuhn, Kath. Dogmatik II. S. 344; Zahn, Marcell. S. 198 f.). A few important notices in Novatian, de trinit. 12 sq.; Method., Conviv. VIII. 10; Arius in ep. ad. Alex. Alexandriæ (Epiph., H. 69. 7); Alexander of Alex. (in Theodoret, H. E. I. 3); Eusebius, c. Marcell. and Præpar. evang.; Basilius, ep. 207, 210, 214, 235; Gregory of Nyssa, λόγος κατὰ Ἀρείου καὶ Σαβελλίου (Mai. V. P. Nova Coll. VIII. 2, p. 1 sq.)—to be used cautiously—; Pseudo-Gregor (Appollinaris) in Mai, l.c. VII. 1., p. 170 sq.; Theodoret. H. F. II. 9; Anonymus, πρὸς τοὺς Σαβελλίζοντας (Athanas. Opp. ed. Montfaucon II., p. 37 sq.); Joh. Damascenus; Nicephorus Call., H. E. VI. 25. For Monarchianism we have a few passages in Gregorius Thaumaturg. The theologians after Origen and before Arius will be cited under.

And the whole was provided by the historians with the same label. At the same time these writers went on drawing inferences, until they have described forms of doctrine which, in this connection, in all probability never existed at all. Accordingly, even after the most careful examination and sifting of the information handed down, it is now unfortunately impossible to write a history of Monarchianism from Sabellius to Marcellus; for the accounts are not only confused, but fragmentary and curt. It is quite as impossible to give a connected history of the Logos Christology from Origen to Arius and Athanasius, although the tradition is in this case somewhat fuller. But the orthodox of the fourth and fifth centuries found little to please them in the Logos doctrine of those earlier disciples of Origen, and consequently they transmitted a very insignificant part of their writings to posterity. This much is certain, however, that in the East the fight against Monarchianism in the second half of the third century was a violent one, and that even the development of the Logos Christology (of Origen) was directly and lastingly influenced by this opposition.[1] The circumstance, that "Sabel-

---

[1] Emendations both to support and to refute Sabellianism were proposed in the valued works of the past; the N. T., as well as other writings belonging to primitive Christian literature, being tampered with. Compare Lightfoot's excursus on I. Clem. II., where Cod. A reads τοῦ Θεοῦ while C and S have τοῦ Χριστοῦ, the latter an emendation opposed to Monarchianism or Monophysitism (St. Clement of Rome, Appendix, p. 400 sq.). The old formulas τὸ αἷμα, τὰ παθήματα τοῦ Θεοῦ and others came into disrepute after the third century. Athanasius himself disapproved of them (c. Apoll. II. 13. 14, I., p. 758), and in the Monophysite controversy they were thoroughly distrusted. Thus in Ignatius (ad. Eph. I.) ἐν αἵματι Θεοῦ and (ad. Rom. VI.) τοῦ πάθους τοῦ Θεοῦ μου were corrected. On the other hand (II. Clem. IX.) the title of πνεῦμα for Christ was changed into λόγος. In the N. T. there are not a few passages where the various readings show a Monarchian or anti-Monarchian, a monophysite or dyophysite leaning. The most important have been discussed by Ezra Abbot in several essays in the " Bibliotheca Sacra " and the "Unitarian Review". But we can trace certain various readings due to a Christological bias as far back as the second century : thus especially the famous ὁ μονογενὴς υἱὸς for μονογενὴς Θεός John I. 18; on this see Hort., Two Dissertations I., on ΜΟΝΟΓΕΝΗΣ ΘΕΟΣ in Scripture and Tradition, 1878; Abbot in the Unitarian Review, June 1875. Since the majority of the important various readings in the N. T. belong to the second and third century, a connected examination of them would be very important from the standpoint of the history of dogma. For dogmatic changes in the western texts, the remarkable passage in Ambrosiaster on Rom. V. 14 falls especially to be noticed.

lianism " was almost the only name by which Monarchianism was known in the East, points, for the rest, to schisms having resulted only from, or, at any rate, after the appearance and labours of Sabellius in the East, therefore at the earliest since about 230—240. So long as Origen lived in Alexandria no schism took place in Egypt over the Christological question. [1]

Sabellius, perhaps by birth a Lybian from Pentapolis, [2] seems after his excommunication to have remained at the head of a small community in Rome. He was still there, to all appearance, when Hippolytus wrote the Philosophumena. Nor do we know of his ever having left the city,—we are nowhere told that he did. Yet he must have, at least, set an important movement at work abroad from Rome as his centre, and have especially fostered relations with the East. When, in Pentapolis, about A.D. 260, and several years after the death of Origen, the Monarchian doctrine took hold of the Churches there (Dionys., l.c.) —Churches which, it is significant, were to some extent Latin in their culture—Sabellius can hardly have been alive, yet it was under his name that the heresy was promoted. [3] But it would seem as if this prominence was given to him for the first time about A.D. 260. Origen at least had not, so far as I know, mentioned the name of Sabellius in his discussions of Monarchianism. These date from as early as A.D. 215. At the time, Origen was in Rome, Zephyrine being still Bishop. From the relations which he then entered into with Hippolytus, it has been rightly concluded that he did not hold aloof from the contentions in Rome, and took the side of Hippolytus. This attitude of Origen's may not have been without influence on his condemnation afterwards in Rome by Pontian, 231 or 232. Origen's writings, moreover, contain many sharp censures on Bishops who, in order to glorify God, made the distinction between Father and Son merely

---

[1] See Dionys. Alex. in Euseb. VII. 6. Dionysius speaks as if the appearance of Sabellian doctrine in his time in the Pentapolis were something new and unheard of.

[2] This information, however, first appears in Basil, then in Philaster, Theodoret, and Nicephorus; possibly, therefore, it is due to the fact that Sabellius' teaching met with great success in Libya and Pentapolis.

[3] Athanas. de sententia Dionysii 5.

nominal. And this again seems to have been said not without reference to the state of matters in Rome. The theology of Origen made him an especially energetic opponent of the Modalistic form of doctrine; for although the new principles set up by him—that the Logos, looking to the content of his nature, possessed the complete deity, and that he from eternity was created from the being of the Father—approached apparently a Monarchian mode of thought, yet they in fact repelled it more energetically then Tertullian and Hippolytus could possibly have done. He who followed the philosophical theology of Origen was proof against all Monarchianism. But it is important to notice that in all places where Origen comes to speak about Monarchians, he merely seems to know their doctrines in an extremely simple form, and without any speculative embroidery. They are always people who "deny that Father and Son are two Hypostases" (they say: ἐν οὐ μόνον οὐσίᾳ, ἀλλὰ καὶ ὑποκειμένῳ), who "fuse together" Father and Son (συγχέειν), who admit distinctions in God only in "conception" and "name", and not in "number", etc. Origen considers them therefore to be untheological creatures, mere "believers". Accordingly, he did not know the doctrine of Sabellius, and living in Syria and Palestine had even had no opportunity of learning it.

That doctrine was undoubtedly closely allied, as Epiphanius has rightly seen (H. 62. 1), to the teaching of Noëtus; it was distinguished from the latter, however, both by a more careful theological elaboration, and by the place given to the Holy Ghost. [1] The opinion of Nitzsch and others, that we must distinguish between two stages in the theology of Sabellius, is unnecessary, whenever we eliminate the unreliable sources. The central proposition of Sabellius ran that Father, Son, and Holy Spirit were the same. Three names accordingly were attached to one and the same being. It was his interest in monotheism that influenced Sabellius. "What shall we say," urge his followers

---

[1] This appears also from our oldest witness, the letter of Dionysius, Eusebius H. E. VII. 6: περὶ τοῦ νῦν κινηθέντος ἐν τῇ Πτολεμαΐδι τῆς Πενταπόλεως δόγματος, ὄντος ἀσεβοῦς καὶ βλασφημίαν πολλὴν ἔχοντος περὶ τοῦ παντοκράτορος Θεοῦ πατρὸς καὶ τοῦ κυρίου ἡμῶν Ἰησοῦ Χριστοῦ, ἀπιστίαν τε πολλὴν ἔχοντος περὶ τοῦ μονογενοῦς παιδὸς αὐτοῦ καὶ πρωτοτόκου πάσης κτίσεως, τοῦ ἐνανθρωπήσαντος λόγου, ἀναισθησίαν δὲ τοῦ ἁγίου πνεύματος,

in Epiphanius (ch. 2), "have we one God or three Gods?" (τί ἂν εἴπωμεν, ἕνα Θεὸν ἔχομεν, ἢ τρεῖς Θεούς;); and Epiphanius (ch. 3) replies: "we do not propound polytheism" (οὐ πολυθεΐαν εἰσηγού-μεθα). Whether Sabellius himself used the comparison between the threefold nature of man and the sun remains a question (one nature, three energies: τὸ φωτιστικόν light giving, τὸ θάλπον heat giving, τὸ σχῆμα the form).[1] The one being was also called by Sabellius υἱοπάτωρ,[2] an expression which was certainly chosen to remove any misunderstanding, to make it impossible to suppose that two beings were in question. This υἱοπάτωρ (son-father) was in Sabellius the ultimate designation for God Himself, and not, say, merely for certain manifestations of a μονάς (unit) resting in the background. Sabellius, however, taught—according to Epiphanius and Athanasius—that God was not at the same time Father and Son; but that he had, rather, put forth his activity in three successive "energies"; first, in the Prosopon (= form of manifestation, figure; not = Hypostasis) of the Father as Creator and Lawgiver; secondly, in the Prosopon of the Son as Redeemer, beginning with the incarnation and ending at the ascension; finally, and up till the present hour, in the Prosopon of the Spirit as giver and sustainer of life.[3] We do not know whether Sabellius was able strictly to carry out the idea of the strict succession of the Prosopa, so that the one should form the boundary of the other. It is

[1] Epiph., l. c.: Δογματίζει γὰρ οὗτος καὶ οἱ ἀπ᾿ αὐτοῦ Σαβελλιανοὶ τὸν αὐτὸν εἶναι πατέρα, τὸν αὐτὸν υἱόν, τὸν αὐτὸν εἶναι ἅγιον πνεῦμα ὡς εἶναι ἐν μιᾷ ὑποστάσει τρεῖς ὀνομασίας, ἢ ὡς ἐν ἀνθρώπῳ σῶμα καὶ ψυχὴ καὶ πνεῦμα, Καὶ εἶναι μὲν τὸ σῶμα ὡς εἰπεῖν τὸν πατέρα, ψυχὴν δὲ ὡς εἰπεῖν τὸν υἱόν, τὸ πνεῦμα δὲ ὡς ἀνθρώπου, οὕτως καὶ τὸ ἅγιον πνεῦμα ἐν τῇ θεότητι. Ἢ ὡς ἐὰν ᾖ ἐν ἡλίῳ ὄντι μὲν ἐν μιᾷ ὑποστάσει, τρεῖς δὲ ἔχοντι τὰς ἐνεργείας κ.τ.λ. Method. Conviv. VIII. 10 (ed. Jahn, p. 37): Σαβέλλιος λέγει τὸν παντοκράτορα πεπονθέναι.

[2] Athanas., de synod. 16; Hilar., de trin. IV. 12.

[3] Epiph. H. 62, c. 1: Πεμφθέντα τὸν υἱὸν καιρῷ ποτέ, ὥσπερ ἀκτῖνα καὶ ἐργα-σάμενον τὰ πάντα ἐν τῷ κόσμῳ τὰ τῆς οἰκονομίας τῆς εὐαγγελικῆς καὶ σωτηρίας τῶν ἀνθρώπων, ἀναληφθέντα δὲ αὖθις εἰς οὐρανόν, ὡς ὑπὸ ἡλίου πεμφθεῖσαν ἀκτῖνα, καὶ πάλιν εἰς τὸν ἥλιον ἀναδραμοῦσαν, Τὸ δὲ ἅγιον πνεῦμα πέμπεσθαι εἰς τὸν κόσμον, καὶ καθεξῆς καὶ καθ᾿ ἕκαστα εἰς ἕκαστον τῶν καταξιουμένων κ.τ.λ. C. 3 Epiphanius says: Οὐχ ὁ υἱὸς ἑαυτὸν ἐγέννησεν, οὐδὲ ὁ πατὴρ μεταβέβληται ἀπὸ τοῦ "πατήρ" τοῦ εἶναι "υἱός" κ.τ.λ.... πατὴρ ἀεὶ πατήρ, καὶ οὐκ ἦν καιρὸς ὅτε οὐκ ἦν πατὴρ πατήρ.

possible, indeed it is not improbable, that he could not fail to
recognise in nature a continuous energy of God as Father.[1] It
is self-evident that the Sabellians would approve of the Catholic
Canon; that they did, is confirmed by Epiphanius. They are
said to have appealed especially to passages like Deut. VI. 4,
Exod. XX. 3, Isa. XLIV. 6 and John X. 38.[2] But Epiphanius
remarks besides that the Sabellians derived their whole heresy
and its strength from certain Apocrypha, especially the so-called
Gospel of the Egyptians.[3] This note is instructive; for it not
only recalls to our recollection a lost literature of the second
century, especially the Gospel of the Egyptians,[4] but it also
shows that the use of an uncanonical Gospel had long continued
among Catholics in the Pentapolis, or at any rate in Egypt.[5]
Finally, it confirms the view that the Christology of Sabellius
cannot have been essentially different from the older, the so-
called Patripassian doctrine. It is distinguished from the latter
neither by the assumption of a transcendental Monas resting
behind the Prosopa, nor by the introduction of the category of
the Logos—which was made use of by Callistus, but not by
Sabellius; nor by a speculative theory, borrowed from the Stoa,
of the Deity, self-contained, and again unfolding itself; nor,
finally, by a doctrine of the Trinity constructed in any fashion
or by the expression υἱοπάτωρ, which, as used by Sabellius, simply
affirmed the single personality of God. As to the doctrine of
the Trinity, a triad was distinctly out of the question in Sabellius. The only noteworthy and real differences are found in
these three points; first, in the attempt to demonstrate the succession of the Prosopa; secondly, as observed above, in the

---

[1] See Zahn, Marcell., p. 213.

[2] Epiph., l. c., c. 2.

[3] L. c.: Τὴν δὲ πᾶσαν αὐτῶν πλάνην καὶ τὴν τῆς πλάνης αὐτῶν δύναμιν ἔχουσιν
ἐξ Ἀποκρύφων τινῶν, μάλιστα ἀπο τοῦ καλουμένου Αἰγυπτίου εὐαγγελίου, ᾧ τινες
τὸ ὄνομα ἐπέθεντο τοῦτο. Ἐν αὐτῷ γὰρ πολλὰ τοιαῦτα ὡς ἐν παραβύστῳ μυστη-
ριωδῶς ἐκ προσώπου τοῦ σωτῆρος ἀναφέρεται, ὡς αὐτοῦ δηλοῦντος τοῖς μαθηταῖς τὸν
αὐτὸν εἶναι πατέρα, τὸν αὐτὸν εἶναι υἱόν, τὸν αὐτὸν εἶναι ἅγιον πνεῦμα.

[4] In the 2nd Ep. of Clement where it is frequently used, though this is disputed
by some, Modalistic formulas occur.

[5] Clemens Alex. knew it; see Hilgenfeld, Nov. Testam. extra can. recept., 2 ed.,
fasc. 4, p. 42 sq.

reference to the Holy Spirit; thirdly, in formally placing the
Father on a parallel line with the two other Prosopa. The
attempt mentioned above may be regarded as a return to the
strict form of Modalism, which it was possible to hold was im-
pugned by formulas like the *compassus est pater filio* (the Father
suffered in sympathy with the Son). In the reference to the
Holy Spirit, Sabellius simply followed the new theology, which
was beginning to take the Spirit more thoroughly into account.
Most important is the third point mentioned. For in ranging
the Prosopon and energy of the Father in a series with the
two others, not only was cosmology introduced into the Modalistic doctrine as a parallel to soteriology, but the preëminence
of the Father over the other Prosopa was departed from in
principle, and thus, in a curious fashion, the way was prepared
for the Athanasian, and still more for the Western and Augustinian Christology. Here, undoubtedly, we have the decisive
advance marked by Sabellianism within Monarchianism. It led
up to the exclusive ὁμοούσιος (consubstantial); for it is probable
that Sabellians employed this expression.[1] They could apply it
with perfect right. Further, while up to this time no evident
bond had connected cosmology and soteriology within Modalistic
theology, Sabellius now made the histories of the world and
salvation into a history of the God who revealed himself in
them. In other words, this Monarchianism became commensurate
in form with that theology which employed the conception of
the Logos, and this fact may have constituted by no means the least
part of the attractiveness which Sabellianism proved itself to
possess in no small degree up to the beginning of the fourth
century and even later.[2] However, it is not to be concealed
that the teaching of Sabellius relative to the Prosopon of the
Father is particularly obscure. The sentence attributed to him
by Athanasius,[3] "as there are diversities of spiritual gifts, but

[1] See above, p. 45.

[2] There were still Sabellians in Neo-Cæsarea in the time of Basilius; Epiphanius
knows of them only in Mesopotamia (H. 62 c. 1). The author of the Acta Archelai (c. 37) also became acquainted with them there; he treats them like Valentinians,
Marcionites, and followers of Tatian as heretics.

[3] Orat. c. Arian IV. 25: ὥσπερ διαιρέσεις χαρισμάτων εἰσί, τὸ δὲ αὐτὸ πνεῦμα,
οὕτω καὶ ὁ πατὴρ ὁ αὐτός μέν ἐστι, πλατύνεται δὲ εἰς υἱὸν καὶ πνεῦμα.

the same spirit, so also the Father is the same, but unfolds
himself in Son and Spirit"—seems at the first glance to contradict the details given above. Yet the different gifts are
certainly the Spirit himself, which so unfolds himself in them
that he does not remain an element behind them, but is completely merged in them. In the same way the Father unfolds himself in the Prosopa. The witnesses to the succession of the
Prosopa in Sabellius are too strong to allow us to infer from this
passage that the Father still remained Father after the unfolding
(πλατυσμός) in the Son. But this passage shows that philosophical speculations could readily attach themselves to the simple
theory of Sabellius. Marcellus rejected his doctrine which he
knew accurately. What he missed in it was the recognition of
the Logos; therefore the idea of God had also not been correctly
apprehended by him.[1] But the form given to Monarchianism
by Marcellus[2] won few friends for that type of doctrine. Alexandrian theologians, or Western scholars who came to their
assistance, had already perfected the combination of Origen's
doctrine of the Logos with the Monarchian Ὁμοούσιος; in other
words, they had turned the category used by Origen against
the λόγος κτίσμα conception (the Logos-created) of Origen himself. The saving formula, "the Logos of the same substance,
not made" (λόγος ὁμοούσιος οὐ ποιηθείς), was already uttered, and,
suspiciously like Monarchianism as it sounded at first, became
for that very reason the means of making Monarchianism superfluous in the Church, and of putting an end to it.[3]

But that only happened after great fights. One of these
we know, the controversy of the two Dionysii, a prelude to
the Arian conflict.[4] In the Pentapolis the Sabellian doctrine
had, soon after the death of Origen, won a great following even

---

[1] Euseb. c. Marcell., p. 76 sq.

[2] See on this Volume IV.

[3] Sabellius seems to have been held a heretic all over the West about A.D. 300;
see the Acta Archelai, Methodius etc.

[4] Hagemann, l.c., p. 411 ff.; Dittrich, Dion. d. Gr. 1867; Förster, in the Ztschr.
f. d. hist. Theol., 1871, p. 42 ff.; Routh, Reliq. S. III., pp. 373—403. The main
source is Athanasius de sentent, Dionysii, a defence of the Bishop, due to the appeal
of the Arians to him; see also Basilius de spiritu, p. 29; Athan. de synod. 43—45.

among the Bishops, "so that the Son of God was no longer preached." Dionysius of Alexandria, therefore, composed various letters in which he tried to recall those who had been misled, and to refute Sabellianism.[1] In one of these, directed to Euphranor and Ammonius, he gave an extreme exposition of Origen's doctrine of the subordination of the Son. This letter seemed very questionable to some Christians—probably in Alexandria, perhaps in Pentapolis. They lodged a complaint, soon after A.D. 260, against the Alexandrian Bishop with Dionysius in Rome.[2] The latter assembled a synod at Rome, which disapproved of the expressions used by the Alexandrian, and himself despatched to Alexandria a didactic letter against the Sabellians and their opponents, who inclined to subordinationism. In this letter the Bishop so far spared his colleague as not to mention his name; but he sent him a letter privately, calling for explanations. The Alexandrian Bishop sought to justify himself in a long document in four books (ἔλεγχος καὶ ἀπολογία), maintained that his accusers had wickedly torn sentences from their context, and gave explanations which seem to have satisfied the Roman Bishop, and which Athanasius at any rate admitted to be thoroughly orthodox. But the letter of the Roman Bishop appears to have had no immediate influence on the further development in Alexandria (see under); the universal collapse of the Empire in the following decades permitted the Alexandrian theologians

---

[1] Euseb., H. E. VII. 26. 1: Ἐπὶ ταύταις τοῦ Διονυσίου φέρονται καὶ ἄλλαι πλείους ἐπιστολαί, ὥσπερ αἱ κατὰ Σαβελλίου πρὸς Ἄμμωνα τῆς κατὰ Βερενίκην ἐκκλησίας ἐπίσκοπον, καὶ ἡ πρὸς Τελέσφορον καὶ ἡ πρὸς Εὐφράνορα, καὶ πάλιν Ἄμμωνα καὶ Εὔπορον. Συντάττει δὲ περὶ τῆς αὐτῆς ὑποθέσεως καὶ ἄλλα τέσσαρα συγγράμματα, ἃ τῷ κατὰ Ῥώμην ὁμωνύμῳ Διονυσίῳ προσφωνεῖ. Dionysius had already called the attention of Sixtus II., the predecessor of the Roman Dionysius, to the revolt in the Pentapolis.

[2] Hagemann maintains that they first turned to the Alexandrian Bishop himself, and that he wrote an explanatory letter, which, however, did not satisfy them; but this cannot be proved (Athanasius de sentent. Dion. 13 is against it). The standpoint of the accusers appears from their appeal to the Roman Bishop, from the fact that he made their cause his own, and from the testimony of Athanasius. who describes them as orthodox Churchmen (de sentent. Dion. 13)—they were orthodox in the Roman sense. It is entirely wrong, with Dorner (Entwickelungsgesch. I., p. 748 f.) and Baur (Lehre v. d. Dreieinigkeit I., p. 313), to identify the accusers with those heretics, who, according to Dionysius' letter, taught there were three Gods; for the heretics meant were rather the Alexandrian theologians.

to continue their speculations, without needing to fear further immediate reproofs from Roman Bishops.

Two facts give a special interest to the controversy of the Dionysii. First, in spite of the acceptance of the sacred Triad, the Romans adhered simply, without any speculative harmonising, to the unity of the Deity, and decided that Origen's doctrine of subordination was Tritheism. Secondly, no scruple was felt at Alexandria in carrying out the subordination of the Son to the Father until it involved separation, though it was well known that such a view was supported, not by the tradition of the Church, but by philosophy alone. The accusers of the Alexandrian Dionysius charged him with separating Father and Son;[1] denying the eternal existence of the Son;[2] naming the Father without the Son and *vice versâ;*[3] omitting to use the world ὁμοούσιος;[4] and finally, with regarding the Son as a creature, related to the Father as the vine to the gardener, or the boat to the shipbuilder.[5] In these censures, which were not inaccurate, it is obvious that Dionysius, continuing the Neoplatonic speculations of his teacher, conceived the λόγος as *portio* and *derivatio* of the μονάς, thus, in order to meet Sabellianism, actually dividing him from the deity. Dionysius sought to excuse himself in his ἔλεγχος (Refutation), and emphasised exclusively the other side of Origen's doctrine, at the same time

---

[1] De sententia 10. 16.

[2] De sententia 14: οὐκ ἀεὶ ἦν ὁ Θεὸς πατήρ, οὐκ ἀεὶ ἦν ὁ υἱός, ἀλλ᾽ ὁ μὲν Θεὸς ἦν χωρὶς τοῦ λόγου, αὐτὸς δὲ ὁ υἱὸς οὐκ ἦν πρὶν γεννηθῇ, ἀλλ᾽ ἦν ποτὲ ὅτε οὐκ ἦν, οὐ γὰρ ἀΐδιός ἐστιν, ἀλλ᾽ ὕστερον ἐπιγέγονεν.

[3] De sententia 16: πατέρα λέγων Διονύσιος οὐκ ὀνομάζει τὸν υἱόν, καὶ πάλιν υἱὸν λέγων οὐκ ὀνομάζει τὸν πατέρα, ἀλλὰ διαιρεῖ καὶ μακρύνει καὶ μερίζει τὸν υἱὸν ἀπὸ τοῦ πατρός.

[4] L. c. 18: προσφέρουσιν ἔγκλημα κατ᾽ ἐμοῦ ψεῦδος ὂν ὡς οὐ λέγοντος τὸν Χριστὸν ὁμοούσιον εἶναι τῷ Θεῷ.

[5] L. c. 18: πλὴν ἐγὼ γενητά τινα—says Dion. Alex.—καὶ ποιητά τινα φήσας νοεῖσθαι, τῶν μὲν τοιούτων ὡς ἀχρειοτέρων ἐξ ἐπιδρομῆς εἶπον παραδείγματα, ἐπεὶ μήτε τὸ φυτὸν ἔφην (τὸ αὐτὸ εἶναι) τῷ γεωργῷ, μήτε τῷ ναυπηγῷ τὸ σκάφος·— 'Ένα τῶν γενητῶν εἶναι—say the opponents of Dion.—τὸν υἱὸν καὶ μὴ ὁμοούσιον τῷ πατρί. The passage in the letter to Euphranor ran (c. 4): ποίημα καὶ γενητὸν εἶναι τὸν υἱὸν τοῦ Θεοῦ, μήτε δὲ φύσει ἴδιον, ἀλλὰ ξένον κατ᾽ οὐσίαν αὐτὸν εἶναι τοῦ πατρός, ὥσπερ ἐστὶν ὁ γεωργὸς πρὸς τὴν ἄμπελον καὶ ὁ ναυπηγὸς πρὸς τὸ σκάφος. καὶ γὰρ ὡς ποίημα ὢν οὐκ ἦν πρὶν γένηται.

admitting that in his incriminated writing he had incidentally
employed somewhat unsuitable similes. Now he said that the
Father had always been Father, and that Christ had always
existed as the Logos and wisdom and power of God; that the
Son had his being from the Father, and that he was related
to the Father as the rays are to the light. [1] He explained that
while he had not used the word ὁμοούσιος, because it did not
occur in Holy Scripture, figures were to be found in his earlier
writings which corresponded to it; thus the figure of parents
and children, of seed or root and plant, and of source and
stream. [2] The Father was the source of all good, the Son the
outflow; the Father the mind (νοῦς), the Son the word (λόγος)—
reminding us very forcibly of Neoplatonism—or the emanating
mind (νοῦς προπηδῶν), while the νοῦς itself remains "and is what
it was" (καὶ ἔστιν οἷος ἦν). "But being sent he flew forth and
is borne everywhere, and thus each is in each, the one being
of the other, and they are one, being two" ('Ο δὲ ἐξέπτη
προπεμφθεὶς καὶ φέρεται πανταχοῦ καὶ οὕτως ἐστὶν ἑκάτερος ἐν
ἑκατέρῳ ἕτερος ὢν θατέρου, καὶ ἕν εἰσιν, ὄντες δύο). [3] But he now
went further: any separation between Father and Son was to
be repudiated. "I say Father, and before I add the Son, I
have already included and designated him in the Father." The
same holds true of the Holy Spirit. Their very names always
bind all three together inseparably. "How then do I who use
these names think that these are divided and entirely separated
from each other? (πῶς οὖν ὁ τούτοις χρώμενος τοῖς ὀνόμασι μεμερ-
ίσθαι ταῦτα καὶ ἀφωρίσθαι παντελῶς ἀλλήλων οἴομαι;). [4] In these
words the retreat was sounded; for what the Roman Bishop
rejected, but Alexandrian theology never ventured wholly to

---

[1] L. c. 15.

[2] L. c. 18.

[3] L. c. 23. The expositions of νοῦς and λόγος which were found both in the
2 and 4 books of Dionysius quite remind us of Porphyry: καὶ ἔστιν ὁ μὲν οἷον
πατὴρ ὁ νοῦς τοῦ λόγου, ὢν ἐφ' ἑαυτοῦ, ὁ δὲ καθάπερ υἱὸς ὁ λόγος τοῦ νοῦ. πρὸ
ἐκείνου μὲν ἀδύνατον, ἀλλ' οὐδὲ ἔξωθέν ποθεν, σὺν ἐκείνῳ γενόμενος, βλαστήσας δὲ
ἀπ' αὐτοῦ. οὕτως ὁ πατὴρ ὁ μέγιστος καὶ καθόλου νοῦς πρῶτον τὸν υἱὸν λόγον ἑρμηνέα
καὶ ἄγγελον ἑαυτοῦ ἔχει.

[4] L. c. 17.

discard, was the "dividing" (μερίζεσθαι).¹ The reservation lies
in the word "entirely" (παντελῶς). Dionysius added in conclusion : "Thus we unfold the unit into the triad without
dividing it, and we sum up the triad again into the unit without diminishing it," (οὕτω μὲν ἡμεῖς εἴς τε τὴν τριάδα τὴν μονάδα
πλατύνομεν ἀδιαίρετον, καὶ τὴν τριάδα πάλιν ἀμείωτον εἰς τὴν μονάδα συγκεφαλαιούμεθα). In this he has accommodated himself
to a mode of looking at things which he could only allege to
be his own under a mental reservation, as in the case of the
qualification "entirely" (παντελῶς). For the terms πλατύνειν and
συγκεφαλαιοῦσθαι were not those current in the school of Origen,
and admit of a different interpretation. Finally, Dionysius denied
the charge of the "sycophants" that he made the Father the
Creator of Christ. ²

The letter of Dionysius of Rome falls midway between these
two manifestoes, which are so different, of the Alexandrian Bishop.
We have to regret very deeply that Athanasius has only preserved one, though a comprehensive, fragment of this document. ³
It is extremely characteristic of the Roman Bishop, to begin
with, that it seeks to settle the sound doctrine by representing
it as the just mean between the false unitarian or Sabellian,
and the false trinitarian or Alexandrian doctrine. ⁴ The second

¹ We see from the passages quoted by Basilius that Dionysius adhered to the
expression "τρεῖς ὑποστάσεις," but discarded the "μερισμένας εἶναι." while his
accusers must have attacked the former expression also: Εἰ τῷ τρεῖς εἶναι τὰς
ὑπαστάσεις μεμερισμένας εἶναι λέγουσι, τρεῖς εἰσί, κἂν μὴ θέλωσιν ἢ τὴν θείαν τριάδα παντελῶς ἀνελέτωσαν. This accordingly is to be translated : "if they maintain
that a separation is necessarily involved in the expression ' three Hypostases,' yet
there are three—whether they admit it or no—or they must completely destroy the
divine triad."

² L.c. 20, 21. It is very noteworthy, that Dionysius has not even brought himself to use the expression ὁμοούσιος in his ἔλεγχος. If he had Athanasius would
have given it in his extracts. For the rest, the attempt of Athanasius to explain
away the doubtful utterances of Dionysius, by referring them to the *human* nature
of Christ, is a makeshift born of perplexity.

³ De decret. synod. Nic. 26 (see besides de sentent. Dion. 13).

⁴ The attack on the latter has alone been preserved by Athanasius along with
the concluding argument ; it is thus introduced: Ὅτι δὲ οὐ ποίημα οὐδὲ κτίσμα ὁ
τοῦ Θεοῦ λόγος, ἀλλ' ἴδιον τῆς τοῦ πατρὸς οὐσίας γέννημα ἀδιαίρετόν ἐστιν, ὡς
ἔγραψεν ἡ μεγάλη σύνοδος, ἰδοὺ καὶ ὁ τῆς Ῥώμης ἐπίσκοπος Διονύσιος γράφων κατὰ
τῶν τὰ τοῦ Σαβελλίου φρονούντων, σχετλιάζει κατὰ τῶν ταῦτα τολμώντων λέγειν
καὶ φήσιν οὕτως.

characteristic of the letter is that it regards the Alexandrian doctrine as teaching that there are three Gods, and draws a parallel between it and the Three principles of the Marcionites. *This proves that the Roman Bishop did not trouble himself with the speculation of the Alexandrians, and simply confined himself to the result—as he conceived it—of three separate Hypostases.*[1] Finally—and this is the third characteristic feature—the letter shows that Dionysius had nothing positive to say, further than that it was necessary to adhere to the ancient Creed, definitely interpreting it to mean that the three, Father, Son, and Spirit, were equally one. Absolutely no attempt is *made to explain or to prove this paradox.*[2] But here undoubtedly

[1] Ἑξῆς δ' ἂν εἰκότως λέγοιμι καὶ πρὸς τοὺς διαιροῦντας καὶ κατατέμνοντας καὶ ἀναιροῦντας τὸ σεμνότατον κήρυγμα τῆς ἐκκλησίας τοῦ Θεοῦ, τὴν μοναρχίαν—thus begins the fragment communicated by Athanasius,—εἰς τρεῖς δυνάμεις τινας καὶ μεμερισμένας ὑποστάσεις καὶ θεότητας τρεῖς· πέπυσμαι γὰρ εἶναί τινας τῶν παρ' ὑμῖν κατηχούντων καὶ διδασκόντων τὸν θεῖον λόγον, ταύτης ὑφηγητὰς τῆς φρονήσεως· οἳ κατὰ διάμετρον, ὡς ἔπος εἰπεῖν, ἀντίκεινται τῇ Σαβελλίου γνώμῃ· ὁ μὲν γὰρ βλασφημεῖ, αὐτὸν τὸν υἱὸν εἶναι λέγων τόν πατέρα, καὶ ἔμπαλιν· οἱ δὲ τρεῖς θεοὺς τρόπον τινὰ κηρύττουσιν, εἰς τρεῖς ὑποστάσεις ξένας ἀλλήλων, παντάπασι κεχωρισμένας, διαιροῦντες τὴν ἁγίαν μονάδα. ἠνῶσθαι γὰρ ἀνάγκη τῷ Θεῷ τῶν ὅλων τὸν θεῖον λόγον, ἐμφιλοχωρεῖν δὲ τῷ Θεῷ καὶ ἐνδιαιτᾶσθαι δεῖ τὸ ἅγιον πνεῦμα, ἤδη καὶ τὴν θείαν τριάδα εἰς ἕνα, ὥσπερ εἰς κορυφήν τινα (τὸν Θεὸν τῶν ὅλων τὸν παντοκράτορα λέγω) συγκεφαλαιοῦσθαί τε καὶ συνάγεσθαι πᾶσα ἀνάγκη. Μαρκίωνος γὰρ τοῦ ματαιόφρονος δίδαγμα εἰς τρεῖς ἀρχὰς τῆς μοναρχίας τομὴν καὶ διαίρεσιν (διορίζει), παίδευμα ὂν διαβολικόν, οὐχὶ δὲ τῶν ὄντως μαθητῶν τοῦ Χριστοῦ... οὗτοι γὰρ τριάδα μὲν κηρυττομένην ὑπὸ τῆς θείας γραφῆς σαφῶς ἐπίστανται, τρεῖς δὲ θεοὺς οὔτε παλαιὰν οὔτε καινὴν διαθήκην κηρύττουσαν According to Dionysius, then, some Alexandrian teachers taught "τρόπον τινά"—this is the only limitation—a form of Tritheism. The whole effort of the Bishop was to prevent this. We recognise here the old Roman interest in the unity of God, as represented by Victor, Zephyrine, and Callistus, but Dionysius may also have remembered, that his predecessors, Pontian and Fabian, assented to the condemnation of Origen. Should we not connect the angry reproach, levelled at the Alexandrian teachers, that they were Tritheists, with the charge made by Callistus against Hippolytus, that he was a Ditheist; and may we not perhaps conclude that Origen himself was also accused of Tritheism in Rome?

[2] The positive conclusion runs: Οὔτ' οὖν καταμερίζειν χρὴ εἰς τρεῖς θεότητας τὴν θαυμαστὴν καὶ θείαν μονάδα, οὔτε ποιήσει κωλύειν τὸ ἀξίωμα καὶ τὸ ὑπέρβαλλον μέγεθος τοῦ κυρίου· ἀλλὰ πεπιστευκέναι εἰς Θεὸν πατέρα παντοκράτορα καὶ εἰς Χριστὸν Ἰησοῦν τὸν υἱὸν αὐτοῦ καὶ εἰς τὸ ἅγιον πνεῦμα, ἡνῶσθαι δὲ τῷ Θεῷ τῶν ὅλων τὸν λόγον· ἐγὼ γάρ, φησί. καὶ ὁ πατὴρ ἕν ἐσμεν. καὶ ἐγὼ ἐν τῷ πατρὶ καὶ ὁ πατὴρ ἐν ἐμοί—these are the old Monarchian proof-texts—οὕτω γὰρ ἂν καὶ ἡ θεία τριὰς καὶ τὸ ἅγιον κήρυγμα τῆς μοναρχίας διασώζοιτο. We see that Dionysius simply

lies the strength of the Roman Bishop's position. When we
compare his letter with that of Leo I. to Flavian and Agatho's
to the Emperor, we are astonished at the close affinity of these
Roman manifestoes. In form they are absolutely identical. The
three Popes did not trouble themselves about proofs or arguments, but fixed their attention solely on the consequences, or
what seemed to them consequences, of disputed doctrines.
Starting with these deductions they refuted doctrines of the
right and left, and simply fixed a middle theory, which existed
merely in words, for it was self-contradictory. This they grounded
formally on their ancient Creed without even attempting to argue
out the connection: one God—Father, Son and Spirit; one
Person—perfect God and perfect man; one Person—two wills.
Their contentment with establishing a middle line, which possessed
the attribute of that known in mathematics, is, however, a proof
that they had not a positive, but merely a negative, religious
interest in these speculations. Otherwise they would not have
been satisfied with a definition it was impossible to grasp; for
no religion lives in conceptions which cannot be represented
and realised. Their religious interest centred in the God Jesus,
who had assumed the *substantia humana*.

The letter of the Roman Bishop produced only a passing
impression in Alexandria. Its adoption would have meant the
repudiation of science. A few years afterwards the great Synod
of Antioch expressly rejected the term ὁμοούσιος (consubstantial)

---

places the "holy preaching of the Monarchy" and the "Divine Triad" side by
side: "stat pro ratione voluntas." Between this conclusion and the commencement
of the fragment preserved by Athanasius given in the preceding note, we have a
detailed attack on those who hold the Son to be a ποίημα like other creatures,
"while the Holy Scriptures witness to his having an appropriate birth, but not to
his being formed and created in some way." The attack on the ἦν ὅτε οὐκ ἦν
touches the fundamental position of the Alexandrian scholars as little as the opposition to three Gods; for Dionysius contents himself with arguing that God would
have been without understanding, if the Logos had not always been with him;
a thing which no Alexandrian doubted. The subtle distinction between Logos and
Logos Dionysius leaves wholly out of account, and the explanation of the Roman
Bishop on Proverbs VIII. 32 (κύριος ἔκτισέ με ἀρχὴν ὁδῶν αὐτοῦ): ἔκτισε ἐνταῦθα
ἀκουστέον ἀντὶ τοῦ ἐπέστησε τοῖς ὑπ' αὐτοῦ γεγονόσιν ἔργοις, γεγονόσι δὲ δι' αὐτοῦ
τοῦ υἱοῦ, must merely have caused a compassionate smile among the theologians
of Alexandria.

as being liable to misconstruction. [1] The followers of Origen in
his training school continued their master's work, and they were
not molested in Alexandria itself, as it seems, up till about
the close of the third century, If we review the great literary
labours of Dionysius, of which we, unfortunately, only possess
fragments, and observe his attitude in the questions debated in
the Church in his time, we see how faithfully he followed in
the track of Origen. The only difference lay in greater laxity
in matters of discipline. [2] He proved, in his work " On Promises "
(περὶ ἐπαγγελιῶν), that he possessed the zeal against all Chiliasm
and the dexterity in critical exegesis which characterised the
school of Origen; [3] and in his work "On Nature" (περὶ φύσεως)
he introduced, and endeavoured to carry out, a new task in
the science of Christian theology, viz., the systematic refutation of Materialism, i.e., of the Atomic theory. [4] Of the
later heads of the training school we know very little; but
that little is enough to let us see that they faithfully preserved the
theology of Origen. Pierius, who also led a life of strict asceticism,
wrote learned commentaries and treatises. Photius [5] testifies that
he taught piously concerning the Father ana Son, " except that

[1] See above, page 45.

[2] See the letter to Fabius of Antioch, and the attitude of Dionysius in the
Novatian controversy, in which he sought at first to act as mediator precisely as
he did in the dispute over the baptism of heretics (Euseb. H. E. VI. 41, 42,
44—46, VII. 2—9).

[3] See the fragments in Euseb. H. E. VII. 24, 25. The criticism of the Apocalypse is a master-piece.

[4] See Euseb. H. E. VII. 26, 2; the fragments of the work in Routh, Reliq. S. IV.,
p. 393 sq. On this, Roch, die Schrift des Alex. Bischofs, Dionysius d. Gr. über
die Natur (Leipzig 1882) and my account of this dissertation in the Th. L. Z. 1883,
No. 2. Dionysius' work, apart from a few Biblical quotations which do not affect
the arguments, might have been composed by a Neo-platonic philosopher. Very
characteristic is the opening of the first fragment preserved by Eusebius. Πότερον
ἕν ἐστι συναφὲς τὸ πᾶν, ὡς ἡμῖν τε καὶ τοῖς σοφωτάτοις Ἑλλήνων Πλάτωνι καὶ
Πυθαγόρᾳ καὶ τοῖς ἀπὸ τῆς Στοᾶς καὶ Ἡρακλείτῳ φαίνεται; there we have in a
line the whole company of the saints with whom Epicurus and the Atomists were
confronted. We notice that from and after Justin Epicurus and his followers were
extremely abhorred by Christian theologians, and that in this abhorrence they felt
themselves at one with Platonists, Pythagoreans, and Stoics. But Dionysius was the
first Christian to take over from these philosophers the task of a systematic refutation.

[5] Photius Cod. 119.

he speaks of two "beings" and two natures; using the words being and nature, as is plain from the context, in place of Hypostasis, and not as those who adhere to Arius" (πλὴν ὅτι οὐσίας δύο καὶ φύσεις δύο λέγει· τῷ τῆς οὐσίας καὶ φύσεως ὀνόματι, ὡς δῆλον, ἔκ τε τῶν ἑπομένων καὶ προηγουμένων τοῦ χωρίου ἀντὶ τῆς ὑποστάσεως καὶ οὐχ ὡς οἱ Ἀρείῳ προσανακείμενοι χρώμενος). This explanation is hardly trustworthy; Photius himself is compelled to add that Pierius held impious doctrines as to the Holy Ghost, and ranked him far below the Father and Son. Now since he further expressly testifies that Pierius, like Origen, held the pre-existence of souls, and explained some passages in the O. T. "economically", i.e., contested their literal meaning, it becomes obvious that Pierius had not parted company with Origen;[1] indeed, he was even called "Origen Junior".[2] He was the teacher of Pamphilus, and the latter inherited from him his un-conditional devotion to Origen's theology. Pierius was followed, in Diocletian's time, by Theognostus at the Alexandrian school. This scholar composed a great dogmatic work in seven books called "Hypotyposes". It has been described for us by Photius,[3] whose account shows that it was planned on a strict system, and was distinguished from Origen's great work, in that the whole was not discussed in each part under reference to one main thought, but the system of doctrine was presented in a continuous and consecutive exposition.[4] Thus Theognostus

---

[1] Routh, Reliq. S. III., pp. 425—435.

[2] Jerome, de vir. inl. 76; see also Euseb. H. E. VII. 32.

[3] Cod. 106.

[4] The first book dealt with the Father and Creator; the second, with the necessity that God should have a son, and the Son; the third, took up the Holy Ghost; the fourth, angels and demons; the fifth and sixth, the possibility and actuality of the Son's incarnation; the seventh, God's creative work. From the description by Photius it appears that Theognostus laid the chief stress on the refutation of two opinions, namely, that matter was eternal, and that the incarnation of the Logos was an impossibility. *These are, however, the two theses with which the Neo-platonic theologians of the 4th and 5th centuries confronted Christian science*, and in whose assertion the whole difference between Neo-platonism, and the dogmatic of Alexandrian churchmen at bottom consisted. It is very instructive to notice that even at the end of the 3rd century the antithesis thus fixed came clearly to the front. If Theognostus, for the rest, rejected the opinion that God created all things from a matter equally eternal with himself, this did not necessarily imply his abandonment of Origen's

invented that form of scientific, Church dogmatic which was to set a standard to posterity—though it was indeed long before the Church took courage to erect a doctrinal structure of its own. Athanasius had nothing but praise for the work of Theognostus, and has quoted a passage from the second book which undoubtedly proves that Theognostus did full justice to the Homoousian side of Origen's Christology.[1] But even the Cappadocians remarked certain affinities between Arius and Theognostus,[2] and Photius informs us that he called the Son a "creature" (κτίσμα), and said such mean things about him that one might perhaps suppose that he was simply quoting, in order to refute, the opinions of other men. He also, like Origen, taught heterodox views as to the Holy Spirit, and the grounds on which he based the possibility of the incarnation were empty and worthless. As a matter of fact, Theognostus' exposition of the sin against the Holy Ghost shows that he attached himself most closely to Origen. For it is based on the well-known idea of the master that the Father embraced the largest, the Son, the medium, and the Holy Spirit the smallest sphere; that the sphere of the Son included all rational beings, inclusive of the imperfect, while that of the Spirit comprehended only the perfect

principle of the eternity of matter; yet it is at any rate possible that in this point he took a more guarded view of the master's doctrine.

[1] The fragment given by Athanasius (de decr. Nic. syn. 25) runs as follows: Οὐκ ἔξωθέν τις ἐστιν ἐφευρεθεῖσα ἡ τοῦ υἱοῦ οὐσία, οὐδὲ ἐκ μὴ ὄντων ἐπεισήχθη· ἀλλὰ ἐκ τῆς τοῦ πατρὸς οὐσίας ἔφυ, ὡς τοῦ φωτὸς τὸ ἀπαύγασμα, ὡς ὕδατος ἀτμίς· οὔτε γὰρ τὸ ἀπαύγασμα οὔτε ἡ ἀτμὶς αὐτὸ τὸ ὕδωρ ἐστὶν ἢ αὐτὸς ὁ ἥλιος, οὔτε ἀλλότριον· καὶ οὔτε αὐτός ἐστιν ὁ πατὴρ οὔτε ἀλλότριος ἀλλὰ ἀπόρροια τῆς τοῦ πατρὸς οὐσίας, οὐ μερισμὸν ὑπομεινάσης τῆς τοῦ πατρὸς οὐσίας· ὡς γὰρ μένων ὁ ἥλιος ὁ αὐτὸς οὐ μειοῦται ταῖς ἐκχεομέναις ὑπ' αὐτοῦ αὐγαῖς, οὕτως οὐδὲ ἡ οὐσία τοῦ πατρὸς ἀλλοίωσιν ὑπέμεινεν, εἰκόνα ἑαυτῆς ἔχουσα τὸν υἱόν. Notice that the μερισμός is here negatived; but this negative must have been limited by other definitions. At all events we may perhaps regard Theognostus as midway between Pierius and Alexander of Alexandria.

[2] See Gregory of Nyssa, c. Eunom. III. in Routh, l.c., p. 412; he proscribes the proposition of Theognostus: τὸν Θεὸν βουλόμενον τόδε τὸ πᾶν κατασκευάσαι, πρῶτον τὸν υἱὸν οἷόν τινα κανόνα τῆς δημιουργίας προϋποστήσασθαι. Stephanus Gobarus has expressly noted it as a scandal that Athanasius should nevertheless have praised Theognostus (in Photius, Cod. 282). Jerome did not admit him into his catalogue of authors, and it is remarkable that Eusebius has passed him over in silence; this may, however, have been accidental.

(τελειούμενοι), and that therefore the sin against the Holy Ghost, as the sin of the "perfect", could not be forgiven. [1] The only novelty is that Theognostus saw occasion expressly to attack the view "that the teaching of the Spirit was superior to that of the Son" (τὴν τοῦ πνεύματος διδασκαλίαν ὑπερβάλλειν τῆς τοῦ υἱοῦ διδαχῆς). Perhaps he did this to oppose another disciple of Origen, Hieracas, who applied himself to speculations concerning Melchizedek, as being the Holy Spirit, and emphasised the worship of the Spirit.[2] This Copt, who lived at the close of the third and in the first half of the fourth century, cannot be passed over, because, a scholar like Origen,[3] he on the one hand modified and refined on certain doctrines of his master,[4] and on the other hand, emphasised his practical principles, requiring celibacy as a Christian law.[5] Hieracas is for us the connecting link between Origen and the

---

[1] See Athanas. Ep. ad Serap. IV., ch. 11; Routh, l.c., pp. 407—422, where the fragments of Theognostus are collected.

[2] See Epiph. H. 67. 3, 55. 5.

[3] Epiphanius (H. 67) speaks in the highest terms of the knowledge, learning, and power of memory, possessed by Hieracas.

[4] H. understood the resurrection in a purely spiritual sense, and repudiated the *restitutio carnis*. He would have nothing to do with a material Paradise; and Epiphanius indicates other heresies, which H. tried to support by a comprehensive scriptural proof. The most important point is that he disputed, on the ground of 2 Tim. II. 5, the salvation of children who died even when baptised; "for without knowledge no conflict, without conflict no reward." Epiphanius expressly certifies his orthodoxy in the doctrine of the Trinity; in fact Arius rejected his Christology along with that of Valentinus, Mani. and Sabellius, in his letter to Alexander of Alex. (Epiph. H. 69. 7). From his short description of it (οὐδ ὡς ʹΙεράκας λύχνον ἀπὸ λύχνου, ἢ ὡς λαμπάδα εἰς δύο—these are figures already employed by Tatian) we can only, however, conclude that H. declared the οὐσια of the Son to be identical with that of the Father. He may have developed Origen's Christology in the direction of Athanasius.

[5] See my Art. in Herzog's R. E. 2 Aufl. VI, p. 100 f. Hieracas recognised the essential difference between the O. and N. T. in the commandments as to ἁγνεία, ἐγκράτεια, and especially, celibacy. "What then did the Logos bring that was new?" or what is the novelty proclaimed and instituted by the Only-begotten? The fear of God? The law already contained that. Was it as to marriage? The Scriptures (= the O. T.) had already dealt with it. Or as to envy, greed, and unrighteousness? All that is already contained in the O. T. ʺΕν δὲ μόνον τοῦτο κατορθῶσαι ἦλθε, τὸ τὴν ἐγκράτειαν κηρύξαι ἕν τῷ κόσμῳ καὶ ἑαυτῷ ἀναλέξασθαι ἁγνείαν καὶ ἐγκράτειαν. ʺΑνευ δὲ τούτου μὴ δύνασθαι ζῆν (Epiph. H. 67, ch. 1). He appealed to 1 Cor. VII., Hebr. XII. 14, Math. XIX. 12, XXV. 21.

Coptic monks; the union of ascetics founded by him may mark the transition from the learned schools of theologians to the society of monks. But in his proposition that, as regards practice, the suppression of the sexual impulse was the decisive, and original, demand of the Logos Christ, Hieracas set up the great theme of the Church of the fourth and following century.

In Alexandria the system of faith and the theology of Origen were fused more and more completely together, and it cannot be proved that the immediate disciples of Origen, the heads of the training-school, corrected their master.[1] The first to do this in Alexandria was Peter, Bishop and Martyr.[2] In his writings "Concerning divinity" (περὶ θεότητος), "Concerning the sojourn of our Saviour" (περὶ τῆς σωτῆρος ἡμῶν ἐπιδημίας), and especially in his books "Concerning (the fact) that the soul does not pre-exist, nor has entered this body after having sinned" (περὶ τοῦ μηδὲ προϋπάρχειν τὴν ψυχὴν μηδὲ ἁμαρτήσασαν τοῦτο εἰς σῶμα βληθῆναι), he maintains against Origen the complete humanity of the Redeemer, the creation of our souls along with our bodies, and the historical character of the events narrated in Gen. III, and he characterises the doctrine of a pre-mundane fall as a "precept of Greek philosophy which is foreign and alien to those who desire to live piously in Christ" (μάθημα τῆς Ἑλληνικῆς Φιλοσοφίας, ξένης καὶ ἀλλοτρίας οὔσης τῶν ἐν Χριστῷ εὐσεβῶς θελόντων ζῆν).[3] This utterance proves that Peter had taken up a position definitely opposed to Origen;[4] but his own expositions show, on the other hand, that he only deprived Origen's doctrines of their extreme conclusions, while otherwise he maintained them, in so far as they did not come into direct conflict with the rule of faith. The corrections on Origen's system were therefore not undertaken silently

[1] Procopius undoubtedly maintains (Comm. in Genes, ch. III., p. 76, in Routh, Reliq. S. IV., p. 50) that Dionysius Alex., in his commentary on Ecc'esiastes, contradicted the allegorical explanation of Gen. II., III; but we do not know in what the contradiction consisted.

[2] Eusebius, H. E. IX. 6: Peter was made a martyr, probably in A.D. 311.

[3] See the fragments of Peter's writings in Routh, l.c., pp. 21—82, especially pp. 46—50. Vide also Pitra, Analecta Sacra IV., p. 187 sq., 425 sq.

[4] Decidedly spurious is the fragment of an alleged Μυσταγωγία of Peter, in which occur the words: τί δὲ εἴπω Ἡρακλᾶν καί Δημήτριον τοὺς μακαρίους ἐπισκόπους, οἵους πειρασμοὺς ὑπέστησαν ὑπὸ τοῦ μανέντος Ὠριγένους, καὶ αὐτοῦ σχίσματα βαλλόντος ἐν τῇ ἐκκλησίᾳ, τὰ ἕως σήμερον ταραχὰς αὐτῇ ἐγείραντα (Routh, l.c., p. 81).

even in Alexandria. A compromise took place between scientific
theology, and the ancient antignostically determined Creed of
the Church, or the letter of Holy Scripture, to which all the
doctrines of Origen were sacrificed that contradicted the tenor
of the sacred tradition. [1] But above all, the distinction made by
him between the Christian science of the perfect and the faith
of the simple was to be abolished. The former must be cur-
tailed, the latter added to, and thus a product arrived at in a
uniform faith which should be at the same time ecclesiastical
and scientific. After theology had enjoyed a period of liberty,
the four last decades of the third century, a reaction seems to
have set in at the beginning of the fourth, or even at the end of
the third century, in Alexandria. But the man had not yet risen
who was to preserve theology from stagnation, or from being
resolved into the ideas of the time. All the categories employed
by the theologians of the fourth and fifth centuries were already
current in theology, [2] but they had not yet received their definite impress and fixed value. [3] Even the Biblical texts which
in those centuries were especially exploited *pro* and *contra*,

---

[1] We have unfortunately no more precise information as to Peter's attitude; we
may determine it, however, by that of Methodius (see under).

[2] So μονάς—τριάς—οὐσία—φύσις—ὑποκείμενον—ὑπόστασις—πρόσωπον—περιγραφή—μερίζεσθαι—διαιρεῖν—πλατύνειν—συγκεφαλαιοῦσθαι—κτίζειν—ποιεῖν—γίγνεσθαι
γεννᾶν—ὁμοούσιος—ἐκ τῆς οὐσίας τοῦ πατρός—διὰ τοῦ θελήματος—Θεὸς ἐκ Θεοῦ—
φῶς ἐκ φωτός—γεννηθέντα οὐ ποιηθέντα—ἦν ὅτε οὐκ ἦν—οὐκ ἦν ὅτε οὐκ ἦν—ἦν ὅτε
οὐκ ἦν—ἕτερος κατ᾽ οὐσίαν—ἄτρεπτος—ἀναλλοίωτος—ἀγέννητος—ἀλλότριος—πηγὴ
τῆς θεότητος—δύο οὐσίαι—οὐσία οὐσιωμένη—ἐνανθρώπησις—θεάνθρωπος—ἕνωσις οὐσιώ-
δης—ἕνωσις κατὰ μετουσίαν—συνάφεια κατὰ μάθησιν καὶ μετουσίαν—σύγκρασις—
ἐνοικεῖν etc. Hipler in the Oesterr. Vierteljahrschrift für kathol. Theol. 1869, p.
161 ff. (quoted after Lösche, Ztschr. f. wiss. Theol. 1884, S. 259) maintains that
expressions occurred in the speculations of Numenius and Porphyry as to the nature
of God, which only emerged in the Church in consequence of the Nicene Council.
Those technical terms of religio-philosophical speculation, common to the Neoplatonists of the 3rd century, the Gnostics and Catholic theologians, require re-
examination. One result of this will be perhaps the conclusion that the philosophy
of Plotinus and Porphyry was not uninfluenced by the Christian system, Gnostic
and Origenistic, which they opposed. We await details under this head from
Dr. Carl Schmidt.

[3] The meaning which was afterwards attached to the received categories was
absolutely unthinkable, and corresponded perfectly to none of the definitions previously
hit upon by the philosophical schools. But this only convinced men that Christianity
was a revealed doctrine, which was distinguished from philosophical systems by
mysterious ideas or categories.

had already been collected in the third. Dionysius of Alexandria had already given warning that the word ὁμοούσιος did not occur in Holy Scripture, and this point of view seems, as a rule, to have been thoroughly decisive even in the third century. [1]

We get an insight into the state of religious doctrine about the middle of the third century and afterwards from the works of Gregory,[2] the miracle-worker, who was one of the most eminent of Origen's disciples, and whose influence in the provinces of Asia Minor extended far into the fourth century. This scholar and Bishop who delivered the first Christian panegyric—one on Origen—and has in it given his autobiography, remained throughout his life an enthusiastic follower of Origen, and adhered, in what was essential, to his doctrine of the Trinity.[3] But Gregory felt compelled, in opposition to Christians whose conception of the Trinity was absolutely polytheistic, to emphasise the unity of the Godhead. He did this in his "Confession of faith",[4] and in a still greater degree, according to the testimony of Basilius, in his lost work διάλεξις πρὸς Ἀιλιανόν (Debate with Ailianus),[5] which contained a proposition, afterwards appealed to by Sabellians, and somewhat to the following effect, viz., Father and Son are two in thought, but one in substance (πατὴρ καὶ υἱὸς ἐπινοίᾳ μέν εἰσι δύο, ὑποστάσει δὲ ἕν). Gregory, on the other hand, described the Logos as creature (κτίσμα)

---

[1] But we have not yet ascertained the method followed in the earlier period of collecting the verdicts of the older Fathers, and of presenting them as precedents; yet it is noteworthy that Irenæus and Clement already delighted in appealing to the πρεσβύτεροι, which meant for them, however, citing the Apostles' disciples, and that Paul of Samosata was accused in the epistle of the Synod of Antioch, of despising the ancient interpreters of the Divine Word (Euseb. VII. 30).

[2] See Caspari IV., p. 10 ff.; Ryssel, Gregorius Thaumaturgus, 1880. Vide also Overbeck in the Th. L.—Z., 1881, No. 12, and Dräscke in the Jahrb. f. protest. Theol. 1881, H. 2. Edition by Fronto. Ducäus, 1621. Pitra, Analecta Sacra III.; also Loofs, Theol. L. Z., 1884, No. 23.

[3] See Caspari's (l.c.) conclusions as to Gregory's confession of faith, whose genuineness seems to me made out. Origen's doctrine of the Trinity appears clearly in the Panegyric. The fragment printed by Ryssel, p. 44 f., is not by Gr. Thaumaturgus.

[4] See Caspari, l.c., p. 10: τριὰς τέλεια, δόξῃ καὶ ἀϊδιότητι καὶ βασιλείᾳ μὴ μεριζομένη μηδὲ ἀπαλλοτριουμένη. Οὔτε οὖν κτιστόν τι ἢ δοῦλον ἐν τῇ τριάδι οὔτε ἐπείσακτον, ὡς πρότερον μὲν οὐχ ὑπάρχον, ὕστερον δὲ ἐπεισελθόν· οὔτε γὰρ ἐνέλιπέ ποτε υἱὸς πατρί, οὔτε υἱῷ πνεῦμα, ἀλλ᾽ ἄτρεπτος καὶ ἀναλλοίωτος ἡ αὐτὴ τριὰς ἀεί.

[5] Basil., ep. 210.

and created ($\pi o i \eta \mu \alpha$)—so Basilius tells us,—and this form of
expression can probably be explained by the fact that he thought
it necessary, in this way and aggressively ($\dot{\alpha}\gamma\omega\nu\iota\sigma\tau\iota\varkappa\tilde{\omega}\varsigma$), to emphasise, on the basis of Origen's idea of the Homoousia of the
Son, the substantial unity of the deity, in opposition to a view
of the divine Hypostases which approximated to polytheism.
On the whole, however, we cannot avoid supposing, that at the
time when theology was introduced into the faith—a work
in which Gregory especially took part,—and in consequence
the worst confusions set in,[1] the tendency to heathen Tritheism
had grown, and theologians found themselves compelled to
maintain the "preaching of the monarchy" ($\varkappa\dot{\eta}\rho\nu\gamma\mu\alpha$ $\tau\tilde{\eta}\varsigma$ $\mu o\nu\alpha\rho\chi\iota\alpha\varsigma$)
to an increasing extent. This is proved by the correspondence
of the Dionysii, the theology of Hieracas, and the attitude of
Bishop Alexander of Alexandria; but we have also the evidence
of Gregory. True, the genuineness of the writing ascribed to
him, on the "essential identity"[2] (of the three Persons), is not
yet decided, but it belongs, at all events, to the period before
Athanasius. In this treatise the author seeks to establish the
indivisibility and uniqueness of God, subject to the hypothesis
of a certain hypostatic difference. In this he obviously approaches
Monarchian ideas, yet without falling into them. Further, the
very remarkable tractate, addressed to Theopompus, on the
incapability and capability of suffering,[3] treats this very subject,
without even hinting at a division between Father and Son
in this connection; on the other hand, the author certainly
does not call it in question. We can study in the works of
Gregory, and in the two treatises[4] just mentioned, which bear
his name, the state of theological stagnation, connected with
the indeterminateness of all dogmatic ideas, and the danger,

[1] It remained a matter of doubt in the East up to the beginning of the fourth
century, whether one ought to speak of three Hypostases (essences, natures), or one.

[2] Ryssel, p. 65 f., 100 f.; see Gregor. Naz., Ep. 243, Opp., p. II., p. 196 sq.,
ed. Paris, 1840.

[3] Ryssel, p. 71 f., 118 f. The genuineness of the tractate is not so certain as
its origin in the 3rd century; yet see Loofs, l.c.

[4] See also the *Sermo de incarnatione* attributed to Gregory (Pitra III., p. 144 sq.,
395 sq.)

then imminent, of passing wholly over to the domain of abstract philosophy, and of relaxing the union of speculation with
the exegesis of Holy Scripture. The problems are strictly confined to the sphere of Origen's theology; but that theology was
so elastic that they threatened to run wild and become thoroughly
secular.[1] If, e.g., we review the Christological tenets of Eusebius of Cæsarea, one of Origen's most enthusiastic followers,
we are struck by their universal hollowness and emptiness, uncertainty and instability. While Monotheism is maintained with
an immense stock of Bible texts and a display of all possible
formulas, a created and subordinate God is, in fact, interposed
between the deity and mankind.

But there was also in the East a theology which, while
it sought to make use of philosophy, at the same time tried to
preserve in their realistic form the religious truths established in
the fight with Gnosticism. There were theologians who, following in the footsteps of Irenæus and Hippolytus, by no means
despised science, yet found the highest truth expressed in the
tenets handed down by the Church; and who therefore, refusing
the claim of philosophical Gnosis to re-edit the principles of
faith, only permitted it to support, connect, and interpret them.
These theologians were necessarily hostile to the science of
religion cultivated in Alexandria, and enemies of its founder
Origen. We do not know whether, during his life-time, Origen
came into conflict in the East with opponents who met him in
the spirit of an Irenæus.[2] From his own statements we must
suppose that he only had to deal with untrained disputants.

---

[1] Origen himself always possessed in his unconditional adherence to the Bible
a kind of corrective against the danger of passing entirely over to philosophy.
Though thoroughly versed in philosophical science, he sought never to be more
than a scriptural theologian, and urged his disciples—witness his letter to Gregor.
Thaum.—to give up their philosophical studies, and devote themselves wholly to
the Bible. No professedly philosophical expositions occur in Origen himself, so far
as I know, like those transmitted by his disciples. For the latter the comprehensive
chapter of Eusebius (H. E. VII. 32) is very instructive. Here we meet with Bishops
who seem to have been scholars first and clerics afterwards. This Eusebius (§ 22)
has to tell of one: λόγων μὲν φιλοσόφων καὶ τῆς ἄλλης παρ᾽ ῞Ελλησι παιδείας παρὰ
τοῖς πολλοῖς θαυμασθείς, οὐχ ὁμοίως γε μὴν περὶ τὴν θείαν πίστιν διατεθειμένος.

[2] It is unknown who was the καλλίων ἡμῶν πρεσβύτης καὶ μακαριστὸς ἀνὴρ
quoted by Epiph. (H. 64, ch. 8 and 67) as an opponent of Origen.

But in the second half of the third century, and at the beginning of the fourth, there were on the side of the Church antagonists of Origen's theology who were well versed in philosophical knowledge, and who not merely trumped his doctrine
with their ψιλὴ πίστις (bare faith), but protected the principles
transmitted by the Church from spiritualising and artificial interpretations, with all the weapons of science.[1] The most important among them, indeed really the only one of whom we have
any very precise knowledge, besides Peter of Alexandria
(see above), is Methodius.[2] But of the great number of treatises
by this original and prolific author only one has been till now
preserved complete in the original—Conviv. decem virg., while
we have the greater part of a second—De resurr.[3] The rest

---

[1] Besides these we have Eastern theologians, who, while they did not write
against Origen, show no signs in their works of having been influenced by Alexandrian theology, but rather resemble in their attitude Irenæus and Hippolytus.
Here we have especially to mention the author of five dialogues against the Gnostics,
which, under the title " De recta in deum fide," bear the name of Adamantius ; see
the editio princeps by Wetstein, 1673, and the version of Rufinus discovered by Caspari
(Kirchenhistorische Anecdota, 1883; also Th. L.—Z. 1884, No. 8) which shows
that the Greek text is interpolated. The author, for whom we have perhaps to look
in the circle of Methodius, has at any rate borrowed not a little from him (and
also from the work of Theophilus against Marcion?). See Jahn, Methodii, Opp. I.,
p. 99, II. Nos. 474, 542, 733—749, 771, 777. Möller in Herzog's R. E., 2 Ed.,
IX., p. 725. Zahn, Ztschr. f. Kirchengesch., Vol. IX., p. 193 ff.: " Die Dialoge des
Adamantius mit den Gnostikern." The dialogues were written ± 300, probably
somewhere in East Asia Minor, or in West Syria, according to Zahn about 300
—313 in Hellenic Syria, or Antioch. They are skilfully written and instructive ; a
very moderate use is made of philosophical theology. Perhaps the Ep. ad Diogn. also
came from the circle of Methodius. Again, there is little philosophical theology to
be discovered in the original edition of the first six books of the apostolic Constitutions, which belongs to the third century. See Lagarde in Bunsen's Analecta
Ante-Nicæna T. II. The author still occupied the standpoint of Ignatius, or the old
anti-gnostic teachers. The dogmatic theology, in the longer recension of the work,
preserved in Greek, belongs entirely to the reviser who lived in or after the middle
of the 4th century (so App. Const. II. 24, VI. 11, 14, 41 [Hahn, Biblioth. der
Symbole, 2 Aufl., §§ 10, 11, 64]; see my edition of the Διδαχή, p. 241 ff. That
Aphraates and the author of the Acta Archelai were unaffected by Origen's theology
will have been clear from what was said above, p. 50 f.

[2] Jahn, S. Methodii Opp., 1865; Pars II. S. Methodius Platonizans, 1865;
Bonwetsch, M. von Olympus I. 1891. Vide also Pitra, Analecta Sacra T. III., IV.
(see Loofs, Th. L.—Z., 1884, No. 23, col. 556 ff.). Möhler, Patrologie, pp. 680—
700. Möller, l.c., p. 724 ff. Salmon Dict. of Christian Biogr. III. p. 909 sq.

[3] Besides smaller fragments are found, increased by Pitra.

has been preserved in the Slavic language, and only very lately been rendered accessible. The personality of Methodius himself, with his position in history, is obscure.[1] But what we do know is enough to show that he was able to combine the defence of the Rule of Faith as understood by Irenæus, Hippolytus, and Tertullian,[2] with the most thorough study of Plato's writings and the reverent appropriation of Plato's ideas. Indeed he lived in these.[3] Accordingly, he defended "the popular conception of the common faith of the Church" in an energetic counterblast to Origen, and rejected all his doctrines which contained an artificial version of traditional principles.[4] But on the other hand, he did not repudiate the basis on which Origen's speculation rested. He rather attempted with its presuppositions and method to arrive at a result in harmony with the common faith. There seems to be no doubt that he took the great work of Irenæus as his model; for the manner in which Methodius has endeavoured to overcome dualism and spiritualism, and to establish a *speculative realism*, recalls strikingly the undertaking of Irenæus. Like the latter, Methodius sought to demonstrate the eternal importance of the natural constitution in spirit and body of the creatures made by God; and he conceived salvation not as a disembodying, not in any sense as a division and separation, but as a transfiguration of the corporeal, and a union of what had been unnaturally divided. He rejected the pessimism with which Origen had, like the Gnostics, viewed the world as it is, the σύστασις τοῦ κόσμου, making it, if a well-ordered and necessary prison, yet a prison after all. This he confronted with the optimistic conviction, that everything which God has created, and as he has created it, is capable of permanence and

---

[1] See Zahn, Ztschr. f. Kirchengesch. Vol. VIII., p. 15 ff. Place: Olympus in Lycia.

[2] He was ranked in later times with Irenæus and Hippolytus (see Andreas Cæs. in præf. in Apoc., p. 2) and that as a witness to the inspiration of John's Apocalypse.

[3] See Jahn, l.c.

[4] See the long fragments of the writing *de resurrectione* which was directed against Origen, as also the work περὶ τῶν γενητῶν. Methodius called Origen a "Centaur" (Opp. I. 100, 101), *i.e.*, "Sophist," and compared his doctrine with the Hydra (I. 86). See the violent attack on the new-fashioned exegetes and teachers in De resurr. 8, 9 (Opp I. 67 sq.) and 20, (p. 74), where the ὀστᾶ νοητὰ and σάρκας νοητάς of Origen's school are ridiculed; ch. 21, p. 75; 39, p. 83.

transfiguration. [1] Accordingly, he opposed Origen's doctrines of the pre-existence of souls, the nature and object of the world and of corporeality, the eternal duration of the world, a pre-mundane Fall, the resurrection as a destruction of the body, etc. At the same time he certainly misrepresented them, as, *e.g.*, Origen's doctrine of sin, p. 68 sq. Like Irenæus, Methodius introduced curious speculations as to Adam for the purpose of establishing realism, *i.e.*, the maintenance of the literal truth of sacred history. Adam was to him the whole of natural humanity, and he assumed, going beyond Irenæus, that the Logos combined the first man created (protoplast) with himself. [2]

---

[1] See the short argument against Origen, De resurr. 28, p. 78: Εἰ γὰρ κρεῖττον τὸ μὴ εἶναι τοῦ εἶναι τὸν κόσμον, διὰ τί τὸ χεῖρον ᾑρεῖτο ποιήσας τὸν κόσμον ὁ Θεός; ἀλλ᾽ οὐδὲν ὁ Θεὸς ματαίως ἢ χεῖρον ἐποίει. οὐκοῦν εἰς τὸ εἶναι καὶ μένειν τὴν κτίσιν ὁ Θεὸς διεκοσμήσατο. Wisdom I. 14 and Rom. VIII. 19 follow. The fight waged by Methodius against Origen presents itself as a continuation of that conducted by Irenæus against the Gnostics. It dealt in part with the same problems, and used the same arguments and proofs. The extent to which Origen hellenised the Christian tradition was in the end as little tolerated in the Church as the latitude taken by the Gnostics. But while Gnosticism was completely ejected in two or three generations it took much longer to get rid of Origenism. Therefore, still more of Origen's theology passed into the "revealed" system of Church doctrine, than of the theology of the Gnostics.

[2] See Conviv. III. 6 (p. 18 sq.): ταύτῃ γὰρ τὸν ἄνθρωπον ἀνείληφεν ὁ λόγος, ὅπως δὴ δι᾽ αὐτοῦ καταλύσῃ τὴν ἐπ᾽ ὀλέθρῳ γεγενυῖαν καταδίκην, ἡττήσας τὸν ὄφιν. ἥρμοζε γὰρ μὴ δι᾽ ἑτέρου νικηθῆναι τὸν πονηρὸν ἀλλὰ δι᾽ ἐκείνου, ὃν δὴ καὶ ἐκόμπαζεν ἀπατήσας αὐτὸν τετυραννηκέναι, ὅτι μὴ ἄλλως τὴν ἁμαρτίαν λυθῆναι καὶ τὴν κατάκρισιν δυνατὸν ἦν, εἰ μὴ πάλιν ὁ αὐτὸς ἐκεῖνος ἄνθρωπος, δι᾽ ὃν εἴρητο τὸ "γῇ εἶ καὶ εἰς γῆν ἀπελεύσῃ," ἀναπλασθεὶς ἀνέλυσε τὴν ἀπόφασιν τὴν δι᾽ αὐτὸν εἰς πάντας ἐξενηνεγμένην. ὅπως, καθὼς ἐν τῷ Ἀδὰμ πρότερον πάντες ἀποθνήσκουσιν, οὕτω δὴ πάλιν καὶ ἐν τῷ ἀνειληφότι Χριστῷ τὸν Ἀδὰμ πάντες ζωοποιηθῶσιν. Still clearer is III. 4, where it is expressly denied that Adam is only a type of Christ: φέρε γὰρ ἡμεῖς ἐπισκεψώμεθα πῶς ὀρθοδόξως ἀνήγαγε τὸν Ἀδὰμ εἰς τὸν Χριστόν, οὐ μόνον τύπον αὐτὸν ἡγούμενος εἶναι καὶ εἰκόνα, ἀλλὰ καὶ αὐτὸ τοῦτο Χριστὸν καὶ αὐτὸν γεγονέναι διὰ τὸ τὸν πρὸ αἰώνων εἰς αὐτὸν ἐγκατασκῆψαι λόγον. ἥρμοζε γὰρ τὸ πρωτόγονον τοῦ Θεοῦ καὶ πρῶτον βλάστημα καὶ μονογενὲς τὴν σοφίαν τῷ πρωτοπλάστῳ καὶ πρώτῳ καὶ πρωτογόνῳ τῶν ἀνθρώπων ἀνθρώπῳ κερασθεῖσαν ἐνηνθρωπηκέναι, τοῦτο γὰρ εἶναι τὸν Χριστόν, ἄνθρωπον ἐν ἀκράτῳ θεότητι καὶ τελείᾳ πεπληρωμένον καὶ Θεὸν ἐν ἀνθρώπῳ κεχωρημένον· ἦν γὰρ πρεπωδέστατον τόν πρεσβύτατον τῶν αἰώνων καὶ πρῶτον τῶν ἀρχαγγέλων, ἀνθρώποις μέλλοντα συνομιλεῖν, εἰς τὸν πρεσβύτατον καὶ πρῶτον τῶν ἀνθρώπων εἰσοικισθῆναι τὸν Ἀδάμ. See also III. 7 8: προγεγύμνασθαι γάρ ... ὡς ἄρα ὁ πρωτόπλαστος οἰκείως εἰς αὐτὸν ἀναφέρεσθαι δύναται τὸν Χριστόν, οὐκέτι τύπος ὢν καὶ ἀπείκασμα μόνον καὶ εἰκὼν τοῦ μονογενοῦς, ἀλλὰ καὶ αὐτὸ τοῦτο σοφία γεγονὼς καὶ λόγος. δίκην γὰρ ὕδατος συγκερασθεὶς ὁ ἄνθρωπος τῇ σοφίᾳ καὶ τῇ ζωῇ τοῦτο γέγονεν, ὅπερ ἦν αὐτὸ τὸ εἰς αὐτὸν ἐγκατασκῆψαν ἄκρατον φῶς.

This union was conceived as a complete incorporation: "God embraced and comprehended in man;" and, starting from this incorporation, the attempt was made to explain redemption in terms of a mystical realism. Salvation was not consummated in knowledge (Gnosis), but it came to light, already achieved for mankind, in the constitution of the God-man.[1] But for this very reason Methodius borders, just like Irenæus, on a mode of thought which sees in the incarnation the necessary completion of creation, and conceives the imperfection of the first Adam to have been natural.[2] Adam, *i.e.*, mankind, was before Christ still in a plastic condition, capable of receiving any impression and liable to dissolution. Sin, which had exclusively an external source, had therefore an easy task; humanity was first consolidated in Christ. In this way freedom is retained, but we easily see that Origen's idea of sin was more profound than that of Methodius.[3] The fantastic realism of the latter's view is carried out in his speculations on the transference of salvation from

[1] Yet see, under, the new turn given to the speculation.

[2] S. Conviv. III. 5: ἔτι γὰρ πηλουργούμενον τὸν Ἀδάμ, ὡς ἔστιν εἰπεῖν, καὶ τηκτὸν ὄντα ταὶ ὑδαρῇ, καὶ μηδέπω φθάσαντα δίκην ὀστράκου τῇ ἀφθρσίᾳ κραταιωθῆναι καὶ παγιωθῆναι, ὕδωρ ὥσπερ καταλειβομένῃ καὶ καπαστάζουσα διέλυσεν αὐτὸ ἡ ἁμαρτία. διὸ δὴ πάλιν ἄνωθεν ἀναδεύων καὶ πηλοπλαστῶν τὸν αὐτὸν εἰς τιμὴν ὁ Θεός ἐν τῇ παρθενικῇ κραταιώσας πρῶτον καὶ πήξας μήτρᾳ καὶ συνενώσας καὶ συγκεράσας τῷ λογῳ, ἄτηκτον καὶ ἄθραυστον ἐξήγαγεν εἰς τὸν βίον, ἵνα μὴ πάλιν τοῖς τῆς φθορᾶς ἔξωθεν ἐπικλυσθεὶς ῥεύμασιν, τηκεδόνα γεννήσας διαπέσῃ. Methodius, like Irenæus, gave much study to Paul's Epistles, because they were especially quoted by Origen and his school (see ch. 51 fin., p. 90); on the difficulties which he felt see De resurr. 26, p. 77; 38, p. 83.

[3] The expositions of concupiscence, sin, and death, are distinguished very strongly from those of Origen. (For death as means of salvation see De resurr. 23, 49). They resemble the discussions of Irenæus, only Methodius maintains—a sign of the times—that sinlessness is impossible even to the Christian. See De resurr. 22 (I., p. 75): ζῶντος γὰρ ἔτι τοῦ σώματος πρὸ τοῦ τεθνήξεσθαι συζῆν ἀνάγκη καὶ τὴν ἁμαρτίαν, ἔνδον τὰς ῥίζας αὐτῆς ἐν ἡμῖν ἀποκρύπτουσαν, εἰ καὶ ἔξωθεν τομαῖς ταῖς ἀπὸ τῶν σωφρονισμῶν καὶ τῶν νουθετήσεων ἀνεστέλλετο, ἐπεὶ οὐκ ἂν μετὰ τὸ φωτισθῆναι συνέβαινεν ἀδικεῖν, ἅτε παντάπασιν εἰλικρινῶς ἀφῃρημένης ἀφ᾽ ἡμῶν τῆς ἁμαρτίας· νῦν δὲ καὶ μετὰ τὸ πιστεῦσαι καὶ ἐπὶ τὸ ὕδωρ ἐλθεῖν τοῦ ἁγνισμοῦ πολλάκις ἐν ἁμαρτίαις ὄντες εὑρισκόμεθα· οὐδεὶς γὰρ οὕτως ἁμαρτίας ἐκτὸς εἶναι ἑαυτὸν καυχήσεται, ὡς μηδὲ κἂν ἐνθυμηθῆναι τὸ σύνολον ὅλως τὴν ἀδικίαν. To this conception corresponds the view of Methodius that Christianity is a cultus of mysteries, in which consecration is unceasingly bestowed on the τελειούμενοι. Methodius also referred Rom. VII. 18 f. to those born again.

Christ to individuals. The deep sleep of the Protoplast is paralleled in the second Adam by the sleep of death. Now as Eve
was formed from, and was part of the being of sleeping Adam,
so the Holy Spirit issued from Christ lying in the sleep of death,
and was part of his being;[1] and from him the Church was
fashioned. "The Apostle has excellently applied the history of
"Adam to Christ. So we will require to say with him that the
"Church is of the bone and flesh of Christ, since for her sake
"the Logos left the Heavenly Father, and came down that he
"might cleave to his spouse; and he fell asleep unconscious
"of suffering, dying voluntarily for her, that he might present
"the Church to himself glorious and faultless, after he had purified
"her by the bath; so that she might receive the spiritual and
"blessed seed, which he himself, instilling and implanting, scatters
"into the depths of the Spirit, whom the Church receives and,
"fashioning, develops like a spouse, that she may bear and
"rear virtue. For in this way the word is also excellently ful-
"filled 'Grow and increase'; since the Church increases daily
"in greatness, beauty, and extent; because the Logos dwells
"with her, and holds communion with her, and he even now
"descends to us, and in remembrance (Anamnesis) of his suffering
"(continually) dies to himself. For not otherwise could the
"Church continually conceive believers in her womb, and bear
"them anew through the bath of regeneration, unless Christ
"were repeatedly to die, emptying himself for the sake of each
"individual, in order to find acceptance by means of his sufferings
"continuing and completing themselves; unless, descending from
"heaven, and united with his spouse, the Church, he imparted
"from his own side a certain power, that all who are edified
"in him should attain growth, those, namely, who, born again
"through baptism, have received flesh of his flesh, bone of his

---

[1] The allegory receives another version Opp. I., p. 119: μή πως ἄρα αἱ τρεῖς
αὗται τῶν προγόνων κεφαλαὶ πάσης τῆς ἀνθρωπότητος ὁμοούσιοι ὑποστάσεις κατ'
εἰκόνα τινά, ὡς καὶ Μεθοδίῳ δοκεῖ—the passage occurs in Anastasius Sin. ap. Mai,
Script. Vet. N. Coll. IX. p. 619—τυπικῶς γεγόνασι τῆς ἁγίας καὶ ὁμοουσίου τριά-
δος, τοῦ μὲν ἀναιτίου καὶ ἀγεννήτου Ἀδὰμ τύπον καὶ εἰκόνα ἔχοντος τοῦ ἀναιτίου
καὶ πάντων αἰτίου παντοκράτορος Θεοῦ καὶ πατρός, τοῦ δὲ γεννητοῦ υἱοῦ αὐτοῦ
εἰκόνα προδιαγράφοντος τοῦ γεννητοῦ υἱοῦ καὶ λόγου τοῦ Θεοῦ. τῆς δὲ ἐκπορευτῆς
Εὔας σημαινούσης τὴν τοῦ ἁγίου πνεύματος ἐκπορευτὴν ὑπόστασιν.

" bone, *i.e.*, of his holiness and glory. He, however, who calls
" bone and flesh wisdom and virtue, speaks truly; but the side
" is the Spirit of truth, the Paraclete, from whom the enlightened
" receiving their portion are born again, in a worthy manner, to
" immortality. But no one can participate in the Holy Spirit,
" and be accounted a member of Christ, unless the Logos has
" first descended upon him, and, falling asleep, has 'emptied'
" himself, that he, rising again and rejuvenated, along with him
" who fell asleep for his sake, and re-fashioned in his own
" person, may participate in the Holy Spirit. For the side ($\pi\lambda\epsilon\upsilon\rho\dot{\alpha}$)
" of the Logos is really the spirit of truth, the seven-formed
" of the prophet, from whom God, in accordance with the self-
" sacrifice of Christ, that is, the incarnation and suffering of Christ,
" takes away something, and fashions for him his spouse, in
" other words, souls fit for him and prepared like a bride." [1]
Methodius accordingly, starts in his speculations from Adam and
Eve as the real types of Christ and the Church; but he then
varies this, holding that the individual soul rather must become
the bride of Christ, and that for each the descent of the Logos
from heaven and his death must be repeated—mysteriously and
in the heart of the believer.

This variation became, and precisely through the instrumentality
of Methodius, of eminent importance in the history of dogma.[2]
We would not have had in the third century all the premises
from which Catholic Christianity was developed in the following
centuries, unless this speculation had been brought forward, or,
been given a central place, by a Christian theologian of the
earlier period. *It marks nothing less than the tapering of the
realistic doctrinal system of the Church into the subjectivity of
monkish mysticism.* For to Methodius, the history of the Logos-
Christ, as maintained by faith, was only the general background
of an inner history, which required to repeat itself in each believer: the Logos had to descend from heaven, suffer, die, and

---

[1] Conviv. III. 8.

[2] It was not altogether absent in earlier times, and on this see ch. V. § 2. As
we have remarked above, individualism in this extreme form occurs also in Origen;
see, *e.g.*, "De orat." 17.: "He who has perceived the beauty of the bride whom
the Son of God loves as bridegroom, namely, the soul."

rise again for him. Nay, Methodius already formulated his view to the effect that *every believer must, through participation in Christ, be born as a Christ.*[1] The background was, however, not a matter of indifference, seeing that what took place in the individual must have first taken place in the Church. *The Church, accordingly, was to be revered as mother, by the individual soul which was to become the bride of Christ.* In a word: here we have the theological speculation of the future monachism *of the Church,* and we see why it could not but pair with the loftiest obedience, and greatest devotion to the Church.

But the evidence that we have really here the fundamental features of the monkish mysticism of the Church, is contained in the correct perception of the final object of the work from which the above details are taken. The whole writing seeks to represent the state of virginity as the condition of Christlikeness (I. 5, p. 13). Everything is directed to this end; yet marriage is not forbidden, but is admitted to possess a mystery of its own. Unstained virginity is ranked high above the married state; towards it all Christians must strive; it is the perfectly Christian life itself. Yet Methodius succeeds in maintaining, beside it, marriage and sin-stained birth from the flesh (II. 1 sq.). He had already arrived at the position of Catholic monasticism; the body belonging to the soul that would be the bride of Christ must remain virgin. The proper result of the work of Christ is represented in the state of virginity of the believers who still walk upon earth, and it is the bloom of imperishableness: "Exceedingly great and wonderful and glorious is virginity, "and to speak plainly, following Holy Scripture, this most noble

---

[1] Conviv. VIII. 8: Ἐγὼ γὰρ τὸν ἄρσενα (Apoc. XII. 1 f.) ταύτῃ γεννᾶν εἰρῆσθαι νομίζω τὴν ἐκκλησίαν, ἐπειδὴ τοὺς χαρακτῆρας καὶ τὴν ἐκτύπωσιν καὶ τὴν ἀρρενωπίαν τοῦ Χριστοῦ προσλαμβάνουσιν οἱ φωτιζόμενοι, τῆς καθ᾽ ὁμοίωσιν μορφῆς ἐν αὐτοῖς ἐκτυπουμένης τοῦ λόγου καὶ ἐν αὐτοῖς γεννωμένης κατὰ τὴν ἀκριβῆ γνῶσιν καὶ πίστιν ὥστε ἐν ἑκάστῳ γεννᾶσθαι τὸν Χριστὸν νοητῶς· καὶ διὰ τοῦτο ἡ ἐκκλησία σπαργᾷ καὶ ὠδίνει, μέχριπερ ἂν ὁ Χριστὸς ἐν ἡμῖν μορφωθῇ γεννηθείς, ὅπως ἕκαστος τῶν ἁγίων τῷ μετέχειν Χριστοῦ Χριστὸς γεννηθῇ, καθ᾽ ὃν λόγον καὶ ἔν τινι γραφῇ φέρεται " μὴ ἅψησθε τῶν Χριστῶν μου" οἱονεὶ Χριστῶν γεγονότων τῶν κατὰ μετουσίαν τοῦ πνεύματος εἰς Χριστὸν βεβαπτισμένων, συμβαλλούσης ἐνταῦθα τὴν ἐν τῷ λόγῳ τράνωσιν αὐτῶν καὶ μεταμόρφωσιν τῆς ἐκκλησίας. Even Tertullian teaches (De pud. 22) that the martyr who does what Christ did, and lives in Christ, is Christ.

"and fair practice is alone the ripe result, the flower and first
"fruits of incorruption, and therefore the Lord promises to admit
"those who have preserved their virginity into the kingdom of
"heaven ... for we must understand that virginity, while walking
"upon the earth, reaches the heavens": μεγάλη τίς ἐστιν ὑπερφυῶς
καὶ θαυμαστὴ καὶ ἔνδοξος ἡ παρθενία, καὶ εἰ χρὴ φανερῶς εἰπεῖν
ἐπομένην ταῖς ἀγίαις γραφαῖς, τὸ οὖλαρ τῆς ἀφθαρσίας καὶ τὸ ἄνθος
καὶ ἡ ἀπαρχὴ αὐτῆς τοῦτο τὸ ἄριστον καὶ κάλλιστον ἐπιτήδευμα
μόνον τυγχάνει, καὶ διὰ ταῦτα καὶ ὁ κύριος εἰς τὴν βασιλείαν εἰσε-
λάσαι τῶν οὐρανῶν τοὺς ἀποπαρθενεύσαντας σφᾶς αὐτοὺς ἐπαγγελ-
λεται..., παρθενίαν γὰρ βαίνειν μὲν ἐπὶ γῆς, ἐπιψαύειν δὲ τῶν
οὐρανῶν ἡγητέον (Conv. I. 1, p. 11).

Methodius started from other premises than the school of
Origen, and bitterly opposed the latter, but in the end he came
to the same practical result—witness the followers of Hieracas.
Their speculations also led to the depreciation of the objective
redemption, and to monachism. But the concrete forms were
very different. In Origen himself and his earliest disciples the
Church was by no means really the mother, or, if it were, it
was in a wholly different sense from that of Methodius. Asceticism and in particular virginity were not in themselves valuable,
an end in themselves, but means to the end. Finally, Gnosis
(knowledge) was different from Pistis (faith), and the ideal was
the perfect Gnostic, who is freed from all that is alien and
fleeting, and lives in the eternal and abiding. Methodius' teaching
was different. Pistis and Gnosis were related to each other as
theme and exposition: there is only one truth, which is the
same for all; but on the soil of the Church there is room for
the state of virginity, *which is the goal of the incarnation*, though
all may not yet reach it. The important and momentous
achievement of Methodius [1] consisted in subordinating a realistic
Church theology, which yet was not destitute of a speculative
phase, and even made a moderate use of the allegorical method,

---

[1] The theology of Methodius was in the Eastern Church, like Tertullian's in
the West, a prophecy of the future. His method of combining tradition and
speculation was not quite attained even by the Cappadocians in the 4th century.
Men like Cyril of Alexandria were the first to resemble him. *In Methodius we
have already the final stage of Greek theology.*

to the practical object of securing virginity, a life in which God and Christ were imitated, (Conv. I. 5, p. 13: to imitate God is to escape from corruption [ὁμοίωσις Θεῷ φθορᾶς ἀποφυγή]; Christ is not only arch-shepherd and arch-prophet [ἀρχιποιμήν-ἀρχιπροφήτης], but also archetypal virgin [ἀρχιπαρθένος]). This doctrine, as well as the practical attitude of Hieracas, and many other features, as, e.g., the considerably earlier Pseudo-Clementine epistles "De virginitate," [1] prove that the great aspiration of the time in the East was towards monachism, and Methodius succeeded in uniting this with a Church theology. In spite of his polemic against Origen he did not despise those phases of the latter's theology, which were at all compatible with the traditional comprehension of religious doctrine. Thus he accepted the doctrine of the Logos implicitly in the form given to it by Origen's school, without, of course, entangling himself in the disputed terminology (see, e.g., De creat. 11, p. 102); so far as I know, he made no express defence of Chiliasm, in spite of the high value he put on the Apocalypse. He is even said by Socrates (H. E. VI. 13) to have admired Origen, in one of his latest writings, "a sort of recantation" (ὡς ἐκ παλινῳδίας). However that may be, the future belonged not to Origen, nor to the scientific religion that soared above faith, but to compromises, such as those, stamped with monachism, which Methodius concluded, to the combination of realistic and speculative elements, of the objectivity of the Church and the mysticism of the monks. [2] The great fight in the next decades was undoubtedly to be fought out between two forms of the doctrine of the Logos; the one, that of Lucian the martyr and his school, which had adopted elements distinctive of Adoptianism, and the other, professed by Alexander of Alexandria and the Western theologians, which with Sabellianism held fast the unity of the divine nature. But, in the case of the majority of Eastern

---

[1] See Funk, Patr. App. Opp. II., pp. 1—27, and Harnack, Sitzungsberichte d. Preuss. Akad. d. Wissensch. 1891, p. 361 ff.

[2] On the authority of Methodius in later times, see the Testimonia Veterum in Jahn, l. c. I., p. 6 sq. The defence of Origen against Methodius by Pamphilus and Eusebius has unfortunately been preserved only to a very small extent. See Routh, Reliq. S. IV., p. 339 sq.

Christians in the 4th century, the background or basis of these opposite views was formed, not by a theology purely Origenist, but by one of compromise, which had resulted from a combination of the former with the popular idea of the rules of faith, and which sought its goal, not in an absolute knowledge and the calm confidence of the pious sage, but in virginity, ecclesiasticism, and a mystical deification. Men like Methodius became of the highest consequence in the development of this theological genus, which, indeed, could not but gain the upper hand more and more, from the elemental force of factors existent in the Church.[1]

But while as regards Origen's theology reservations may have gradually grown stronger and more numerous in the course of the next decades, theological speculation aimed in the East, from about 250—320, at a result than which nothing grander or more assured could be imagined. In the West the old, short, Creed was retained, and, except in one case,[2] the Christological conflicts did not induce men to change it. *But in the leading Churches of the East, and during the given period, the Creeds were expanded by theological additions,[3] and thus exegetical and speculative theology was introduced into the Apostolic faith itself.*[4] Thus, in the Catholic Churches of the East, this

---

[1] It is instructive to notice how Athanasius has silently and calmly shelved those doctrines of Origen which did not harmonise with the wording of the rule of faith, or allegorised facts whose artificial interpretation had ceased to be tolerated.

[2] See above, p. 75.

[3] It is possible, and indeed probable, that Creeds were then set up for the first time in many Churches. The history of the rise of Creeds—further than the Baptismal formula—in the East is wholly obscure. Of course there always were detailed Christological formulas, but the question is whether they were inserted into the Baptismal formula.

[4] It has been already pointed out on p. 48, note 1, that the Biblical character of some of those additions cannot be used against their being regarded as theological and philosophical formulas. The theology of Origen—witness his letter to Gregory—was throughout exegetical and speculative; therefore the reception of certain Biblical predicates of Christ into the Creeds meant a desire to legitimise the speculation which clung to them as Apostolic. The Churches, however, by setting up theological Creeds only repeated a development in which they had been anticipated about 120 years before by the "Gnostics." The latter had theologically worked out Creeds as early as in the second century. Tertullian, it is true, says of the Valentinians (adv. Valent. I.) "*communem fidem affirmant,*" i.e., they adapt

8

theology was for ever fused with the faith itself. A striking example has been already quoted; those six Bishops who wrote against Paul of Samosata in the seventh decade of the third century, submitted a Rule of Faith, which had been elaborated philosophically and theologically, as the faith handed down

themselves to the common faith; but he himself relates (De carne, 20; see Iren. I. 7, 2) that they preferred "διὰ Μαρίας" to "ἐκ Μαρίας"; in other words, of these two prepositions, which were still used without question even in Justin's time, they, on theological grounds, admitted only the one. So also they said "Resurrection from the dead" instead of "of the body." Irenæus as well as Tertullian has spoken of the "blasphemous" regulæ of the Gnostics and Marcionites which were always being changed (Iren. I. 21 5, III. 11 3, I. 31 3; II præf.; II. 19 8, III. 16, 1, 5; Tertull., De præscr. 42; Adv. Valent. 4; Adv. Marc. I. 1, IV. 5, IV. 17). We can still partly reconstruct these "Rules" from the Philosoph. and the Syntagma of Hippolytus (see esp. the regula of Apelles in Epiphan. H. XLIV. 2). They have mutatis mutandis the most striking similarity to the oriental confessions of faith published since the end of the third century; compare, e.g., the Creed, given under, of Gregorius Thaumaturgus with the Gnostic rules of faith which Hippolytus had before him in the Philosoph. There is, further, a striking affinity between them in the fact that the ancient Gnostics already appealed in support of their regulæ to secret tradition, be it of one of the Apostles or all, yet without renouncing the attestation of these rules by Holy Scripture through the spiritual (pneumatic) method of Exegesis. Precisely the same thing took place in the Eastern Churches of the next age. For the tenor and phrasing of the new Creeds which seemed to be necessary, the appeal to Holy Scripture was even here insufficient, and it was necessary to resort to special revelations, as in the case alluded to, p. 115, note 3, or to a παράδοσις ἄγραφος of the Church. That the new theology and Christology had found their way into the psalms sung in the Church, can be seen from the Synodal document on Paul of Samosata (Euseb. VII. 30, 11), where it is said of the Bishop: ψαλμοὺς τοὺς μὲν εἰς τὸν κύριον ἡμῶν Ἰ. Χρ. παύσας ὡς δὴ νεωτέρους καὶ νεωτέρων ἀνδρῶν συγγράμματα; i.e., Paul set aside those Church songs which contained the philosophical or Alexandrian christology. In this respect also the Church followed the Gnostics: compare in the period immediately following, the songs of Arius, on the one hand, and the orthodox hymns on the other; for we know of Marcionite, Valentinian, and Bardesanian psalms and hymns. (See the close of the Muratorian Fragment, further my investigations in the Ztschr. f. wissensch. Theol., 1876, p. 109 ff.; Tertull., De Carne Chr. 17 ; Hippol., Philos. VI. 37; the psalms of Bardesanes in Ephraim ; the Gnostic hymns in the Acts of John and Thomas, in the Pistis Sophiæ, etc.). It is self-evident that these psalms contained the characteristic theology of the Gnostics; this also appears from the fragments that have been preserved, and is very clearly confirmed by Tertullian, who says of Alexander the Valentinian (l. c.) : "sed remisso Alexandro cum suis syllogismis, etiam cum Psalmis Valentini, quos magna impudentia, quasi idonei alicuius auctoris interserit." The scholastic form of the Church was more and more complete in the East in the second half of the third century, after one school, that of the Alexandrian Catechists, had finally succeeded in partly insinuating its teaching into

n the holy Catholic Church from the Apostles. [1] But we possess numerous other proofs. Gregory of Nyssa tells us that from the days of Gregory Thaumaturgus till his own, the Creed of the latter formed the foundation of the instruction given to catechumens in Neo-Cæsarea. But this Creed [2] was neither more nor less than a compendium of Origen's theology, [3] which, here,

he Church. Where Valentine Basilides, etc., had absolutely failed, and Bardesanes partly succeeded, the School of Origen had been almost entirely successful. It is very characteristic that the ecclesiastical parties which opposed each other in the third century applied the term "school" (διδασκαλεῖον) as an opprobrious epithet to their antagonists. This term was meant to signify a communion which rested on a merely human, instead of a revealed doctrine. But the Church nearly approximated, in respect of doctrine, to the form of the philosophic schools, at the moment when her powerful organisation destroyed every analogy with them, and when the possession of the two Testaments marked her off definitely from them. Much might be said on " schola" and "ecclesia"; a good beginning has been made by Lange, Haus und Halle, 1885, p. 288 ff. See also v. Wilamowitz-Möllendorff, " Die rechtliche Stellung der Philosophenschulen," 1881.

[1] See also the document in Eusebius, H. E. VIII. 30, 6, where it is said of Paul: ἀποστὰς τοῦ κανόνος ἐπὶ κίβδηλα καὶ νόθα διδάγματα μετελήλυθεν.

[2] Caspari, l. c. IV., p. 10. 27. Hahn, § 114.

[3] It runs: Εἷς Θεός, πατὴρ λόγου ζῶντος, σοφίας ὑφεστώσης καὶ δυνάμεως καὶ χαρακτῆρος ἀϊδίου, τέλειος τελείου γεννήτωρ, πατὴρ υἱοῦ μονογενοῦς, Εἷς κύριος, μόνος ἐκ μόνου, Θεὸς ἐκ Θεοῦ, χαρακτὴρ καὶ εικων τῆς θεότητος, λόγος ἐνεργός, σοφία τῆς τῶν ὅλων συστάσεως περιεκτικὴ καὶ δύναμις τῆς ὅλης κτίσεως ποιητική, υἱὸς ἀληθινὸς ἀληθινοῦ πατρός, ἀόρατος ἀοράτου καὶ ἄφθαρτος ἀφθάρτου καὶ ἀθάνατος ἀθανάτου καὶ ἀΐδιος ἀϊδίου. Καὶ ἓν πνεῦμα ἅγιον, ἐκ Θεοῦ τὴν ὕπαρξιν ἔχον καὶ δι' υἱοῦ πεφηνὸς [δηλαδὴ τοῖς ἀνθρώποις], εἰκὼν τοῦ υἱοῦ, τελείου τελεία, ζωὴ ζώντων αἰτία, [πηγὴ ἁγία] ἁγιότης ἁγιασμοῦ χορηγός, ἐν ᾧ φανεροῦται Θεὸς ὁ πατὴρ ὁ ἐπὶ πάντων καὶ ἐν πᾶσι, καὶ Θεὸς ὁ υἱὸς ὁ διὰ πάντων-τριὰς τελεία, δόξῃ καὶ ἀϊδιότητι καὶ βασιλείᾳ μὴ μεριζομένη μηδὲ ἀπαλλοτριουμενη. Οὔτε οὖν κτιστόν τι ἢ δοῦλον ἐν τῇ τριάδι, οὔτε ἐπείσακτος, ὡς πρότερον μὲν οὐχ ὑπάρχον, ὕστερον δὲ ἐπεισ·ελθόν· οὔτε γὰρ ἐνέλιπέ ποτε υἱὸς πατρί οὔτε υἱῷ πνεῦμα, ἀλλ' ἄτρεπτος καὶ ἀναλλοίωτος ἡ αὐτὴ τριὰς ἀεί. It ought to be distinctly noticed that the genuineness of this Creed is, in spite of Caspari's brilliant defence, not raised above all doubt. But the external and internal evidence in support of its authenticity seem to me overwhelming. According to Gregory of Nyssa it was said to have been revealed to Gregory Thaumaturgus immediately before entering on his Bishopric, by the Virgin Mary and the Apostle John. If this legend is old, and there is nothing to show it is not, then we may regard it as proving that this confession of faith could only be introduced into the Church by the use of extraordinary means. The abstract, unbiblical character of the Creed is noteworthy ; it is admirably suited to a follower of Origen like Gregory; but it is less suited to a post-Nicene Bishop. Origen himself would hardly have approved of so unbiblical a Creed. It points to a time in which there was imminent danger of theological speculation relaxing its connection with the Books of Revelation.

was thus introduced into the faith and instruction of the
Church. Further, it is clear from the letter of Alexander of
Alexandria to Alexander of Constantinople, that the Church of
Alexandria possessed at that time a Creed which had been
elaborated theologically.[1] After the Bishop has quoted extensive
portions of it, which he describes as "the whole pious Apostolic
doctrine" (πᾶσα ἡ ἀποστολικὴ εὐσεβὴς δόξα), he closes with the
words "these things we teach and preach, that is the Apostolic
dogmas of the Church" (ταῦτα διδάσκομεν, ταῦτα κηρύττομεν,
ταῦτα τῆς ἐκκλησίας τὰ ἀποστολικὰ δόγματα). But these dogmas
belong to Origen's theology. Finally, we perceive from the
Nicene transactions, that many Churches then possessed Creeds,
which contained the Biblical theological formulas of Origen.
We may assert this decidedly of the Churches of Cæsarea,
Jerusalem, and Antioch.[2] The entire undertaking of the Fathers

[1] See Theodoret, H. E. I. 4; Hahn, l. c., § 65: Πιστεύομεν, ὡς τῇ ἀποστολικῇ
ἐκκλησίᾳ δοκεῖ, εἰς μόνον ἀγέννητον πατέρα, οὐδένα τοῦ εἶναι αὐτῷ τὸν αἴτιον
ἔχοντα... καὶ εἰς ἕνα κύριον Ἰησοῦν Χριστόν, τὸν υἱὸν τοῦ Θεοῦ τὸν μονογενῆ, γεννηθέντα οὐκ ἐκ τοῦ μὴ ὄντος, ἀλλ᾽ ἐκ τοῦ ὄντος πατρός... πρὸς δὲ τῇ εὐσεβεῖ ταύτῃ
περὶ πατρὸς καὶ υἱοῦ δόξῃ, καθὼς ἡμᾶς αἱ θεῖαι γραφαὶ διδάσκουσιν, ἐν πνεῦμα ἅγιον
ὁμολογοῦμεν, τὸ καινίσαν τούς τε τῆς παλαιᾶς διαθήκης ἁγίους ἀνθρώπους καὶ τοὺς
τῆς χρηματιζούσης καινῆς παιδευτὰς θείους. μίαν καὶ μόνην καθολικήν, τὴν ἀποστολικὴν ἐκκλησίαν, ἀκαθαίρετον μὴν ἀεί, κἂν πᾶς ὁ κόσμος αὐτῇ πολεμεῖν βουλεύηται...
Μετὰ τούτων τὴν ἐκ νεκρῶν ἀνάστασιν οἴδαμεν, ἧς ἀπαρχὴ γέγονεν ὁ κύριος ἡμῶν
Ἰ. Χρ., σῶμα φορέσας ἀληθῶς καὶ οὐ δοκήσει ἐκ τῆς θεοτόκου (one of the earliest
passages, of which we are certain, for this expression; yet it was probably already
used in the middle of the third century; a treatise was also written περὶ τῆς θεοτόκου by Pierius) Μαρίας, ἐπὶ συντελείᾳ τῶν αἰώνων, εἰς ἀθέτησιν ἁμαρτίαςέ πιδημήσας
τῷ γένει τῶν ἀνθρώπων, σταυρωθεὶς καὶ ἀποθανών, ἀλλ᾽ οὐ διὰ ταῦτα τῆς ἑαυτοῦ
θεότητος ἥττων γεγενημένος, ἀναστὰς ἐκ νεκρῶν, ἀναλημφθεὶς ἐν οὐρανοῖς, καθήμενος
ἐν δεξιᾷ τῆς μεγαλωσύνης.

[2] The Cæsarean Creed in Athanasius, Socrates, Theodoret and Gelasius, see
Hahn, § 116 and Hort, Two Dissertations, pp. 138, 139. It runs: Πιστεύομεν εἰς
ἕνα Θεὸν πατέρα παντοκράτορα, τὸν τῶν ἀπάντων ὁρατῶν τε καὶ ἀοράτων ποιητήν.
Καὶ εἰς ἕνα κύριον Ἰ Χρ., τὸν τοῦ Θεοῦ λόγον, Θεὸν ἐκ Θεοῦ, φῶς ἐκ φωτός, ζωὴν
ἐκ ζωῆς, υἱὸν μονογενῆ, πρωτότοκον πάσης κτίσεως, πρὸ πάντων τῶν αἰώνων ἐκ τοῦ
πατρὸς γεγεννημένον, δι᾽ οὗ καὶ ἐγένετο τὰ πάντα· τὸν διὰ τὴν ἡμετέραν σωτηρίαν
σαρκωθέντα καὶ ἐν ανθρώποις πολιτευσάμενον, καὶ παθόντα, καὶ ἀναστάντα τῇ τρίτῃ
ἡμέρᾳ, καὶ ανελθόντα πρὸς τὸν πατέρα, καὶ ἥξοντα πάλιν ἐν δόξῃ κρῖναι ζῶντας καὶ
νεκρούς. Καὶ εἰς πνεῦμα ἅγιον. This Creed is also remarkable from its markedly
theological character. On the Creeds of Antioch and Jerusalem, which are at any
rate earlier then A.D. 325, see Hort, (l.c. 73) and Hahn, § 63. We cannot appeal,
as regards the phrasing, to the so-called Creed of Lucian (Hahn, § 115). Yet it is
extremely probable that it is based on a Creed by Lucian.

of the Nicene Council to set up a theological Creed to be observed by the whole Church, would have been impossible, had
not the Churches, or at least the chief Churches, of the East
already been accustomed to such Symbols. These Churches
had thus passed, in the generations immediately preceding
the Nicene, through a Creed-forming period, to which little
attention has hitherto been paid. In its beginning and its
course it is wholly obscure, *but it laid the foundation for
the development of theological dogmatics, peculiar to the
Church, in the fourth and fifth centuries.* It laid the foundation
—for the following epoch was distinguished from this one by
the fact that the precise definitions demanded by the doctrine
of redemption, as contained within the frame-work of Origen's
theology, were fixed and made exclusive. Thus the dangers
were guarded against, which rose out of the circumstance, that
the philosophical theory of God, and the idea of the Logos
which belonged to it, had been received into the system of
religion, *i.e.*, the Neo-platonic method and circle of ideas had
been legitimised, without the traditional tenets of the faith having
been sufficiently protected against them. In the new Creeds of
the period 260—325 we find the conditions to hand for a system
of religion based on the philosophical doctrine of God, a system
specifically belonging to the Church, completely expressed in
fixed and technical terms, and scientific. We find the conditions ready—but nothing more, or less. But it was also due to
the Creeds that in after times every controversy of the schools
necessarily became a conflict that moved and shook the Church
to its very depths. The men, however, who in the fourth and
fifth centuries made orthodox dogma, were undoubtedly influenced,
to a greater degree than their predecessors of from A.D. 260—
315, by specifically Church ideas; and their work, if we measure
it by the mixture of ideas and methods which they received
from tradition, was eminently a conservative *reduction* and
securing of tradition, so far as that was still in their possession.
It was really a new thing, a first step of immeasurable
significance, when Athanasius staked his whole life on the recognition of a single attribute—*the consubstantiality*—of Christ,
and rejected all others as being liable to pagan misinterpretation.

At the beginning of the fourth century, Rules of Faith and theology were differently related to each other in the Churches of the East and West. In the latter, the phraseology of the primitive Creed was strictly adhered to, and a simple antignostic interpretation was thought sufficient, by means of formulas like "Father, Son, and Spirit: *one God*"—"Jesus Christ, God and man"—"Jesus Christ, the Logos, wisdom, and power of God"— In the former, theological formulas were admitted into the Confession of Faith itself, which was thus shaped into a theological compendium ostensibly coming from the Apostles. But in both cases, the personal reality, and, with it, the pre-existence of the divinity manifested in Christ, were recognised by the vast majority;[1] they were included in the instruction given to Catechumens; they furnished the point of view from which men sought to understand the Person of Christ. And, accordingly, the accurate definition of the relation of the Deity to that other divine nature which appeared on earth necessarily became the chief problem of the future.

[1] See the interesting passage in Eusebius' letter to his Church, in which he (sophistically) so defends the rejection of the οὐκ ἦν πρὸ τοῦ γεννηθῆναι, as to fall back upon the universally recognised pre-existence of Christ (Theodoret, H. E. I. 12).

DIVISION II.

THE DEVELOPMENT OF THE DOGMA OF THE CHURCH.

BOOK I.

THE HISTORY OF THE DEVELOPMENT OF DOGMA AS THE DOCTRINE OF THE GOD-MAN ON THE BASIS OF NATURAL THEOLOGY.

Τὰ κρατούμενα τῷ λόγω τῆς φύσεως οὐκ ἔχει ἔπαινον,
τὰ δὲ σχέσει φιλίας κρατούμενα ὑπεραινεῖται.

PAUL OF SAMOSATA.

Ohne Autorität kann der Mensch nicht existiren,
und doch bringt sie ebensoviel Irrthum als
Wahrheit mit sich; sie verewigt im Einzelnen,
was einzeln vorübergehen sollte, lehnt ab und
lässt vorübergehen, was festgehalten werden
sollte, und ist hauptsächlich Ursache dass die
Menschheit nicht vom Flecke kommt.

BOOK I.

THE HISTORY OF THE DEVELOPMENT OF DOGMA AS THE DOCTRINE OF THE GOD-MAN ON THE BASIS OF NATURAL THEOLOGY.

CHAPTER I.

HISTORICAL SITUATION. [1]

THE first main division of the history of dogma closed with the adoption of the Logos doctrine as the central dogma of the Church, and with the accompanying revision in the East of the old formulas of the faith under the influence of philosophical theology. The testament of primitive Christianity—the Holy Scriptures—and the Testament of Antiquity—Neoplatonic speculation—were intimately and, as it seemed, inseparably connected in the great Churches of the East. The system of doctrine established by the Church in the third century corresponded to the Church whose structure appeared complete in the same period. As the political powers of the Roman Empire were conserved in the Catholic Church, so also were the spiritual forces of Antiquity in its faith. Both required to be invested with divine lustre in order to live through storms and amid universal ruin. [2] But Christianity was by no means completely Hellenised in Catholicism; that is proved, if we needed proof, by the attacks of

---

[1] Walch, Entw. einer vollst. Historie der Ketzereien, 1762 ff. Hefele, Konciliengesch., 2 Bd. I.—IV. Histories of the Roman Empire by Tillemont, Gibbon, Richter und Ranke (Weltgesch., Bd. IV. und V.). Réville, Die Religion z. Rom unter den Severern (German translation by Krüger, 1888). V. Schultze, Gesch. des Untergangs des griechisch-römischen Heidenthums, 2 Bde., 1887 f. Boissier, La fin du paganisme, 2 Bde. 1891. Dorner, Entw.-Gesch. d. L. v. d. Person Christi, II., 1853. H. Schultz, Die L. v. d. Gottheit Christi, 1881. Gass, Symbolik d. griech. Kirche, 1872. Kattenbuch, Lehrbuch d. vergleichenden Konfessionskunde. 1 Bd., 1890. Denzinger, Ritus Orientalium, 2 Bde. 1863 f.

[2] Tiele, Kompendium der Relig. Gesch. (German transl.), p. 283: "the Catholic Church is the secular Roman rule, modified and consecrated by Christian ideas."

Porphyry and Julian. Undoubtedly all the institutions and ideas felt to be necessary were included in the "Apostolic tradition" to an increasing extent. But since a place had been given in that tradition to the O. T. and the written memorials of primitive Christianity, these really furnished aids to the comprehension of the Gospel, which had certainly been obscured in the "*Gnosis*" as well as in the "*New Law*". The theology of Origen, in spite of some very earnest attacks upon it, was held in the East to be the pattern and the inexhaustible source of the theology of the Church, so far as a scientific system was desired. Even its opponents, like Methodius, could not escape its influence. From its rich store of formulas were more fully elaborated, in opposition to what was called Ebionitism and Sabellianism, those confessions which were employed in the cultus and instruction of the Church, and which, thus enriched, were then invested with some sort of Apostolic authority. [1] The West did not go so far; yet it was perfectly defenceless against the "advances" made by the Church in the Eastern half of the Empire; for certain theological and Christological conceptions to which it also clung, made any counter-movement impossible, though many teachers, preachers, and apologists went ways of their own, and in their doctrines of Christ and salvation mixed up obselete Christian traditions with the popular philosophy of the West. Looking to theological metaphysics as wrapped up in the official formulas of the Church, the difference was finally only one of degree. It showed itself among those less interested and scholarly, who were therefore conservative in their instincts and looked with distrust on the theology of Origen; they thought with perfect simplicity that their own formulas: "Father, Son, and Spirit; one God", "Christ, the Logos, wisdom, and power of God", "*duæ substantiæ, una persona*", "Jesus Christ, God and man", constituted the "faith" which needed no explanation. The element of speculative philosophy was as a rule weak in the system of religion of the West. In place of it, the West of Tertullian possessed a series of juristic "plans" which were destined to have a great future.

In spite of many far-reaching differences in their practical and

[1] See above p. 47 ff., 113 ff.

theoretical interests, in spite of the development in ecclesiastical affairs, Christians in East and West felt that they belonged to one united Church. The Novatian and Samosatian controversies ultimately resulted in strengthening the consciousness of unity,[1] even though a not altogether insignificant part of Christendom cast itself adrift. These controversies showed plainly that the Western and Eastern communities held substantially the same position in the world, and that both required to use the same means to maintain it. Communities everywhere adopted the character of the Church of the world. Their union preserved all the features of a political society, and, at the same time, of a disciplinary institution, equipped with sacred sanctions and dreadful punishments, in which individual independence was lost. [2] Of course, in proportion as this confederacy of Christians adapted itself to civic, national, and political relationships, in order to maintain and strengthen itself, the integrity of the Church was most gravely imperilled, when these very relationships lost their last shreds of unity in the collapse of the Empire. Above all, the great cleavage between the Eastern and Western halves of the Empire could not fail to be prejudicial to the Church. But about the close of the third century the latter, in spite of discontent in its midst, held more firmly together than the Empire, and its unity was still maintained after the fourth century by great Emperors and influential theologians. [3]

In addition to the episcopal constitution, uniformly and strictly carried out, the common basis of the Churches was due to the recognition of the same authorities and designs, the uniform appreciation of sacramental rites, and the strong tendency to asceticism for the sake of a future life. It was, at first, too stable for the different forces which threatened to shatter the Empire, and also, in consequence, beat upon the Imperial Church. But this basis . was nevertheless insufficient. It can be easily shown that the elements composing it were as incapable ot

---

[1] See on this the correspondence between the oriental Bishops and Julius of Rome; Socr., H. E., II. 15; Ep. Julii ap Athan., Apolog. c. Arian, ch. 21 sq.

[2] See Vol. II., p. 122 f.

[3] Reuter, Augustinische Studien, in the Zeitschr. f. K.-Gesch. V., p. 349 ff., VI., p. 155 ff., 190.

guaranteeing the unity, as of protecting the Christianity, of the
Church, through a prolonged period.

Among the authorities the two Testaments, combined by the
evidence of prophecy and allegorical explanation, took the first,
indeed, strictly speaking, a unique place. But not only was their
extent not absolutely decided, but their interpretation was wholly
uncertain. In addition to this, the scope to be left to the "Apostolic tradition", *i.e.*, the illusion of "antiquity", and to the decision
of episcopal synods, was by no means defined; for the sufficiency
of Holy Scripture was placed, theoretically, beyond doubt.
But where elementary wants, felt by the great majority, were
to be satisfied, where a reassuring sanction was required for the
advancing secularisation, men did not rack their brains, if no
inconvenient monitors were in the way, to find precedents
in Holy Scripture for what was novel. They went right back
to the Apostles, and deduced from secret traditions what no
tradition ever possessed. Huge spheres of ecclesiastical activity
embracing new and extensive institutions—the reception of national customs and of the practices of heathen sects—were in
this way placed under "Apostolic" sanction, without any
controversy starting worth mention. This is true, *e.g.*, of the
ritual of worship and ecclesiastical discipline, "The sacred
canons" or "the apostolic canons" constituted from the close of
the third century, a court of appeal, which practically held the
same rank as the sacred writings, and which, especially in the
East, cast its protection to an increasing extent over national
customs and traditional morals in the face of attacks of every
kind. It is obvious that authorities so obtained were likely, in
the end, to divide the Churches of the different nations.

The crudest superstition was thus consecrated by "apostolic"
decrees, or legitimised, after the event, from the O. T.,[1] and
from the middle of the third century it ascended from the lower
strata of Christians to the upper, which had lost all spiritual
stability. And now in the fourth century, when Church and
State were fused into one, everything was assigned to the former
which had ever, or anywhere been regarded as venerable or
holy. As it had submitted to the Church, it demanded indulgent

---

[1] See my Edition of the Διδαχή, Prolegg. pp. 222 ff., 239 ff.

treatment. The religion of pure reason and of the strictest morality, the Christianity which the ancient apologists had once portrayed, had long changed into a religion of the most powerful rites, of mysterious means, and an external sanctity. The historical tradition of Christ and the founding of Christianity was turned into a romance, and this historical romance, which was interwoven with the religion, constantly received new chapters. The stream of the history of salvation ended in a waste swamp of countless and confused sacred tales, and in its course took in heathen fictions and the stories of gods and heroes. Every traditional holy rite became the centre of new sacred ceremonies, and every falling off in morality was covered by increasing the religious apparatus. The idea of forgiveness of sins was to many a cloak for frivolity and wickedness. Up to the middle of the third century, every Catholic Christian was, in all probability, a genuine monotheist. That can no longer be said of the generations who afterwards pressed into the Church. Polytheism had lost its name, indeed, but not its influence in the Church of the fourth century. Great masses preserved, in spite of their baptism, the piety to which they had been accustomed. Christian priests had to respect and adjust superstition, in order to keep the leadership in their hands, and theologians had no difficulty in finding, in the O. T. and in many views and usages of Christian antiquity, means of justifying what was most novel, alien, and absurd. Miracles, were of everyday occurrence, and they were barbarous and detestable miracles, directed to meet the meanest instincts, and offensive to even moderately clear heads. [1] The Christian religion threatened to become a new

[1] Compare the criticism by Julian and his friends of the Christian religion and the worship paid to saints and relics, or read the writings in which Sulpicius Severus attempts to recommend Christianity to the refined society of Aquitania. We can study in the works of the historians Socrates and Sozomen the attitude of cultured Catholic Christians, after the complete triumph of the Church over paganism. Even Sozomen cannot be regarded as having reached the stage of the "dry tree," and yet into what a superstition the Christian faith is transformed in his pages! We see how paganism thrust itself into worship, in—to quote a well-known instance—August. Confess. VI. 2 ff. Let us, above all, remember that from the beginning of the fourth century special chapels and churches were built to the different saints. The saints took the place of the local deities; their festivals of the old provincial services of the gods. We have just begun to investigate the

paganism;[1] while, at the same time, making shipwreck of its own unity and common character. For even if priests and theologians were always to be in a position to keep the reins in their hands, dissolution threatened the one undivided Church which girt the Empire, if the local rites, customs, usages of men were consecrated as Christian in every province, and might establish themselves without any decided counterpoise.

But where was such a counterpoise to be found? In the constitution? That was indeed a firm structure, binding Christendom strongly together; but even it presented sides on which the centrifugal forces, destructive of unity, found entrance. Love of rule and ambition were encouraged by the episcopal chair. And when the danger of dismemberment into independent bishoprics was met by a rigid metropolitan leadership, the way was opened up to that lofty ambition which desired the first place and the highest influence in the province, and which sought to domineer over the civil powers and to master neighbouring provinces. The Patriarchs and Metropolitans who—to use an expression of

transformation of heathen tales of gods and heroes into legends of the saints, and ancient light literature has contributed its quota in works of travel and adventure by land and sea. These researches promise, if instituted critically and soberly, to give interesting results; yet I doubt if the state of our materials will admit of confident conclusions. Besides the worship of the saints, the cultus of the Emperor threatened in the fourth century to intrude itself into the Church. Philostorgius relates (H. E. II. 17) that Christians presented offerings to the picture of Constantine, and honoured it with lanterns and incense; they also seem to have offered *vota* to him that they might be protected from calamities.

[1] Besides the worship of saints, martyrs, and relics, we have to notice the new forms of faith in demons. It would be impossible to believe more sincerely in demons than Christians did in the second century. But that age was yet ignorant of the fantastic tricks with them, which almost turned Christendom into a society of deceived deceivers. (The expression was first applied to Christians by Plotinus: see Vita Plot. by Porphyrius 16: ἐξηπάτων καὶ αὐτοὶ ἠπατημένοι). When we reflect that the Vita Antonii was written by an Athanasius, nothing can again surprise us. Spiritualism with all its absurdity, which we are once more conversant with in the nineteenth century, had long been familiar in heathen circles, and then, as now, it was connected with religious ideas on the one hand, and physical experiments and speculations on the other. It forced its way into the Church, in spite of all protests, from the third, still more, however, from the fourth century, after it had long been wide-spread in "Gnostic circles." As a religious phenomenon it signified a renaissance of the lowest forms of religion. But even the most enlightened minds could not keep clear of it. Augustine proves this.

Socrates—played at being "hereditary lords" (Dynastai) no longer protected, but undermined the unity of the Church. The great Bishops of Rome and Alexandria, who sought to rule over the Church in order to preserve its unity and independence, entangled themselves in an ambitious policy, and produced division. The Emperors were really patrons of unity, and the supreme means at their disposal, the Œcumenical Synod, was their contrivance; in all cases it was a political institution, invented by the greatest of politicians, a two-edged sword which protected the endangered unity of the Church at the price of its independence.

But was not the bond of unity, the common ground, to be found in the common ideal, in the certain hope of a future life, and in asceticism? This bond was assuredly a strong one. The Church would hardly have succeeded in following out the free path opened up to it by Constantine had it not had in its midst, besides its transcendent promises, a power to which all, Greek and barbarian, polytheist and monotheist, learned and unlearned required ultimately, if reluctantly, to bow. And that power was the asceticism which culminated in monachism. The ancient world had arrived, by all the routes of its complicated development, at the bitterest criticism of and disgust at its own existence; but in no other faith was religion itself as effectively combined with asceticism, in none did the latter come so powerfully to the front, yet in none did it submit itself so pliably to Church government, as in Catholicism. A religion comprehended in a mere sacramental communion could not have gained the allegiance of the more clear-sighted and earnest. One that imposed on all, as an inalienable duty, the perfect fulfilment of the positive moral law, could not have held its ground. One that commanded all alike to renounce the world would have closed the world against it. But a religion which graded its members as priests, monks, and laity, embraced a threefold piety of initiated, perfect, and novices, and succeeded in the hardest task of all, that of reconciling priest with monk, [1] and of admitting the layman to a share in the

---

[1] The order of the monks had to pass through crises and conflicts before it was able to establish itself side by side with, and to influence a secularised priesthood; we possess the key to this struggle in the East in the writings of the forger who

blessings of both, was superior to all others, and possessed in its organisation, generally established, a strong bond of association.

Protestants at the present day can hardly form a conception of the hold which asceticism possessed over the mind in the fourth and fifth centuries, or of the manner in which it influenced imagination, thought, and the whole of life. At bottom only a single point was dealt with, abstinence from sexual relationships; everything else was secondary; for he who had renounced these, found nothing hard. Renunciation of the servile yoke of sin (servile peccati iugum discutere) was the watchword of Christians, and an extraordinary unanimity prevailed as to the meaning of this watchword, whether we turn to the coptic porter or the learned Greek teacher, to the Bishop of Hippo, or Jerome, the Roman presbyter, or the biographer of Saint Martin. Virginity was the specifically Christian virtue, and the essence of all virtues: in this conviction the meaning of the evangelical law was summed up.[1]

composed the Apostolic constitutions and the longer recension of the Ignatian Epistles; in the West in the works, written from the opposite standpoint, of Sulpicius, as also in those of Jerome, Augustine, and the Gallican authors of the fifth century. Compare Hauck, K.-Gesch. Deutschlands, I., p. 49 ff. The order of the monks was imported into the West. It was not till about the middle of the fifth century that its opponents, inside and outside the ranks of the clergy, were silenced. For a time—at the end of the fourth century—it was in danger of being included in the condemnation of the Ascetics who held dualistic views.

[1] The Fathers of the fourth century could not proceed so consistently as Hieracas (see above, p. 98, n. 5) since they had to sanction the "lower" morality in the Church. The Eustathians who condemned marriage—see the decrees of the Synod of Gangra in Hefele, Concil. Gesch., I. 2, p. 777 ff.—were therefore opposed. But the numerous tractates " De virginitate " show how near the great Fathers of the Church came to the Eustathian view. We can hardly point to one who did not write on the subject. And the same thing is, above all, proved by Jerome's polemic against Jovinian, in spite of its limitation, in the Ep. (48) ad Pammachium. For the rest, Augustine did not differ from Jerome. His Confessions are pervaded by the thought that he alone can enjoy peace with God who renounces all sexual intercourse. Like Hieracas, Ambrose celebrated virginity as the real novelty in Christian morality; see De virginibus, I. 3 sq.: "Since the Lord wrapped himself in a bodily form, and consummated the marriage of deity with humanity, without the shadow of a stain, he has infused poor frail men with heavenly life over the whole globe. That is the race which the angels symbolised when they came to serve the Lord in the wilderness... That is the heavenly host which on that holy Christmas the exulting choirs of angels promised to the earth. We have the testimony of antiquity therefore from the beginning of time, but complete submission only since the word became flesh. This virtue is, in fact, our exclusive possession. The heathens had

But not only did the evangelical law culminate in virginity, but to it also belonged all promises. Methodius' teaching that it prepared the soul to be the bride of Christ, was from the fourth century repeated by everyone. Virginity lies at the root of the figure of bridegoom (Christ) and bride (the soul) which is constantly recurring in the greatest teachers of East and West, and it is the key to the corresponding exposition of the Song of Songs, in which often appear a surprising religious individualism and an impassioned love of Christ. [1]

it not; it is not practised by the still uncivilised barbarians; there are no other living creatures among whom it is to be found. We breathe the same air as they do, we share in all the conditions of an earthly life, we are not distinguished from them in birth, and so we only escape from the miseries of a nature otherwise similar to theirs through the virgin chastity, which, apparently extolled by the heathens, is yet, even if placed under the patronage of religion, outraged by them, which is persecuted by the barbarians, and is known to no other creatures." Compare with this Chrysostom's tractate on the state of virginity. Much thought was given after the middle of the fourth century to the relation of priest and monk, especially by those who wished to be monks and had to be priests. The virgin state (of the monks) was held by the earnest to be the easier and safer, the priestly condition the more perilous and responsible; yet in many respects it was regarded as also loftier, because the priest consummated the holy sacrifice and had to wield authority (Chrysostom de sacerdotio, esp. VI. 6—8 and III. 4—6, VI. 4). But the danger to which priests and bishops were subject of becoming worldly, was felt, not only by men like Gregory of Nasianzum and Chrysostom, but by countless earnest minded Christians. A combination of the priestly (episcopal) office and professional asceticism was therefore early attempted and carried out.

[1] See Vols. II., III., p. 109. The allegory of the soul of the Gnostic as the bride received its first lofty treatment in the Valentinian school. Thence Origen got it. The sources drawn upon by later writers were Origen's homilies and commentary on the Song of Songs (Lommatzsch. XIV., p. 233 sq.): the prologue of the latter in Rufinus begins with the words: "Epithalamium libellus hic, id est, nuptiale carmen, dramatis in modum mihi videtur a Salomone conscriptus, quem cecinit instar nubentis sponsæ, et erga sponsum suum, qui est sermo dei, cœlesti amore flagrantis. Adamavit enim eum, sive anima, quæ ad imaginem eius facta est, sive ecclesia." Jerome, who has translated the book, says that Origen surpassed himself in it. Methodius' writing "Convivium" in which the same thought often occurs, was also much read. The purest and most attractive form of the conception in the East appears in Gregory of Nyssa; see e g., his homilies on the Song of Songs, and his description of the life of Macrina (Ed. Oehler, 1858, p. 172 sq.); we read p. 210 sq.: Διὰ τοῦτό μοι δοκεῖ τὸν θεῖον ἐκεῖνον καὶ καθαρὸν ἔρωτα τοῦ ἀοράτου νυμφίου. ὃν ἐγκεκρυμμένον εἶχεν ἐν τοῖς τῆς ψυχῆς ἀπορρήτοις τρεφόμενον, ἔνδηλον ποιεῖν τότε τοῖς παροῦσι καὶ δημοσιεύειν τὴν ἐν καρδίᾳ διάθεσιν, τὸ ἐπείγεσθαι πρὸς τὸν ποθούμενον, ὡς ἂν διὰ τάχους σὺν αὐτῷ γένοιτο τῶν δεσμῶν ἐκλυθεῖσα τοῦ σώματος. Besides Gregory we have to mention Macarius with his "Spiritual

But the ascetic ideal did not succeed in establishing itself,
especially in the West, without severe conflicts, and it concealed within it dangers to the Church. Asceticism threatened
to become an end in itself, and to depart from the historical
foundation of the Christian religion. When the Church authorised

Homilies" (Migne T. XXXIV.; see Floss, Macarii Aegypt. epp. etc., 1850,
German translation by Jocham, Kempten, 1878); compare especially the 15th homily
which contains already the figure, repeated a hundred times afterwards, of the soul
as the poor maiden who possesses nothing but her own body and whom the
heavenly bridegroom loves. If she worthily cherishes chastity and love for him,
then she becomes mistress of all the treasures of her Lord, and her transfigured
body itself shares in his divinity. Further, Hom. IV., ch. 6 sq., 14 sq. Compare
also Ep. 2. "A soul which has cast aside the ignominy of its outward form, which
is no longer ruled by shameful thoughts or violated by evil desires, has manifestly
become a partner of the heavenly bridegroom; for henceforth it has only one
requirement. Stung by love to him it demands and, to speak boldly, longs for the
immediate fulfilment of a spiritual and mysterious union that it may enter the
indissoluble embrace of communion in sanctification." See Cyril Catech. III., ch. 16 ;
καὶ γένοιτο πάντας ὑμᾶς ἀμώμως τῷ νοητῷ νυμφίῳ παραστάντας κ.τ.λ. Before this:
ἡ γὰρ πρότερον δούλη ψυχὴ νῦν ἀδελφιδοῦν αὐτὸν τὸν δεσπότην ἐπεγράψατο, ὃς τὴν
ἀνυπόκριτον ἀποδεχόμενος προαίρεσιν ἐπιφωνήσει· Ἰδοὺ εἶ καλὴ ἡ πλησίον μου, ἰδοὺ
εἶ καλή· ὀδόντες σου ὡς ἀγέλαι τῶν κεκαρμένων (Cantic. 4, 1). διὰ τὴν εὐσυνείδητον
ὁμολογίαν. We can point to very few Greek Fathers in whom the figure does not
occur.   All the greater is the contrast presented by the depreciatory verdict of
Theodore of Mopsuestia on the Song of Songs (Kihn, Theodor v. M. 1880, p. 69 f.).
It may be expressly noticed, besides, that Clement of Alex. as well as Methodius
and Macarius had already transferred the figure of the bride to the married woman.
Indeed, Macarius was conscious that he was acting boldly in doing so. Western
nuns and monks were distinguished by lavishing those sexual feelings which were
forbidden them on Christ (and Mary). Ambrose especially taught the West the
conception of the soul as the bride of Christ; while Augustine was, apart from a
few passages, more reserved, and Jerome wanted strength in sentiment and language.
Not only in Ambrose's tractate "De Isaac et anima", really a commentary on the
Song of Songs, but in innumerable passages in his works—even when it is least
expected, as in the consolatory discourse on Valentinian's death (ch. 59 sq.)—the
idea of a special tie between the virgin soul and Christ comes to the front. But
Ambrose gave it a colouring of his own due to the deep sentiment of a great
man, and his peculiar faculty of giving a warm expression to his personal love of
Christ (see also Prudentius); compare passages like De pœnit. II. 8.   We cannot
appreciate too highly the important influence exerted on after times, and first on
Augustine, by Ambrose's expression of his personal religion. The light that dawned
in Augustine's confessions already shone from the works of Ambrose, and it was
the latter, not the former, who conducted western piety to the specific love of
Christ. On the mysticism of Macarius, who was in many respects allied to these
western Christians, compare also the details in Förster (in the Jahrb. f. deutsche
Theol. 1873, p. 439 f.). Bigg (the Christian Platonists of Alex., p. 188 f.) has very

the Christianity of 'the perfect', it really declared the great mass of its divine and apostolic institutions to be mere apparatus, meaningless to him who had resolved to renounce the world, and to prepare for eternity. Those settlers in Egypt, who sought to obtain redemption by torturing themselves, in the end imperilled religion not less than the great crowds who simply submitted to certain sacramental observances, and with the approval of the priests dragged into Christianity whatever pleased them. It was possible, and in fact the danger was imminent, for the ascetic ideal to lose any assured connection with Jesus Christ. Asceticism had also been proclaimed indeed by Greek science. But in that case the common character of religion disappeared; for a merely negative ideal of life, which at the same time was without a close dependence on history, could not form a lasting bond of connection among men.

Our information is exceptionally bad, and not from accident, as to the internal state of the Church, at the time when Constantine chose it to be the support of the Empire. But what we know is enough to establish the fact that the internal solidity by no means corresponded to the external. We may with greater propriety affirm that the Churches of the East were in danger of relapsing into worldliness, and that not only in the form of worldly modes of action. [1] The peril went deeper. Theology, the power which, as matters then were, could alone

rightly seen that Origen's homilies on the Song of Songs were at the root of Christian mysticism: "This book gave welcome expression to what after the triumph of Athanasius was the dominant feeling, and redeemed in some degree the name of its author, damaged by his supposed inclination to Arianism. And thus Origen, the first pioneer in so many fields of Christian thought, the father in one of his many aspects of the English Latitudinarians, became also the spiritual ancestor of Bernard, the Victorines, and the author of the De Imitatione, of Tauler, and Molinos and Mme. de Guyon."

[1] Church history has at this point in its investigations to collect the numerous data which prove how deeply members of the Church had become involved in heathen polytheistic morals, usages, customs, and conceptions, how strong reliance on sacred witchcraft, amulets, and sacramental vehicles had grown, and how far stability and peace of heart and mind had been lost. For the latter we can especially compare Eusebius (H. E. VIII. 1), (further the epitaph of Damasus on Euseb. the Roman Bishop, in Duchesne, Le liber Pontificalis, Tom. I., 1885, p. 167); of a later date, Cyril, Catech. 15, ch. 7. As regards syncretism, see the work on the Egyptian mysteries (ed. Parthey).

give an energetic protection to the distinctive character of
religion, was at the point of dissolving it and abandoning it to
the world.

We have already described in this volume the state of
Eastern theology at the beginning of the fourth century. Conceptions of the faith which began and ended with the historical
personality of Jesus Christ were equally condemned with the
attempts, whether unstudied or philosophical, to identify the
Person of Jesus with the Deity. [1] The realistic and eclectic
theology of Irenæus had probably very few defenders in the
West. The theology of the Apologists had triumphed, and all
thinkers stood under the influence of Origen. But the genius
of this great man was too powerful for the Epigoni. The importance of his system lay in a threefold direction : first, in the
sharp distinction between Pistis and Gnosis, which he kept
apart, and connected only by unity of aim; secondly, in the
abundant material in his speculations, the conservatism that he
showed in inweaving all that was valuable, and the balance
which he knew how to preserve between the different factors
of his system, relating them all to one uniform aim; thirdly, in
the Biblical impress which he gave his theology by strict adherence to the text of Holy Scripture. In all these respects the
Epigoni introduced changes. The most important in its consequences was the mingling of Pistis and Gnosis, of faith and
theology. Origen had not published his system, in which the
faith of the Church was reconciled with science, as Church
doctrine. To him the distinction between the faith of the Church
and the science of faith remained fixed. But in the next period
— following the precedent of Methodius [2] and opposing Basil's
principle — it was thought necessary to identify them. Reactionary
and progressive tendencies met in these efforts. The Pistis

---

[1] See the short disclaimers in the fourth Catechism of Cyril of Jerusalem,
(ch. 7. 8): Οὐχ, ὡς τινες ἐνόμισαν, ὁ υἱὸς μετὰ τὸ πάθος στεφανωθεὶς ὥσπερ ὑπὸ
τοῦ Θεοῦ διὰ τὴν ὑπομονὴν ἔλαβε τὸν ἐν δεξιᾷ θρόνον, ἀλλ᾽ ἀφ᾽ οὗπέρ ἐστιν ἔχει τὸ
βασιλικὸν ἀξίωμα ... Μήτε ἀπαλλοτριώσῃς τοῦ πατρὸς τὸν υἱόν, μήτε συναλοιφὴν
ἐργασάμενος υἱοπατρίαν πιστεύσῃς. Further, the 11th Catechism. So also Athanasius steadily disavows the heresy of the Adoptians as well as of the Sabellians.

[2] See Vol. III, p. 103.

(faith) was supplied with the formulas of Origen's theology, and Gnosis was to stop short at certain tenets of tradition, and to receive them without revision. The point was to find a new medium which should be at once tradition and speculation, Pistis and Gnosis. This endeavour was undoubtedly justified by an actual change accomplished before this and promoted by Origen himself, viz., the incorporation of the doctrine of the Logos in the faith of "the simple." These simple Christians already possessed a dogma which was shaped by exegesis and speculation, and confronted them as an external authority, a law of faith. This creation had forced its way from the circumference of the ecclesiastical system into its centre. Besides, the sharp distinction between a traditional doctrine of the Church and a science of religion contradicted the whole ecclesiastical tradition as established in the fight with Gnosticism. But the intermingling at first produced a kind of stagnation. It threatened to make faith lose its certainty, speculation its reasoning power, and the Church the unity of its confession. If we review the new religious formulas, which were brought into circulation about the year 300, and if we compare the theologies of the period—which unfortunately we only know in part—the theologies, namely, of the Alexandrian teachers, Gregory Thaumaturgus, Lucian, Methodius, Hieracas etc., we see a wealth of forms which, if blood-relations, are extremely different. How could the unity of the Church continue under their sway? and if it continued, was it Christianity after all that furnished the common element?

And this has brought us to the second point　Origen had recognised the full significance of the historical Christ for the stage of Pistis; while he directed the Gnostic to the eterna! Logos. Now uncertainties arose here also. The historical Christ threatened to fall entirely into the background. We can observe this in the works of two of the Epigoni, which have no affinity to each other. Gregory Thaumaturgus has in his famous Symbol dealt only with the Logos "apart from the flesh" (λόγος ἄσαρκος),[1] and Methodius intended to declare the loftiest

---

[1] See Vol. III., p.115, the words run: εἷς κύριος, μόνος ἐκ μόνου, Θεὸς ἐκ Θεοῦ, χαρακτὴρ καὶ εἰκὼν τῆς θεότητος, λόγος ἐνεργός, σοφία τῆς τῶν ὅλων συστάσεως

truth when he demanded that Christ should be born in every man 'consciously' (νοητῶς), and that each must become a Christ by participation in Christ.[1] Further, in Origen the cosmological and soteriological interests balanced each other. We recognise this in his formulas which relate to the Logos. But here also a displacement was introduced, one that favoured cosmology. The word Ὁμοούσιος (consubstantial) was, indeed, retained by some, perhaps by many theologians; but as it was in itself ambiguous, so also it was no evidence of an interest in soteriology. The crowd of rhetorical and philosophical predicates heaped upon the Logos, did not serve to illustrate and establish the significance of the Logos as the principal factor in redemption; it was rather a term for the reason and order reigning in the universe, and for the spiritual forces with which humanity had been gifted. Men indeed held firmly, on all hands, to the incarnation; nay, it was regarded, as is proved by the great work of Theognostus, as being, next to the doctrine of the creation of matter, the feature that distinguished the speculation of the Church from that of the Neo-platonists. But the whole stress was laid on the question, what idea was to be formed of the constitution of the subject of which incarnation was predicated. A great school, that of Lucian of Antioch, distinguished, in the manner of Paul of Samosata, between wisdom proper, eternal, existent in God, and a created wisdom or Logos; and identified the latter alone with the incarnate Son— 'wisdom arose through wisdom according to the will of the wise God'. But in drawing this line, not only was the incarnation of the Deity rendered impossible, but every form of His personal activity on earth. The theological interest in Christ threatened to resolve itself entirely into cosmology and morality, or, as in Methodius, to be deprived of its meaning by a mystical alloy.

The liberty which theology enjoyed in the East up to the beginning of the fourth century, and the influence which it exerted on the Church in the same period, could not but produce complete confusion and loss of meaning. All the elements

περιεκτικὴ καὶ δύναμις τῆς ὕλης κτίσεως ποιητική, υἱὸς ἀληθινὸς ἀληθινοῦ πατρός, ἀόρατος ἀοράτου καὶ ἄφθαρτος ἀφθάρτου καὶ ἀθάνατος ἀθανάτου καὶ ἀΐδιος ἀϊδίου.

[1] See Vol. III., p. 110.

united by Origen in his vast system sought to establish them
selves independently. Even tritheistic tendencies were not wanting; but, above all, the idea of a subordinate God and semi-
divine beings began to be familiar. The idea of the subordinate
God is indeed as old as the theology of the Christian Church;
even the Apologists shared it, and Origen, with all caution,
adopted and justified it in working out his doctrine of the Son.
But in the earlier period the *simplices et rudes* (the simple and
uncultured) were still startled at the suggestion; theologians provided the idea with strong safe-guards, and Origen himself, who
in many points bordered on Polytheism, on the other hand
restored the Logos to the being of God, and united Father and
Son as closely as possible. But opposition to 'Sabellianism'
evidently rendered a later age much more careless. And it is
indubitable that the idea of the created God, the God who
came into being, coalesced with ancient polytheistic inclinations.
The claims of Monotheism were considered to be satisfied by
the effort to protect the supreme Deity, as against Modalism,
from change and plurality; and the Logos and other beings
entitled to worship were suffered calmly to spring up side by
side with God; they could not, it was presumed, endanger
Monotheism, because they belonged to the domain of the created. Add that theologians dealt in their speculations with a
plethora of philosophical categories destitute of a fixed impress,
or fixed value; [1] further, that this terminology, unsifted and un-
controlled, everywhere forced its way into the faith of the
community, and we can form a conception of the danger which
hovered over the Church. We find a Monotheism which did not
exclude polytheism, a Logos-Christ, who, as a cosmological
quantity, was of shifting nature and origin, ideas of the incarnation and redemption as designed to "enlighten" the human
race, and to effect an incarnation of God in every individual
soul. All this, too, was clothed in a rank growth of artificial
philosophical expressions, identical with that used in contemporary science. And we may well ask whether such a theology
was in a condition to protect even the scanty remains of the

---

[1] See Vol. III., p. 102.

evangelic tradition, above all, at the moment when the partition
between State and Church was torn down and the Church was
brought face to face with its greatest task. A deism—if the
term may be allowed—was at hand, surrounded by the shifting
forms of a speculation which had neither a settled boundary
nor an assured object. It almost seemed as if the special characteristics of the Christian religion were to be reduced to the
evidence of antiquity and prophecy, what Porphyry called
'foreign fables'. Yet even Scriptural proof was no longer everywhere called for and given with the zeal so noticeable in Origen;
although it was just the school of Lucian which neglected it
least. But what could Scripture avail against the method? If
a Bishop so capable and learned, and so well versed in tradition as Eusebius of Cæsarea was satisfied in his Christology
with the formulas we read there, if he could praise the religious
edicts and manifestoes of his Emperor, though they substantially
celebrated "God in nature", as brilliant specimens of his
Christian conviction, we must conclude that the Logos doctrine
settled in the Church was the strongest means of completely
effacing the figure of the historical Christ, and of resolving
everything into mist.[1] Even the rationalist, who in his study
of the history of religions always follows with sympathy the
progress to 'natural' religion, would require to restrain his
sympathy here. For the pure religion of humanity could not
have resulted from this development, but one that was wholly
indefinite, and therefore capable of being influenced from any
quarter, one in whose centre was throned that hollow and
helpless figment of thought, the $\ddot{o}\nu$, the $\pi\rho\dot{\omega}\tau\eta\ o\dot{\upsilon}\sigma\dot{\iota}\alpha$ (being—
primal being). And men would have gone on proclaiming this

---

[1] On Eusebius' Christology see Dorner, Lehre v. d. Person Christi, I. (1845)
p. 792 ff. Lee, on the Theophan. 1843, Preliminary Dissert. The Christology of
Euseb. is that of the ancient apologists, approximating in its terms to Neoplatonic
speculations and richer in its phases on account of the many antitheses. In spite
of his dependence on Origen, Euseb. was chary of receiving all the ideas and
predicates which the former applied to the Son and to which orthodoxy afterwards
appealed. That is of consequence. Euseb. was more convinced than Origen that
the idea of deity was completely exhausted in that of the strictly one and un-
changeable $\ddot{o}\nu$ the $\pi\rho\dot{\omega}\tau\eta\ o\dot{\upsilon}\sigma\dot{\iota}\alpha$; he separated the $\delta\epsilon\dot{\upsilon}\tau\epsilon\rho\sigma\varsigma\ \Theta\epsilon\dot{\sigma}\varsigma$ much further from
God than the Apologists; see Zahn, Marcell., p. 37 f.

religion to be Christianity, simply because they possessed in Holy Scripture the means of proving it, and of dating it back to the beginning of the world as the universal religion. And they would have adopted sacred media, charms, and intermediary powers more and more boldly, because they were incapable of understanding and applying either to God or to Jesus Christ the tradition that God redeemed men through Jesus Christ.

The Bishops and theologians in the East about A.D. 320, whose views were similar to those of Eusebius, had on their side the strongest power to be found in an ecclesiastical communion—tradition: *they were the conservatives.* Conservative theology, the theology that took its stand on Origen, limited the idea of Deity to the primal being ($\pi\rho\acute{\omega}\tau\eta$ $o\mathring{v}\sigma\acute{\iota}\alpha$), inoperative and really incapable of being revealed, *i.e.*, to the Father. It accordingly ignored the Logos and Christ in determining the conception of God. Further, it deduced, like the Neoplatonists, a second or third Ousia (being) from the first, and adorned the Logos created by the will of the Father with the loftiest, yet vacillating, predicates. It taught the incarnation of the Logos, and celebrated its result, yet once more in indefinite, in high-sounding and meaningless, Biblical phrases. Finally, it subordinated everything spiritual and moral to the thought of free-will and human independence. Any attempt at precision could not fail, on this domain, to be regarded as an innovation. Anything might establish itself as long as it did not claim to be exclusive.[1] There never did exist in the Church a general tendency to form new dogmas—the terms 'new' and 'dogma' are mutually exclusive; least of all did it exist in the East; there was either indifference to philosophical speculation, or a desire that it should have liberty, or it was regarded with suspicion. For the

---

[1] Gwatkin says very justly in Studies of Arianism (1882), p. 52: "In fact Christendom as a whole was neither Arian nor Nicene. If the East was not Nicene, neither was it Arian, but conservative: and if the West was not Arian, neither was it Nicene, but conservative also. Conservatism, however, had different meanings in East and West." In the East it was considered conservative to uphold the formulas of Origen strengthened against Sabellianism. On the doctrine of the Logos and Christ in Origen Bigg says very truly (The Christian Platonists of Alex., p. 182): "What struck later ages as the novelty and audacity of Origen's doctrine was in truth its archaism and conservatism."

rest, men reverenced in the cultus the mystery, *i.e.*, the complex of formulas whose origin had already become obscure. [1]

Nevertheless, there probably never was a time in the East when a reaction did not exist against the development of the

[1] When theology is engaged in forming dogmas, it has never, as is really self-evident, enjoyed the sympathy of any large section in the Church. There is nothing to support the contention that the Christian Church passed through a period—from Origen up to the Synod of Chalcedon or A.D. 431—during which there prevailed universally, or even to a great extent, a supreme interest in the abstract form of the contents of Religion, and an effort, with all the means at hand, to expound it as exactly as possible. The great mass of Bishops, monks, and laity, were then wholly occupied in satisfying themselves with what had been given. This was the highest demand of the Catholic religion itself, which presupposed the "Apostolic" as its foundation, which called everything else "heresy" (νεωτε-ρισμός), and as an institution for worship did not permit changes. Undoubtedly, the period from Origen, or say, from Athanasius up to the Ephesian Council, appears unique in the history of the Church. But that was an episode enacted in opposition to the great body of Christians, and the theological leaders themselves, in proportion to their piety, conceived their task to be compulsory, dangerous, and ensnaring them in guilt. To prove the former read Socrates' Church History (see my discussion in Herzog R. E., Vol. XIV. p. 408 ff.). This man was, on the one hand, orthodox at every point, on the other, an enthusiastic partisan of Ἑλληνικὴ παιδεία, full of veneration for the great Origen and his science, which he held was to be fostered continually. But the production of dogma by scientific theology was repugnant to him in every sense, *i.e.*, he accused and execrated dogmatic controversies as much in the interest of a dogma fixed once for all as in that of science. The Nicene Symbol belonged sufficiently to the past to be accepted by him as holy and apostolical; but beyond this every new formula seemed to Socrates pernicious, the controversies sometimes fights in the dark (nyktomachies), sometimes an outflow of deceptive sophistry and ambitious rivalry: σιωπῇ προσκυνείσθω τὸ ἄρρητον, *i.e.*, the mystery of the trinity. Had Socrates lived 100 years earlier, he would not have been a Nicene, but a Eusebian Christian. He therefore passes very liberal judgments on, and can make excuses for, the latest "heretics", *i.e.*, theologians who have been recently refuted by the Church. In this he stood by no means alone. Others, even at a later date, went still further. Compare Evagrius (H. E. I. 11) whose argument recalls Orig. c. Cels. III. 12.

Dogma has been created by the small number of theologians who sought for precise notions, in the endeavour to make clear the characteristic meaning of the Christian religion (Athanasius, Apollinaris, Cyril). That these notions, separated from their underlying thought, fell into the hands of ambitious ecclesiastical politicians, that the latter excited the fanaticism of the ignorant in their support, and that the final decision was often due to motives which had nothing to do with the case, is admittedly undeniable. But the theologians are not therefore to blame, who opposed in the Church a lazy contentment with mystery, or an unlimited pursuit of scientific speculation. Their effort to make clear the essence of Christianity, as they understood it, and at the same time to provide a λογικὴ λατρεία, was rather, next to the zealous order of monks with whom they were intimately

Logos doctrine towards complete separation of the Son from the Father.[1] It sprang not only from Modalists, but also from disciples of Origen, and it celebrated at Nicæa an amazingly rapid triumph. In opposition to a school which had ventured too far forward, and had embroidered the doctrines of Paul of Samosata with questionable tenets of Origen, the term Ὁμοούσιος, once banned at Antioch, was successfully elevated to the dignity of the watchword of faith.

The importance of this rapid triumph for the history of dogma cannot be rated too highly. But procured as it was by the Emperor, the victory would have been resultless, had it not been for the man whose biography coincides with the history of dogma of the fourth century—Athanasius.

The second division of the history of dogma, the account of its development, opens with Athanasius, but his conception of the faith also dominated following centuries. Augustine alone surpassed him in importance; for Augustine was an Origen and Athanasius in one—and he was still more.[2] However, the connected, the sole great feature in the epoch. They set themselves to stem the *vis inertiæ* of the pious, and with the highest success. When indolence in the end held the field, an important result had at any rate been attained. The period from Athanasius till about the middle of the fifth century was in many respects the brilliant epoch of theology in the Church. Not even the age of Scholasticism can compare with it. That the work of the theologians became faith according to the Church—a thing Origen never thought of—involved its strength and weakness alike. The fanaticism of the masses for dogmatic and philosophical catch-words— see the amusing narrative of Gregory of Nyssa, Opp. ed. Paris, 1638, T. III. p. 466—affords no information as to the measure of their comprehension; for the dogmatic catch-word is merely a fetish in wide circles.

[1] Origen's doctrine of subordination was felt in the West simply to constitute ditheism; see Vol. III., p. 85 ff.

[2] See Ranke, Weltgeschichte Vol. IV. 1, p. 307: "Augustine's system is, if I mistake not, the second that arose in the Church; it set aside the peculiar characteristics of the first, that of Origen, and then made good its position." We can only admit that it held its ground in a modified sense. In fact we see here a parallel of the highest significance in the history of the world. The Church has produced two fundamental systems, Origen's and Augustine's. But the history of theology in the East is the history of the setting aside of Origen's system, and the same is to be said of the Augustinian in the Catholic West. Only the procedure in the East was more thorough-going and open than in the West. In the former Origen was condemned, in the latter Augustine was constantly celebrated as the greatest *Doctor ecclesiæ*. In both cases, however, the rejection of the theological system caused the loss of a coherent and uniform Christian conception of the world.

future course of history has yet to decide whether Athanasius'
thought will not in the end live longer than the conceptions of
Augustine.   At the present day at least Augustine is given up
sooner than Athanasius in the Churches.

But it is really not permissible to compare these great men.
Augustine was a loftier genius, a man of inexhaustible wealth
of ideas and sentiment; Athanasius' greatness consisted in *reduction*, in the energy with which, from a multitude of divergent speculations claiming to rest on tradition, he gave exclusive
validity to those in which the strength of religion then lay.
Augustine opened up a new view of the highest blessings and
of human nature in the Church, he scattered a thousand germs
for the future; Athanasius, like every reformer, *reduced*, he first
secured a sphere of its own to the Christian religion on the
soil, already won, of Greek speculation, and he referred everything to the thought of redemption. Augustine invented a new
speculation, and the fascinating language of the deepest religious
feeling, beyond which changed times and manners seem unable to
go; Athanasius was unable to put forward either gifts of speculation or of eloquence on behalf of the thought in which he
lived.   His strength arose out of his conviction and his office.

Athanasius was a reformer, though not in the highest sense
of the word.   Behind and beside him existed a speculation
which led on a shoreless sea, and the ship was in danger of
losing its helm. [1]   He grasped the rudder.   We may compare
the situation with that in which Luther found himself when
confronting the mediæval Church and Scholasticism. It was not
for a word, or a formula, [2] that he was concerned, but a crucial

---

[1] It might seem as if we ought to grant the same credit to Arius of having
reduced and given fixity to vacillating and divergent speculations. But apart from
the contents and value of his doctrine, Arius was always disposed to make concessions, and as semi-opponents defended him, so he unhesitatingly accepted half
friends for complete allies. This very fact proves, however, that he would never
have succeeded in clearing up the position.

[2] Athanasius always made a sparing use of the catch-word ʽΟμοούσιος in his works.
The formula was not sacred to him, but only the cause which he apprehended
and established under cover of the formula. His conduct at the Synod of Alexandria
shows that he laid no stress on words. For his theology he needed no Creed. The
existence of one in the Nicene was valuable to him, but he was far from wor-

thought of his faith, the redemption and raising of humanity
to divine life through the God-man. It was only from the certainty that the divinity manifest in Jesus Christ possessed the
nature of the Deity (unity of being) and was for this reason
alone in a position to raise us to divine life, that faith was to
receive its strength, life its law, and theology its direction.
But Athanasius in thus giving the chief place to faith in the
God-man who alone delivers from death and sin, furnished practical piety, then almost exclusively to be found in monkish
asceticism, with its loftiest motive. To speak briefly, this combined as closely as possible the Ὁμοούσιος (consubstantial), which
guaranteed the deification of human nature, with monkish asceticism, and raised the latter from its still under-ground or, at least,
insecure realm to the public life of the Church. While fighting
against the phrase the created Logos (λόγος-κτίσμα) as heathen
and as a denial of the power of the Christian religion, he at the
same time as strenuously opposed worldly pursuits. He subordinated Scripture, tradition, and theology to the thought that
the Redeemer was God by nature, but he also strove to work
out the Christian life which received its motive from close
communion with the God-Christ,[1] and the prospect of being
invested both the divine nature. If we would do justice to
Athanasius, both these facts must be kept in mind. He became
the father of Catholic orthodoxy and the patron of ecclesiastical
monachism, and that he never would have been, had he not
also set the practical ideal of the piety of the time 'on the
candlestick'.[2]

There is here nothing new in the common sense of the word;
Athanasius had really on his side, the best part of the tradition
of the Church, to which he also appealed. Irenæus had already
given the central place to the object, nature, and accomplish-

shipping Symbols. While many of his friends sought support in the authority of
the formula, he sought and found it solely in the cause.

[1] Bigg (l. c., p. 188) has very rightly called attention to the high value attached
by orthodox Fathers after Athanasius' triumph to the Song of Songs in Origen's
exposition.

[2] See the Vita Anton. of Athanasius and Gregory of Naz., Orat. 21. It is noteworthy that Paul of Samosata and the Eusebians were worldly Christians. On the
other hand, the puritanism of Arius is, of course, famous.

ment of redemption in the categories: Logos, incarnation, God-
man, deification, and sons of God. Athanasius could refer to
a series of ideas in Origen and other Alexandrian catechists in
support of his distinctive treatment of the Logos doctrine. New
alone was *the fact*, the energy and exclusiveness of his view
and action at a time when everything threatened to undergo
dissolution.

Athanasius was no scientific theologian in the strict sense of
the term; from theology he descended to piety, and found the
exact word required. A man of authority, and attached to the
tradition of his school, he was not in a position to disentangle
the problem from the context in which the Apologists and
Origen had set it. He was a disciple of Origen, but his attitude
first to Marcellus, and then to the recent defenders of Ὁμοούσιος,
the Cappadocians, proves that he was as destitute of scientific
interest in a philosophical theory of life, as of the obstinacy of
theologians. He had to deal with that which transcended theology. He was the first to raise to honour in the Church in all
its force the old maxim that we must think of Christ as God
(ὡς περὶ θεοῦ), and therefore he paved the way for the new
principle, that we must think of God as in Christ (ὡς ἐν Χριστῷ).

In this he stood aloof from the rational thought of his time.
While admitting its premises, he added an element, which
neutral speculation was incapable of assimilating completely.
Nothing certainly was more unintelligible to it, than the assumption of an essential unity of the quiescent and the active Deity.
Athanasius fixed a gulf between the Logos of the philosophers,
and the Logos whose redeeming work he proclaimed. What
he said of the latter, declaring the mystery strongly and
simply, and by no means committing himself to new distinctions, could not but appear to the Greeks 'an offence and folly'.
But he did not shrink from reproach; with firm hand, though
in awkward lines, he marked off a sphere of its own for the
Christian faith. [1]

---

[1] The Cappadocians, theologians who reconciled the faith of Athanasius with
the current philosophy, and apprehended it abstractly, did not retain his teaching
pure and simple. This is especially shown by their doubtful contention that the
Christian idea of God was the true mean between the Jewish and Greek. They

And this man respected science and its free development.
We can observe this in his criticisms of Origen and the Alexandrian catechists. Undoubtedly it must have been important
to him to obtain reliable witnesses (testes veritatis) for his
doctrine, and the effort to do this explains frequently his practice of making the best of everything. But it does not entirely
explain his conduct. Christian faith was in his view exhausted
in faith in the God-man, the incarnation, and the redemption
which constituted a divine nature; for this reason he permitted
liberty in everything else. It would seem that he had no desire
to abolish Origen's distinction between the Christian science of
the perfect and the faith of the imperfect. He did not sit as
a judge of heretics on Origen's doubtful tenets and correct
them by the *regula fidei*, nor did he follow the course first
taken by Bishop Peter, one of his predecessors, in Alexandria. [1]
This is all the more remarkable, as for his own part he could
hardly find a single point in the Gnostic heterodoxies of Origen
with which he could agree.

Athanasius did not see beyond the horizon of his own time.
He attributed the highest efficacy to the mysteries of the cultus.
He regarded them as the personal legacy of Christ, immediate
emanations of his life as God-man, and as containing the means
of applying salvation. If in succeeding centuries the religious
interest attached itself more and more closely to ritual, that
did not imply any contradiction of the conception of the great
Alexandrian. He also laboured on behalf of the dogma which
was to obtain its practical and effective presentation in the

boldly characterised the plurality of Hypostases, *e.g.*, as a phase of truth preserved in
Greek polytheism. Athanasius, therefore, did not take unmixed pleasure in their
work. Cf. the λόγος κατηχητικός of Gregory of Nyssa (ch. 4, ed. Oehler): "Jewish
dogma is refuted by adoption of the Word, and by faith in the Spirit, but the
illusion of the Greeks (Ελληνίζοντες) in worshipping a multiplicity of Gods is
dispelled by the (doctrine of the) unity of nature which destroys the extravagant
opinion of a (divine) plurality. We must, in turn, retain the unity of being from
the Jewish type of faith, and only the distinction of personal (divine) existences
from the Greek; and by this means godless conceptions are met on the left and
right in correspondingly salutary ways. For the trinity is a corrective for those
who err as to unity, just as the doctrine of the unity (of God) is for those who
have made shipwreck by belief in plurality."

[1] See Vol. III., p. 99 ff.

monks on the one hand, and in ritual on the other, until the transitory was exalted into the permanent.

Athanasius' importance to posterity consisted in this, that he defined Christian faith exclusively as faith in redemption through the God-man who was identical in nature with God, and that thereby he restored to it fixed boundaries and specific contents.[1] *Eastern Christendom has been able to add nothing up to the present day. Even in theory it has hit on no change, merely overloading the idea of Athanasius; but the Western Church also preserved this faith as fundamental. Following on the theology of the Apologists and Origen, it was the efficient means of preventing the complete Hellenising and secularisation of Christianity.*

The history of dogma in the East after the Nicene Council reveals two interlacing lines of development. First, the idea of the God-man from the point of view of the redemption and elevation of the human race to divine life, in other words, the faith of Athanasius, was elaborated on all sides. In this the history of dogma, in the strict sense of the term, exhausted itself, for dogma was faith in the God-man. But with this a second development was closely connected, one which dealt

[1] In the cleverly written introduction to his description of "Western Church architecture" (Stuttgart, 1884), Dehio works out the idea that the classical period of ancient Christian architecture, the fourth century, was distinguished not by the multiplicity of ideas and forms of construction, but rather by the simplification or reduction of the forms. The Church, confronted by the number of models in ancient architecture, laid hold of one of them, the Basilica, and transmitted it alone to the Middle Ages. That, however, meant not a loss, but an advance. "The genius of Christianity contributed nothing new to the architectural creations of Rome and Alexandria. The great revolution it evoked lay in another direction. It consisted in the reduction of the multiplicity of styles to one dominant and sole form, not so much by a metamorphosis of artistic feeling, as by making religion once more the central motive of life. It thus assigned to the future architecture of the Middle Ages conditions analogous to those which governed the beginnings of Greek art; and thus the birth of Gothic art was possible at the climax of the Middle Ages—for the second time in history, a true organic style, like that of the Greek temple." This observation is extremely instructive to the historian of dogma. The thought of Athanasius corresponds in theology to the meaning of the Basilica in the history of architecture in the fourth century. Both were happy simplifications from a wealth of ideas—reductions which concealed full and varied contents.

with the relations of dogma and theology. Here also one man can be named: it was the science that Origen had cultivated which formed the centre of interest. However, since his days the problem had become more complicated, for theological principles that penetrated deeply had been received into faith itself, and the great development up to the Council of Chalcedon, and still later, consisted in the incorporation of theological results and formulas in the general belief of the Church. The question, accordingly, was not merely whether a freer and more independent theology, like Origen's in spirit and method, could receive an acknowledged position and latitude in the Church; whether, in general, the phases of criticism and idealistic spiritualism, included in Origen's science, were to be tolerated. It was a much harder problem that arose, though one that from its nature was always half concealed. If the theological dogma, at the moment when it became a creed of the Church, received the value of an apostolic doctrine which had never been wanting in the Church, how were the theologians to be regarded who had really created it, and how were the most venerated men of the past to be looked upon who had either been wholly ignorant of the dogma, or had incidentally, or avowedly, contradicted it? The conclusion is clear. The former were to receive special honour as witnesses to, but not as creators of, the truth. The latter it was necessary to abandon, however real and constructive their labours may once have been, or their works were to be coloured, corrected, or even amended by the insertion of glosses. But how long will a theology receive room to work on dogma, if the work is again and again to be disguised and how long will theologians be found to continue the dangerous business? "Theology is the most thankless of sciences. It crushes its builders with the very stones which they have helped to erect." The relation of theology to dogma recalls the myth of Chronos. But here it is not the father who swallows his children, it is the creature that devours its creators up to the third and fourth generations. As, moreover, the age from the fourth to the sixth centuries is the classic period of all dogma, so in no other period does it so clearly exhibit to the historian its characteristic of demanding living sacrifices.

10

Accordingly we observe two phenomena in these centuries. First, we have a continuous fight against the free theology of Origen, against the heterodoxies which it embraced, its critical phase, and its idealistic speculation. At any rate, more than two centuries elapsed before it was finally refused all right of citizenship in the Church, and at the same time Ἑλληνικὴ παιδεία (Greek culture) was deprived of any greater influence on dogma, than what the latter required for its correct exposition and justification. [1] But, in the second place, a traditionalism arose which looked distrustfully on theology taking any share in the work of the Church at the time, which substituted authority for science, while it either exalted ancient teachers to heaven as saints, or hurled them down to hell as heretics. It was due to the secret logic of events that such a tendency gained strength and finally triumphed; for if even the most capable and independent theologians were compelled to live under the delusion that what was new in their teaching could never be true, or that the true could not possibly be new, it necessarily followed that fewer and fewer would be found to undertake their dangerous work. [2] Accordingly, after dogma had developed to

[1] The prestige of Origen in the Church was still in the first half of the fifth century almost absolute and incomparable in wide circles. As we have above remarked, the Church history of Socrates is in this respect particularly instructive. The belittlers and enemies of this man were vain and ambitious obscurantists, hero-levelling fellows; against them—Methodius, Eustathius, Apollinaris, and Theophilus—he appealed to the testimony of Athanasius on behalf of Origen's orthodoxy (VI. 13). Even the view that Origen's works and utterances required to be sifted, appeared to him folly (VI. 17). He defended everything that the master wrote. It was incomprehensible to him how the Arians could study and value Origen, without becoming orthodox (VII. 6)—to the Arians the opposite was incomprehensible—and he declares with absolute conviction that Porphyry and Julian would not have written what they did if they had read the great teacher (III. 23). Further, Origen was once more quoted in the Monophysite controversies. Apart from special uses of it, his name represented a great cause, namely, no less than the right of science, Ἑλληνικὴ παιδεία, in the Church, a right contested by traditionalism in conjunction with the monks.

[2] It was pointed out above, p. 138, note 1, that even orthodox theological leaders were not comfortable in their dogmatic work, so that the position from the middle of the sixth century, the sovereign rule of traditionalism, was really the goal desired from the beginning. The works of all prominent theologians testify to this. Some deplored the fact that the mystery could not be worshipped in silence, that they were compelled to speak; and the rest say explicitly, that the

a certain extent, held a certain number of conceptions capable
of employing the intelligence, and was adapted to scholastic
treatment, it became so sensitive that it ceased to tolerate a
theology that would carry it further, even under all possible
safe-guards. The theology that did independent work, that at
no time professed to produce dogma, and therefore really had
not existed, now came actually to an end. The date coincides
with that at which Origen was condemned (the sixth century).
The history of this process ran its course very gradually. On
the other hand, there was no want of important actions in the
history of the ejection of Origen's doctrine. We have here to
mention the 'Origenist controversies', though we must not limit
them, as has been customary, to a few decades. Along with
them the opposition to the school of Antioch and its condemnation come before us. But we must not look at the victory of
the creed of the Church over theological liberties merely from
the point of view of a decline of science in the Church. We
have rather to consider what a more liberal speculative and
critical science had to offer at the time to the Church. In view
of the way in which the pursuit of theology and the exposition
of the faith were intertwined, there were gifts which the Church
had to decline in order to maintain its tradition, *i.e.*, the standard left to it of its Christianity. But the heterodoxies of the
theologians presented neither an incentive to nor the means for a
revision of the whole doctrine in its possession. Besides, the
entire process of expelling the freer theology was carried out
without crises worth mentioning, as if spontaneously. That is
the strongest evidence of the weakness of the speculations and
critical views which sought to hold their ground alongside the
doctrine of the Church. The condition of affairs at the close,
when we have (1) dogma (2) a theology of scholastic mysticism,
and (3) antiquarian and formal science not confused with religion,

truth of their propositions lay in their negations alone. Hilary expresses himself perhaps most strongly (De trinit. II. 2): " Compellimur hæreticorum et blasphemantium
vitiis illicita agere, ardua scandere, ineffabilia eloqui, inconcessa præsumere. Et cum
sola fide explorari, quæ præcepta sunt, oporteret, adorare scilicet patrem et venerari
cum eo filium, sancto spiritu abundare, cogimur sermonis nostri humilitatem ad ea,
quæ inenarrabilia sunt extendere et in vitium vitio coarctamur alieno, ut, quæ
contineri religione mentium oportuisset, nunc in periculum humani eloquii proferantur."

was in many respects an improvement, and the value of the product received its strongest attestation in the duration of the system. Leaving out of account a few oscillations, that had been actually attained, which the 'conservatives', *i.e.*, the great majority in all phases of violent dogmatic conflicts, had longed for, and had therefore always contemplated. A mysterious dogma had been arrived at, one elevated above the schools, which gave theologians liberty to be antiquarians, philologists, or philosophers; for what independent work was left in the pursuit of dogma was subject to the jurisdiction of these specialists, so far as it did not come under the review of the experts in mysteries and liturgies. But the great loss consisted in the fact that men no longer possessed a theological system complete in itself. Origen's was the only one that the Greek Church had produced. After its rejection there existed, besides dogma, a vast sum of incongruous fragments, bound artificially together by quotations from Scripture and tradition and from Aristotelian scholasticism. The great dogmatic work of John of Damascus only appears to be a logically connected system; it is in reality far from that.

As regards the periods, the dividing lines are formed by the Œcumenical Synods, namely, the so-called 2nd, then the 4th, 5th, 6th and 7th. But we can also use the names of Theodosius I., Pope Leo I., Justinian, and Pope Agatho. The unification of the Churches was rendered possible by the fact that they obtained a *forum publicum* (a public tribunal) in the universal Synods.[1] For the Creeds of the provincial Churches, which agreed only in the main points, and not even in all these, the Councils substituted a dogmatic confession whose proclamation, enactment, and extension excited the most violent conflicts. At the same time the confederation of the Churches

[1] But for Constantine the Nicene Council would not have been carried through, and but for the Emperor's uniform creeds would not been arrived at. They were Athanasius' best coadjutors. Nay, even the Emperors hostile to him helped him; for they used every effort to unite the Church on the basis of a fixed confession. It is therefore absurd to abuse the State Church, and yet to regard the establishment of the orthodox creed as a gain.

became a reality through the imperial policy, which sought to come into touch with the strongest dogmatic currents, though not infrequently it supported trivialities. The last traces of independence possessed by individual communities were destroyed; along with unity, uniformity in doctrine, discipline, and worship was almost re-established, and the constitution of the Church, even in the higher ranks, was gradually so adapted to that of the empire that the hierarchical organisation and administration of the Church corresponded to the order of the State. But this re-arrangement required, in part, to be carried out by force (τυραννίς of the Emperors and a few great Bishops), and speaking strictly, was a reality for only a few decades. It excited counter-movements; in opposition to it nationalistic feeling first really gained strength, especially in the East, and the great schisms of the national Churches there were also a consequence of the absolutist attempts at unification. [1] In the West the State collapsed under the storms of the tribal migration at the moment when, in the East, the dismemberment of the imperial Church into national Churches began. The attempts of the East Roman

---

[1] See Hatch, The Councils and the Unity of the Church, in his Social Constitution of the Christian Churches, p. 172 ff.; he has given an excellent account of the share of the State in this unity and its limitations; compare also my Analekten, p. 253 ff. In the process by which Christendom was united externally and ecclesiastically, we can distinguish in the East three, and in the West four, epochs. The first three were common to the Churches of both East and West. The first was characterised by the recognition of the apostolic rule of faith in opposition to the erroneous creeds of heretical associations, after a common ideal and a common hope had united Christians up to the middle of the second century. The κανὼν τῆς πίστεως became the basis of ἀδελφότης. The second epoch, in which organisation became already of supreme importance, was represented in the theory of the episcopal office, and in the creation of the metropolitan constitution. While this was struggling to establish itself amid violent crises, the State of Constantine brought about the third epoch, in which the Church, by becoming completely political, was united, and thus arrived at an external and uniform unity, so that in it the essential nature of the Empire was continued. The Church became the most solid organisation in the Empire, because it rested on the imperial order of the ancient kingdom. It got no further than this organisation in the East; indeed, several great provincial Churches soon separated from it; for the creation of Constantine concealed germs of dissolution; see Zahn, Konstantin d. Gr. 1876, p. 31 f. In the West, on the contrary, the Roman Bishop began to engage in those enterprises which, favoured by circumstances, succeeded in the course of centuries in substituting a new and distinctively ecclesiastical unity for that created by the state.

emperors to recover the Western half of the realm, or at least parts of it, more than once thwarted the oriental policy imperatively required of them, and are also, from the complications to which they led, of great importance for the history of dogma. While the Emperors of Byzantium were involved in a double task, which constituted an insoluble dilemma, the Roman Bishops served themselves heirs to the West Roman kingdom. In the revolution in political and social affairs, Christians and Latins were compelled to postpone their separate interests and to attach themselves closely to the most powerful defender of the old institutions. The Germans, who apparently broke up the Empire, brought about the internal unity of all that was Catholic and Latin, and strengthened the position of ecclesiastical Rome. The East, on the contrary, which had been less endangered actually did break up. In the Western Catholic Church the ancient Roman Empire was preserved after a fashion with its order and culture. This Church had no longer beside it a state similar in character and closely related to itself and thus its Bishop could train the new peoples to his service, and soon undertook an independent policy against the Western schemes of the East Roman Emperors. The internal separation between East and West was complete, when neither understood the language of the other. Yet the West still took an active interest in the controversy of the 'Three Chapters', and at the same time obtained, in the translation of the Antiochene and Persian *Instituta regularia divinæ legis*, and in the great works translated at the instigation of Cassiodorus, valuable gifts from the East which stand comparison with those made by Hilary, Ambrose, Rufinus, and Jerome. Even in the seventh century Rome and the East were for a time engaged in a lively correspondence. But the rule of Byzantium over Rome was felt to be that of the foreigner, and conversely the Roman spirit was alien to the Orientals. Their relations were forced. *Augustine hardly left a trace in the Eastern Church*. That was its greatest calamity. Of course it was less disposed by its past to understand him than the Western Church, and it was at no time really inclined to accept instruction from its rival.

The first period of the History of Dogma closes with the

Synods of Constantinople (381—383). At them faith in the complete divinity of the Redeemer was finally settled as the creed of the Catholic Church, and his complete humanity was also expressly acknowledged. Next to Athanasius the chief part in the decision was taken by the Cappadocians on the one hand, and by the Roman Bishop and Ambrose on the other. It would not have been arrived at, however, so early, if it had not been carried through in Constantinople by a powerful ruler who came from the West. The theologians, so far as any took part in it, were men who were equipped with the full culture of the period, and were also devoted to the ideals of monastic piety. The Cappadocians were still relatively independent theologians, worthy disciples and admirers of Origen, using new forms to make the faith of Athanasius intelligible to contemporary thought, and thus establishing them, though with modifications, on a secure basis. Beside them stood Apollinaris of Laodicea, a man who anticipated the problems of the future, who was their equal in scholarship, and surpassed them in many respects in theology. But Arianism revealed its weakness by nothing more than its rapid decline after it ceased to possess the imperial favour. The impression made by it on the German nations, and its prolonged popularity with them, must be described as an 'accident' in history. Catholicism was first made a reality by Theodosius I.—'the idea of a communion which should unite East and West in the same confession, beyond which no other form of confession was recognised.' But Ranke remarks rightly [1] that the Christian idea (of Nicene orthodoxy) gained the upper hand over Hellenistic and heretical systems, not from the doctrine alone, but from the course of events. The victory of the Nicene Council was also decided at the Tigris by the defeat of Julian, and at Adrianople by the death of Valens. In this first period the Christian Church was still in constant touch with Hellenism, and adopted from it whatever it could use. But the history of dogma can only give a very meagre view of these relations. Its boundaries gradually become altogether more restricted. In the first three centuries it can hardly be separated

---

[1] Weltgeschichte IV. 1, p. 305 f.

from the universal history of the Church; in those following the general life of the Church is less and less clearly reflected in it. He who desires to become acquainted with that life, must study the monachism, worship, ethics, and especially the theological science of the age. There is nothing in the history of dogma to require us to portray a figure like that of Synesius, and, if we define our task strictly, we can make little use of the rich epistolary literature of the time.

The second period extends to the Council of Chalcedon (451). Its first and longer half covers the time in which the imperial Church, resting on the Nicene basis and directed by emperor, priest, and monk, established itself. But after a time of comparative peace, [1] the question again emerged as to the relation of the divine and human in the person of the Redeemer. The opposition between the school of Antioch and the new Alexandrian theology, which felt itself to be the sole teaching of the Church, culminated in this question, and the Alexandrian Bishop succeeded in making it the centre of ecclesiastical interest. The theologians of the school of Antioch still wrought in freedom; nay, even among their opponents there were to be found men who defined the faith by its aim, and were not overawed by traditionalism. Yet traditionalism grew more and more powerful. Under the leadership of Epiphanius the great reaction against Origen began, [2] and not only the Alexandrian Bishop, but the greatest scholar of the age took part in

---

[1] On these decades, which are to be described as in many respects the most prosperous period of the Byzantine Church, see Herzog R. E., Vol. XIV., p. 403 ff. Heathenism was then first completely overthrown, and the heretics, even finally the Novatians, were hard pressed. The regime of Chrysostom seems to have been especially signalised by the suppression of heretics in the patriarchate of Constantinople; see the account of Socrates. We know of other Bishops who were active in extirpating heresy in the first half of the fifth century, a work in which Theodoret took part. The reigns of Gratian and Theodosius, on the one hand, the indefatigable labours of Epiphanius on the other, laid the foundation. Their programme was carried out from the end of the fourth century. But from about the middle of the fifth century, when the last traces of the ancient Gnostics, Novatians and Manichæans were substantially removed, great schisms began to take place on the basis of the Chalcedonian decree.

[2] See before this Demetrius, Peter, Methodius, Eustathius, Marcellus, and Apollinaris.

it. [1] To this was added another fact. The constitution of the Patriarchate began to reveal its effect in threatening the unity of the Church. The Cappadocian Churches of Asia Minor receded into the background simply because they possessed no patriarch of their own, dogmatics began to constitute an instrument of provincial ecclesiastical policy, and the dogmatic formula to be a mark of the diocese and nationality. In proportion as this took place, the state was compelled to intervene. Dogmatic questions became vital to it, and the appointment in the capital to the Patriarchate, which it had fostered, was now a political problem of the first rank; for the occupant of the chair stood at the head of the spiritual affairs of the empire. The great controversy was not settled at the two Synods of Ephesus (431, 449), but it was, ostensibly, at the Synod of Chalcedon (451) by means of a long formula. This formula was proposed and dictated by the West in the person of Bishop Leo and was approved by the Emperor; it was regarded in the West as the simple and unchanged creed of the Fathers, in the East as a compromise which was felt by some not to be sufficiently orthodox, and by others to require interpretation. Meanwhile the East hardly possessed as yet the rudiments of a theology capable of interpreting it. Therefore the formula of Chalcedon has not unjustifiably been called a 'national misfortune' for the Byzantine Empire. But even as regards the Church its advantages no more than balanced its disadvantages. During this period the monks obtained the mastery over the Church. Although their relations with the hierarchy were not infrequently strained, they added very greatly to its strength. The clergy would have been completely eclipsed in the world and the state, if they had not obtained a new support from the 'religiosi' and 'religiosity'. But while monachism became an important element in the Church, the prestige of the state declined in the minds of men; nothing was left to the Emperors but to adopt certain monkish fashions for themselves, and along with the state the life of social morality was depreciated in favour of 'religiosity' and a magical cultus. For monachism merely pro-

---

[1] "Babylon is fallen, fallen,"—with these words of triumph did Jerome accompany the overthrow of Chrysostom in the Origenist controversy (Ep. 88).

motes itself and next to that a religion of idol-worship; it quits the field where a vigorous morality arises. On the other hand, however, the State was delivered at the close of this period from its most powerful opponent, the Bishop of Alexandria, though at much too high a cost.

The third period extends up to the fifth Œcumenical Council (Constantinople A.D. 553). The disadvantages of the Chalcedonian formula made themselves felt in the first half of this century. Great ecclesiastical provinces were in revolt, and threatened to secede from the membership of the universal Church. Greek piety everywhere showed itself to have been unsettled by the decree of Chalcedon. Theology could not follow it; nay, it appeared to be stifled by the decision, while in Monophysitism life and movement prevailed. The perplexed Emperors were at their wits' end, and tried provisionally to recall, or at any rate to tone down, the formula, but in doing so they prejudiced the union with the West. This was changed under Justin I., but above all under Justinian I. As the reign of the latter was signalised politically by the restoration of the Byzantine supremacy, and the codification of its laws, it was ecclesiastically distinguished by the restoration and establishment of the constitution and dogmatics of the Church. The creed of Rome was recognised so far as its wording was concerned, but Rome itself was humbled; the Chalcedonian formula remained in force, but it was interpreted in terms of Cyril's teaching, and its future position was assured by the condemnation of the writings of the Antiochene schools on the one hand, and of Origen on the other. Thus was the theology of the past judged: 'solitudinem faciunt, pacem appellant'. The Justinian Church condemned the glorious Fathers, and the fifth Œcumenical Council blotted out the freer theological science. However, this measure was only possible because an orthodox Church theology had developed in the first half of the sixth century. [1] It presupposed the Chalcedonian formula, which had become more venerable by age, and explained it by means of the philosophy of Aristotle, which had then come once more

[1] See Loofs, Leontius von Byzanz in the "Texten und Unters. z. alt-christl. Literaturgesch.," Vol. III., parts 1 and 2, p. 37 ff., 303 ff.

to the front, in order to reconcile it with the spirit of Cyril's theology, and to make it in some measure comprehensible. *Here we have the rise of ecclesiastical scholasticism* which now took its place beside the mystical Neo-platonic theology that had been most comprehensively stated by the Pseudo-areopagite, and which corrected and defined it, uniting with and balancing it. The effect of this development was extremely significant. Men now began for the first time to feel themselves at home on the ground of the Chalcedonian formula; piety also was reconciled to it. Productive dogmatic work ceased entirely; its place was taken by the mystical theology of scholasticism based on the inheritance from antiquity and the enumeration of authorities. Justinian in reality closed not only the school of Athens, but also that of Origen, the schools, *i.e.*, of productive theological science and criticism.[1] Henceforth theology only existed as a servant to the tradition of Justinian and Chalcedon. It was served in turn by the dialectic of Aristotle on the one hand, and the Neo-platonic mysticism of the Areopagite on the other. It did important work in the way of elaboration and adaptation; we are not warranted in passing a sweeping verdict of stultification and sleep;[2] but it made no further change in the creed of the Church and was bound hand and foot.[3]

---

[1] The closing of the school of Athens has been disputed. It was certainly not a great, formal action; see Krummacher, Gesch. d. Byzant. Litt., p. 4.

[2] See the works of Gass and Gelzer, especially the latter's interesting lecture: "Die politische und kirchliche Stellung von Byzanz."

[3] Noteworthy, but not surprising, is the parallel capable of being drawn between the history of theology and that of (heathen) philosophy during the whole period from Origen to Justinian. The history of Greek philosophy finds its limits in the middle of the fifth century, and again in the age of Justinian; the same is true of the science of the Church. In the general history of science Plato comes to be supplanted by Aristotle from the close of the fifth century; in dogmatics the influence of the Stagirite makes itself felt to an increased extent from the same date. Justinian's epoch-making measures, the codification of the law, the closing of the school of Athens, and the restoration of the Byzantine Church and Empire, point to an inner connection. This has not escaped Ranke. On account of the importance of the matter I give here his excellent discussion (Vol. IV. 2, p. 20 ff.): "Justinian closed the school of Athens ... An event of importance for the whole continued development of the human race; any further development in a direct line on the basis laid in classical antiquity was rendered impossible to the Greek

As regards the history of dogma the fourth period possesses
no real independence. The dogmatic activity which characterised it was exclusively political; but since it created a new
formula, we may here assume a special period. It ends with

spirit, while to Roman genius such an advance was left open and was only now
rendered truly possible for after ages by means of the law-books. The philosophical
spirit perished in the contentions of religious parties; the legal found a mode of
expression which, as it were, concentrated it. The close of Greek philosophy recalls
its beginning; nearly a thousand years had elapsed during which the greatest
transformations in the history of the world had taken place. May I be permitted to
add a general reflection, as to which I merely desire that it may not be rejected
by the general feeling of scholars.

The Christian religion had risen upon earth in the conflict of religious opinions
waged by nations, and had then in opposition to these developed into a Church.
Christian theology which set itself to appropriate the mysterious and to come to
terms with the intellect had grown up in constant contact, sometimes of a friendly,
more often of a hostile kind, with Greek philosophy. That was the business of
those centuries. Then appeared the great Christian theologians from Origen onwards; as we said in passing, they passed through, without exception, Greek or
closely related Latin schools, and framed their doctrines accordingly. Greek philosophy had produced nothing comparable to them; it had, as regards public life,
been thrust into the background and now it had perished. But it is striking that
the great Christian theologians also came to an end. Never again do we find in
later times men like Athanasius, the Gregories of Cappadocia, Chrysostom, Ambrose and Augustine. I mean that along with Greek philosophy the original development of Christian theology also came to a stand-still. The energy of the Church
doctors, or the importance of the Church assemblies in these centuries cannot be
paralleled by analogous phenomena belonging to later times. Different as they are
in themselves we find a certain resemblance in the state of Roman law and of
Christian theology. The old Roman jurisprudence now appeared as universally
valid law in a redaction which while historical was yet swayed by the conditions
of the day. At the same time, limits were set by the triumph of orthodoxy, especially of the dogmas declared in the Chalcedonian resolutions, to all the internal
divisions of theology in which the divergent opinions were also defended with
ability and thoroughness ... Justinian who reinstated orthodoxy, and gave the force
of law to juridical conceptions, takes a high place in the rivalry of the centuries.
Yet, while he raised his government to such a pinnacle of authority, he felt the
ground shake momentarily under his feet." Greek science and the monkish view
of the world, leagued as they were, dominated the spiritual life of the Church
before as well as after the Justinian age; they were at bottom indeed far from
being opposed, but possessed a common root. But how differently it was possible
to combine them, what variations they were capable of! If we compare, e.g., Gregory of Nyssa with John of Damascus it is easy to see that the former still really
thinks independently, while the latter confines himself to editing what is given.
It is above all clear that the critical elements of theology had been lost. They
only held their ground in the vagaries of mystical speculation; in all ages they
are most readily tolerated there.

the sixth Œcumenical Council (A.D. 680). 'Justinian's policy of conquest was in the highest degree unstable, and went far beyond the resources of the Empire'. Whether his dogmatic policy was correct, which maintained union with the West at the cost of losing a large section of the Oriental Churches, is a question which may be debated. But whether an open and consistently monophysite policy was then still possible in Constantinople is very doubtful. Egypt, Syria, and Armenia were lost, not only to the state, but also to Greek language and culture. In order to keep them, or win them back from the Persians and Arabians, an energetic Emperor resolved to publish a monophysite rallying cry without prejudicing the wording of the Chalcedonian Creed. Monothelitism on the basis of the doctrine of the two natures is in itself no artificial creation; it is founded on the old consideration rising out of the doctrine of redemption; but at that time it had its origin in policy. Yet this still-born child of politics set the Eastern Church in an uproar for more than two generations. To prevent the loss not only of the East but of Italy also, the Emperor required the help of the Roman Bishop. Justinian's success in curbing the latter's authority had only continued for a little under his successors. The pontificate of Gregory I. still exerted an influence, and, at the sixth Council, Agatho, repairing the fault of one of his predecessors, dictated the formula, as Leo had done at Chalcedon. This bore the impress of the West, and did not correspond perfectly to the eastern conception. It further became manifest at the Council that, when it was a question of defining dogma, theology had been completely transformed into a rehearsal of authorities. Next to the older synodal decisions, the decisive precedent was formed by the immense, and frequently forged, collection of the *dicta patrum*.

After the sixth Council, orthodoxy and Monophysitism were definitively separated, though attempts were not wanting to harmonise them in the following centuries, in keeping with the monophysite tendencies, never wholly destroyed, of eastern orthodoxy. The mystery was firmly established, and obtained further definition; for the doctrine taught by John of Damascus of the enhypostasis of the human nature in the Logos)

had been accepted, even in the age of Justinian, to be
the correct interpretation of the doctrine of the two natures.
The movement of thought in the Church passed accordingly to
a new sphere; or, more correctly, the old absorbing interest of
the Church in the mysteries of the cultus [1] now came to light
undisguised, because the pursuit of theology, converted as it
was into scholasticism, had become the business of scholars and
experts in the mysteries, and it was only temporarily that a
controversy springing out of it agitated the Church. Dogma,
designed by the Nicene and Chalcedonian Creeds to be looked
at and treated formally, henceforth revealed this its character
thoroughly. The philosophy appropriate to it was found, or
invented—that compound of Neoplatonism and Aristotelianism,
with which no one could dispense who desired to unfold or
comment on dogma orthodoxly. [2] He who passed over the
philosophy of the Church stood in danger of becoming a heretic. [3]

---

[1] It is said of Polycarp in his Vita per Pionium (sæc. IV.): ἑρμηνεῦσαί τε
ἱκανὸς μυστήρια, ἃ τοῖς πολλοῖς ἦν ἀπόκρυφα, οὕτω φανερῶς αὐτὰ ἐξετίθετο, ὥστε
τοὺς ἀκούοντας μαρτυρεῖν, ὅτι οὐ μόνον ἀκούουσιν ἀλλὰ καὶ ὁρῶσιν αὐτά. That was
accordingly the supreme thing; to be able also to see the mystery, the Christian
possession of salvation.

[2] The fight between Platonism and Aristotelianism was accordingly acute among
theologians in the following centuries; they often indeed made heretics of one
another. Up till now we only know these disputes in part; they are important for
the later conflicts in the West, but they do not belong to the history of dogma

[3] Even to-day simple-minded Catholic historians of dogma exist who frankly
admit that he becomes necessarily a heretic who does not, e.g., use the conceptions
"nature" and "person" correctly; and they even derive heresy from this starting-
point. Thus Bertram (Theodoreti, Ep. Cyrensis, doctrina christologica, 1883) writes
of Theodore of Mopsuestia: "Manifesto declarat, simile vel idem esse perfectam
naturam et perfectam personam... Naturæ vox designat, quid sit aliqua res, vel
essentiam vel quidditatem; hypostasis vero modum metaphysicum existendi monstrat.
Ex quo patet, ad notionem perfectæ naturæ modum illum perfectum existendi non
requiri. Hac in re erravit Mopsuestenus, et hæresis perniciosa ex hoc errore nata
est. What a quid pro quo! The ignorance of the terminology, which was yet first
created ad hoc, in order to escape Scylla and Charybdis, is held to be the real
ground of the origin of the heresy. Such a view of things, which is as old as
scholasticism, undoubtedly needed mysticism as its counterpoise, in order not to
perish wholly from the religious sphere. Atzberger (Die Logoslehre d. h. Athan.,
1880) has expressed himself still more unsophisticatedly, and therefore more
instructively, on the relation of philosophy and dogma (p. 8, 29). But see also
Hagemann (Röm. Kirche, p. 361): "The Patripassians arrived at their doctrines of

But dogmatics, undoubtedly the foundation, did not dominate the Church as a living power. The conception of the natures of Christ found its continuation in that of the sacraments and sacramental things by which men became participators in Christ. The perceived (αἰσθητόν) thereby obtained side by side with the conceived (νοητόν) an ever loftier, and independent significance. Symbolism was more and more expunged; the mystery became more and more sensuous. But, in proportion as the latter was made operative in the cultus, the cultus itself was regarded, in all its setting and performance, in the light of the divino-human.[1] All its sensuous side, which was presented for his benefit to the worshipper, was regarded as deified and as promoting deification. Now in so far as the believer derived his life entirely from this cultus, a ritual system, to which the character of the divino-human attached, took the place of the God-man, Christ. Piety threatened to be submerged in a contemplation of wonders, the spiritual in the sensuous, and theology, in so far as not identified with scholasticism and polemics, in a science of mysteries.[3] From this point of view we can understand the worship of images and the reaction of icono-

God, his attributes, his creation, and incarnation, because they took their stand on Stoic logic and with it cherished the most extreme nominalism, and because they absolutely rejected the objective existence of ideas."

[1] For the history of the development of the Greek liturgy after the fourth century, Swainson's The Greek Liturgies, chiefly from original authorities (London 1884), is the standard work. For the doctrine of the mysteries cf. Steitz' Abhandlungen in the Lehrbb. f. deutsche Theol. 1864 ff.

[2] If we collect the fourth-century evidence of crude sensuous superstition intimately combined with Christian piety, we might believe that it could go no further. And yet it did go further from century to century, as anyone can easily convince himself by reading the tales of saints and relics, among which those of the oriental monophysites are the worst. But apart from this increase, we have to call attention to the fact that this barbarous superstition ascended into higher and more influential circles and was systematically cultivated by the monks, while the corrective of a more rational theology grew ever weaker. Theology became more defenceless, because it had to adapt itself to sacred ceremony. The worst gift bequeathed by moribund antiquity to the Church was the ritual of magic and the monstrous number of great and little aids in need and means of atonement. It is not the case that this state of matters was produced by the inrush of barbarian peoples; on the contrary, the decomposition of ancient culture and religion takes the first place in the process, and even the Neo-platonic philosophers are not free from blame. In view of this circumstance it is natural to conclude that the reforma-

clasm which opened the fifth period. But this explanation is
not complete; another factor coöperated. This was the relation
of Church and State which was also involved in the controversy
about images. There always were discords between them; but
these became more and more acute when the priesthood fell
completely under the sway of the monks. Even from the fifth
century the practice had begun of transferring monks to episcopal chairs, and it had almost become the rule in the following
centuries. But the monks both strove zealously to make the
Church independent and claimed sovereignty among the people,
and as a rule, though interested on behalf of the *nations*, they
also cherished a strong hostility to the *State :* in other words
they endangered the settlement of Church and State established
in the fifth and sixth centuries. Their most powerful instrument
was the sensuous cultus which had captivated the people, but
which undoubtedly, barbarous and mechanical as it was with
all its appliances and amulets, was yet connected with the ideal
forces still to be credited to the age, with science, art, and
especially piety. Here we have the miserable dilemma of the
period, and of the Church; the worship of images was barbarous,
but iconoclasm threatened to introduce an increased degree of barbarism. For the 'enlightened' (Aufklärung) were at the disposal of
an iron military despotism, and despised science, art, and religion.

tion of Athanasius bore little fruit, that it only checked for a time the polytheistic
under-current, and, in a word, that the Church could not have got into a worse
state than, in spite of Athanasius, it did, as regards the worship of Mary, angels,
saints, martyrs, images and relics, and the trickery practised with amulets. But even
if we were to go further and suggest that the later development of dogma itself, as
e.g., in the worship of Mary and images, directly promoted religious materialism,
yet we cannot rate too highly the salutary importance of this dogma. For it kept
the worship of saints, images and the rest at the stage of a christianity of the
second order, invested with doubtful authority, and it prevented the monks from
cutting themselves wholly adrift from the *religio publica*. Finally, it is to be
pointed out that superstition has brought with it at all times ideas and conceptions
extremely questionable from the point of view of dogmatics, ideas which seem to be
affected by no amount of censure. Overbeck (Gött. Gel.- Auz. 1883, no. 28, p. 870)
has rightly described it as a phenomenon requiring explanation that the gnat-
straining centuries which followed Nicæa, could have swallowed such camels as,
e.g., delighted the readers of the Acts of Thomas (even in the Catholic edition) or
of the numerous Apocalypses (see the edition of the Apoc. Apocal. by Tischendorf
and James, Apocrypha anecdota, 1893).

The Church of Byzantium was at that time engaged in a life
and death struggle. Its existence was really at stake, and with
it the existence of the old form of society and culture, in
opposition to forces which as yet had no positive policy, but
at first merely ruled by brute force. The priestly caste was
arrayed against the military, the hosts of shaven monks against
the standing army, which from the fourth century had played
a great rôle, but now sought to be master in the state. These
fearful fights ended in the restoration of the *status quo ante*,
in so far as dogma and cultus were concerned, and the old
order seemed all the more sacred after the attacks that had
been made upon it. But on the political side, the state supported by the army carried off the victory—and this was not
without consequences for the system and life of the Church.
The monks were given a free hand in dogma, but their activity
as ecclesiastical politicians was checked. The Emperor remained
chief priest, in spite of some patriarchs who, until after the
eleventh century, attempted to maintain an independent and
equal position side by side with him. With the support of his
army he resisted them. The independence of the Church was
gone, in so far as it sought to rise above the level of an institution devoted to ritual and worship. Its activity was completely restricted to the mysteries and the preparation for death.
It became an institution of the state, impressing it only by the
unchangeableness of its doctrine and ceremonies. To the new
peoples to whom this Church came, the Slavs, it was far more
than to the Greeks an unchangeable, heavenly creation. A
thousand years have passed away since the Slavs were hellenised; and they have not yet ventured, like the Germans, to think
and feel freely and at their ease in the Church, although they
recognise in it a main defence of their national characteristics
against the West. From the West these 'Greek Slavs' were
spiritually separated, after Augustine's ideas were admitted
there. The external cleavage, though only complete in the
eleventh century, began immediately after the image controversy.
The states in the territory of the Greek Church still really stand
under a military dictatorship: where this has fallen, as in the
kingdom of Greece, a final stage has not yet been reached.

States like the former support an ecclesiastical department, but
no Church.

The path into which Athanasius led the Church has not been
abandoned; but the other forces of life completely restricted it.
Orthodox dogma corresponds on the whole to the conception of
Athanasius; but the balance which he held between the religious
creed and the cultus has been disturbed to the disadvantage of the
former. The creed still shows life when it is called in question,
or when the nation it serves requires a flag. In other cases it
lives in the science of scholastic mysticism, which has already
become by degrees stereotyped and sacred, and in its presentation
in public worship. Theology also is bound to the latter; it has
thus received a standard of which Athanasius knew nothing. [1]

Our sources are the works of the Church Fathers and the
Acts of Councils (Mansi). We still want a history of Greek
ecclesiastical literature after Eusebius, capable of satisfying the
most reasonable demands. Of more recent works on the subject that of Fessler is the best (Instit. Patrologiæ, 1850—52),
Alzog's is the most familiar, and Nirschl's the newest.

---

[1] It is very characteristic as regards this, that while Cyril of Jerusalem described
the Christian religion as μάθημα τῶν δογμάτων καὶ πράξεις ἀγαθαί, Photius defined
it as μάθησις καὶ μυσταγωγία. From the fourth century interest was more and more
transferred from the regulation of the whole life by religion, to its external consecration through the mysteries. The distinctions are indeed only gradual, but the
descent was very significant. The Greek Church ultimately gave up the regulation
of moral social life, and therewith renounced the power to determine private
morality so far as the latter was not dominated by fear of death. The ultimate
reason of this is to be sought in the order of the monks and the constitution of
the Græco-Slavic states.

CHAPTER II.

THE FUNDAMENTAL CONCEPTION OF SALVATION AND GENERAL OUTLINE OF THE DOCTRINAL SYSTEM.

I. THE dogmatic conflicts in the East from the fourth up to the seventh century have this in common, that they centred almost entirely in Christology in the narrower sense, as well as in the incarnation of the Deity. Since men of all parties were meanwhile conscious that they were contending for the essence of Christianity, it follows that the conception of the salvation offered in the Christian religion is to be deduced from the formulas over which they fought, and which then made good their ground. This conclusion is, however, made further certain from the fact that the oriental Church took no interest in dogma, apart from those formulas, at least in the time of these conflicts. [1] Anything else, therefore, outside of the formulas, which was either fixed as *matter of course*, or maintained in ambiguous propositions in opposition to Manichæism, Fatalism, and Epicureanism, did not possess the value of a dog-

---

[1] Very instructive in this respect is the Church History of Socrates. A man's orthodoxy is completely decided for him by his attitude to the dogma of the Trinity (see H. E. III. 7, VI. 13, VII. 6, 11). The Cappadocians and the theologians after Socrates held similar views; see Gregory of Naz. Orat. XXVII. 10: "Philosophise about the world and worlds, matter, the soul, rational beings, good and bad alike, about resurrection, judgment, and retribution, and the sufferings of Christ. For if on these points you hit on the truth it is not without service, but if you fail, you can suffer no harm" (cf. Ullmann, Gregory of Naz., 1867, p. 217 f.). We have also to consider here the contents of the oriental symbols, creed-decalogues etc. The interest taken to an increasing extent from the fifth century in the tenets levelled against Origen was biblical and traditional. It only became dogmatic at a time when in theology and Christology the influence of "antiquity" had taken the place of that of dogma. On the place and importance of the doctrine of the Trinity in Gregory, see Ullman, p. 232 ff.

matic declaration in the strict sense.   Remembering this, there can be no doubt that the essence of the Christian religion, and therefore the contents of its creed, are summed up in the following proposition. *The salvation presented in Christianity consists in the redemption of the human race from the state of mortality and the sin involved in it, that men might attain divine life, i.e., the everlasting contemplation of God, this redemption having already been consummated in the incarnation of the Son of God, and being conferred on men by their close union with him: Christianity is the religion which delivers from death and leads to the contemplation of God.*[1]   This proposition can be more precisely defined as follows: the highest blessing bestowed in Christianity is adoption into the divine sonship, which is assured to the believer, and is completed in participation in the divine nature, or more accurately, in the deification of man through the gift of immortality.   This gift includes the perfect knowledge and the lasting vision of God, in a blessedness void of suffering, but it does not do away with the interval between Christ and the believer.[2]   From this

---

[1] I share fully the view of Kattenbusch (Confessionskunde I., p. 296) that the dogma was not merely supported by one idea, and that in the Greek Church of to-day the idea of redemption held by the ancient Church no longer rules directly; but this view does not contradict the exposition given in the text.

[2] The fact that the idea of deification was the ultimate and supreme thought is not a discovery of recent times, but it is only in recent times that it has been appreciated in all its importance. After Theophilus, Irenæus, Hippolytus, and Origen, it is found in all the Fathers of the ancient Church, and that in a primary position. We have it in Athanasius, the Cappadocians, Apollinaris, Ephraem Syrus, Epiphanius and others, as also in Cyril, Sophronius, and late Greek and Russian theologians. In proof of it Psalm LXXXII. '6 is very often quoted—"I said ye are gods and all sons of the most High." Just as often are θεοποίησις and ἀθανασία expressly combined. Some Fathers feel the boldness of the formula; but that is very rare.   I select merely a few from my collection of passages: Athanas. de incarn. 54: "Αὐτὸς ἐνηνθρώπησεν, ἵνα ἡμεῖς θεοποιηθῶμεν, καὶ αὐτὸς ἐφανέρωσεν ἑαυτὸν διὰ σώματος, ἵνα ἡμεῖς τοῦ ἀοράτου πατρὸς ἔννοιαν λάβωμεν, καὶ αὐτὸς ὑπέμεινεν τὴν παρ' ἀνθρώπου ὕβριν, ἵνα ἡμεῖς ἀθανασίαν κληρονομήσωμεν, cf. Ep. ad Serap. I. 24, Orat. c. Arian. I. 38, 39, and often; Vita Antonii, c. 74, Ephraem, Comment. in Diatess., init. (ed. Moesinger, p. 1): "Quare dominus noster carnem induit? Ut ipsa caro victoriæ gaudia gustaret et dona gratiæ explorata et cognita haberet.   Si deus sine carne vicisset, quæ ei tribuerentur laudes? Secundo, ut dominus noster manifestum faceret, se initio creationis nequaquam ex invidia prohibuisse, quominus homo fieret deus, quia maius est, quod dominus noster in homine humiliabatur, quam quod in eo,

it follows: (1) *that redemption, as seen in its final effect, was conceived to be the abrogation of the natural state by a miraculous transformation of our nature;* that accordingly (2) the supreme good was definitely distinguished from the morally good; and that (3) an atonement was not included in it. For atonement can only be thought of where the division between God and man is regarded as an opposition of the will. But it further follows from this that this theology, in agreement with the apologetic and old Catholic doctrine, admitted no independent object to our present life. The work of the Christian consisted wholly in preparing for death (τὸ ἔργον τοῦ Χριστιανοῦ οὐδὲν ἄλλο

---

dum magnus et gloriosus erat, habitabat. Hinc illud: 'Ego dixi, dii estis'." Gregory of Nyss., Colloq. cum Macrina (ed. Oehler, p. 170): Τῶν οὖν τοιούτων ταῖς διὰ τοῦ πυρὸς ἰατρείαις ἐκκαθαρθέντων τε καὶ ἀφαγνισθέντων, ἕκαστον τῶν πρὸς τὸ κρεῖττον νοουμένων ἀντεισελεύσεται, ἡ ἀφθαρσία, ἡ ζωή; ἡ τιμή, ἡ χάρις, ἡ δόξα, ἡ δύναμις, καὶ εἴ τι ἄλλο τοιοῦτον αὐτῷ τε τῷ Θεῷ ἐπιθεωρεῖσθαι εἰκάζομεν. Gregory of Naz., Orat. 40, c. 45 (Decalogus fidei, ed Caspari, Alte und Neue Quellen, 1879, p. 21): πίστευε τὸν υἱὸν τοῦ Θεοῦ ... τοσοῦτον ἄνθρωπον διά σε, ὅσον σὺ γίνῃ δι᾿ ἐκεῖνον Θεός. So also Orat. I. 5: "We become like Christ, since Christ also became like us; we become gods on his account, since he also became man for our sake." On the other hand, compare Orat. XLII. 17: μεθ᾿ ἡμῶν τὸ κτίσμα, τῶν οὐ Θεῶν· εἰ κτίσμα δέ, οὐ Θεός, and XXXIX. 17: "How should he not be God, *to insert in passing a bold deduction,* by whom thou also dost become God?" Apollinaris Laod., Κατὰ μέρος πίστις (ed. Lagarde, p. 110): φαμὲν ἄνθρωπον γεγενῆσθαι τὸν τοῦ Θεοῦ λόγον, ἵνα τὴν ὁμοίωσιν τοῦ ἐπουρανίου λάβωμεν καὶ θεοποιηθῶμεν. Macar., hom. 39. Pseudo-hippolytus, Theophan. (ed. Lagarde, p. 41, 21): εἰ οὖν ἀθάνατος γέγονεν ὁ ἄνθρωπος, ἔσται καὶ θεός. Dionys. Areopag., saepissime, *e.g.*, de caelesti hierar. c. 1: ἡ ἡμῶν ἀνάλογος θέωσις. Sophronius, Christmas Sermon (ed. Usener, Rhein. Mus. für Philologie, 1886, p. 505): θεωθῶμεν θείαις μεταβολαῖς καὶ μιμήσεσιν. Leo, Patriarch of Russia (Pawlow, p. 126): ἐθεώθημεν Θεοῦ τῇ μεταλήψει. Gennadius, Confess. (ed. Kimmel, p. 10): " dixit deus: Induam me carne ... et erit omnis homo tamquam deus non secundum naturam sed secundum participationem." We have, however, to notice that this deification, as understood by the Greek Church, did not by any means signify roundly "Becoming like God". The Greeks in the main did not connect any clear conception with the thought of the possession of salvation (felicity) further than the idea of imperishableness; and this very fact was their characteristic feature. It is the ineffable, the transcendent which may therefore be described as the θεία φύσις, because it is enjoyed for ever. The interval between Christ—who was born, and did not become, Son of God—and the sons by adoption is always very strongly emphasised; compare (the precise expositions in Augustine, De remiss. pace. II. 24) and above all, Athanasius' third discourse against the Arians; further, Cyril Catech. II., ch. 4—7 and 19. Yet the θέωσις of Mary forms a kind of exception. The idea of deification is also found in Western writers, especially Augustine. But if I am not deceived Augustine himself brought it to an edifying end.

ἐστὶν ἢ μελετᾷν ἀποθνῄσκειν). In the present there only existed a preliminary possession of salvation. This was represented (1) in the knowledge of God and of the accomplished incarnation of the Son of God, and therewith in the certain hope of being deified; (2) in power over demons; (3) in the call to salvation and perfect acquaintance with the conditions of its reception; (4) in certain communications of divine Grace which supported believers in fulfilling those conditions—the forgiveness of sin in baptism, the power of certain holy rites, and holy vehicles, the example of the God-man etc.; and (5) in participation in the mysteries—worship and the Lord's supper—and in the enjoyment of the consecration they imparted, as also, for ascetics, in a foretaste of the future liberation from the senses and deification. [1]

The certainty of faith in the future deification, however, because its possibility and reality, rested exclusively on the fact of the incarnation of the Son of God. The divine had already appeared on earth and had united itself inseparably with human nature.

This conception formed the universal foundation for the development of dogmas in the fourth to the seventh century, though all might not equally understand it or see its consequences clearly. Only thus can we comprehend how the Church could perceive, define, and establish the nature of salvation in the constitution of the incarnate Son of God. Faith simply embraces the correct perception of the nature of the incarnate Logos, because this perception of faith includes the assured hope of a change of human nature analogous to the divinity of Jesus Christ, and therewith everything worth striving for. 'We become divine through him, because for our sake he became man'. But the dogmatic formulas corresponding to this conception only established their position after severe fights; they never arrived at a perfectly exact expression; and they never obtained the exclusive supremacy which they demanded.

---

[1] Athanasius (Ep. encycl. ad episc. Ægypt. et Lib. ch. I.) mentions as the gifts of grace already possessed by Christians: (1) the type of the heavenly mode of life, (2) power over demons, (3) adoption to be sons, (4) and what is exalted and rises high above every gift—the knowledge of the Father and the Word himself and the grant of the Holy Spirit. This list is not quite complete.

The reasons for this delay, inexactness, and failure to obtain supremacy are numerous and various. The most important deserve to be emphasised.

Firstly, every new formula, however necessary it might appear, had the spirit of the Catholic Church against it, simply because it was new; it could only gain acceptance by deceiving as to its character of novelty, and as long as the attempt to do so was unsuccessful, it was regarded by the pious with suspicion. [1] Secondly, the ability of the Catholic Fathers really to explain their faith, and to deduce dogmatic consequences, was extremely slight. Grown up in the schools of philosophy and rhetoric, they never clearly felt it to be their duty to give an abstract account of their faith, however they might understand it. Far from describing the system of doctrine as a statement of the nature and contents of Christian piety, and from evolving the latter from its distinctive conditions, they found it difficult even to make a simple inference from their conception of salvation to the person of Christ and *vice versa*. Their reasoning was always being disturbed by apologetic or other considerations foreign to it. Energetic men, to whom the matter of religion should be all in all, were accordingly required, if an advance were to take place in the work of formulating it. But such men have been extremely rare. There have been few in all periods of the history of dogma who clearly perceived and duly appreciated the final interests which moved themselves. This is true of the ancient Church, though then matters were a little better than in later centuries. Thirdly, the formulas required conflicted with every kind of philosophy; they amounted to an offence to the thought of the schools. This circumstance undoubtedly might afterwards prove an advantage; it was possible to show the divinity and sacredness of the formulas by referring to their inscrutability and therefore to the mystery that surrounded them. But as long as the formula was still new, this confirmation encountered doubts, and even afterwards, in spite of the 'mystery', it was impossible to do without a philosophy which should interpret it, and should restore confidence,

[1] See above, p. 137, f.

as to the contradictions, by new combinations of categories. Now, as long as no such philosophy was created, faith was not satisfied, and the formula was not guaranteed permanence. Fourthly, it was of the highest importance that by almost all the Fathers their conception of the salvation procured by the God-man (deification) was appended to, or bolstered up by, the system of 'natural theology'. But under this system knowledge and virtue were the highest blessings, and God was exclusively the judge who rewarded the good and punished the wicked. Now, it was undoubtedly possible so to combine these two lines of thought that neither was prejudiced, and we will see that such a combination alone corresponded to the ideas of those Christians, and was actually brought about. But it was impossible to prevent natural theology from intruding more and more into dogmatics, and from interfering with the success of the mystical doctrine of redemption—for so we may well name it. Men were not in a position to strike at the roots of those views of Christian salvation which did not definitely conceive the latter to be distinctive, and which therefore did not sufficiently differentiate it from virtue and the natural knowledge of God.

Fifthly, the complete acceptance of the mystical doctrine of redemption was imperilled from another side, and this menace also could never be completely averted. The picture of the life of Jesus contained in the Gospels, in spite of all the arts of exegesis, contradicted in a way it was impossible to disregard the Christological formulas called for by the doctrine. The life even influenced the form given to the dogma of the incarnation and its consequences[1] to an extent which, from the standpoint of the theory of redemption, was questionable; and it subsequently always accompanied the dogmatic formulas,

---

[1] In the introductory fourth Catechism in which Cyril summarises the main points of the faith, he says (ch. IX.): πίστευε δὲ ὅτι οὗτος ὁ μονογενὴς υἱὸς τοῦ Θεοῦ διὰ τὰς ἁμαρτίας ἡμῶν ἐξ οὐρανῶν κατῆλθεν ἐπι τῆς γῆς. (ch. X.) : οὗτος ἐσταυρώθη ὑπὲρ τῶν ἁμαρτιῶν ἡμῶν. Nothing is said of the abolition of death. So also in the Homilies of Chrysostom who generally tried to follow Paul, sin comes to the front. The saying "Let us not fear death, but only sin," is often repeated with variations by Chrysostom. Alexander of Alex. also in his letter to Alexander (Theodoret H. E. I. 4) gives as the only ground of the incarnation of the Son of God, that he came εἰς ἀθέτησιν ἁμαρτίας, but he is unable to carry out the thought.

keeping alive in the Church the remnant of a conception of the Redeemer's personality which did not agree with them. The Church indeed never lost recollection of the human individuality of Jesus in its simple loftiness, its heart-winning love, and its holy earnestness; it never forgot the revelation of God in humanity. Scripture reading and, in part also, preaching preserved the memory, and with and by it thought was ever again led to the simplest and highest of facts, the love of God which is loftier than all reason, the rendering of service to our neighbour, sincere humility, and patience. But as the gospel prevented dogma from obtaining an exclusive supremacy, so also Pauline theology, and kindred views found in Holy Scripture, exerted an important influence, which maintained its ground side by side with the dogma, and often very strongly decided its exposition. That the work of Christ consisted in what he achieved, culminating in his sacrificial death, and signifying the overcoming and removal of guilt; that salvation accordingly consisted in the forgiveness, justification and adoption of men, are ideas absolutely wanting in none of the Church Fathers, and very prominent in a few, while in the majority they find their way into the exposition of the dogma of redemption. They do not agree with the latter, nay, in this combination can hardly be held to have deepened the conception in any point; for they rather menaced the finality of the fundamental dogmatic thought in which men lived. In fact they wrought mischief, *i.e.*, they led to moral laxity, as in all cases where they are only allowed a secondary authority. But their existence must be expressly stated if our view is to be complete. New Testament reminiscences and thoughts and in general Biblical theological ideas of the most varied kind, always accompanied and impinged on dogma growing or full-grown. [1] They helped to delay its reduction into formulas, and prevented the mystical doctrine of redemption and its corresponding dogmas obtaining a completely exclusive supremacy in the Eastern Churches.

Sixthly and finally, the scheme of Christology, distinctive of the

---

[1] The contradictions and inconsistencies were not felt if it was possible to support the separate propositions by an appeal to Holy Scripture; see on this Vol. II., p. 331, n. 1.

West, forced on the Church by the policy of the emperors, brought a
disturbing and confusing influence into the Eastern history of dogma.
The Eastern Church, left to itself, could only, if it had simply
given expression to its own idea of redemption, have raised to
a dogma the one nature, made flesh, of God, the Logos (μία
φύσις θεοῦ λόγου σεσαρκωμένη), and must have left the paradox
standing that the humanity of Christ was consubstantial (ὁμοούσιος)
with ours, and was yet from the beginning not only without
sin, but free from any kind of corruption (φθορά). This dogma
was condemned as heretical in the process, as we know, of
forming an exclusive authoritative doctrine, and another was
set up in its place which it required the most elaborate efforts
of theologians to connect closely with the idea of redemption.
Conversely, as regards the doctrine of the Trinity in the fourth
century, while the correct formula—correct, i.e., when gauged
by the conception of redemption—triumphed, yet the considerations springing from natural theology and science were here
so strong that the Eastern Church could only reconcile itself
to the doctrine by the aid of a complicated theology, which in
this case, however, was really heterodox, because it weakened
the meaning of the formula. *In the fourth century the correct
formula triumphed, but the triumph was procured by a theology
really heterodox; in the fifth and up to the seventh an incorrect
formula, if gauged by the idea of redemption, became supreme,
but theology was able to treat it orthodoxly.* In view of these
incongruities one is almost tempted to believe in the 'cunning
of the idea'; for this development alone made possible, or demanded, the application of the whole apparatus of Platonic and
Aristotelian philosophy to dogma. Neither the conception of
the ὁμοούσιος (consubstantial) as given by Athanasius, nor the
strictly Monophysite form of the incarnation dogma, would have
conjured philosophy anew to its aid, and to a greater extent
than was contained in the dogma itself. This happened and
could not but happen, because men would not understand
ομοούσιος as ταυτούσιος (of the same substance); and because
they were forced to fit the two natures into their system. Dogmatics (the doctrines of the Trinity and the Incarnation) became
the high school of Philosophy. By them the Middle Ages

received all that they ever did of philosophical thought. And these facts were due to the circumstance that the idea of redemption was not expressed purely and absolutely in dogma, that rather in the doctrine of the Trinity, as well as in the Christology, the formula overlapped its support, or the support the formula, and therefore necessarily called for endless exertions. Where would Plato and Aristotle have been in the Church or the Middle Ages if the East had honoured Athanasius and Julian of Halicarnassus as the sole authoritative Fathers of the Church, and how nearly was this the case with both! How much the East owes to the interference of the West, and yet, on the other hand, how greatly did the same West disturb it! But it is to be described as a gain from another point of view, that the correct formulas—those which corresponded to the Greek idea of redemption—did not establish their position. *The evangelical conception of Christ was preserved to a greater degree in the Byzantine and Nestorian Church, based on the doctrine of the two natures, than in the Monophysite Churches.* The latter only prove that the consistent development of the materialistic idea of redemption reduces Christianity to barbarism. The Arabians taught Aristotle to the Nestorians and not to the Monophysites. But those Churches also show that the Christ who possessed one incarnate nature—that phantom—reduced the historical Christ almost to the vanishing point. All the features of the man Christ of history, which the Byzantine and Nestorian Church still kept alive in their communities, are so many evidences that the old idea of redemption was forced to submit to limitations.

But in spite of this the dogma of the God-man which sprang from the doctrine of redemption assumed a unique and predominant position and alone constituted dogma in the strict sense. Theology = the doctrine of the Trinity, Economy = the idea and realisation of the Incarnation. The course of development also shows by its inner logic, which indeed, as already pointed out, was not so stringent as more recent scholars would have us believe, that it was in this dogma that the strongest interest was taken. After Athanasius had proved the necessity and realisation of redemption through the incarnation of the

Son of God, the consubstantiality (Homoousia) of the Son of God with God himself was first established. Then the fact was emphasised that the Incarnate was constituted similarly with man, and finally, the unity of deity and humanity in the incarnate Son of God was settled. The historian of dogma has here simply to follow the course of history. It is in this connection by no means clear how besides this the work of the God-man is to be treated. As regards the work of Christ we can only deal with 'conceptions' which are not firmly allied to the dogma. But we have to remark finally, that not only in theory was the dogma planned eschatologically, *i.e.*, with a view to the future life, but that also in practice faith in the imminent approach of the end of the world still influenced the pious. In a few Fathers this faith undoubtedly held a subordinate place; but yet it formed the rule, and the storms caused by the invasion of the tribes as well as the political revolutions constantly gave it strength.

II. In relation to the blessing of salvation man is receptive and passive. He receives it in this world in the hope of his faith, and enjoys it in the other as a transcendently glorious gift of grace. God alone can grant it, and no human effort can deserve it. As we have already noticed, this religious blessing of salvation is wholly different from moral goodness; for moral goodness cannot be presented, but must be gained by our own actions. On the other hand, Christianity as a religion cannot take up a neutral attitude to moral goodness, but must rather embrace the loftiest morality. That was also the universal conviction of the Greek Church and its theologians. The problem which thus arose was solved without noteworthy vacillations, and in the sense of the theology of the apologists and Origen. It was assumed that freedom in the moral sphere corresponded to receptivity in the domain of religion and the blessings of salvation conferred by it; and that God attached the grant of the religious blessing of salvation to the achievement of a perfectly moral life, whose law, though not new, had first found expression in the Christian religion as something perfect and capable of being easily recognised. The scheme of nature and grace current in the West since Augustine, was not entirely unknown in the East, so far as words were concern-

ed.[1] But the latter already found "grace" in "nature", *i.e.*,
in the inalienable natural disposition to freedom, and, on the
other hand, conceived "grace" to be the communication of a
higher nature. Hence the above scheme was not adapted to
express Greek thought. Christianity was rather, on the one hand,
the perfect law of goodness, and, on the other, a promise and sure
pledge of immortality.[2] It was therefore holy living and correct
faith. The convictions that God himself is the good; that he is
the creator of the inalienable reason and freedom of man; that
the perfect morality of man represents the only form of his
similarity to God attainable in the sphere of the temporal and
created; that the supreme law of goodness, hitherto obscured,
has been once more revealed to men in the Christian religion,
and that in the most impressive way imaginable—by the deity
in a human form; finally, that the religious blessing of salvation
procured by Christ contains the strongest motive to practise
morality,[3] while it also includes mysterious forces which promote
it: these convictions, according to the conception of Greek theologians, bound religion and morality together as closely as
possible, and, since only the good man could receive salvation,
guaranteed the character of Christianity as the moral religion.
The monk Sophronius (seventh century) says in his Christmas
Sermon: "Therefore the Son of God assumed human poverty,
that he might make us gods by grace; and the divine father
David sings in his psalms ... I said, ye are gods and all sons
of the highest. God is in us; let us become gods by divine

---

[1] It occurs, *e.g.*, in the Homilies of Macarius. If elsewhere he speaks of χάρις,
it is as a rule the substantial grace imparted in the sacraments (baptism) that is
meant. The beginning of Cyril's first Catechism is very instructive: Καινῆς διαθήκης
μαθηταὶ καὶ Χριστοῦ μυστηρίων κοινωνοί, νῦν μὲν τῇ κλήσει, μετ᾽ ὀλίγον δὲ καὶ τῇ
χάριτι, καρδίαν ἑαυτοῖς ποιήσατε καινὴν καὶ πνεῦμα καινόν, ἵνα εὐφροσύνης ὑπόθεσις
γένησθε τοῖς οὐρανοῖς.

[2] See Cyril, Catech. 4, c. 2: Ὁ τῆς θεοσεβείας τρόπος ἐκ δύο τούτων συνέστηκε,
δογμάτων εὐσεβῶν καὶ πράξεων ἀγαθῶν. Καὶ οὔτε τὰ δόγματα χωρὶς ἔργων ἀγαθῶν
εὐπρόσδεκτα τῷ Θεῷ, οὔτε τὰ μὴ μετ᾽ εὐσεβῶν δογμάτων ἔργα τελούμενα προσδέ-
χεται ὁ Θεός ... μέγιστον τοίνυν κτῆμά ἐστι τὸ τῶν δογμάτων μάθημα.

[3] Cyril begins his 18th Catechism with the words "The root of every good
action is the hope of the resurrection. For the expectation of obtaining a corresponding reward is a spur to incite the soul to practise good works." The way to
morality is made easy by removal of the fear of death.

transformations and imitations" (Διὰ τσῦτο ὁ υἱὸς τοῦ Θεοῦ ἀνθρω-
πίνην πτωχείαν ἐνδύεται ἵνα θεοὺς ἡμᾶς ἀπεργάσηται χάριτι. καὶ
ταῦτα μελῳδῶν ὁ θεοπάτωρ Δαβίδ .... Ἐγὼ εἶπα· Θεοί ἐστε καὶ
υἱοὶ ὑψίστου πάντες. Θεὸς ἐν ἡμῖν· θεωθῶμεν θείαις μεταβολαῖς καὶ
μιμήσεσιν). [1] In the last phrase the Greek fundamental thought is
put into a classic form. Only we must not take "μεταβολαῖς"
and "μιμήσεσιν" to be equivalent. The former signifies the actual
process, the latter its condition and form; not the sufficient
reason, as is proved by "χάριτι." [2] There is, however, a form of
morality which does not appear to be merely subordinate to
religious faith and hope, but which anticipates the future blessings,
or puts man into the condition of being able to receive them
immediately. This is negative morality, or asceticism. It corresponds
in a true sense to the characteristic of the religious gift of salvation; it is also therefore no longer a mere adjunct to the latter,
but it is the adequate and essential disposition for the reception
of salvation. But in so far as ecstasy, intuition, and the power
of working miracles can be combined with it, it forms the anti-
cipation of the future state. The ultimate rule of this conception
of Christianity may accordingly be compressed, perhaps, into the
saying: "Dost thou desire the supreme good, incorruption
(ἀφθαρσία), then divest thyself of all that is perishable." Side
by side with this we have the more general rule "Dost thou

---

[1] Ed. Usener, l. c. Once more we have to compare Cyril of Jerusalem. After
he has limited the "creed" to the ten sections of the Symbol he continues: μετὰ
δὲ τὴν γνῶσιν τῆς σεμνῆς καὶ ἐνδόξου ταύτης καὶ παναγίας πίστεως καὶ σεαυτὸν
γνῶθι λοιπὸν ὅστις εἶ. Accordingly, faith is that given from without, divine. Moral
self-knowledge and self-discipline are independent of it.

[2] The Greek Fathers speak not infrequently of the new birth in connection
with N. T. passages and it is to be admitted that some succeed in reproducing
the thought satisfactorily, but only—so far as I know—when they adhere closely to
the sacred texts. At all events we must not let ourselves be misled by the mere
title. This is shown most clearly by the closing chapters of Gregory of Nyssa's
Orat. catechet. (ch. 33 sq.). By regeneration Gregory understands the mysterious
birth in us of the divine *nature*, which is implanted by baptism. As the natural
man is born of moist seed, so the new undying man is born of water at the
invocation of the Holy Trinity. The new immortal nature is thus begun in germ
by baptism and is nourished by the Eucharist. That this conception has nothing
in common with the new birth of the New Test., since it has a physical process
in view, needs no proof. According to Cyril, regeneration only takes place after
man has voluntarily left the service of sin (see Catech. I., ch. 2).

desire the supreme good, then first be good and nourish the
new nature implanted in thee in Baptism by the Eucharist and
the other mysterious gifts." The extent to which all this was
connected with Christ is shown by the saying of Clemens Alex.
(Protrept. I. 7)—a saying which retained its force in after times :
" Appearing as a teacher he taught the good life, in order that afterwards as God he might grant everlasting life " (τὸ εὖ ζῆν ἐδίδαξεν
ἐπιφανεὶς ὡς διδάσκαλος, ἵνα τὸ ἀεὶ ζῆν ὕστερον ὡς Θεὸς χορηγήσῃ).

This whole conception of the importance of morality needed,
however, no doctrinal and specific description, any more than
the nature of morality and the principles of natural theology in
general. All that was already settled in its fundamental lines;
man knew it by his own reason; it formed the self-evident presupposition of the doctrine of redemption. The very freedom
used by the Church Fathers in dealing with details shows that
here they were treating matters generally recognised and only
called in question by Manichæans, Fatalists, etc., and that it
was therefore unnecessary to have recourse to revelation. In
describing the dogma of the Greek Fathers, therefore, we have
to consider their views of the nature of salvation, [1] of God as

---

[1] The fundamental conception of the nature of the blessing secured by salvation
is yet not wholly unknown to rational theology, since the latter supposed, though
with some uncertainty, that it could perceive a divine element in the original constitution of men (see, e g., Gregory of Nyssa). Even for the doctrine of the Trinity
recourse was had here and there to reason and the philosophers. But we must go
still farther. If the doctrine of redemption has been characterised above as mystical,
this does not exclude the fact that faith confers redemption in so far as it confers
a knowledge which in and by itself includes liberation. As long as men dealt independently with dogma, this conception was by no means wanting; indeed it
was really the hidden mystery in dogma which was clearly expressed by Clement
and Origen, but only dimly shadowed by later teachers. From this point, however,
faith and ethics were intimately combined; for ethics was also intellectual. No
later writer has stated and known the thought so clearly expressed by Clement of
Alex. (Strom. IV. 23, 149): Διόπερ ὁ Δημόκριτος εὖ λέγει "ὡς ἡ φύσις τε καὶ διδαχὴ
παραπλήσιον ἐστι"... καὶ γὰρ ἡ διδαχὴ μεταρρυθμίζει τὸν ἄνθρωπον, μεταρρυθμί-
ζουσα δὲ φυσιοποιεῖ καὶ διήνεγκεν οὐδὲν ἡ φύσει πλασθῆναι τοιόνδε ἡ χρόνῳ καὶ
μαθήσει μετατυπωθῆναι· ἄμφω δὲ ὁ κύριος παρέσχηται, τὸ μὲν κατὰ τὴν δημιουργίαν,
τὸ δὲ κατὰ ἐκ τῆς διαθήκης ἀνάκτισίν τε καὶ ἀνανέωσιν. The whole matter gradually
became really mystical, i.e., indescribable and inconceivable in every sense in the
Fathers; the intellectual phase and intention almost disappeared. Conversely, the
reality of the blessing in salvation was thought of from the beginning as something
supernatural, surprising, and bestowed from without.

the Good and the Giver of salvation, of the state and duties of man, etc., on the one hand, as a kind of *a priori* presuppositions of the doctrine of redemption ; but, on the other, as individual conceptions, framed partly from contemporary philosophy, and partly from the Bible. They certainly have a right to a place in a description of the complete view taken by the ancient Church of Christianity ; but as certainly they cannot be called dogmas; for dogmas are as essentially different from self-evident presuppositions as from fluctuating conceptions. Our only reason for discussing them in the history of dogma is that we may guard dogma from misunderstanding and correctly mark off the space due to it. [1] The Greek conception of Christianity has, like an ellipse, two centres: the doctrine of liberty, which embraces the whole of rational theology, Stoic and Platonic, and the doctrine of the actual redemption, which is supranatural. Supranatural as it was it admitted a relationship to natural theology, just as, conversely, freedom was regarded as a gift of divine grace. We find, indeed, that the two centres were first brought into the greatest possible proximity by the negative morality. Therefore from this point also the achievements of positive morality necessarily appear as a *minimum* to which the shadow of essential imperfection always clings.

It follows from the above exposition that the doctrines of God, the world, and man—with freedom and sin, are to be prefixed, as presuppositions and conceptions, to dogma, *i.e.*, the doctrines of the godman, while they are only to be discussed in so far as

---

[1] One might be disposed to assume that the dogmatic of the ancient Church also contained *articuli puri et mixti*, but this designation would be misleading. In the opinion of the Fathers, the gospel must have made *everything* clear; conversely, there is hardly anything in the dogmatics which able philosophers had not foreshadowed. The *realisation* was the mystery. Socrates says (H. E. III. 16): Πολλοὶ τῶν παρ' Ἕλλησι φιλοσοφησάντων οὐ μακρὰν τοῦ γνῶναι τὸν Θεὸν ἐγένοντο, καὶ γὰρ καὶ πρὸς τοὺς ἀπρονοησίαν εἰσάγοντας, οὔτε Ἐπικουρίους, ἢ ἄλλως ἐριστικούς, μετὰ τῆς λογικῆς ἐπιστήμης γενναίως ἀπήντησαν, τὴν ἀμαθίαν αὐτῶν ἀνατρέποντες, καὶ διὰ τούτων τῶν λόγων χρειώδεις μὲν τοῖς τὴν εὐσέβειαν ἀγαπῶσι κατέστησαν· οὐ μὴν τῆς κεφαλῆς τοῦ λόγου ἐκράτησαν, τοῦ μὴ γνῶναι τὸ ἀποκρυπτόμενον ἀπὸ τῶν γενεῶν καὶ ἀπὸ τῶν αἰώνων κατὰ Χριστὸν μυστήριον· Socrates had already in view violent opponents of the intrusion of Ἑλληνικὴ παιδεία into theology; but the dispute so passionately conducted never really weakened the confidence placed in natural theology. The actual position is correctly described in Eusebius' phrase (H. E. IV. 7, 14): ἡ καθ' ἡμᾶς ἐπὶ θείοις τε καὶ φιλοσόφοις δόγμασι διδασκαλία.

such discussion is required for the comprehension of dogma. But this does not complete the list of our tasks; the whole presentment of dogma must be prefaced by a chapter treating of the sources of our knowledge and our authorities, *i.e.*, Scripture, tradition, and the Church. So also we must at the close examine the mysterious application of redemption—the mysteries —and all that is connected with it.

The following arrangement of our material, in which a systematic exposition forms the basis of the historical, because the foundations of our view have not changed since the time of Origen, will thus be appropriate.

Ch. III. Of the sources of knowledge and the authorities, or of Scripture, tradition, and the Church.

A. The Presuppositions of the Doctrine of Redemption, or Natural Theology.

Ch. IV. The presuppositions and conceptions of God the Creator as bestower of salvation.

Ch. V. The presuppositions and conceptions of man as recipient of salvation.

B. The Doctrine of Redemption in the Person of the God-man in its Historical Development.

Ch. VI. The doctrine of the necessity and realisation of redemption through the incarnation of the Son of God.

Appendix. The ideas of redemption from the devil and atonement through the work of the God-man.

Ch. VII. The doctrine of the consubstantiality of the Son of God with God himself.

Appendix. The doctrine of the Holy Spirit and the Trinity.

Ch. VIII. The doctrine of the perfect similarity of constitution between the incarnate Son of God and humanity.

Ch. IX. Continuation. The doctrine of the personal unity of the divine and human nature in the incarnate Son of God.

C. The Foretaste of Redemption.

Ch. X. The mysteries and the like.

Ch. XI. Conclusion. Sketch of the history of the genesis of the orthodox system.

Supplement 1.—The Greek conception of Christianity appears undoubtedly to be exceedingly compact and clear, as long as we do not look too deeply into the heart of it. The freeing of dogmatics of all matters which do not fall within the scope of the doctrine of redemption is very remarkable. But these advantages are purchased, first, by abandoning any attempt to establish an inner unity between the supreme notions of "moral good" and "blessedness" (imperishableness); secondly, by the depreciation of positive morality in favour of asceticism; thirdly, by completely caricaturing the historical Christ. But the knowledge of the Christian faith possessed by the Fathers up to the middle of the fifth century was still far from being in the desolate state in which theology makes no resolute attempt to deduce the consequences of a doctrine, while it does not venture to abandon it, but contents itself with perceiving "a profound element of truth" in any or every theologoumenon brought to it by tradition. The idea of the Greek Fathers, to which everything was subordinate, that Christianity is the religion which delivers from perishableness and death, was derived from the ancient Catholic Church. It presents itself as a specific limitation of primitive Christian hopes under the influence of views held by the ancients. It is possible to express it in a grand and awe-inspiring form, and this the Greek Fathers understood. Further, where misery, mortality, and finitude are felt to be the heaviest burdens laid upon men, the supreme good can be nothing but endless, blessed rest. In so far as the Greek Fathers perceived and firmly believed in this gift being conferred by the Christian religion, while they connected its bestowal with Jesus Christ, they assigned to Christianity the highest conceivable significance, and to its founder the highest conceivable dignity, within their range of vision. But the mood which looked on Christianity from this point of view and regarded it as consolatory, was that of the fall and ruin of the ancient world, which no longer possessed the power to turn earnestly to an energetic life. Without premising this the dogmatic developments are not intelligible. But we cannot retain the formulas of the Greek faith without self-deception, if we change or refuse to admit the validity of its premises. But if we are ready

honestly to retain them, then let us clearly understand to
what Orthodoxy and Monophysitism came in the East. After
they had piled one monstrosity on the top of the other, they
were—to use a strong figure of Goethe's—almost choked in
chewing the cud of moral and religious absurdities. Originally
their doctrine was good for nothing in the world but for dying;
afterwards they became deadly sick on this very doctrine.

Supplement 2.—If the conception of the supreme good may
be regarded as a revised version, made by Greek philosophy, of
the ancient Christian hopes of the future, yet this philosophy
always rejected the idea of the incarnation of God, and therefore could not, in its definition of the supreme good, attain the
certainty which was given in the Christian conception. In the
fourth and fifth centuries, however, there were even Christian
theologians—Synesius, for example—who would not admit the
incarnation of God without revision, and yet held by the thought
of deification; who accordingly approached, not rationalistic, but
rather pantheistic views. At any rate, faith in the incarnation of
God, along with the idea of creation, formed the dividing line
between Greek philosophy and the dogmatics of the Church.
"For what," says Athanasius, de incarn. 41, "is absurd or ridicu-
lous in our teaching, except merely our saying that the Logos
was made manifest in a human body?" (τί γὰρ ἄτοπον, ἢ τί
χλεύης παρ' ἡμῖν ἄξιον, ἢ πάντως ὅτι τὸν λόγον ἐν σώματι πεφαν-
ερῶσθαι λέγομεν;). [1] On the other hand, the Christian says (Cyril,
Catech. 4, ch. 9): "If the incarnation was a dream, then salvation is also a dream." (Εἰ φάντασμα ἦν ἡ ἐνανθρώπησις, φάντασμα
καὶ ἡ σωτηρία). That is the confession which in the Greek
Church was the equivalent of 1 Cor. XV. 17 f.

Supplement 3.—In order to learn the classical form of Greek
piety, the strongest root of dogma, it is necessary to study the
literature of asceticism. For it seldom comes clearly to light
in the dogmatic, apologetic, and polemical works, with the exception of the writings of Athanasius, and in the homiletic

---

[1] Compare Gregory Nyss., Orat. catech. 5: Τὸ μὲν εἶναι λόγον Θεοῦ καὶ πνεῦμα
διά τε τῶν κοινῶν ἐννοιῶν ὁ Ἕλλην καὶ διὰ τῶν γραφικῶν ὁ Ἰουδαῖος ἴσως οὐκ ἀντι-
λέξει, τὴν δὲ κατὰ τὸν ἄνθρωπον οἰκονομίαν τοῦ Θεοῦ λόγου κατὰ τὸ ἴσον ἑκάτερος
αὐτῶν ἀποδοκιμάσει ὡς ἀπίθανόν τε καὶ ἀπρεπῆ περὶ Θεοῦ λέγεσθαι.

literature, apart from Chrysostom, it is always greatly disguised by rhetoric. But a distinction must be made even in ascetic literature. The descriptions of the piety of monkish heroes lose themselves as a rule in extravagance and eccentricity, and are not typical because the writers set out to prove the already supramundane character of those heroes. We have especially to examine numerous writings on "the resurrection," "virginity," "perfection," and similar subjects, and also the practical homilies. We obtain perhaps the clearest and truest impression of the piety of the Greek Church from reading the biography of sister Macrina, by Gregory of Nyssa (Oehler, Biblioth. d. KVV. I. 1, 1858, p. 172 ff.). The dying prayer put in her lips (p. 213 f.) is given here because it expresses inimitably the hopes and consolation of Greek Christianity, yet without omitting the characteristic warmth of feeling which belonged to its very essence.

"Her prayer was such that one could not doubt that she was with God, and heard his voice. She said: Thou, Lord, hast for us destroyed the fear of death. Thou hast made the end of this earthly life the beginning of the true life. Thou makest our bodies rest for a time in sleep, and dost awaken them again with the last trumpet. Thou givest our clay, which Thou didst fashion with Thy hands, to the earth to keep it, and Thou takest again what Thou didst give, and dost transform into imperishableness and beauty that which was mortal and unseemly. Thou hast snatched us from the curse and sin, having Thyself become both for us. Thou hast crushed the heads of the dragon, which had grasped man with its jaw in the abyss of disobedience. Thou hast paved the way of the resurrection for us, having shattered the gate of Hades, and destroyed him who had the power of death. Thou has given those who fear Thee the image of Thy holy cross for a sign for the destruction of the adversary and the safety of our life. Eternal God, to Whom I was dedicated from the womb, Whom my soul has loved with all its power, to Whom I have consecrated my flesh and my soul from my youth and till now! Place Thou an angel of light by my side to lead me to the place of quickening where is the source of rest in the bosom of the Holy Fathers.

Oh Thou who didst break the flaming sword, and didst restore
to Paradise the man crucified with Thee who begged Thy
mercy. Remember me, too, in Thy kingdom, because I also
am crucified with Thee, piercing my flesh ·with nails from fear
of Thee, and fainting in dread of Thy judgments! May the
awful abyss not divide me from Thine elect, nor the calumni-
ator block my way; may my sin not be found before Thine
eyes, if I, having failed through the weakness of our nature,
should have sinned in word, or deed, or thought! Thou who
hast power on earth to forgive sins, grant me forgiveness, that
I may be quickened, and when I put off my body may I be
found by Thee without stain in my soul, so that my soul,
spotless and blameless, may be received into Thy hands like
a sacrifice before Thy presence."

Supplement 4.—For centuries after the great work of Theognostus, which we only know very imperfectly, no complete system
of scientific theology was written in the East. The idea of a
system was in itself a philosophical one, and for its execution
all that was in existence were examples whose authority was
already shaken. Platonism only contributed to form a heterodox system. Aristotelianism with its formal logic, which triumphed
over all difficulties, first succeeded in creating an orthodox system. Systematic works, in the period up to Johannes Damascenus, fall into the following lists.

(1) *On the incarnation of the Logos*—or Son of God. In these
works the central question of Greek dogma is discussed. The title
varies, or is more precise, according to the standpoint of each:
"On the two natures", "On not confounding the natures", etc.
Under this head come also the polemical, dogmatic tractates—
against Arius, Marcellus, Eunomius, Apollinaris, Nestorius, etc.—
as well as dogmatic monographs—on the Holy Ghost, the Trinity,
etc. We have to notice finally the *Expositiones veritatis* at the close
of the writings against the heretics, like those found, after the
precedent of Hippolytus, in, *e.g.*, Epiphanius and Theodoret.

(2) *Exposition of Christian doctrines in catechetical form.*
Here Cyril's catechisms are especially important. [1] The catechism

---

[1] The plan of Cyril's catechisms is very instructive. First, there is in the preface
an inquiry as to the aim and nature of the instruction. It begins with the words

was always bound by the Symbol, but the Symbol necessitated the treatment of the main points of Jesus' history as points of doctrine, and the expiscation of their exact value for faith. Thus dogma gained an important supplement from the exposition of the Symbol. The decalogue of the creed by Gregory of Nazianzus also falls to be mentioned here. In the great catechism of Gregory of Nyssa catechetic treatment is combined with apologetic. Instructions how to pursue theological science came from the Antiochene school and thence penetrated into the West—Junilius —where Augustine had already written his work De doctrina Christiana. So far as I know, the older Byzantine Church possessed no such instructions.

(3) *Apologetic works in reference to heathens and Jews.* In these, natural theology—the monotheistic faith and doctrine of freedom —is unfolded, and the Christian view of history, as well as the proof of its antiquity, presented in opposition to polytheism and ceremonial religions; so in several works by Eusebius, Apollinaris, Cyril of Alexandria, etc.

Ἤδη μακαριότητος ὀσμὴ πρὸς ὑμᾶς. Compare also ch. VI: Βλέπε μοι πηλίκην σοι ἀξίαν ὁ Ἰησοῦς χαρίζεται... μὴ νομίσῃς ὅτι μικρὸν πρᾶγμα λαμβάνεις· ἄνθρωπος ὢν οἰκτρός, Θεοῦ λαμβάνεις προσηγορίαν... τοῦτο προβλέπων ὁ Ψαλμῳδὸς ἔλεγεν ἐκ προσώπου τοῦ Θεοῦ, ἐπειδὴ μέλλουσιν ἄνθρωποι Θεοῦ προσηγορίαν λαμβάνειν· Ἐγὼ εἶπα, θεοί ἐστε καὶ υἱοὶ ὑψίστου πάντες, c. 12: ἐάν σε κατηχούμενος ἐξετάσῃ, τι εἰρήκασιν οἱ διδάσκοντες, μηδὲν λέγε τῷ ἔξω· μυστήριον γάρ σοι παραδίδομεν καὶ ἐλπίδα μέλλοντος αἰῶνος· τήρησον τὸ μυστήριον τῷ μισθαποδότῃ. Then follow three Catechisms which impart information concerning sin, baptism, and penitence in general, and are meant to awaken the right disposition. In the fourth a sketch is given of the system of faith according to the Symbol. Ten systems are distinguished, whose numbering, however, can no longer be established with certainty. The exposition contained in Catechisms 5—18 do not agree with the sketch, seeing that to the latter is appended a didactic section on the soul, the body, food, and clothing, a section which is wanting in the exposition; the latter rather in the last catechism deals with the Church, which is not mentioned in the sketch. The whole is concluded by five catechisms which explain the secret rites of the mysteries to the baptised. The decalogue of the faith by Gregory contains, in the first commandment, the doctrine of the Trinity; in the second, the creation out of nothing and the providence of God; in the third, the origin of evil from freedom, not from an evil matter or God; in the fourth, the doctrine of the incarnation and constitution of the Redeemer; in the fifth, the crucifixion and burial; in the sixth, the resurrection and ascension; in the seventh, the return of Christ in glory to act as judge; in the eight and ninth, the general resurrection and retributive judgment; the tenth runs: Δέκατον ἐργάζου τὸ ἀγαθὸν ἐπὶ τούτῳ τῷ θεμελίῳ τῶν δογμάτων, ἐπειδὴ πίστις χωρὶς ἔργων νεκρά, ὡς ἔργα δίχα πίστεως.

(4) *Monographs on the work of the six days*, on the human soul, the body, the immortality of the soul, etc. In these, also, natural theology is developed and the scientific cosmology and psychology in the oldest sources of the Bible stated.

(5) *Monographs on virginity, monachism, perfection, the virtues, the resurrection.* Here the ultimate and supreme practical interests of piety and faith find expression.

(6) *Monographs on the mysteries, cultus and priesthood.* These are not numerous in the earlier period—yet instruction in the sacraments and their ritual was regularly attached to the training in the Symbol; see the Catechisms of Cyril which form a guide to the mysteries. Their number, however, increased from the sixth century.

Copious, often intentionally elaborated, dogmatic material, finally, is also contained in scientific commentaries on the Biblical books and in the Homilies.

The right use for the history of dogma of these different kinds of sources is an art of method for which rules can hardly be given. The rhetorical, exegetical, philosophical, and strictly dogmatic expositions must be recognised as such and distinguished. At the same time we have to remember that this was an age of rhetoric which did not shrink from artifices and untruths of every kind. Jerome admits that in the works of the most celebrated Fathers one must always distinguish between what they wrote argumentatively (διαλεκτικῶς), and what they set down as truth. Basilius also (Ep. 210) was at once prepared to explain a heterodox passage in Gregory Thaumaturgus, by supposing that he had been speaking not dogmatically (δογματικῶς), but for the sake of argument (ἀγωνιστικῶς). So also Athanasius excuses Origen on the ground that he wrote much for the sake of practice and investigation (De decretis synod. Nic. 27, cf. ad Serap. IV. 9); and while completely defending the Christology of Dionysius Alex., he remarks that the latter in many details spoke from policy (κατ' οἰκονομίαν). The same stock excuse was seized upon by the Fathers at Sardica in the case of Marcellus. According to this, how often must the great writers of the fourth and fifth centuries themselves have written for the sake of argument (ἀγωνιστικῶς)! Moreover, Gregory of Nazianzus speaks of a necessary and salutary οἰκονομηθῆναι τὴν ἀλήθειαν, *i.e.*, of the politic and prudent disguise and the gradual communication of the truth; and he appeals in support of this to God himself who only revealed the truth at the fitting time, οἰκονομικῶς (Orat. 41. 6, Ep. 26). Cyrus declares, in the monothelite controversy, that one must assume κατ᾽ οἰκονομίαν a not altogether correct dogma, in order to attain something of importance.

Some, however, went much farther in this matter. As they did not hold themselves bound to stick to the truth in dealing with an opponent, and thus had forgotten the command of the gospel, so they went on in theology to impute untruthfulness to the Apostles, citing the dispute between Paul and Peter, and to Christ (he concealed his omniscience, etc.). They even charged God with falsehood in dealing with his enemy, the devil, as is proved by the views held by Origen, Gregory of Nyssa, and most of the later Fathers, of redemption from the power of the devil. But if God himself deceived his enemy by stratagem (*pia fraus*), then so also might men. Under such circumstances it cannot be wondered at that forgeries were the order of the day. And this was the case. We read even in the second century of numerous falsifications and interpolations made under their very eyes on the works of still living authors. Think of the grievances of the Church Fathers against the Gnostics, and the complaints of Dionysius of Corinth and Irenæus. But what did these often naïve and subjectively innocent falsifications signify compared with that spirit of lying which was powerfully at work even in official compositions in the third and fourth centuries? Read Rufinus' De adulterat. libr. Origenis, and weigh Rufinus' principles in translating the works of Origen. And the same spirit prevailed in the Church in the fifth and sixth centuries; see a collection of the means employed to deceive in my altchrist. Litt.-Gesch. I., p. xlii ff. In these centuries no one continued to put any trust in a documentary authority, a record of proceedings, or protocol. The letters by Bishops of this period throng with complaints of forgeries; the defeated party at a Synod almost regularly raises the charge that the acts of Synod are falsified; Cyril and the great letter-writers complain that their letters are circulated in a corrupt form; the

epistles of dead Fathers—*e.g.*, that of Athanasius to Epictetus—
were falsified, and foreign matter was inserted into them; the followers of Apollinaris and Monophysites, *e.g.*, systematically corrupted the tradition. See the investigations of Caspari and Dräseke.
Conversely, the simplest method of defending an ancient Church
Father who was cited by the opposition, or on whose orthodoxy
suspicion was cast, was to say that the hereties had corrected
his works to suit themselves and had sown weeds among his
wheat. The official literature of the Nestorian and Monophysite
controversy is a swamp of mendacity and knavery, above which
only a few spots rise on which it is possible to find a firm
footing. Gregory I. (Ep. VI. 14) at once recalls in a given case
the forging of the acts of the Ephesian Synod. What was not
published as Nicene in later times, and to some extent very
soon! Much indeed was even then dismissed as mendacity and
deceit, much has been laid bare by the scholars of the seven-
teenth century. But if one considers the verdicts, anxieties,
and assertions of suspicion of contemporaries of those conflicts,
he cannot avoid the fear that present-day historians are still
much too confiding in dealing with this whole literature. The
uncertainties which remain in the study precisely of the most
important alterations of the history of dogma, and of the Church
of the Byzantine period, necessarily awaken the suspicion that
we are almost throughout more or less helpless in face of the
systematically corrupted tradition. All the same I would not
recommend so bold a handling of the sources as that formerly
practised by the Jesuits, and to-day by Vincenzi (Ketzertaufstreit,
Acten des 5 Concils, Honoriusfrage).

Supplement 5.—The form assumed by the substance of the
faith in the Greek Church shows very clearly the characteristic
point of view. First, namely, it was conceived—though, so far
as I know, seldom—as law; indeed Gregory of Nazianzus sketched
a decalogue of faith. This form must not be misunderstood.
The faith appears as law only in so far as its contents constitute a revealed ordinance of God to which man has to submit;
we must not let it suggest to us a parallel to the moral law.
Secondly, however, the creed is regarded in its formulas as a
mystery to be kept secret. Men were initiated into the faith

as they were initiated into the sacred rites.[1] Secrecy was, according to ancient ideas, the necessary nimbus of all consecration. The conceptions of the creed as law and as mystery have this in common, that in them the content of the faith appears as something strictly objective, something given from without.[2] But in so far as the authority of any formula whatever conflicts with original Christianity as much as this secrecy, the dependence of the Greek Church on the practice of the ancient mysteries and schools of philosophy is here manifest.

Supplement 6.—Ideas of the realisation of the supreme good in the world beyond had to attach themselves to the phrases of the creed known in the Symbols, and were not permitted to disregard the numerous and diversified statements of Holy Scripture. The motley and manifold conceptions which resulted were owing to harmonising with primitive Christian eschatology on the one hand, and Origen's doctrine of the consummation on the other, subject to due regard for the sacred writings. Origen's doctrine was more and more regarded as heretical from the end of the fourth century, while previously recognised theologians, like Gregory of Nyssa, had reproduced it in all its main points. Its rejection marks the first decisive victory of traditionalism—itself indeed impregnated with speculation—over spiritualising speculation. In the fifth century, there were counted as heretical, (1) the doctrine of apokatastasis (universalism) and the possibility of redemption for the devil;[3] (2) the doctrine of the complete annihilation of evil; (3) the conception of the penalties of hell as tortures of conscience; (4) the spiritualising version of the resuscitation of the body; and (5) the idea of

---

[1] See the investigations into the so-called Arcan-Disciplin, by Rothe, Th. Harnack, Bonwetsch, and Von Zezschwitz.

[2] Constantine delighted in applying the name "law" to the whole of the Christian religion. This is western (nostra lex = nostra religio); it is rare in the East. On the other hand, the whole Bible was not infrequently "the law" in the one Church as well as in the other.

[3] Gregory of Nyssa still defended it, appealing to 1 Cor. XV. 28; see the second half of his writing περὶ ψυχῆς καὶ ἀναστάσεως, and Orat. catech. 8, 35. So also—for a time—Jerome and the older Antiochenes; even in the fifth century it had numerous defenders in both East and West. It was definitively condemned with the condemnation of Origen under Justinian. See under, ch. XI.

the continued creation of new worlds. On the other hand, the doctrines of Christ's reign on earth for a thousand years, and the double resurrection, etc., were in the East in part shelved, in part absolutely characterised as Jewish heresies.[1] The return of Christ, which was still described as imminent, though for many theologians it had lost its essential significance, the judgment of the world, the resurrection of the body,[2] the eternal misery (θάνατος ἐν ἀθανασίᾳ—undying death) of the wicked, were maintained, and even the conception of a transfiguration of heaven and this earth was not everywhere rejected. Retained accordingly were only those points enumerated in the symbols, and therefore no longer to be passed over. To these were added the expectation of Antichrist, which, however, only emerged, as a rule, during exceptional distress, as in the times of Arian emperors, Julian, barbarous nations, Mohammed, etc., and by no means now belonged to the solid substance of theological eschatology; (yet see Cyril, Catech. 15, ch. 11 f., the pseudo-hippolytan work περὶ συντελείας, and the late apocalypses of from the fourth to the seventh century). Blessedness was regarded as a state of freedom from suffering, of the perfect knowledge, and the intuitive and entrancing enjoyment, of God. Yet the majority recognised different degrees and stages of

---

[1] The last important theological representative of Chiliasm in the East was Apollinaris of Laodicea; see Epiph. H. 77, ch. 37, Jerome de vir. inl. 18. Jerome labours to prove (Ep. 129) that the *terra promissionis* was not Palestine, but a heavenly place. The Apocalypse was, as a rule, not included in the Canon in the East (in older times). With this state of matters is contrasted very strongly the fact that in the lower ranks of priests, monks, and laity apocalypses continued to be eagerly read, and new ones were ever being produced on the basis of the old.

[2] The doctrine of the resurrection of man in spirit and body still always formed a main point in Apologetic evidences, and was, as formerly, proved from the omnipotence of God, from various analogical inferences, and from the essential importance of the body for human personality. The Cappadocians and some later Greek theologians still held, though in a much weakened form, to the spiritualistic version of the doctrine attempted by Origen. But, following Methodius, Epiphanius (H. 64, ch. 12 ff.) especially insisted that there was the most perfect identity between the resurrection body and our material body, and this faith, enforced in the West by Jerome, soon established itself as alone orthodox. There now arose many problems concerning the limbs and members of the future body, and even Augustine seriously considered these. He experimented on the flesh of a peacock, and confirmed his faith in the resurrection by the discovery of its preservation from decay.

blessedness, a conception in which we perceive the moralist encroach upon the ground of religion,[1] since it put a high value on special earthly achievements, such as asceticism and martyrdom. As regards the blessed dead, it was supposed in wide circles that their souls waited in Hades, a subterranean place, for the return of Christ;[2] there Christ had also preached the gospel to the good who had died before him.[3] Not a few Fathers of the fourth century maintained, following Origen, that the souls of the pious at once enter Paradise, or come to Christ,[4] and this opinion gained ground more and more. It was universal in regard to saints and martyrs. Besides, the conceptions of the intermediate state, like everything else in this connection, were altogether vague, since Greek theologians were only inter-

---

[1] The assumption of various degrees of blessedness (and damnation) must have been almost universal; for the divergent opinion of Jovinian was felt to be heretical; see Jerome adv. Jovin. I. 3, II. 18—34. Still it excited more real interest in the West than in the East (Augustine, De civitate, XXII., ch. 30). As regards the idea of future existence, some Fathers supposed that men would positively become angels, others that they would be like the angels.

[2] The different conceptions as to the relations of Hades, Hell, Paradise, the bosom of Abraham, etc., do not come in here. According to Gregory of Nyssa, Hades is not to be held a place, but an invisible and incorporeal state of the life of the soul.

[3] This old theologoumenon (see Vol. I., p. 203) occurs in western and eastern theologians. Those who would have become Christians if they had lived later, *i.e.*, after Christ's appearance, were redeemed. The phrase *descendit ad inferna* came into the Symbols from the fourth century. We find it in the West first, in the Symbol of Aquileia, in the East in the formula of the fourth Synod at Sirmium (359 εἰς τὰ καταχθόνια κατελθόντα). It is at least questionable whether it was already in the Jerusalemite Symbol at the same date. Compare Hahn, Bibliothek d. Symbole, 2 Aufl. §§ 24, 27, 34, 36, 37, 39—41, 43, 45, 46—60, 93, 94, 96, 108; Caspari, Ueber das Jerus. Taufbekenntniss in Cyrillus' Katechesen, with an excursus: Hat das Jerus. Taufbekenntniss den *descensus ad inferos* enthalten, in the norweg. Theol. Ztschr. Vol. I.

[4] With this it could be and, as a rule, was understood that their felicity up to the last judgment was only preliminary. Two interests met here: those of a spiritualising religion and of primitive Christian eschatology; see Vol. I., p. 129 f. The latter required that blessedness should be attached to the return of Christ and the last judgment; the former demanded that it should be complete as soon as the believing soul had parted from the mortal body. Therefore, in spite of Jerome's polemic against Vigilantius and Augustine's against Pelagius, no fixed Church doctrine could be arrived at here, however much piety desired an absolute decision. See for details Petavius and Schwane D. Gesch. d. patrist Zeit, p. 749 ff.

ested ultimately in the hope of deification.[1] In the West, on the contrary, the entire primitive Christian eschatology was upheld pretty nearly intact during the fourth century, and even the idea of Nero returning as Antichrist had numerous supporters. The reason of this lies in the fact that Neoplatonic speculation, and speculation generally, obtained at first no footing here, and the specific import of Christianity at the same time was still always expressed in the dramatically conceived eschatology. But the distinction between West and East goes at this point much deeper. Strongly eschatological as was the aim of the whole dogmatics of the East, it cannot be overlooked that the heart of the matter—the thought of the judgment—had been torn away from the eschatology since Origen. This thought which expresses the fearful responsibility of every soul to the God of holiness, and without which the forgiveness of sins must remain an enigma and an empty word, dominated the gospel, and determined ancient Christianity. But " scientific" theology had shelved it.[2] The name is not wanting in Origen's system, but the thing had disappeared. In spite of all the emphasis laid on freedom, nothing exists but a cosmic process, in which the many issues from the one, in order to return into the one. In such a scheme the Judgment has been deprived of its meaning. In subsequent times apokatastasis—universalism—was indeed condemned in the East, and Origen's system was rejected; but any one who studies closely Greek Byzantine dogmatics will see how profound was the attachment to this most important point in Origenism and Neoplatonism. The problems to which the creed gave birth in the fourth to the seventh century, and which men laboured to solve, discountenance any effective reference to the judgment. Again and again we have deification as a hyperphysical and therefore physical

---

[1] Clement and Origen had assumed a purgatory in the shape of a cleansing fire (see Vol. II., p. 377, n. 5); the Greek Fathers, however, have, so far as I know, dropped the idea, with the exception of Gregory of Nyssa (περὶ ψυχῆς καὶ ἀναστάσεως, Oehler, Vol. I., p. 98 f.). From Origen and Gregory the conception passed to Ambrose who established it in the West, after the way had been prepared for it by Tertullian. The Scriptural proof was 1 Cor. III. 13 f.; compare Augustine De civitate dei, XXI. 23 sq. Enchir. 68 sq. (ignis purgatorius).

[2] It still lived in the popular views of Christianity held by the Orientals.

process, but dogmatics tell us little of the tenet that it is appointed unto man to die and after that the judgment. For this reason also the strict connection with morality was lost, and therefore in some regions even Islam was a deliverer. It was different in the West. What has been named the "Chiliasm" of the West, possessed its essential significance in the prospect of the judgment. If we compare West and East in the Middle Ages— the theologians, not the laity—no impression is stronger than that the former knew the fear of the judge to which the latter had become indifferent. It was the restless element in the life of faith of the West; it sustained the thought of forgiveness of sins; it accordingly made the reformation of Catholicism possible. And any reformation, if it should ever take place in the Greek Church, will begin by restoring the conviction of the responsibility of every individual soul, emphasising the judgment, and thus gaining the fixed point from which to cast down the walls of dogmatics.

Literature.—Hermann, Gregorii Nysseni sententiæ de salute adipiscenda, 1875. H. Schultz, Die Lehre von der Gottheit Christi, 1881. Kattenbusch, Kritische Studien der Symbolik, in the Studien und Kritiken, 1878, p. 94 ff. Ritschl, Die Christl. Lehre v. d. Rechtfertigung und Versöhnung, 2 Ed., Vol. I., pp. 3—21. Kattenbusch, Konfessionskunde I., p. 296 ff. On Monachism, especially in Russia, see Frank, Russ. Kirche, p. 190 ff.

CHAPTER III.

THE extent and authority of the Catholic authorities were already substantially fixed at the beginning of the fourth century, though their mutual relations and the manner of using them in detail were not.[1] Among the parties which contended over the correct definition of the dogma of redemption, they had to a certain degree become undoubtedly subjects of controversy. The great opposition between a more liberal theology and pure traditionalism was based upon a difference in the way of looking at the authorities. But this opposition never culminated in a clear contrast of principles. Consequently, theologians had no occasion to frame a special doctrine of the Church and the authorities—Scripture and tradition. The need was not, as in the case of the dogma of redemption, so pressing as to lead men to adopt the perilous and obnoxious course of formulating laws of faith anew. The petty skirmishes, however, with more or less obscure theologians and reformers, who point-blank objected to this or that portion of the traditional basis, did not come before the great tribunal of the Church, and the conflict with Manichæans, Paulicians, Euchites, and Bogomilians, has left no trace in the history of dogma.[2]

---

[1] See the account given in Vol. II., pp. 18—127, and elsewhere.

[2] The opposition to the Eustathians and Andians (see the Acts of the Synod of Gangra and Epiph. H. 70) does not belong to this section; for it arose from a different conception of the obligatoriness of the monk's life on Christians. On the contrary, it is noteworthy that Aërius, once a friend of Eustathius (Epiph. H. 75) not only maintained the original identity of bishops and presbyters—that had also been done, and supported from the N. T., by Jerome and the theologians of Antioch—

Still, changes took place in the period between Eusebius and
Johannes Damascenus. They followed simply the altered requirements of the Church. They gave utterance to the increased
traditionalism. Necessity became a virtue, *i.e.*, every new point
which was felt to be needed in order to preserve the unity of
the Church, or to adapt its institutions to the taste of the time,
was inserted in the list of authorities. This method was in
vogue even in the third century. It was now only further and
further extended. But it is hard to fix its results, since at that
time there was no fixity and there could be none, from the
nature of the principle that the state of the Church at any time
was to be declared as in every respect the traditional one. [1]

1. *Holy Scripture.* [2]

To the two Testaments a unique authority was ascribed.
They were the Holy Scriptures κατ' ἐξοχήν; every doctrine had

but he made the question an *articulus stantis et cadentis ecclesiæ*. We cannot now
determine what motive influenced him. The attack of Marcellus of Ancyra on the
foundations of the prevalent theology, and his argument that the dogma was
essentially ἀνϑρωπίνης βουλῆς τε καὶ γνώμης, are of incomparably greater significance
in principle. But his arguments were not understood, and produced no effect. Meanwhile, the basis of the whole structure of the Catholic Church in the East was at
no time left unassailed. The Church has never embraced everything which was,
and might be, named Christian. After the Marcionites and the older sects had
retired from the stage, or had fused with the Manichæans, Paulicians, Euchites, and
Bogomilians, etc., came upon the scene. These Churches contested the Catholic
foundations as the Marcionites and Manichæans had done; they accepted neither
the Catholic Canon, nor the hierarchical order and tradition. They succeeded, in
part, in creating lasting, comprehensive, and exclusive systems, and afforded work
to Byzantine theologians and politicians for centuries. But important as it is to
assert their existence, they have no place in the history of dogma; for at no time
had they any influence whatever on the formation of dogma in the East; they have
left no effect on the Church. Therefore general Church history has alone to deal
with them.

[1] The view held of the apostolate of the twelve first fully reached its Catholic
level in the fourth and fifth centuries. The Apostles were (1) missionaries who had
traversed the whole world and performed unheard of miracles, (2) the rulers of the
Churches, (3) teachers and law-givers in succession to Christ, having given in speech
and writing to the least detail all the regulations necessary to the Church for faith
and morals, (4) the authors of the order of worship, the liturgy, (5) heroic ascetics
and fathers of monachism, (6) though hesitatingly, the mediators of salvation.

[2] See histories of the Canon by Holtzmann, Schmiedel (in Ersch and Gruber
"Kanon"); Weiss, Westcott, and especially Zahn. Overbeck, Z. Gesch. des Kanons,

to be proved out of them, in other words, opinions that held something necessary to faith which did not occur in Scripture, had no absolute validity. Any one who declared that he took his stand on Scripture alone did not assume an uncatholic attitude. This view of the Holy Scriptures presupposed that their extent was strictly defined, and placed beyond all doubt. But this supposition was for centuries contradicted by the actual facts, which, however, were concealed, partly because men neither would nor dared look at them, partly because they really did not see them. The theologians of Antioch, and especially Theodore, criticised on internal and external grounds the contents of the Canon, as these were gradually being fixed; but in doing so even they were guided by an ecclesiastical tradition. Their criticism still had its supporters in the sixth century, and its influence extended not only to Persia, but even, through Junilius, to the West. But neither the spirit of the criticism nor its results ever made any impression whatever on the great Church. [1]

As regards the O. T., the oldest and most revered of the Greek Fathers followed Melito and Origen, and only recognised the 22—24 books of the Hebrew Canon, [2] according to the others in the Alexandrian Canon only a secondary validity, or none at all. While there was some hesitation about the Book of Esther, and that not only in Antioch, this decision obtained

---

1880. The controversy with the Jews as to the possession and exposition of the O. T. still continued in the Byzantine period; see on this McGiffert, Dialogue between a Christian and a Jew, entitled ’Αντιβολὴ Παπίσκου καὶ Φίλωνος κ.τ.λ. . . . together with a discussion of Christian polemics against the Jews. New York, 1889.

[1] On the attitude of Theodore and his disciples to the Canon, see the thorough investigations of Kihn (Theodorus von Mopsuestia und Junilius Africanus, 1880). Theodore rejected from the O. T., Job, the Song of Songs, Chronicles, Ezra and Nehemiah, Esther, and the inscriptions of the Psalms; see Leontius Byz. Contra Nestor. et Eutych. L. III., ch. 13—17, Migne T. 86, p. 1365 sq. The fifth Synod expressly condemned Theodore's criticism and interpretation of Job and the Song of Songs, as well as his idea of inspiration in reference to Solomon's writings, and his exposition of some of the Psalms. On Theodore's prestige in Nisibis, see Kihn, p. 333 f.; on Junilius' dependence on him, l. c., 350—382. For the dependence of the Nestorian Canon on Theodore's, see Noeldeke in the Gött. Gel. Anz. 1868, St. 46, p. 1826 and Kihn, l. c., 336.

[2] Authoritative were especially the views of Athanasius, Cyril of Jerus. and Gregory of Nazianzus, who reckoned only 22 Books; see also the sixtieth Canon of the Council of Laodicea (363? inauthentic?).

in the Greek Churches, though divergences were not wanting
in provincial communities. But it was always in danger of
being disregarded, for the sacred books were continually transcribed from the LXX.; and so, as a rule, those writings, ex-
cluded in theory, were copied along with the others. The legend
of the genesis of the LXX., again, was always highly valued,
and it seemed to imply the sacredness of the whole translation.
Yet it was only in consequence of the attempts at union with
the Roman Church in the Middle Ages, and still more after
the ill-fated enterprise of Cyrillus Lucaris (17th century),
that the Greek Church was persuaded to give up the Hebrew
and adopt the Alexandrian and Roman Canon. But a binding,
official declaration never followed; the passiveness and thought-
lessness with which it changed, or upturned its position in so
important a question, is extraordinarily characteristic of the
modern Græco-Slavic Church. The question is not even yet
decided, and there are distinguished Russian theologians, who
regard the books of the Hebrew Canon as being alone strictly
canonical. They are, however, growing ever fewer. [1] In the
Western Church a state of complete uncertainty still prevailed
in the fourth century as to the extent of the O. T. But the
Latin Bible, complete copies of which may not have been very
common, was a translation of the LXX. This fact was more
potent than the historical views which found their way into the
West from the East, in a disjointed form, and for whose
triumph Jerome had laboured. Augustine, who was ignorant of
Biblical criticism, held to the current Latin collection (see, *e.g.*,
his list in De doct. christ. II., 8), and at the Synods of Hippo,
A.D. 393 (can. 36), and Carthage, A.D. 397 (can. 47), the Alexandrian Canon was adopted. The decision that the Roman
Church was to be asked for a confirmation of this conclusion
does not seem to have been carried out. From that date the
Hebrew Canon was departed from in the West, though the
view of Athanasius, conveyed to it by Rufinus, and the decision
of Jerome, exerted a quiet influence, and even apart from this

---

[1] See Gass, Symbolik der griechischen Kirche, p. 97 ff.; Strack, Kanon des
A. T. in Prot. R.-E., Vol. VII. 2, p. 412 ff. The reader is referred to this article and
to Introductions to the O. T. for details. Kattenbusch, Confessionskunde I., p 292.

some uncertainty—*e.g.*, in the case of 4 Esra, the Pastor of Hermas, etc.,—still remained.[1] Cassiodorus seems to have taken a very important part in finally shaping the Latin Bible. But we cannot by any means describe the attitude of the West as uncritical. It only avoided the inconsistency into which scholars had fallen in extolling the LXX. as a divinely composed and authentic work, while they ranked the Hebrew Bible above it.

As regards the N. T., the Alexandrian Church accepted the Western collection in the time of Origen, and in the course of the third century most of the others, though not yet all,[2] seem to have followed its example. In so far as any reflection was given to their historical characteristics, the Scriptures were regarded as Apostolic-catholic, and were acknowledged to contain the real sources of evidence for Christian doctrine. But the principle of apostolicity could not be strictly carried out. In many national Churches apostolic writings were known and revered which were not found in the Western collection, and conversely, it was not always possible to perceive the Apostolic origin and Catholic recognition of a received book. Origen already therefore adopted the idea, consonant to the spirit of antiquity, that the collection embraced those books about whose title a general agreement had prevailed from the earliest times. Canonicity was decided by unanimous testimony. But even this principle did not meet the whole case; Origen himself violated it in forming the group of seven Catholic Epistles. Yet it became the established rule, and put an end to any consideration of the question based on criticism of the facts.

[1] Gregory I. (Moral XIX. 13) thought it necessary to excuse himself for arguing from Maccabees.

[2] Thus Syrian Churches still used Tatian's Diatessaron in the fourth century; and in a few circles among them there were retained in the Canon, the apocryphal correspondence of the Corinthians and Paul, the two Epp. of Clement, nay, even the Ep. of Clement de virginitate. On the other hand, some books were wanting. Not a few apocryphal writings held an undefined rank in the Syrian Patriarchate. In a word, the old Roman Canon, expanded in the course of the third century in Alexandria, did not get the length of being acknowledged in vast territories of the East proper. In spite of the association of the Apostolic Epistles with the Gospels, the higher rank peculiar to the latter was not done away with as late as the fourth century. Alexander of Alexandria (in Theodoret H. E. I. 4) describes the contents of Holy Scripture briefly as 'Law, Prophets, and Gospels.'

Eusebius, who was a very important authority, and who—if we are to understand the passage so—had been commissioned by the Emperor to prepare standard Bibles, followed the view of Origen; yet in the case of one book, the Apocalypse, he expressed his dislike in a way that ran counter to the principle of the Canon. The three, or four, categories, in which he required to arrange the books, show that men were struggling with a difficulty not to be solved in this way, which could only be solved by time with its power to hallow all inconsistencies. [1] If we collected statistically all the Eastern information we possess concerning the extent of the N. T. from the date of Eusebius up to the destruction of Constantinople—direct and indirect statements by Church Fathers, Synodal decisions, Bible manuscripts and indices from the Churches of various provinces, and especially Syria—we would be forced to the conclusion that complete confusion and uncertainty prevailed. [2] But this view would be erroneous. We have to multiply by hundreds the lists which enumerate 26 (27) books, *i.e.*, the *Acknowledged* and the *Disputed melioris notæ* of Eusebius.—Athanasius' Festival Epistle, A.D. 367, was of paramount importance in settling the complete equality of these two classes in the Patriarchates of Alexandria and Constantinople and in the West.—On the other hand, apart from the Syrian Churches, [3] the lists which diverge

[1] On the efforts of Eusebius to fix the extent of the N. T., see Texte und Untersuch. zur altchristl. Litteratur-Geschichte, Vol. II. 1, 2, p. 5 ff.

[2] Almost everything which was esteemed in quite different circumstances in the earliest period, is to be again found somewhere or other in the Byzantine age. Most instructive is the history of Clement's Epistles and Hermas. Conversely, the old doubts also remain and even new ones emerge (Philemon, see Jerome in his preface to the Epistle).

[3] The N. T. had a peculiar history in the Syrian Churches, which has not yet been written; see Nestle, 'Syrische Bibelübersetzungen' in the Prot. R.-E. Vol. XV.; Bäthgen's work on the Syrus Cureton. 1885, and my 'das N. T. um das Jahr 200' (1888). It is more than questionable whether Theodore of Mopsuestia did any independent criticism on the extent of the N. T. He, probably, simply adhered to the Canon of his Church, which then of the Catholic Epistles only admitted 1 Peter and 1 John, and rejected the Apocalypse; see Kihn, l. c., 65 ff. and the Canon of Chrysostom. While the whole Church was substantially agreed about the extent of the N. T., from the end of the fourth century, wide districts in the Patriarchate of Antioch retained their separate traditions. Only we must not forget

from the above owe their existence either to a badly applied scholarship, or to individual reminiscences, in rare cases to a divergent usage on the part of provincial Churches. From the end of the fourth century real unanimity prevailed, in the main, as to the contents of the N. T. and the authorship of the separate books, in Constantinople, Asia Minor, Alexandria, and the West. Apart from doubts of long standing, yet ineffectual and isolated, about the Catholic Epistles (and Philemon?), the one exception was John's Revelation, for which Eusebius' verdict was momentous.[1] But even in this case attempts to come to a decision were given up: the book was shelved, and re-emerged, from the circles in which it had maintained its ground, without exciting any controversy worth mentioning. The disquieting distinction between Acknowledged and Disputed books, abolished by Athanasius, was but very seldom of any consequence in practice; but scholars still recalled it here and there. When the collection was limited to 26 (27) books, the reading of others in the Church was, from the end of the fourth century, more strictly prohibited. But even at the beginning of the fifth, men in a position to know, like Jerome and Sozomen, can tell us that the prohibition was here and there unknown or disregarded. Some primitive Christian writings were thus in use in the Churches down to the fifth century and later; but the Monophysite Churches preserved, as a monkish protest against the spiritualism of Origen, Jewish Apocalypses revised by Christians and belonging to the earliest period, and the barbarism into which they fell spread a protective covering over these writings.[2]

The details are obscure of the way in which the Western

that the vast majority even of these had accepted the Roman Canon of undisputed books in the second half of the third century. But the agreement went no further; for from the fourth century they would take no more instruction from Alexandria.

[1] For the rest, Weiss has rightly shown (Einleitung in das N. T., p. 98) that the extent to which the Apocalypse was rejected, has been somewhat exaggerated. Extremely noteworthy is the view of Didymus on 2 Peter (Enarrat. in epp. cathol.): "Non est ignorandum præsentem epistolam esse falsatam, quæ licet publicetur non tamen in canone est."

[2] In the Byzantine Church also Apocalypses continued to be read, and new ones were constantly being produced.

Church obtained the Epistle of James, second Peter, and third John. The Epistle to the Hebrews, not unknown to it from the first, it received in the fourth century as a Pauline composition, from the East, through the famous intermediaries. Those same men did away with all uncertainty at the close of the fourth century on the ground of the decisions given by Eusebius and Athanasius. The 27 books, *i.e.*, the Canon of Athanasius, were alone recognised at the Synods of Hippo and Carthage (397), and this result was confirmed by Augustine's authority (see, *e.g.*, De doctr. christ. II. 8) without any general declaration having been made.[1] But the sharper the line drawn between the collection and all other writings, the more suspicious must those have appeared whose title could lead, or had once admittedly led, to a claim for recognition as Catholic and Apostolic. The category of "apocryphal" in which they had formerly been placed, solely in order to mark the alleged or real absence of general testimony in their favour, now obtained more and more an additional meaning; they were of unknown origin, or 'fabricated', and this was often supplemented by the charge of being 'heretical'. But however great the gulf between the canonical and uncanonical books, it is impossible to con-

---

[1] See also under this head the verdict, freer because dependent on Theodore, which Junilius passed on the Catholic Epistles. Critical investigations have not yet arrived at a final result regarding the Decretum Gelasii. Augustine himself has not failed, besides, to notice the doubts that existed in his time; see Retractat. II. 4, 2. In his De pecc. mer. I. 27, he still leaves the Ep. to the Hebrews unassigned. In De doctr. christ. II. 8, he writes: "In canonicis autem scripturis ecclesiarum catholicarum quam plurimum auctoritatem sequatur, inter quas sane illæ sint, quæ apostolicas sedes habere et epistolas accipere meruerunt." Accordingly, this principle still holds. "Tenebit igitur hunc modum in scripturis canonicis, ut eas quæ ab omnibus accipiuntur ecclesiis catholicis, præponat eis quas quædam non accipiunt; in iis vero quæ non accipiuntur ab omnibus, præponat eas, quas plures gravioresque accipiunt eis, quas pauciores minorisque auctoritatis ecclesiæ tenent. Si autem alias invenerit a pluribus, alias a gravioribus haberi, quamquam hoc facile inveniri non possit, æqualis tamen auctoritatis eas habendas puto." Since the older copies of the Bible continued to be transcribed, uniformity had not been secured. It is true we no longer possess western Bibles whose contents are limited to the earliest Roman Canon—Gospels, Acts, 13 Pauline Ep., 1 and 2 John, 1 Peter, Jude, Revelation—but we have them with an Ep. to the Laodiceans, the Pastor (though in the O. T.), and even with the apocryphal correspondence of the Corinthians and Paul.

ceal the fact that the Church never published a general decision, excluding all doubt, on the extent of the Canon in ancient times. The Canon of Augustine was adopted by Pope Innocent I. (Ep. 6, ch. 7, ad Exsuperium).

With the complete elaboration of the conception of canonical books, every other description applied to them gave way to the idea of their divinity.[1] What could any predicate signify compared with the conviction that they had been composed by the Holy Ghost himself? Therefore the categories of canonical and inspired writings coincided, nay, inspiration in its highest sense was limited to the canonical books. The belief in inspiration was necessarily attended by the duty of pneumatic or allegorical exegesis. This sacred art was then practised by all, who were able thus to disregard the results of any other kind of exposition. The problems which pneumatic exegesis, praised even by cultured Hellenists,[2] had to solve, were mainly the following. It had (1) to demonstrate the agreement between the two Testaments, in other words; to christianise the O. T. completely, to discover prophecy everywhere, to get rid of the literal meaning where it was obnoxious, and to repel Jewish claims;[3] (2) to harmonise the statements of Holy Scripture with the prevailing dogmatics; (3) to furnish every text with a profound meaning, one valuable for the time. Exegesis became a kind of black art, and Augustine was not the only man who was delivered from Manichæan, by Biblical, Alchemy.

But while these tasks were generally fixed, a sure and unvarying method was still wanting.[4] Even the principles of

[1] The conception that the canonical books were solemnly set apart, occurs first in Athanasius; the Alexandrians, however, including Origen, had the idea and even the word before him (Orig. Prolog. in Cantic.). Athanasius writes in his Festival Ep. τὰ κανονιζόμενα καὶ παραδοθέντα πιστευθέντα τε θεῖα εἶναι βιβλία.

[2] The Neoplatonic opponents of the Church were not quite honest, they were rather talking διαλεκτικῶς, when they objected to the allegorical method of interpreting Holy Scripture. They treated their own sacred writings in exactly the same way.

[3] Sozomen says (H. E. V. 22) that the Jews were more readily seduced to heathenism, because they only interpreted Holy Scripture πρὸς ῥητόν, and not πρὸς θεωρίαν.

[4] Thus Arians and Orthodox sometimes appealed to the same texts. But the impossibility of drawing up a rule deciding how far the letter of Scripture was

Origen were not strictly retained. [1] On the other hand, the historical antiquarian interest, which he had awakened, in Holy Scripture, continued to exert its influence. It not only lasted up to the fifth century, [2] but it also exerted a critical and re-

authoritative, caused more anxiety. Had God a human form, eyes, or voice; was Paradise situated on the earth; did the dead rise with all their bodily members, even with their hair, etc.?—to all these and a hundred similar questions there was no sure answer, and consequently disputes arose between adherents of one and the same confession. All had to allegorise, and, in turn, all had to take certain texts literally. But what a difference existed between an Epiphanius and a Gregory of Nyssa, and how many shades of belief there were between the crude anthropomorphists and the spiritualists! The latter, as a rule, had reason to dread the arguments, and frequently the fists, of the former; they could not but be anxious about their own orthodoxy, for the old *regula* was on the side of their opponents, and the most absurd opinion had the prejudice that it was the most pious in its favour. Ultimately, in the course of the fifth century, a sort of common sense established itself, which could be taken as forming, with regard to the anthropomorphists, a middle line between the exegetic methods of Chrysostom and Cyril of Alexandria, and which had been anticipated by a few Fathers of the fourth century. Yet not many concessions were made to the anthropomorphists. Even Antiochians like Theodore had become suspected of an anthropomorphism incompatible with the honour of God (see Johannes Philoponus, De creat. mundi, I. 22. in Gallandi XII., p. 496). He who did not rise from the *turpitudo litteræ ad decorem intelligentiæ spiritalis* (Jerome ad Amos. 2) might come under suspicion of heresy. But, on the other hand, the Cappadocians themselves opposed those who allegorised "too much", and thus approximated too closely to heathen philosophers; and after a part of Origen's expositions had passed into the traditional possessions of the Church, the rest was declared heretical. Even before this Epiphanius had written (H. 61, ch. 6): Πάντα τὰ θεῖα ῥήματα οὐκ ἀλληγορίας δεῖται, ἀλλὰ ὡς ἔχει, ἔχει; θεωρίας δὲ δεῖται καὶ αἰσθύσεως. Origen's thorough-going principle that "God can say and do nothing, which is not good and just", by which he criticised and occasionally set aside the letter of Scripture, was too bold for the Epigoni with their faith in authority. God had done what Scripture said of him, and what God did was good. This principle not only ruined all lucid science, but also deprived the Church of the intrinsic completeness of her creed. Yet we must not minimise the result of the compromise made in the fourth and fifth centuries, between the literal, allegorical, and typical methods of interpreting Scripture; for it has held its ground up to the present day in a way really identical in all Churches, and it seems to possess no small power to convince.

[1] For Origen's principles see Vol. II., p. 346.

[2] Origen, Eusebius, and Jerome are links in a chain of scholarly tradition and work. The succession, however, marked a descent not only in point of time. The attitude of Jerome and the conflicts in which he was involved show at the same time that the age no longer tolerated independent scholarship in historical criticism. Therefore it ceased after Jerome; such work was confined to registering antiquarian notices, even doubtful ones, which were accepted without reflection, since, having entered into the stock of tradition, they no longer roused criticism.

strictive influence on pneumatic exegesis. [1] This was the case among the scholars of Antioch. Diodorus and Theodore tried, following the precedent set by Lucian and Dorotheus, to form an inner connection between the pneumatic and the grammatico-historical exegesis. It cannot be held that this gave rise to a more rational method, or one more tenable from the critical standpoint. Yet in detail they followed sound principles. These again had been already pared down by Chrysostom and Theodoret in favour of the dominant method, but they lasted in the Nestorian Church and its schools as long as science existed there at all, and their influence extended into the West through Junilius. [2]

[1] Besides, when driven by necessity, *i.e.*, when brought face to face with inconvenient passages of Scripture, a way was found out of the difficulty in the demand that the historical occasion of the text must be carefully weighed. Thus Athanasius writes (Orat. c. Arian. I. 54), when setting himself to refute the Scriptural proofs of the Arians, and finding that he is in considerable straits: δεῖ δέ, ὡς ἐπὶ πάσης τῆς θείας γραφῆς προσήκει ποιεῖν καὶ ἀναγκαῖόν ἐστιν, οὕτω καὶ ἐνταῦθα, καθ᾿ ὃν εἶπεν ὁ ἀπόστολος καιρὸν καὶ τὸ πρόσωπον καὶ τὸ πρᾶγμα, διόπερ ἔγραψε, πιστῶς ἐκλαμβάνειν, ἵνα μὴ παρὰ ταῦτα ἢ καὶ παρ᾿ ἕτερόν τι τούτων ἀγνοῶν ὃ ἀναγιγνώσκων ἔξω τῆς ἀληθινῆς διανοίας γένηται. The same contention was often upheld in earlier times by Tertullian when driven into a corner by the exegesis of the Marcionites (see De præscr. adv. Marc. II.—V.). The exegetical "principle" of the Fathers gradually became the *complexus oppositorum ; i.e.*, when the literal meaning was disturbing, then it was, in the words of Gregory of Nazianzus, (Orat. XXXI. 3): ἔνδυμα τῆς ἀσεβείας ἐστὶν ἡ φιλία τοῦ γράμματος: or men spoke of the *turpitudo litteræ*, the Jewish understanding of Scripture, the necessity of considering historical circumstances or the like. But if "advanced" theologians produced suspected allegorical explanations, then the cry was raised ὡς ἔχει, ἔχει, Holy Scripture is not to be understood according to Plato, etc.

[2] The distinction between Alexandrian—Origenistic—and Antiochene exegesis does not consist in the representatives of the latter having rejected wholesale the spiritual meaning. They rather recognised it, but they tried to determine it typically from the literal meaning. While the Alexandrians avowedly set aside the literal meaning in many passages, and attached the pneumatic sense to texts by some sort of device, the Antiochenes started from the literal meaning, seeking to discover it by all the means of a sound exegesis, and then showed that the narrative concerned was a σκιὰ τῶν μελλόντων, a type created by God, which had been fulfilled by Jesus Christ. They set up definite rules for the discovery of the literal meaning as well as for that of the typical and allegorical sense (θεωρία, not ἀλληγορία), which lay not in the words, but the realities, persons, and events designated by the words. The rules are strikingly like those of the Federal theologians—Cocceius—and the school of Hofmann; the method of the author of the Hebrews furnished their model. This procedure had various results. First, the

The West received through Hilary, Ambrose, Jerome, and
Rufinus, the erudite pneumatic method of the Greeks, as practised especially by the Cappadocians. Before this, and for a
few decades afterwards, the exegesis of the West was mainly

method of Philo and Origen followed by the Alexandrians was strenuously opposed
both in independent treatises, and in connection with exegesis. Secondly, an effort
was made to give the literal meaning in all cases its due; thus Diodorus says in
the Catena of Nicephorus (Leipz. 1772, I. p. 524): τοῦ ἀλληγορικοῦ τὸ ἱστορικὸν
πλεῖστον ὅσον προτιμῶμεν. Thirdly, a real covenant was accordingly recognised
between God and the Jewish people, and that nation was accorded its significant
place in the history of salvation: the " history of salvation" which thus originated
differed essentially from that of Irenæus (see Vol. II., p. 305). Fourthly and finally,
the number of directly Messianic passages in the O. T. became extraordinarily
limited; while, according to pneumatic exegesis, everything in the O. T. was in a
sense directly Messianic, i.e., Christian, the Antiochenes only retained a few such
passages. The horizon of O. T. authors was more correctly defined. Theodore
decidedly disputed the presence of anything in the O. T. about the Son of God
or the Trinity. Further, the Antiochenes distinguished grades of inspiration, namely,
the spirit of prophecy, and that of wisdom, and they placed the former far above
the latter. Although the advance of this exegesis on the Alexandrian is obvious,
yet it is seriously defective in completeness and consistency in method. First, the
Antiochenes, in spite of their polemic against the older expositors—Hippolytus, Origen,
Eusebius, Apollinaris, Didymus, and Jerome—could not altogether divest themselves of the old principle of the authoritative interpretation of Scripture; "they
regarded the old traditional doctrine, the exposition given by the Fathers, and the
definitions of Synods, as the standard and touch-stone of agreement with the creed
of the Church, and they made of this rule what use they pleased"; from this source
their attitude became somewhat uncertain. Secondly, they only rarely succeeded in
criticising the literal meaning historically; where they did, they employed rationalistic interpretations, and accordingly their procedure approximated to Origen's
speculative exegesis, yet without following any fixed principle. Thirdly, their typolo-
gical exegesis also often bordered very closely on the allegorical, and since they assumed
a double sense in Scripture, they did not remove, but only disguised, the fundamental
error of current exegesis. Fourthly, they could not make clear the difference between the
O. T. and the N. T., because, in spite of their assumption of different degrees of
inspiration, they placed the O. T. prophets on a level with the Apostles; see
Theodore, Comment. on Neh. I. in Migne, T. LXVI., p. 402: τῆς αὐτῆς τοῦ ἁγίου
πνεύματος χάριτος οἵ τε πάλαι μετεῖχον καὶ οἱ τῷ τῆς καινῆς διαθήκης ὑπηρετούμενοι
μυστηρίῳ. Finally, by assuming directly Messianic passages in the O. T. they gave
up their own position, and placed themselves at the mercy of their opponents.

See later for the history of the school of Antioch, especially its relation to
Aristotle. Diestel, Gesch. des A. T. in der christl. Kirche, p. 126 ff. Fritzsche, de
Theod. Mops. vita et scriptis, Halae, 1836. Above all, the works of Kihn, Die
Bedeutung der Antioch. Schule a. d. exeget. Gebiete (1866), and Theodor von
Mopsuestia und Junilius als Exegeten (1880), where the older literature is given.
Swete, Theodori ep. Mops. in epp. Pauli Comment. Cambridge, 1880, 1881.

characterised by absence of system; along with reverence for
the letter we find all sorts of allegorical explanations, and in
turn a predilection for a dramatic close to earthly history.
Jerome was far from having fixed exegetic principles, since he
allegorised against his better knowledge wherever the orthodox
confession required it. In his time Tychonius, a Donatist, drew
up for the interpretation of Holy Scripture seven rules which
were to remove all difficulties (Augustine, De doctr. christ. III.
30 sq.).[1] These were adopted by Augustine in his work 'On
Christian Science', which, subject as it is to the errors of the
age, is a glorious memorial of the great Bishop's love of truth,
and evangelical feeling. Of evangelical feeling, in so far as
Augustine, in opposition to all biblicism, declared the study of
Holy Scripture to be merely the path towards love; he who
possessed love, no longer needed the Scripture, he lived with
Christ and God; accordingly he had ceased to require separate
'saving truths', for he lived in truth and love.[2]

---

[1] These rules are of material importance (for theology). The first treats of the
Lord and his body: *i.e.*, we must and may apply the truth concerning the Lord
to the Church, and *vice versa*, since they form one person; only in this way do
we frequently get a correct sense. The second deals with the bi-partite body of
the Lord: we must carefully consider whether the true or the empirical Church is
meant. The third takes up the promises and the law, *i.e.*, the spirit and letter;
the fourth treats of genus and species: we must observe the extent to which texts
apply; the fifth, of the dates: we must harmonise contradictory dates by a fixed
method, and understand certain stereotyped numbers as symbolical. The sixth
discusses repetition: *i.e.*, we have frequently to refrain from assuming a chronolo-
gical order, where such an order appears to exist, and the seventh deals with the
devil and his body, *i.e.*, the devil and the godless, many things referring to the
latter which are said of the devil and *vice versa*—see the first rule.

[2] The thought wavers between that of Origen, who also elevates himself above
the historical Christ, and the genuinely evangelical idea that the Christian must
stop short at "means of salvation"; see De doctr. I. 34: "Nulla res in via (ad
eum) tenere nos debet, quando nec ipse dominus, in quantum via nostra esse
dignatus est, tenere nos voluerit, sed transire; ne rebus temporalibus, quamvis ab
eo pro salute nostra susceptis et gestis, hæreamus infirmiter, sed per eas potius
curramus alacriter etc." In ch. 35 love is held up as the exclusive goal: ch. 36
teaches that no one has understood Scripture who has not been led by it to love
God and his neighbour; but if he has been led to this love, then he loses nothing
by failing to hit on the correct sense of detached texts: in that case he is deceived,
but without guilt: "Quisquis in scripturis (I. 37) aliud sentit quam ille qui scripsit,

But this thought of the book does not give its prevailing colour; this is furnished, on the contrary, by the other ideas that Scripture is the only way by which to come to God and Christ, that it is to be interpreted by the rule of faith, that obscure passages are to be explained by clear ones, and that the literal meaning, where offensive, must yield to the deeper sense. The numerous hermeneutic rules set up by Augustine,[1] which are so many expedients and very like Origen's methodic principles, determined the nature of exegesis in later periods in the West. In connection with whatever else was derived from the East, the view that there was a triple and fourfold meaning in Scripture became a fixed doctrine.[2] The little book by Junilius which

---

[1] illis non mentientibus fallitur; sed tamen, ut dicere cœperam, si ea sententia fallitur, qua ædificet caritatem, quæ finis præcepti est, ita fallitur ac si quisquam errore deserens viam, eo tamen per agrum pergat, quo etiam via illa perducit." Augustine says indeed (l. c.): " titubabit fides, si divinarum scripturarum vacillat auctoritas," but, on the other hand (I. 39): "Homo, fide, spe et caritate subnixus eaque inconcusse retinens, *non indiget scripturis nisi ad alios instruendos.* Itaque multi per hæc tria etiam in solitudine sine codicibus vivunt ... Quibus tamen quasi machinis tanta fidei, spei et caritatis in eis surrexit instructio, ut perfectum aliquid tenentes, ea quæ sunt ex parte non quærant; perfectum sane, quantum in hac vita potest." This forcible way of assigning a practical purpose to the reading of Scripture and the understanding at the root of it, viz., that it was *the whole* that was of importance, is the opposite of the conception that Scripture embraces innumerable mysteries; but an affinity exists far down between them, inasmuch as Augustine seems to reserve to the monks the state in which Scripture is not required, and he borders on the belief of Origen (I. 34) that the Christ of history belongs to the past for him who lives in love. The whole conception is first found, besides, in the description by the Valentinian school of the perfect Gnostic; see Excerpta ex Theodoto, ch. 27: ποῦ δὲ ἔτι γραφῆς καὶ μαθήσεως κατόρθωμα τῇ ψυχῇ ἐκείνῃ τῇ καθαρᾷ γενομένῃ, ὅπου καὶ ἀξιοῦται πρόσωπον πρὸς πρόσωπον Θεὸν ὁρᾶν ; besides Augustine expressly argued against those who supposed they could dispense with Scripture from the start, and appealed to an inner revelation (see the Præfat. to De doctr. christ.). He puts it beyond doubt that he who uses Scripture must bow to its authority even where he does not understand it.

[1] See the second and especially the third book of the work quoted. The second contains a short and precise review of all branches of knowledge which are collectively perceived to spring from heathenism, and it states which may and must be used by the Christian, and to what extent. The third book contains the hermeneutic proper.

[2] See Eucherius of Lyons, liber formularum spiritalis intelligentiæ ad Veranium filium, in Migne, Ser. lat. T. 50, p. 727. In later times the mnemonic formula wa composed: *Littera* gesta docet, quid credas *allegoria,*
                 Moralis quid agas, quo tendas *anagogia.*

contained the Antiochene system of hermeneutics as handed down at Nisibis, although much read, made few changes. But it was exceedingly significant that Augustine, in spite of his view that it was only a means, had placed the Bible on such a pinnacle that all theologians who afterwards took their stand upon it alone as against tradition, were able to appeal to him. As a matter of fact Scripture held quite a different place in the Church life of the West from that in the East: it came more into the foreground. That also is to be explained, above all, by the influence of Augustine,[1] and the deficiency of the West in speculative ability.[2]

As the Church had never published a general decree, exclusive of all doubt, on the extent of Scripture, it had also failed to publish one concerning its characteristics. Freedom from error was generally deduced from inspiration, and it was, as a rule, referred to the very words. But on the other hand, an attempt was made here and there to leave room for the individuality and historical limitation of the authors; minor inconsistencies were not wholly denied (see even Aug., De consensu evang.); and exegesis was often practised as if the strict dogma of inspiration did not exist.[3] A clear idea of the suffi-

[1] The work "On Christian Science" points to Scripture as its sole object, and does not discuss tradition at all. However, the latter receives its due inasmuch as Augustine regards the propositions of the rule of faith—based on the Symbol—as the *matters*, which constituted the essential contents of Scripture. In this definition we find the reason why dogmatics never ceased to waver between Scripture and the rule of faith. Yet we know that Augustine was by no means the first to hold this view. Even the writer of the Muratorian fragment and Irenæus knew no better.

[2] Origen taught that Christian science was the science of Scripture; Augustine stands upon his shoulders. But afterwards, in the East, the interest in dogmatic formulas became uppermost, while in the West, the Bible remained pre-eminently the direct source of knowledge of the faith.

[3] Even the men of Antioch, by whom, Chrysostom not excepted, human elements were aknowledged to exist in the Bible, maintained the inspiration of other passages *quoad litteram*, just like Origen and the Cappadocians. Augustine accepted this freedom from error in its strictest sense; see Ep. 82. 3 (ad Hieron.): "Ego fateor caritati tuæ, solis eis scripturarum libris, qui iam canonici appellantur, didici hunc imorem honoremque deferre, ut nullum eorum auctorem scribendo aliquid errasse irmissime credam. Ac si aliquid in eis offendero litteris, quod videatur contrarium veritati, nihil aliud quam vel mendosum esse codicem, vel interpretem non assecuum esse quod dictum est, vel me minime intellexisse non ambigam." In his vork *De consensu evang.*, which is particularly instructive as regards his whole

ciency of Scripture was certainly not reached; it was maintained in general phrases, and was violated in generalities and in details. [1] Finally, as regards the relation of the two Testaments to each other, three views existed side by side. The Old Testament was a Christian book as well as the New: it was throughout the record of prophecy: it contained the true creed under certain limitations and imperfections, and led and still leads educationally to Christ. These points of view were adopted alternately as the occasion required. It was recognised that the Jewish nation had possessed a covenant with God, yet the consequences of this were far from being admitted.. The same method of employing the Bible was still upheld in apologetic arguments as was followed by the Apologists of the second century. [2] For the rest, even Cyril of Alexandria still brought "heathen prophecy" to bear in this matter, while in other respects—speaking generally—the assumption of heathen 'prophets' and inspired philosophers excited suspicion.

attitude to Holy Writ, he declares that the Apostles' writings make up sufficiently for the absence of any by our Lord; for the Apostles were the Lord's hands, and had written what he commanded. It is extremely surprising that this being the view taken of the Bible—and even the translation of the LXX. was held to be inspired—yet no one ever *ex professo* reflected on how the Canon was formed. No miracle was assumed. Even Augustine quite naively stated, *sancti et docti homines* had formed the N. T. (c. Faustum XXII. 79). Here the authority of the Church comes in.

[1] The early Catholic Fathers had already maintained the sufficiency of Holy Scripture, as well as the necessity of proving everything out of it; see for the latter point Orig. in Jerem., Hom. I. c. 7 (Lomm. XV. p. 115): Μάρτυρας δεῖ λαβεῖν τὰς γραφάς. Ἀμάρτυροι γὰρ αἱ ἐπιβολαὶ ἡμῶν καὶ αἱ ἐξηγήσεις ἄπιστοί εἰσιν. Cyril of Jerusalem has expressed himself similarly (Cat. 4, 17: Δεῖ γὰρ περὶ τῶν θείων καὶ ἁγίων τῆς πίστεως μυστηρίων μηδὲ τὸ τυχὸν ἄνευ τῶν θείων παραδίδοσθαι γραφῶν· καὶ μὴ ἁπλῶς πιθανότησι καὶ λόγων κατασκευαῖς παραφέρεσθαι. Μηδὲ ἐμοὶ τῷ ταῦτά σοι λέγοντι, ἁπλῶς πιστεύσῃς· ἐὰν τὴν ἀπόδειξιν τῶν καταγγελλομένων ἀπὸ τῶν θείων μὴ λάβῃς γραφῶν· Ἡ σωτηρία γὰρ αὕτη τῆς πίστεως ἡμῶν οὐκ ἐξ εὑρεσιλογίας, ἀλλὰ ἐξ ἀποδείξεως τῶν θείων ἐστὶ γραφῶν); cf. Athanasius (Orat. adv gentes init.: Αὐτάρκεις μέν εἰσιν αἱ ἅγιαι καὶ θεόπνευστοι γραφαὶ πρὸς τὴν τῆ ἀληθείας ἀπαγγελίαν). So also the Antiochenes, moreover Augustine De doctr. II. 9 "In iis quæ aperte in scriptura posita sunt, inveniuntur illa omnia, quæ continer fidem moresque vivendi, spem scilicet et caritatem." Vincent., Commonit. 2.

[2] All the more did the use made of the O. T. for the constitution of the Churc differ from the apologetic view. Very many of the regulations of the O. ceremonial law came once more to be highly valued by the Church, not as spi itually understood, but as directly applied to ecclesiastical institutions of every sor

2. *Tradition.*

The authority of Holy Scripture frequently appears in the Fathers as something wholly abstract and despotic. It contained, in fact, a latent tendency to assert its independence of the conditions out of which it had arisen. But the revolution which was characterised by the isolation of the Bible, its deliverance from the authority of ecclesiastical tradition, and the annihilation of the latter, only took place in the sixteenth century, and even then it was, we know, not completely successful. In ecclesiastical antiquity, on the contrary, the bond was by no means severed which connected Scripture with the maternal organism of the Church. The Church, its doctrine, institutions, and constitution, were held, in and by themselves, to constitute the source of knowledge and the authoritative guarantee of truth. As the holy, Apostolic, and Catholic institution, it possessed nothing whatever untrue or capable of amendment either in its foundations or its development. Everything in it, rather, was apostolic, and the guidance of the Church by the Holy Ghost had preserved this apostolic fabric from any change. This thought was necessarily emphasised more and more strongly in consequence of the development undergone by Church affairs in the fourth and following centuries. Since at the same time, however, the independent authority and the sufficiency of the Bible were also emphasised, there arose difficulties, in part even manifest inconsistencies, which were never removed. [1] But they were not clearly felt, because men always possessed the power, when confronted by inconvenient monitors, to carry through ultimately, whether in the form of dogma, or in that of order, whatever was required. In face of traditions become obsolete an appeal was made to other traditions, or to the Bible; where written testimony was uncertain or awanting, recourse was had to tradition; *i.e.*, that was declared to be tradition which was

[1] The Orientals, especially the Antiochenes, but Cyril of Jerus. also, adhered more exclusively to Scripture; the Alexandrians, and even the Cappadocians relied more strongly on tradition. Yet the differences are only in degree. At any rate, the difference comes out more strongly on a comparison of Theodoret and Cyril of Alexandria.

not to be justified under another title. Hence it is already clear that tradition never was and never could be systematised and catalogued, that an authentic declaration never was and never could be published as to its extent and scope. There was no single deliverance on the application of tradition, which would not, if consistently carried out, have thrown the Church into confusion. If Augustine therefore (De bapt. c. Donat. II. 3, 4) declared—certainly against his better knowledge—that 'canonical Scripture was contained within fixed limits of its own' (scriptura canonica certis suis terminis continetur), yet it never occurred to him or any one else to maintain as much about tradition. The latter was in antiquity a wholly elastic category, as we see when we look at its use in individual cases; in *summa* it was, however, an extremely rigid and clear notion: meaning simply that the Church was determined, in spite of all changes, to regard itself as the unchangeable creation of the Apostles. It derived its claim to this view partly from the divine promises, partly from the organisation instituted for it, yet without alleging confidently any empirical factor within the Church which should be the bearer of its infallibility.[1] The most important consequences of this view held by the Church regarding itself have been already stated in the second-volume; but others came to be added in the post-Constantinian period.

A. The creed of the Church was always held to be the most important part of its tradition. The anti-gnostic formulas which the creed had preserved passed over in the East, along with theorems, half biblical half speculative, and here and there with purely philosophical or polemical discussions, into the Symbols.[2] These Symbols, which had been adopted for use

---

[1] Reuter's excellent explanation of Augustine's position (Ztschrft. für K.-Gesch., Vol. VIII., pp. 181 f., 186 f.) was then true of very wide circles: "The Episcopate and the Roman *sedes apostolica*, the whole relatively coördinated *sedes apostolicæ*, the relative and the absolute plenary councils were held to be representations of the (infallible) Church; but not one of these factors, not all of them combined, formed the (infallible) representation of the (infallible) Church. The latter possessed no indubitably sure institution or organs indubitably representative of it." The decrees of councils were only placed on a complete equality with Scripture in the East, after councils had ceased to be held, and when the latter therefore were seen, like Scripture, in a nimbus of hoary antiquity.

[2] See Vol. II., p. 20 f. and III., pp. 48 ff., 111 ff.

in the Church, were regarded as apostolic testimonies. Their
phrasing was not considered in the East to be due to the
Apostles, but the honour paid them was justified from the
Apostles' preaching.[1] These Symbols of the provincial Churches
were supplanted in the period between the first and third (fourth)
Œcumenical Councils by the Nicene, or soon thereafter by the
so-called Constantinopolitan Symbol.[2] This confession[3] had
already been held at Chalcedon to be *the creed* pure and simple,
and it never lost this place of honour. If it had already been
constantly assumed that the doctrine of the Church was the
theme, or the matter, constituting the real contents of Scripture,
then this assumption was now definitely transferred to the
Nicene or the Constantinopolitan Symbol. All subsequent
dogmatic conclusions were accordingly regarded solely as explanations of this Symbol,[4] which was not maintained, however, to be of Apostolic origin—in its language. *Tradition, in
the strictest sense of the term, consisted in the contents of the
Symbol for the time being.* Cyril says of this (Cat. V. 12):
'In these few paragraphs the whole dogma of the faith (is)
comprised' (ἐν ὀλίγοις τοῖς στίχοις τὸ πᾶν δόγμα τῆς πίστεως

---

[1] The Symbol of Gregory Thaumaturgus was derived from a special revelation;
see Vol. III., p. 115.

[2] There were two symbol-constructing periods in the East before a universal
Confession was framed. The former of these embraced A.D. 250—325, the second,
A.D. 325 up to the beginning or the middle of the fifth century. In the latter
period the attempt was made either to transform the Nicene Creed into a baptismal
Confession, or to displace it by parallel formulas; sometimes the leading words of
the Nicene Symbol were inserted in those of the provincial Churches. See on the
history of this, the part played by the Bishops of Asia Minor in these develop-
ments, and the history of the so-called Constantinop. Symbol, my art. "Konstantinop.
Symbol" in Herzog's R.-E. 2, Vol. VIII.; Caspari's works, Hort's investigations,
Two Dissertations, Cambridge, 1876, and Kattenbusch, Confessionskunde I., p. 252 ff.

[3] It was originally the Baptismal Confession of the Church of Jerusalem, revised
soon after the middle of the fourth century, and furnished with a *regula fidei*
concerning the Holy Spirit; it came thus to be honoured first through the authority
of Epiphanius, and then through the energy of the Bishop of Constantinople, which
also led to its supplanting the Nicene Symbol.

[4] Monophysites and orthodox believers always professed to be able to read their
Christological formulas word for word in the Symbol. The Greek Church maintains
to the present day that the Nicene-Constantinopolitan Symbol contains everything
we require to believe.

περιλαμβανόμενον). As the Church had obtained in the Nicene
Creed a complete and uniform Symbol, the view was transferred to it. There were two sides meanwhile to the relations of
Scripture and Symbol. You might not believe the contents of
the Symbol unless you could convince yourself of their truth
from Scripture; [1] but on the other hand, your interpretation of
Scripture had to be regulated by the creed laid down in the
Symbol. [2] In the West a unique djgnity was retained by the
old Roman Symbol (or its parallel forms in the provincial
Churches) which was regarded as being composed of twelve
articles. From the fourth century at least it was held to be
the *Apostolic Creed* in the strict sense of the term. [3] Its brevity
and simplicity long preserved the Roman Church from extravagant theological speculations, but they could not barricade it
against the theological development of the East. An industri-
ous attempt was made, or at least professed, to derive the
decision of dogmatic questions, as they emerged, from this
Apostolic Symbol, and to rest upon it the whole of the ever
increasing material of dogmatics. [4] It was only after the begin-

[1] So, above all, Cyril and the Antiochenes.

[2] No hesitation prevailed in the Church on this point; yet Synods simply forbade certain expositions of Scriptural texts as heretical. The Church alone furnished
the *gubernaculum interpretationis* (see Vincent., Commonit. 2, 41) and that in its
concise guide to faith, the Symbol. After the Constantinopolitan Symbol had been
placed on an inaccessible height, we no longer find the blunt assertion that the
creed is compiled from the Holy Scriptures. But this contention was also historically
false. (For it see Cyril, Cat. V. 12): οὐ γὰρ ὡς ἔδοξεν ἀνθρώποις συνετέθη τὰ τῆς
Πίστεως· ἀλλ᾽ ἐκ πάσης γραφῆς τὰ καιριώτατα συλλεχθέντα μίαν ἀναπληροῖ τὴν
τῆς Πίστεως διδασκαλίαν. "Canon" was originally the rule of faith; the Scripture
had in truth intervened, yet so that its authority had a support placed still further
back, namely, the O. T. and the Lord's sayings.

[3] See my art. "Apostolisches Symbol" in Herzog's R.-E. 2 B. I. The opinion that
the Apostles had composed the Symbol jointly (Rufinus) cannot be traced earlier
than the middle of the fourth century, but it may be much older. Yet we must
not date it too soon; for if the Churches of the western provinces had received
the Symbol with this legend attached, they would hardly have ventured to propose
changes on it. It was certainly not extolled even in Rome in the third century,
so exuberantly as it was afterwards by Ambrose.

[4] This point falls to be discussed in the next book. Augustine had to rest his
distinctive theology on the Symbol, though the latter was only imperfectly adapted
for the purpose.

ning of the fifth century that the Constantinopolitan Symbol
supplanted the apostolic in Church use in Rome and the West, [1]
yet without the latter losing its prestige. This was of course
transferred in part to the new Symbol, but the old remained,
though latent, in force. [2] *The twelve articles of the Apostolic
Symbol, to be explained by the Constantinopolitan, constituted
in the West the ecclesiastical tradition* κατ᾽ ἐξοχήν. Justinian's
legislation confirmed this conception, though, indeed, that was
not needed. [3]

B. At the beginning of the fourth century there already
entered into the composition of the Church, not only its creed,
but a *cultus* fixed in its main features; there were further
disciplinary and *ceremonial provisions*—still differing, indeed, in
part in the various provincial Churches [4]—and finally, a settled
constitution. It was only in a very late period that the notion
of apostolicity was applied, in the strict sense, to the whole of
these elements; [5] but not only did the foundations of these
ordinances come to be characterised as apostolic, but as a rule,
and to an increasing extent, everything which there was a desire
to assure of permanence. Different methods were adopted,
however, of establishing the apostolic character of these institutions. First, it was maintained that regulations observed by the
whole Church required no proof that they were Apostolic. [6]

---

[1] See my art. on the Constantinop. Symbol, l. c.

[2] The history of the Apostolic Symbol between the fifth and sixth centuries
urgently requires investigation.

[3] Justinian's law-book is headed by the art. " De summa trinitate et de fide catholica
et ut nemo de ea publice contendere audeat " ; but see also the famous decree of
the Emperors, Gratian, Valentinian and Theodosius, A.D. 380, with which the
law-book begins.

[4] See, *e.g.*, Socrates, H. E. V. 22.

[5] When this occurred a very exact distinction had already been made between
faith and disciplinary law. Apostolic faith was something different from and higher
than apostolic laws (διατάξεις, νόμοι, κανόνες ἐκκλησιαστικοὶ διὰ τῶν ἀποστόλων).
This corrected the equality apparently attributed to the two branches of tradition
by the common predicate "apostolic."

[6] See August., De bapt. c. Donat. II. 7, 12: "Multa, quæ non inveniuntur in
litteris apostolorum neque in conciliis posteriorum, et tamen quia per universam
custodiuntur ecclesiam, non nisi ab ipsis tradita et commendata creduntur." IV.
24. 31: "Quod universa tenet ecclesia, nec conciliis institutum sed semper retentum

Secondly, advantage was taken in the East, of the numerous legends of the Apostles current in the Churches; they began to be used in connection with the government and cultus of the Churches in such a way that definite detailed regulations were attributed to the Apostles, individually or collectively, whenever they were required for the discipline or cultus of the time. [1] Thirdly, men began in the fourth century—not un-influenced by Clement and Origen—to introduce the notion of a παράδοσις ἄγραφος (unwritten tradition), in whose wholly un-defined contents were even included dogmatic theories which it was not everyone's business to understand; yet it dealt extremely seldom with the trinitarian and Christological catch-words. This idea of an 'unwritten tradition' crept in in a very real sense; for it conflicted with more than one main point in the fundamental positions of the Church. But it attained high honour, and its existence absolutely became a dogma. But

est, non nisi auctoritate apostolica traditum rectissime creditur." V. 23. 31: " Multa, quæ universa tenet ecclesia et ob hoc ab apostolis præcepta bene creduntur, quam-quam scripta non reperiantur."

[1] The Apologists had exhibited Christianity as the worship of God in Spirit and in truth, and as an alliance regulated by equality and fraternity. But there had grad-ually developed a complicated cultus round the mysteries, and a comprehensive and detailed code of discipline had become necessary. For both of these appeal was made to an increasing extent to apostolic authority. Compare the Apostolic Con-stitutions, the κανόνες ἐκκλησιαστικοί, the Apostolic Canons, in general the mass of material, partly published, partly discussed, by Bickell, Pitra, and Lagarde; further, the designation of the Liturgies of the provincial Churches as by Mark, James, etc. The history, still partly unwritten, of these Eastern forgeries under apostolic names is closely connected with the general history of the legends of the Apostles (see Lipsius, Die apokryphen Apostelgesch.). The O. T. commandments were again introduced into the Church by means of apostolic fictions, until the ancient awe of Moses, the law-giver, was surmounted. After apostolic commandments of this sort had been allowed to spring up luxuriantly for a time, the Church had no little trouble to exorcise the spirits it had conjured. A sifting process began from the sixth century—at least in the Byzantine Church—to which, e.g., the Constitutions fell a victim. In the law books of the Monophysite and Nestorian Churches, much more comprehensive matter had been preserved, under apostolic names, as possessed of the value of law. Yet it did not receive the same honour as the Holy Scriptures. In order to realise the possibility of such an unabashed invention of regulations cloaked with the authority and name of the Apostles, we must remember that, from the second century, writings bearing on discipline were in existence, called διδαχαί or διατάξεις τῶν ἀποστόλων, and that these, having no individual impress, were thoroughly adapted for constant remodelling and expansion.

because it really made all else unnecessary and was a dangerous
drastic expedient, it was not defined, nor was its extent ever
determined. And it did not banish Scriptural proof or the
appeal to familiar and demonstrable tradition. *The existence
was maintained of a tradition which dispensed with all criteria
—and that was what the παράδοσις ἄγραφος was; but a prudent
use was made of it.* Unwritten tradition was preferentially
applied to the development of ritual and the sacramental performance of the mysteries, while the secret truths of the creed
were based exclusively on Scripture and the Councils. [1] But

---

[1] The assumption of a secret apostolic tradition—that is, the παράδοσις ἄγραφος
—first appeared among the Gnostics, *i.e.*, among the first theologians, who had to
legitimise as apostolic a world of notions alien to primitive Christianity. It then
was found quite logically among the Alexandrians, and from them passed to Eusebius, who not only accepted it (H. E. II. 1, 4), but also vindicated it against Marcellus (lib. I. c. 1): ἐκκλησίας τὰς ἀπὸ τῶν θείων γραφῶν μαρτυρίας ἐξ ἀγράφου
παραδόσεως σφραγιζομένης. But the Cappadocians first established it in their conflict
with the Eunomians and Pneumatomachoi, yet the bold use made of it by them in
defence of the dogma of the Trinity, was not afterwards parallelled. Basil (De
spiritu sancto, 27) referred the orthodox doctrine of the Holy Ghost to the unwritten tradition, placing the latter on an equality with the public tradition; but
he endeavoured at the same time to retain the old Alexandrian distinction between
κήρυγμα and δόγμα, δόγμα being meant to embrace the theological formulation of
the faith (τῶν ἐν τῇ ἐκκλησίᾳ πεφυλαγμένων δογμάτων καὶ κηρυγμάτων τὰ μὲν ἐκ
τῆς ἐγγράφου διδασκαλίας ἔχομεν, τὰ δὲ ἐκ τῆς τῶν ἀποστόλων παραδόσεως διαδο-
θέντα ἡμῖν ἐν μυστηρίῳ παρεδεξάμεθα, ἅπερ ἀμφότερα τὴν αὐτὴν ἰσχὺν ἔχει πρὸς
τὴν εὐσέβειαν ... ἄλλο γὰρ δόγμα, καὶ ἄλλο κήρυγμα, τὰ μεν γὰρ δόγματα σιω-
πᾶται, τὰ δὲ κηρύγματα δημοσιεύεται). The latter distinction was opposed to the
tendency of the age, and remained without effect. (With that which Basil named
dogma, the μυστικὴ παράδοσις was identical, of which Pamphilus and Eusebius
speak, and by the aid of which they defended the orthodoxy of Origen; see
Socrates III. 7.) But it is important that in order to prove the existence of a
παράδοσις ἄγραφος, Basil appeals merely to matters of ritual—signs of the Cross,
prayers of consecration, and baptismal rites. To these the unwritten tradition was in
later times almost exclusively applied. Gregory of Nazianzus advanced in a different
direction from Basil: he admitted to his opponents (Orat. 37) that tradition was
defective in reference to the doctrine of the Spirit, but he believed he could
assume a progressive development of the truth of revelation. But, as far as I know,
he only once expressed himself so imprudently, and he found absolutely no imitators.
His attempt only proves the difficulty caused by the defence of the dogma of the Trinity
in the fourth century. In Cyril of Jerusalem (see his view so divergent from that of the
Cappadocians, Cat. 16, ch. 2) and the older Antiochenes the παράδοσις ἄγραφος does
not occur, but it does in Epiphanius (H. 61, ch. 6: δεῖ καὶ παραδόσει κεχρῆσθαι.
οὐ γὰρ πάντα ἀπὸ τῆς θείας γραφῆς δύναται λαμβάνεσθαι· διὸ τὰ μὲν ἐν γραφαῖς,
τὰ δὲ ἐν παραδόσεσιν παρέδωκαν οἱ ἅγιοι ἀπόστολοι). It is also found in Chrysostom,

this distinction was not sufficient, nor was it firmly held to be unalterable.

C. All conceptions of the authority of tradition, of which many Fathers—*e.g.*, Cyprian—described Scripture to be the main element, [1] were based ultimately on the conviction *that the Church had been invested with authority through its connection with the Holy Spirit himself.* [2] At this point two problems arose, which, though hardly ever clearly formulated, were yet felt, and which attempts were made to solve. I.—By whom and when did the Church speak? II.—How were novelties to be explained in the Church, especially in the sphere of doctrine, if the authority of the Church had its root exclusively in its apostolic character, that is, its ability to preserve the legacy of the Apostles?

As to I. It was a settled doctrine from the third century, that the representation of the Church was vested in the

Cyril of Alexandria, and others down to John of Damascus, who says plainly (De fide orthod. IV. ch. 12): ἄγραφός ἐστιν ἡ παράδοσις αὕτη τῶν ἀποστόλων, πολλὰ γὰρ ἀγράφως ἡμῖν παρέδοσαν (see details in Langen, Joh. von Damaskus, 1879, p. 271 ff.). So also the Greek Church of to-day teaches : διωρεῖται τὸ θεῖον ῥῆμα εἰς τε τὸ γραπτὸν καὶ ἄγραφον (see Gass, Symbolik der griech. Kirche, p. 107 ff.) Quotations are especially taken from Pauline texts in which παραδόσεις occur, and thus a sort of Scriptural proof is led in support of what does not occur in Scripture. The unwritten tradition is hardly again applied to the creed, since it was thought to be sufficiently supported by Scripture and the Symbol. In the West, Augustine was in the same doubtful position, with regard to certain theses which he defended against Donatists and Pelagians, as the Cappadocians were in reference to the orthodox doctrine of the Holy Ghost. Hence he derived, *e.g.*, the doctrine of original sin, which could not be otherwise proved out of tradition, from the rite of exorcism, declaring this to have been an apostolic tradition; (see c. Julian. VI. 5, 11): "Sed etsi nulla ratione indagetur, nullo sermone explicetur, verum tamen est quod antiquitus veraci fide catholica prædicatur et creditur per ecclesiam totam; quæ filios fidelium nec exorcizaret, nec exsufflaret, si non eos de potestate tenebrarum et a principe mortis erueret, etc). So also he appealed against the Donatists in the controversy as to Baptism by Heretics (against Cyprian's authority) to the unwritten testimony of the whole Church (see note 6, p. 211).

[1] Cyprian calls Scripture "*divinæ traditionis caput et origo*" (Ep. 74, ch. 10). This designation is not common.

[2] The universal conviction is expressed in the famous sentence of Augustine (C. ep. Manich. 6) which he has given in various forms in the Confessions and elsewhere : *Ego vero evangelio non crederem, nisi me catholicæ ecclesiæ commoveret auctoritas.* Even Cyril of Jerusalem, who has emphasised most strongly the authority of Scripture, could not pass over that of the Church (Cat. IV., ch. 33).

Episcopate, though the strict conception of the latter, as first taught by Cyprian, that it was the main support of the Church, was for a long time not universally held.[1] We find, meanwhile, even, *e.g.*, from the plan of Eusebius' Church History, that the Bishops, the successors of the Apostles, were regarded as guarantors of the legitimacy of the Church. The conception never emerged that the Bishop was infallible as an individual;[2] but a certain inspiration was already—though not without differences of opinion—attributed to the provincial Synods.[3] Constantine was the first to form the idea of a universal Synod,[4] and he

---

[1] In his studies on Augustine, Reuter has shown that Augustine fell short of Cyprian (see his theses in the Ztschr. f. K.-Gesch., Vol. VIII., p. 184, and the relative discussions in Vol. VII.). In the East the compiler of Apostolic Constitutions took substantially the view of the Episcopate held by Ignatius, but not by Irenæus and Cyprian. Even Chrysostom's work, περὶ ἱερωσύνης, tends in the same direction as the Constitutions. It is very remarkable that Cyril of Jerusalem (Cat. XVIII., ch. 27) makes no mention of the hierarchy, but only of the Apostles, prophets, teachers and other office-bearers enumerated in the well-known passage in the Ep. to the Corinthians. That is a memorable archaism; yet see even Vincentius, Commonit. 40. He also says very little about Bishops, and nothing at all about the apostolic succession.

[2] On the contrary, the fallibility of individual bishops was always admitted from Irenæus down (III. 3, 1): "*Valde perfectos et irreprehensibiles in omnibus eos volebant esse (apostoli), quos et successores relinquebant, suum ipsorum locum magisterii tradentes, quibus emendate agentibus fieret magna utilitas, lapsis autem summa calamitas.*"

[3] Cyprian (Ep. LVII., ch. 5) introduces the decree of the provincial Council of Carthage with the words, "*Placuit nobis spiritu sancto suggerente.*" Acts XV. 28 certainly influenced this phrase. On the other hand, we must not allow it too much weight, for Cyprian often appeals to instructions given to him personally by the Holy Ghost. See also the Votum of Bishop Lucius of Ausafa, No. 73 of the sentent. episcoporum LXXXVII. at the Carthaginian Council: "*Secundum motum animi mei et spiritus sancti.*" The Synod of Arles, A.D. 314, also used the formula, "*Placuit ergo, præsente spiritu sancto et angelis eius*" (see Mansi, Collect. Concil. II. p. 469, and Hefele, Conciliengesch. I. 2, p. 204); and Constantine wished to have its decision regarded as "*cæleste iudicium*": this judgment by priests was to have the same honour as if it had been pronounced by the Lord himself (Mansi, l.c. p. 478). For the rest, we may here recall the fact that ἡ ἱερὰ σύνοδος had long been a technical term in common use among the Greeks (see also "holy senate" in Justin). On the origin of the ecclesiastical Synods see Sohm's excellent discussions in Kirchenrecht. I. p. 247 ff.

[4] This is now almost universally admitted; yet the idea was introduced by the great Oriental Synods in the cases of Novatian and Paul of Samosata, as well as by the Synod of Arles already indeed summoned by Constantine. The latter has

also supposed such a body to be under the special guidance
of the Holy Spirit, and therefore incapable of error. [1] In the
course of the fourth century the idea that the Nicene Synod
possessed an infallible authority became slowly established; [2]
it was transferred in the following centuries to the Œcumenical Synods generally, yet so that one—the second—was
only subsequently stamped as Œcumenical. [3] From the sixth

been looked on in the West as a General Council for more than a century, and can
also be regarded as such in many respects. On the Councils see Hatch's fine lecture
in his book "The Social Constitution of Christian Churches," p. 172 f.

[1] See Constantine's letter to the Bishops after the Council of Nicæa (in Theodoret
H. E. I. 9 *fin*) : "Whatever is determined in the holy assemblies of the Bishops,
may be attributed to the divine will." Further, Socrates H. E. I. 9, who contrasts
the recognition by the Emperor of the divine character of the Synod, with the
aspersions of Sabinus the Macedonian.

[2] The orthodox party made use of the advantage presented by the decision of
a Synod which none could refuse to recognise as a wholly extraordinary event.
On the other hand, nothing but such an event could atone for the unusual forms
given to the creed, and thus attest a new theory. For in spite of everything
which it had been hitherto possible to relate of Synods being under divine leadership, it was a novelty to raise the decision of a Synod to the level of an authority above discussion. Of such a thing even Bishop Julius of Rome, *e.g.*, knew
nothing. And it was all the more startling when the decision was supported
neither by the letter of Scripture, nor a clear tradition, nor even an analogy of
any sort. But this very fact promoted the assumption of an absolute authority,—
though not yet in the case of Athanasius (see Gwatkin, Stud. of Arianism, p. 50);
a virtue was made of necessity. With the first victory over Arianism, the view
arose that the dogma of the Trinity was a certain truth because it had been affirmed at Nicæa by 318 Bishops inspired by the Holy Ghost—thus the Cappadocians, Cyril of Alex. etc. It is, however, extremely paradoxical, that even up to
the middle of the fourth century the Eusebians laid greater stress on the authority of Synodical decisions than the orthodox party. In order to get the West to
accept the deposition of Athanasius, they continued to appeal to their Antiochene
Synod, and declared its decisions to be irreversible. Although their tactics compelled them also to admit the validity of the Nicene Creed, they did so in the
hope that after the removal of Athanasius they would be able to carry an interpretation of it suitable to their own views.

[3] The latter fact is admitted also by Hefele (l. c. Vol. I., p. 3). Besides, nothing
could be more incorrect than the opinion that the distinction between Œcumenical
and other Synods, as regards dogmatics, was established soon after the Nicene
Council. The greatest variety of opinion prevailed till past the middle of the fifth
century as to what Synods were œcumenical and might be ranked along with the
Nicene. Gregory of Nazianzus we know, *e.g.*, to have spoken very contemptuously
of the Constantinopolitan Synod, and, indeed, of Synods in general. Conversely,
a certain authority was still ascribed to Provincial Synods in dogmatic questions.

century there gradually ceased to be any doubt that the
resolutions of Œcumenical Synods possessed an absolute authority.[1] Whoever rebelled against them refused to admit that the
Synods in question were regular, but did not dispute the

Further, there is a passage in Augustine which infers not only a relatively binding authority on the part of Provincial Councils, but also uncertainty as to the
absolute authority of General Councils. The passage is extraordinarily characteristic of the unsteadiness of the whole structure of tradition. Meanwhile Reuter
(Zeitschr. f. K.-Gesch. VIII. p. 167, 173, 176, 186) has rightly decided that we
must keep steadily in view the special circumstances under which Augustine has
here written; De bap. c. Donat. II. 3, 4 : "Quis nesciat sanctam scripturam canon-
icam tam veteris quam novi testamenti certis suis terminis contineri, eamque omnibus posterioribus episcoporum litteris ita præponi, ut de illa omnino dubitari et
disceptari non possit, utrum verum vel utrum rectum sit, quidquid in ea scriptum
esse constiterit: episcoporum autem litteras quæ post confirmatum canonem vel
scriptæ sunt vel scribuntur, et per sermonem forte sapientiorem cuiuslibet in ea re
peritioris, et per aliorum episcoporum graviorem auctoritatem doctioremque pruden-
tiam et per concilia licere reprehendi, si quid in eis forte a veritate deviatum est:
et ipsa concilia quæ per singulas regiones vel provincias fiunt, plenariorum conciliorum auctoritati quæ fiunt ex universo orbe Christiano, sine ullis ambagibus cedere:
ipsaque plenaria sæpe priora posterioribus emendari, cum aliquo experimento rerum
aperitur quod clausum erat, et cognoscitur quod latebat." *Emendari* can only
mean here actual emendation—not merely explanation, as Catholic historians of
dogma have to assume. It is also worthy of note, that Augustine assigned
Œcumenical rank to several Synods—*e.g.*, that of Arles—which afterwards were
not held to be Œcumenical. On the other hand, it is instructive that he himself
did not, like the Orientals, regard the Nicene decree as the foundation of the
doctrine of the Trinity; see Reuter's arguments on the relation of the work " De
trinitate" to the Nicene Symbol, (Ztschr. f. K.-Gesch. V. p. 375 ff.). The Council
of Chalcedon first put an end to dubiety as to the number, and the authority, of Œcumenical Councils in the East (even at the Robber Synod, A.D. 449,
only two had been recognised). Up till then the Nicene stood alone on an inaccessible height; moreover, in after times the uniqueness of this Council was still
remembered, though others were added beside it. For the rest, Roman Bishops
spoke very depreciatorily of, or even refused to recognise, many canons of later
councils; so Leo I. of the third of Constantinople (Ep. 106 [al. 80]), to say nothing
of the twenty-eighth of Chalcedon. But Leo did not recognise the second Council
as legitimate. Even Felix III. and Gelasius knew only of three Œcumenical Councils. General Synods Leo I. declared to be inspired (see Ep. 114, 2, to the Bishops
assembled at Chalcedon); but it is more than questionable whether he therefore
held all their resolutions to be absolutely irreversible.

[1] After the Council of Chalcedon, it was, above all, Justinian's legislation which
confirmed and popularised, even in the West, the view that there had been four
Œcumenical Councils: see his edict on the Three Chapters, 131: Οἱ ὑπὸ τῶν τεσσάρων
συνόδων, τῶν ἐν Νικαίᾳ καὶ Κωνσταντινουπόλει, ἐν Ἐφέσῳ καὶ ἐν Χαλκηδόνι τιθέντες
ὅροι νόμων τάξιν ἐχέτωσαν καὶ τὰ δόγματα αὐτῶν ὡς αἱ θεόπνευστοι τιμάσθωσαν

authority of regular Synods in general.   After the seventh Synod it was a settled principle in the orthodox Church of the East that Scripture and the decisions of the seven Œcumenical Councils formed the sources of the knowledge of Christian truth. [1]   They were characterised simply as the tradition, nay, men spoke, and not infrequently speak and act up to the present day, as if the Church possessed and required no other sources of knowledge or authorities.   As a rule, the παράδοσις ἄγραφος is not included when Holy Scripture and the seven Councils are spoken of.

This apparently simple, consistent development, seemingly corresponding to all requirements, did not, however, solve all difficulties, either after it had come to an end, or still less during its course. But it had further to reckon with authorities, some of which were of long standing, while others emerged in the contemporary organisation of the Church. What position was to be taken up in doctrinal controversies in which an Œcumenical Synod had not pronounced its decision? Must there not

---

γραφαί, Accordingly, this development was inaugurated by Constantine and closed by Justinian. After him Gregory I. (Ep. L. I. 25) wrote: "Sicut sancti evangelii quattuor libros, sic quattuor concilia suscipere et venerari me fateor." But this very utterance proves that the West only slowly accepted this whole development; for Gregory leaves out of account the fifth Œcumenical Council held meanwhile. Again, the attitude of the North African Church in the sixth century proves that there the dubiety felt by Augustine had not yet been wholly overcome. But the attempts of the papal theologian Vincenzi to dispute the independent authority of the councils generally—even for the above date—are thoroughly biassed, and carried out with the most daring indifference to historical fact. See his "In St. Gregorii Nyss. et Origenis scripta et doctrinam nova defensio", 5 T., 1865 f. and "De processione spiritus s. ex patre et filio", 1878.

[1] This is taught without any variation by the later so-called Symbols of the Greek Church and the most distinguished theologians up to the present day; see, e.g., Damalas, Ἡ ὀρθόδοξος πίστις, Athens, 1877, p. 3 ff.: οὐδεὶς πιστεύει εἰς μίαν ἐκκλησίαν ὁ μὴ ὁμολογῶν ὅτι τὰς ἐκπροσωπούσας ταύτην οἰκουμενικὰς συνόδους τὸ πνεῦμα τὸ ἅγιον ὁδηγεῖ εἰς πᾶσαν ἀλήθειαν. καὶ ὅτι ἡ ἐκκλησία αὕτη δὲν δύναται νὰ ᾖ ἄλλη παρὰ τὴν ἐπῳκοδομημένην ἐπὶ τῆς μόνης ἑνοποιοῦ ἀρχῆς τῶν οἰκουμενικῶν συνόδων· διότι ἡ ἀρχὴ τῶν μερικῶν ὑποχρεωτικῶν ὁμολογιῶν, ἣν καθιέρωσαν αἱ λοιπαὶ ἐκκλησίαι, ἐστὶν ἡ μήτηρ τῆς διαιρέσεως... ἡ προμνημονευθεῖσα ἀναγνώρισις τῶν ἑπτὰ οἰκουμενικῶν συνόδων ἐστὶ γεγονὸς ἱστορικόν, μηδεμίαν πλέον ἐκκλησιαστικὴν ἀναψηλάφησιν ἐπιδεχόμενον. According to present Greek ideas, the whole period of the Councils belongs to the classical antiquity of the Church; this period has long run its course.

be forthcoming in the Church *at any moment* a clear testimony to the truth, solving all doubtful questions, and giving forth no uncertain sound? What importance was due to the occupants of the great episcopal chairs, the Bishops of the apostolic communities, and especially of Rome? Decisions were not reached in all these questions, but a certain *common sense* arose. First, the Church speaks also by a unanimous testimony, audible from the earliest days, and this testimony never has been and never for a moment is, lacking. What has been always, everywhere, and by all, believed is inerrant tradition, even if it has not been solemnly and formally attested, or laid down in primitive authorities. This leads to a procedure similar to that followed by Eusebius in settling the N. T., viz., that the antiquity, unanimous attestation, and catholicity of a doctrine are to be expiscated in order that it may be certified a doctrine of the Church. The notion of 'antiquity' had now been extended and shifted with the advance of the Church. In the fourth century all the teachers held orthodox before Origen had been regarded as ancient, or *vicini apostolorum* (neighbours of the Apostles); the latter predicate especially had gradually been extended to the beginning of the third century: men like Irenæus, Apollinaris of Hierapolis and Hippolytus even were called γνώριμοι τῶν ἀποστόλων (friends of the Apostles).[1] Then the whole period of the martyrs came to be considered sacred as the ancient time. But the Church was compelled to recognise to an increasing extent, that not much was to be gained for its purposes from its theological 'witnesses' before Athanasius, from those before as well as after Origen. Their names were still held in sacred memory—with the exception of those who seemed too greatly compromised, or had even fallen into bad odour with their own contemporaries; but their works disappeared more and more, or gave place to forgeries. Accordingly, from the fifth century, Athanasius and orthodox teachers of similar views of the fourth century, appeared as the "Fathers" proper.[2]

[1] See as to this the Introduction to my History of Ancient Christian Literature up to Eusebius, Vol. I. 1893.

[2] Athanasius was not indeed so frequently quoted as one would believe. His works have been comparatively eclipsed by those of the Cappadocians, and the

When controversies arose, and soon even at Synods, the votes
of these men were *counted*. Doctrines were looked on as armed
with the testimony of antiquity, when they could be supported
from the Fathers from Athanasius to Cyril. Nor were forgeries
wanting here. The disciples of Apollinaris of Laodicea practised
these frauds to a vast extent, in order to rediscover their master's teaching in antiquity; they were afterwards imitated by
others. In any case, the tribunal of the 'Fathers' remained
an uncertain one; great as was the scope assigned to it, its
place and value were not dogmatically detailed. It was not
even really decided what relation the inspiration of the Councils
held to the *consensus patrum*, [1] (see under). Such a *consensus*
had often enough to be first restored; this was done by exegesis, or even by fabrications, because it was necessary to pre-
suppose it. References of an opposite character remained of
no effect; but when needs must a want of accuracy (akribeia)
and detached errors were admitted in the case of individual
Fathers, without the general conception being modified by these
concessions. The Fathers were just read backwards—so to
speak—*i.e.*, from the standpoint of the dogma of the time being,
and their undeveloped or divergent doctrines were interpreted
in accordance with the principle of making the best of everything. [2]

---

final statement arrived at in the East, A.D. 381, of the dogma of the Trinity was
more favourable to them than to Athanasius. The Synod of Constantinople, A.D.
383, (see *in loco*) furnishes the first example of the authority of the Fathers being
made decisive, and of the Scriptures themselves being ignored. But the attempt
miscarried at the time.

[1] To the "teachers" the predicate "Θεόπνευστος" was also applied. Thus
Athanasius writes (De incarn. verbi 56): Αἱ γραφαὶ μὲν γὰρ διὰ θεολόγων ἀνδρῶν
παρὰ Θεοῦ ἐλαλήθησαν καὶ ἐγράφησαν. ἡμεῖς δὲ παρὰ τῶν αὐταῖς ἐντυγχανόντων
θεοπνεύστων διδασκάλων, οἳ καὶ μάρτυρες τῆς Χριστοῦ θεότητος γεγόνασι, μαθόντες
μεταδίδομεν καὶ τῇ σῇ φιλομαθίᾳ. Similarly, though very rhetorically, Arius in his
Thalia (Athanas. Orat. c. Arian I. 5): κατὰ πίστιν ἐκλεκτῶν Θεοῦ, συνετῶν Θεοῦ,
παίδων ἁγίων, ὑρθοτόμων, ἅγιον Θεοῦ πνεῦμα λαβόντων, τάδε ἔμαθον ἔγωγε ὑπὸ τῶν
σοφίης μετεχόντων, ἀστείων, θεοδιδάκτων, κατὰ πάντα σοφῶν τε.

[2] It would take us too far to give detailed instances of the points discussed
under this head. We only emphasise the following. (1) The attestation of a doctrine
by the Councils was often set side by side with that given by the "Fathers", the
"ancient" or "holy doctors", in such a way that the former seemed often to be
merely a special case of the latter. And this was quite natural. The Church

Secondly, a peculiar reverence was inherited from the past for Apostolic Churches or their bishops, entwined with the evidence based on history and dogmatics. Although the theory of Cyprian, which allowed no special importance to the Bishops

possessed no continuous testimony in the Councils; from its distinctive character, however, it required one. And this could only be furnished by the unbroken chorus of orthodox doctors. Even taken historically this court of appeal was the older. Irenæus and especially Clemens Alex. had already referred to deceased presbyters as authoritative teachers; and Eusebius' conception of Church History embraced the idea—see preface and outline—that side by side with the *successio episcoporum* there stood a series of witnesses who, in uninterrupted succession, had declared the true doctrine orally and in writing. (2) No definitions were arrived at of the manner in which the authority of the Bishops was related to that of the doctors. It was possible to shut one's eyes to this question, because in most cases the teachers were also bishops. As a rule, the Greeks spoke not of bishops, but the ancient doctors, when appealing to the witnesses to the truth. It was otherwise with the majority of the Latins after Cyprian (see p. 214). (3) As the usual procedure at the Councils was to set up no doctrinal tenet unless it was believed to have the support of the doctors, and as the claim was made that this course should always be adopted, the idea that the Councils were inspired was already abolished, and they were subordinated to the continuous testimony of the Church (see under). (4) The practice of consulting authorities began at the Ephesian Council; it played a more prominent part in every succeeding Synod. Athanasius and the Arians had undoubtedly disputed before this over passages in the Fathers, but their disputes were of slight importance compared with those that took place afterwards. (5) The notion of ecclesiastical antiquity gradually became more and more comprehensive; meanwhile the real ancient period of Christianity became more obscure, and bit by bit came to be forgotten. After the seventh the whole period of the Councils was looked on as the classical antiquity of the Church. If even in the fourth, nay, up to the middle of the fifth century, Councils were held to be an innovation, their absence was now considered a characteristic of the age of the Epigoni; indeed they were thought to be unnecessary, because everything was already settled. (6) The opinion held by faith that the "Fathers" had decided every disputed point beforehand, was a strong challenge to produce forgeries, and resulted in objective and and subjective falsehood. Caspari (Alte und neue Quellen, etc., 1879) has shown that the followers of Apollinaris were the first to forge on a large scale; but the Acts of Councils, and the examination of writings circulated under the names of celebrated Fathers, show that they had numerous imitators in the ranks of all parties. The practice of compiling collections of extracts, which was so much favoured after the middle of the fifth century, was, besides, especially adapted to conceal forgeries or inaccuracies. (7) But the limits, authority, and character of the Court of Appeal of the "Fathers" were never determined. It was taught that the orthodox Fathers agreed in all matters, nay, this theory was treated as a dogma. Stephen Gobarus' attempt (Photius, Cod. 232) to demonstrate the contradictions of the Fathers was felt to be profane, just as Eusebius had condemned as unchurchmanlike the attitude of Marcellus of Ancyra, who had censured the consultation, without

of Apostolic communities within the general authority of the
Episcopate, had weakened this prestige, it still held its ground.
Augustine still recalled it in the question of the extent of the
Holy Scriptures. [1]   But there now grew up, in consequence of

independent examination, of the "wisest" Fathers. But even John of Damascus had
to admit that Fathers—otherwise orthodox—held divergent opinions on single
points (De imag. I. 25), and Photius actually was more than once compelled, in
the course of his learned studies, to notice mistakes committed by them (see his
Bibliotheca). Therefore the question was never decided who constituted the orthodox Fathers. It became the custom to prefer (Athanasius), Gregory of Nazianzus,
Chrysostom, Cyril, and afterwards also John of Damascus. In the fourth century
the orthodox were much troubled by the fact that the Synod of Antioch (A.D. 268)
rejected, while that of Nicæa accepted, the term Ὁμοούσιος. The treatment of this
difficulty in Athanasius, "De synod." 43 sq., shows that no one had hit on the idea that
the later decision made the earlier obsolete. It was rather held on the contrary:
οἱ προλαβόντες ἀφανίζουσιν τοὺς μετὰ ταῦτα γενομένους. Therefore Athanasius
sought and found evidences of the word Ὁμοούσιος before the Samosatian controversy. Ultimately, however, he had to adopt a different treatment of the whole
question, i.e., to show that Ὁμοούσιος had only been rejected at Antioch as against
Paul, in order not to admit a contradiction in the chorus of the Fathers. The
same difficulty was caused about the middle of the fifth century by the term "δύο
φύσεις", for it was hard to find an instance of that in antiquity. Of Eutyches the
following expression is recorded (Mansi VI., p. 700): τὸ ἐκ δύο φύσεων ἑνωθεισῶν
καθ᾽ ὑπόστασιν γεγεννῆσθαι τὸν κύριον ἡμῶν Ἰησοῦν Χριστὸν μήτε μεμαθηκέναι ἐν
ταῖς ἐκθέσεσι τῶν ἁγίων πατέρων μήτε καταδέχεσθαι, εἰ τύχοι τι αὐτῷ τοιοῦτο παρά
τινος ὑπαναγινώσκεσθαι, διὰ τὸ τὰς θείας γραφὰς ἀμείνονας εἶναι τῆς τῶν πατέρων
διδασκαλίας. He afterwards disowned this expression as being distorted, his advocate
corrected it in his name thus: "The Fathers have spoken in different ways, and
I accept everything they say, but not as a rule of faith" (εἰς κανόνα δὲ πίστεως
οὐ δέχομαι). That is very instructive. The words excited the greatest consternation
in the assembly in which they were uttered, and the speaker felt himself compelled
at once to excuse them on the ground of a momentary confusion.

[1] See above, Note 1, p. 198, and compare "De peccator. mer. et remiss." I., 50.
Here the *auctoritas ecclesiarum orientalium* is mentioned (in reference to the Ep.
to the Hebrews), and to Augustine this *auctoritas* was exalted, because Christianity
had come from the Apostolic Churches, from the communities to which John and
Paul had written, *above all, from Jerusalem* (*unde ipsum evangelium coepit prædicari*). The fact that the Donatists had been separated from Apostolic Churches
proved to him that they were wrong; see especially the Liber ad Donat. post
collat. c. 4, c. 29; also Ep. 52, c. 3 and c. Lib. Petil. l. II., c. 51 (Reuter in the
Ztschr. f. K.-Gesch. V., p. 361 ff.). Optatus had already held the same view as
Augustine; see the important details "De schism. Donat." II., 6, VI., 3. But even
after the middle of the sixth century a Roman Pope, Pelagius I., singled out the
fact in praise of Augustine, that he, "mindful of the divine teaching which founded the
Church *on the Apostolic Chairs*, taught that those were schismatics who seceded
from the doctrine and communion of *these Apostolic Chairs*" (Mansi, Concil. IX.,

the Metropolitan and Patriarchate form of government, a new
aristocracy among the Bishops, which received its importance
from the size and influence of the episcopal cities. Rome, Alexandria—the founding of whose Church by Mark was undisputed
about A.D. 300—and Antioch were not affected by the rivalry
involved in this new principle; for in these cases the special
connection with the Apostles coincided with the greatness of the
city. But the political factor prevailed so strongly that the
Chairs of Corinth, Thessalonica, etc., and finally, even that of
Ephesus, [1] lost all peculiar prestige—only that of Jerusalem, in
spite of the political insignificance of the city, was ranked with
those more distinguished [2]—but Constantinople was added to
the list of the outstanding episcopates. In the East this was
frankly justified by the political position of the city; [3] but this
justification was so far insufficient as the chair, by its co-ordin-
ation with the Apostolic sees, participated in the attributes

p. 716). Pelagius even declared that when doubts as to the faith arose it was
necessary to conform to *the Apostolic Chairs* (l. c. p. 732). This form of expression is all the more remarkable since the Roman Bishops of the fifth century spoke,
as a rule, as if the designation *sedes apostolica* belonged peculiarly to their Chair.

[1] At the transition from the fourth to the fifth century; see Hefele II., pp. 77 ff.,
495 f., 528 ff.

[2] See the 7th Canon of Nicæa, and in addition, Hefele's details, Vol. I., p. 403 f.;
II., p. 213. Jerusalem was first raised to a Patriarchate at Chalcedon, see Hefele
II., pp. 477, 502. Jerusalem became once more the 'holy city' in the fourth cen-
tury; see Epiphanius and others.

[3] See the 3rd Canon of Constantinople, Hefele, II., p. 17 f. and the 28th of Chalcedon, Hefele, II., p. 527 f.; τῷ θρόνῳ τῆς πρεσβυτέρας ῾Ρώμης διὰ τὸ βασιλεύειν
τὴν πόλιν ἐκείνην, οἱ πατέρες εἰκότως ἀποδεδώκασι τὰ πρεσβεῖα, καὶ τῷ αὐτῷ σκοπῷ
κινούμενοι οἱ ἑκατὸν πεντήκοντα θεοφιλέστατοι ἐπίσκοποι τὰ ἴσα πρεσβεῖα ἀπένειμαν
τῷ τῆς νέας ῾Ρώμης ἁγιωτάτῳ θρόνῳ, εὐλόγως κρίναντες, τὴν βασιλείᾳ καὶ συγκλήτῳ
τιμηθεῖσαν πόλιν καὶ τῶν ἴσων ἀπολαύουσαν πρεσβείων τῇ πρεσβυτέρᾳ βασιλίδι
῾Ρώμῃ, καὶ ἐν τοῖς ἐκκλησιαστικοῖς, ὡς ἐκείνην, μεγαλύνεσθαι πράγμασι, δευτέραν
μετ᾿ ἐκείνην ὑπάρχουσαν. Constantinople was factitiously promoted to the place of
Ephesus by reason of this unexampled act of legitimation. At the Robber Synod,
nevertheless, it still held the fifth place. As regards the historical interpretation of
the sixth Canon of Nicæa and the third of Constantinople, I agree substantially with
the excellent arguments of Kattenbusch (l. c. I., p. 81 ff.); only it must be still
more strongly emphasised that the Canons of A.D. 381 bore a clearly marked
hostility to Alexandria. Even then it was considered necessary to suppress the
authority of the Alexandrian Church, which was on the point of developing into
the premier Church of the East.

which the latter possessed in virtue of their apostolic character. [1] Such attributes continued to be ascribed to those chairs without it being stated, however, in what they really consisted. They were nothing tangible, and yet they were held to exist. [2] But even in the view of Orientals they belonged in a preëminent degree to Rome. The works of the only western author before Jerome who was also read in the East—*i.e.*, Cyprian—could not fail to heighten the prestige of Rome. [3] But that was already great enough in itself. As the ancient capital of the Empire, as the city of the two chief Apostles, of the *Cathedra Petri*, as the only apostolic community of the West, that which had done more for the whole Church than any other, Rome even in the East enjoyed a unique prestige. [4] But as early as the fourth century, and certainly from the fifth onwards, Rome meant the Roman Bishop, with whose spiritual dignity were fused the memories of the ancient city that had ruled the world. These memories overhung the place, after the Emperor had left, and the most of them clung to the Bishop. In the momentous Arian conflict the great Eastern sees, except Alexandria, became compromised or dishonoured; the orthodox Orientals sought and found their support in Rome. [5] The Emperor

[1] An energetic protest was admittedly raised, especially by Leo I. and his successors. Leo at the same time also advocated the rights of the Apostolic Churches in general (Ep. 106). We cannot here follow out the controversy, although it reflects the revivification of the Byzantine Church and State, and the attitude of the Roman Bishops, which was purely ecclesiastical, though it did rest on fictions: see Hefele II., pp. 408, 539 ff., 549 ff., and Sohm l. c. I., pp. 377—440. It was not until the fourth Lateran Synod (Can. 5), when a Latin Patriachate existed at Constantinople (1215), that Rome recognised the 28th Canon of Chalcedon.

[2] Although all Bishops were held to be successors of the Apostles, yet Leo I. singles out very distinctly those who had inherited the chairs of the Apostles; see his letter to the Emperor Marcian (Ep. 104).

[3] Not only Eusebius, but also Theodore of Mopsuestia had read Cyprian's Epistles. At the Council of Ephesus evidence taken from him was read; see Vincent, Commonit. 42. Of the Westerns, after Cyprian, Ambrose was especially esteemed in the East. Augustine also possessed a certain authority.

[4] See Vol. II., p. 149 f.

[5] On the authority of the Roman Bishop in the fourth century, see Hauck, Der römische Bischop in 4 Jahrh., 1881; Rade, Damasus, 1881; Langen, Gesch. der römischen Kirche, 2 Vols., 1881, 1885; Sohm, l. c. In what follows we only discuss Rome's prestige in the East. Even Hefele (l. c. I., p. 8) admits that the first eight

in Constantinople who brought the great controversy to an end
was a Western, full of veneration for Rome. The promotion
which he afterwards assigned to Constantinople was no equivalent—at first, at least,—for the advance in political power
secured to Rome by the Arian controversy.¹ The role˙ of

Synods were not appointed and convoked by the Roman Bishops. His arguments
as to the presidency at the Synods are, however, biassed (pp. 29—44). It was at
Chalcedon that the legates of the Roman Bishop first occupied a special position.
The sixth Canon of Nicæa, when correctly interpreted, gives no preference to Rome,
but refers merely to the fact that it was the ecclesiastical metropolis for the Churches
of several provinces. It is credible that Julius I. uttered the principle (Socrates
H. E. II. 17): μὴ δεῖν παρὰ γνώμην τοῦ ἐπισκόπου Ῥώμης κανονίζειν τὰς ἐκκλησίας.
The peculiar authority of the Roman Chair showed itself in the fourth century in
the following facts. First, Constantine transferred to the Roman Bishop the duty
of presiding over the commission to examine the case of the Donatists. Secondly,
the oppressed adherents of the Nicene Symbol in the East turned to him for
protection (see even Langen, l. c. I., p. 425 f.). Thirdly, we have the request of
the Eusebians that Julius should decide the dogmatic question; it is true that very
soon—when they foresaw their defeat in Rome—they changed their tone. They
still conceded a peculiar dignity to Rome; it does not seem to me possible to
translate φιλοτιμίαν (Sozom. III. 8) with Langen by "ambition." Yet they pointed
out that Rome had received its Christianity from the East, and that it was as little
entitled to review the decision of a dogmatic question given in the East, as the
Oriental Bishops would have been to take up the Novatian affair after Rome had
spoken. (The letter is to be reconstructed from Sozom. III. 8, and Athanas. apolog.
c. Arian. 25—35.) Fourthly, we have evidence of Rome's position also in Julius'
epistle to the Orientals (Athanas. l. c.); fifthly, in Canons 3 and 5 of the Synod
of Sardica; and sixthly, in the request of the Antiochenes, or Jerome, to Damasus,
for a decision in the Antiochene schism (Ep. 16).

¹ Damasus' policy did not at once succeed in raising the prestige of the Roman
Chair in the East (see Rade, l. c., p, 137 f.), but the manner in which Theodosius I.
at first decided the Arian controversy there, did. "Cunctos populos, quos clementiæ
nostræ regit temperamentum, in tali volumus religione versari, quam divinum
Petrum apostolum tradidisse Romanis religio usque ad nunc ab ipso insinuata
declarat," etc. Besides, the new style adopted by Damasus in his letter to the
Oriental Bishops (Theodoret H. E. V. 10) was not without effect in the East. He
calls them my "sons" instead of my "brethren," and he no longer speaks, like
other Bishops, as commissioned by the Synod—though the question at issue was
a decision of the Synod—or as representing the Western Church. On the contrary,
he addresses them in virtue of the authority of his "Apostolic Chair," which he
connects solely with Peter and without any reference to Paul. "The first rank is
due to the Holy Church, in which the Holy Apostle had his seat, and taught
how we should fitly guide the helm which we have undertaken to control." Rade
has, besides, here rightly conjectured (p. 136) that Jerome had a share in this letter,
which did a great deal to raise the influence of the Roman Chair in the East.

observer and arbiter, which the Roman Bishop was able to play
in the Christological controversies, made it possible for him to
maintain for a time the lofty position he had won. [1] (On the
aspirations of the Alexandrian Bishops, Athanasius, Peter, etc.,
and the successful opposition to them by Leo, see chap. IX.)
There can be no doubt that even in the eyes of the Orientals
there attached to the Roman Bishop a special something, which
was wanting to all the rest, a nimbus which conferred upon
him a peculiar authority. [2] Yet this nimbus was not sufficiently

---

[1] From and after Siricius I., the Roman Bishops maintained that it was their
province to care for all Churches (Constant., p. 659. Ep. 6, ch. 1). On the relation
of Leo I. to the East, and to the fourth Council, see Langen, l. c. II., pp. 10 f., 50 ff.
The phrase "our fatherly solicitude" occurs frequently even in the letters of his
predecessors to the East. The appeal of Cyril to Coelestine is very important in
its bearing on the dignity of the Roman Chair; compare the language of the
Roman legate at the Council of Ephesus (Mansi III., p. 1279 sq.).

[2] In the work "Der Papst und das Concil von Janus" (1869), p. 93, we find
this passage. "In the writings of the doctors of the Greek Church, Eusebius,
Athanasius, Basil the Great, the two Gregorys, and Epiphanius, not a word is to
be found of peculiar pregrogatives being assigned to a Roman Bishop. Chrysostom,
the most prolific of the Greek Fathers, is absolutely silent on the point, and so also
are the two Cyrils. Basil (Opp. ed. Bened. III. 301, Ep. 239 and 214) has expressed
his contempt for the writings of the Popes in the strongest terms [in the affairs of
Marcellus]: 'these proud and conceited westerns, who would only fortify heresy';
even if their letters descended from heaven, he would not accept them." It is true
that, seeing the now wide-spread view of the apostolic succession of all Bishops,
the prestige of the Roman Bishop is hardly perceptible in the East at the beginning of the fourth century, and that he had to fight, i.e., to wrest for himself
the position which had formerly belonged to the Roman Church. Therefore the
testimonies to a special dignity being possessed by the Roman Bishops in the East
in the fourth century are in fact comparatively scanty, But they are not wanting—
see, e.g., Greg. Naz., Carmen de vita sua T. II., p. 9, and Chrysostom, Ep. ad
Innocent I.—and from A.D. 380 this dignity bulked more largely in the eyes of
Orientals, though indeed, without receiving a definite and fixed meaning. Very
characteristic in this respect are the Church Histories of Socrates and Sozomen,
who on this point are free from partiality, and reflect the universal opinion. But
it does not occur to them to doubt that the Roman Bishop had a special authority
and a unique relation to the whole Church (see, e.g., Socrat. II. 8, 15, 17; Soz.
III. 8; also Theodoret's letter to Leo I.). Instructive here are the collections of Leo
Allatius and in the Innsbrucker Theol. Ztschr., 1877, p. 662 f.; see also three
treatises by the Abbé Martin: "Saint Pierre, sa venue et son martyre à Rome,"
in the Rev. des quest. historiq., 1873 (principally from oriental sources); "S. Pierre
et S. Paul dans l'église Nestorienne," Paris, 1875; "S. Pierre et le Rationalisme
devant les églises orientales," Amiens, 1876. These discussions, though in part uncritical, are very full of matter. Matt. XVI. 18, John XXI. 18, were undoubtedly

bright and luminous to bestow upon its possessor an unimpeach-
able authority; it was rather so nebulous that it was possible
to disregard it without running counter to the spirit of the
universal Church. And it gradually became fainter. The more
completely, after the middle of the fifth century, the internal
relations of West and East ceased, and the more strongly the
distinctively Byzantine spirit could assert itself in the diminished
Church of the East, so the more rapidly declined the prestige
of the Roman Bishop. Constantinople put an end to it in its
own midst, when the Roman Bishop set up claims which in the
fourth and fifth centuries had been palliated by actual circumstances and the necessities of the time, but which 500 years
afterwards could not fail to be felt as the intrusion of an alien
spirit. [1] Yet, in spite of this, the idea of the unity of the Church
still held its ground for a long time. After Synods ceased to
be held, the influence of the great Patriarchates throughout the
whole Church in the East increased [2]—though, indeed, the
orthodox Patriarchs of Alexandria, Antioch, and Jerusalem, had
lost their real importance; and theoretically the dignity of the

never referred in the East to the primacy of Rome (see Janus, p. 97). Still in any
case it is saying too little—even for the period about the year A.D. 380—to
remark as Rade does (l. c., p. 137). To the Orientals the Bishop of Rome was like
the rest, only, thanks to his situation, the natural representative of the Churches of
the western half of the Empire, acting, as it were, as correspondent in the name
of the Christians of the West.

[1] The prestige of the Roman Bishop in the East was accordingly on the increase from the beginning of the fourth till the middle of the fifth century, remained at its height till about the time of Justinian, when, however, it lost its
practical importance, and then, apart from the events about A.D. 680 and the next
decades, slowly declined, yet without ever being wholly destroyed. The Roman
Chair was now held to be schismatic; if not that, it would still have been the
first. Undoubtedly there was a strong inclination in later times to oppose it by
advancing the see of Jerusalem, the seat of James, but it was not possible to gain
any confidence in the claim of the latter to the first place. See on the criticism
of the papacy by the Greeks, Pichler, Gesch. der kirchl. Trennung zwischen Or.
u. Occ., 1864; Hergenröther, Photius, 3 Vols. 1867 ff ; Gass, Symbolik, p. 216 ff.;
Kattenbusch, l. c., pp. 79—124. It was a settled doctrine of the Church in the East,
that the Church has no visible head.

[2] The terms τυραννίς and δυναστεία are first used, so far as I know, in reference
to Antioch, i.e., against Paul of Samos. (Eus. H. E. VII. 30), after Origen had already
complained of the ambition of the Great Bishops. Socrates has expressed himself
very frankly about this matter.

Roman Bishop as *primus inter pares,* though not unassailed, was embraced in that of the great Eastern sees. But it was never made clear how far the Patriarchs in their collective capacity really constituted an authority in dogma: there is not even an explicit statement that they did form such an authority. There was an uncertainty of opinion as to their position alongside of and in the Œcumenical Synods. [1] Here also there was an absence of fixed definitions. The Church as it is, with its graduated orders, crowned by the Patriarchs, constituted the tradition and the authority. But the authority of no factor in this system possessed, when isolated, any significance whatever. It might not assert itself at the expense of the rest. Its dignity was founded on its being a part of *antiquity.*

As to II. This at once involves the answer to the second question (see p. 214). The assumption that the Councils were inspired did not imply any power on their part to deliver new revelations to the Church. On the contrary, they proved their peculiar possession of the Holy Spirit by their unfailing testimony to the ancient doctrinal tradition. [2] But in that case the new formulas created by the Councils could not but cause

---

[1] The importance of the four Patriarchs—of Constantinople, Alexandria, Antioch, and Jerusalem—was celebrated here and there in lofty expressions; it was especially prominent in the later Symbols, so-called, of the Greek Church (see Gass, l. c., p. 222 f.). Their presence or that of their representative was even held to be absolutely necessary at an Œcumenical Synod; but not only was the extent of their authority never defined, but the essential equality of all Bishops was steadily maintained in the East; and the latest development of the Greek Church, *i.e.,* its disruption into perfectly independent National Churches, has thrown overboard the whole 'Constitution of the Patriarchate', which in all ages was more a matter of assertion than reality. The Bishop of Alexandria, undoubtedly, nearly succeeded in becoming in the fifth century supreme Bishop of the East, but Leo and Pulcheria overthrew him. Kattenbusch (l. c. p. 357 ff.) furnishes further details as to the "five Patriarchs as symbolical figures." Has the Patriarchate of Rome come to an end in the view of the Greek Church? In the abstract, no; in the concrete, yes.

[2] See above, p. 215 f. Augustine gives utterance to a very remarkable statement in De bapt. c. Donat. II., 4, 5: "Quomodo potuit ista res (the baptism by heretics) ·tantis altercationum nebulis involuta, ad plenarii concilii luculentam illustrationem confirmationemque perduci, nisi primo diutius per orbis terrarum regiones multis hinc atque hinc disputationibus et collationibus episcoporum pertractata constaret?" Accordingly, only a matter which had already become ripe for decision through frequent deliberations could be submitted to and decided by a Council.

offence. How far they did is shown by the history of the dogmatic controversies. Above all, the unbiblical catch-word 'consubstantial' ('Ομοούσιος), for a time directly rejected by the
Church, only won acceptance under great difficulties, even
among those who had little or no objection to the cause it
represented. These formulas had to be proved in some way or
other to have been anciently held. For 'Ομοούσιος it was of the
highest importance that a Council had made it an accomplished
fact. As the word gradually made good its ground, the Council lay far enough in the past to be itself regarded as belonging to antiquity. The evidence was got by reasoning in a
circle; the authority of the Council supported the word which
was anything but old, but the authority of any Council was
dependent on its rejection of all innovations. Numerous passages in the Fathers furnished material in confirmation of the
later formulas — which were never, so far as I know, bluntly
deduced from unwritten tradition (παράδοσις άγραφος); but a
strong preference was shown for understanding them as a repetition of the Nicene Symbol, the explication being disregarded,
just as Irenæus in his time had passed off the Symbol unfolded
in an antignostic sense, the *regula fidei*, for the Symbol itself,
i.e., for the ancient repository of the truth. In spite of all novelties, it was thus contended that novelties were not forthcoming
in the Church. Nay, even the power of the Councils to *unfold*
doctrines authoritatively was not plainly asserted in the East;
on the other hand, a Western, Vincentius of Lerinum, did
maintain it, and essayed to furnish a theory on the subject.
After the uncertainties of the Greeks over the conception of
tradition, we really breathe freely when we study the attempt
of this man to introduce light and certainty into the question.
However, even in the East, the younger generation now and
then gave the older Fathers the benefit of looking at their
words as having been uttered at a time when dogma was
not yet explained, or sharply formulated. Strictly speaking,
this expedient was not tenable on Greek ground. Only a
very sparing use therefore was made of it there, [1] while the

---

[1] The more common way of putting it in the East was that the writer in
question had failed in the necessary "Akribeia" (exactness), *i.e.*, he could, and

Catholic West employs it to a great extent up to the present day. [1]

The conception of tradition is accordingly quite obscure. The hierarchical element does not *in theory* play the leading

should, have done it better (see, above all, the views of Photius). But it was rarely admitted that the Church at the time referred to did not yet possess complete *akribeia* in dogma. But we have further to notice here that a distinction was still drawn both in East and West between questions of faith, in the strict sense of the term, and theological doctrines, and that unity in the former was alone demanded. But as this distinction was in itself obscure, since in fact questions of faith had been transformed into theological and scientific ones, so in the East it became more and more restricted, though it was never wholly effaced. Augustine, besides, still laid great stress on this distinction, and accepted a whole group of theological doctrines in which differences did not endanger unity; the passages are given in Reuter, Ztschr. f. K.-Gesch. V., p. 363 ff. But if " faith " is itself a doctrine, where does it cease and the doctrine begin? Besides the excuse of want of accuracy, which, indeed, involves censure, that of ἁπλούστερον γεγραφέναι was asserted. It involved no fault. Thus Athanasius writes (De Synod. 45) of the Fathers who in A.D. 268 rejected the term Ὁμοούσιος at Antioch : περὶ τῆς τοῦ υἱοῦ θεότητος ἁπλούστερον γράφοντες οὐ κατεγένοντο περὶ τῆς τοῦ ὁμουσίου ἀκρίβειας. Precisely in the same way the Homoiousians at Nice excused the Nicene Fathers. Unique, so far as I know, is the statement of Gregory of Naz. (Orat. 31. 28), which is only explicable from the still wholly confused state of the doctrine of the Holy Ghost in his time. "As the O. T. declared the Father clearly, but the Son more vaguely, so the N. T. has revealed the Son, but only suggested the divinity of the Spirit " [compare the contentions of the Montanists]. "Now, however, the Spirit reigns among us, and makes himself more clearly known to us; for it was not advisable to proclaim the divinity of the Son, so long as that of the Father was not recognised, or to impose upon the former—if we may use such a bold expression—that of the Spirit, while it (viz., the divinity of the Son) was not accepted." We may in this passage study the distinction between Gregory the theologian and Athanasius.

[1] So, above all, Augustine, who excused Cyprian in this way, and further, set up the general rule that as long as no unequivocal decisions had been given in a question, the bond of unity was to be maintained among the dissentient Bishops (De bapt. c. Donat. II. 4, 5). Augustine thus admitted that ecclesiastical tradition did not at every moment solve all questions pending in the Church. The Donatist and Pelagian controversy roused Western theologians to reflect on tradition. One fruit of this reflection was the Commonitorium of Vincentius of Lerinum, unique, because it deals professedly with the question of tradition. The arguments are decisive of Western views, but the book did not extend its influence into the East; there the ideas about tradition remained characteristically indefinite. A short analysis of the Commonitorium is necessary. Let it be noticed that it is ultimately aimed at Augustine's doctrine of grace and predestination, but that a large part of the rules are taken from that theologian.

After a preface, in which Vincentius remarks that he is only sketching out what he had received from the past, he sets side by side the two foundations of the

part in it. The apostolical succession has in theory had no such thorough-going importance even in the West for the proof of tradition as one would expect. After the time of the Councils the authority of the Bishops as bearers of tradition was wholly

faith, the divine law (Holy Scripture) and the tradition of the Catholic Church (1). The former is sufficient by itself, but it requires the latter for its correct explanation (2). The latter embraces what had been believed *everywhere, at all times,* and *by all*—or, at least, by almost all priests and doctors (3). Accordingly, the following criteria were to be applied: (a) When a section of the Church renounced the communion of the Catholic faith, the Christian followed the great communion; (b) when a heresy threatened danger to the whole Church, he held by antiquity, "which, certainly, could not now be seduced"; (c) when he came upon heresy in antiquity itself, in a few men, or in a city or province, he followed the decision of a General Council; (d) if no such Council had spoken, he examined and compared the *orthodox* doctors and retained what—not two, or three—but all, had alike taught clearly, frequently, and persistently, in one and the same sense (4). These rules are illustrated by reference to the dangers, which had threatened the Church from Donatism, Arianism, and the Anabaptists (5—10). At this point, however, it is conceded that orthodox teachers might have and had fallen into error on one point; nevertheless they were blessed, but hell received the Epigoni, who, in order to start a heresy, took hold of the writings of one or other of the ancients (as the Donatists did of Cyprian's) which were composed in obscure language, and which, owing to the obscurity prevailing in them, seemed to coincide with their teaching, so that the views brought forward by these heretics bore not to have been maintained for the first time and exclusively by them. Such people were like Ham in uncovering the shame of their father (11). After this excursus the author adduces proofs from Paul's Epistles, that changes in the creed, in short, any kind of innovation, constituted the worst evil (12—14). In order to prove and tempt his own, God had permitted teachers belonging to the Church, and therefore not foisted in from without, to essay the setting up of new tenets in the Church; examples are taken from Nestorius, Photinus, and Apollinaris; their heresy is described, and contrasted with the true faith (15—22). But the greatest temptation of the Church was due to the innovations of Origen, who was so famous (23), and of the no less distinguished Tertullian (24). Here follows a detailed practical application; those who have been seduced by the great heretics should unlearn to their salvation, what they have learned to their destruction; they must apprehend as much of the doctrine of the Church as can be grasped by the mind, and believe what they cannot understand; all novelty is wickedness and folly; in making innovations ignorance cloaks itself under the 'scientific spirit', imbecility under 'enlightenment', darkness under 'light'. The pure science of the worship of God is only given in the Catholic, ancient, and harmonious tradition 25—27). Antiquity is really the thorough-going criterion of the truth.

This is followed by the second part, which contains the most original matter. It opens with the question whether there is any progress in the Church of Christ in religion. This is answered in the affirmative; the progress is 'very great'; but it consists in deepening, not in altering. It is *organic growth of knowledge* both on the part of individuals and the Church (28). In order to illustrate this,

spent on that proof. Yet even that is perhaps saying too much
Everything was really obscure. So far, however, as the Greek
Church has not changed since John of Damascus, the Greek has at
present a perfectly definite sense of the foundation of religion.

use is made figuratively of the growth of the child and plants; religion is fortified
with years, expanded with time, and developed more subtly with age; yet every
thing remains really what it was, no innovation takes place, for a single novelty
would destroy everything (29—31). The Church is intent only on clearness, light
a more subtle differentiation and invigoration of doctrine. What then did it ever
seek to attain by the decrees of Councils, except that simple belief should become
more definite, supine preaching be rendered more urgent, and that a wholly in
dolent conduct of affairs should give place to a correspondingly anxious perform
ance of duty? "Hoc inquam semper neque quidquam præterea, hæreticorum novitati
bus excitata [that then is admitted], conciliorum suorum decretis catholica perfeci
ecclesia, nisi ut quod prius a majoribus sola traditione susceperat, hoc deinde pos
teris etiam per scripturæ chirographum consignaret, magnam rerum summam pauci
litteris comprehendendo *et plerumque propter intelligentiæ lucem non novum fide
sensum novæ appellationis proprietate signando*" (32). As compared with this ad
mission, the author attacks all the more vigorously the 'wicked verbal innovations
practised by all heretics (33, 34). But it was still more necessary to be on one's
guard when heretics appealed to Scripture—as *e.g.*, the Arians did to predicates
taken from the Bible against the term 'Ομοούσιος—for they were the real wolves
in sheeps' clothing, sons of the devil, for the devil also quoted the Bible (35—37)
All that was necessary to meet their exposition and obtain the correct sense, was
simply to apply the criteria given in ch. 4. (38). The last of these was the search
for the concordant views of many and great teachers, when a Council had not
yet decided the question concerned. Then follows a particular instruction which
betrays very clearly the uncertainty of that citerion. It was to be applied, not to
every unimportant question, but only, at least for the most part only, in the case
of the rule of faith; it was, further, only to be used when heresies had just arisen
"before they had time to falsify the standards of the ancient creed, before they
could by a wider diffusion of the poison adulterate the writings of the forefathers
Heresies already circulated and deeply rooted were not to be attacked in this
way, because in the long lapse of time they had had sufficient opportunity to pur
loin the truth" (!!). Christians must try to refute these ancient heresies by the
authority of Scripture alone—accordingly the principle of tradition is declared in
solvent; or they must simply be avoided as having been already condemned. But
even the principle of the *consensus* of the teachers is to be used with the greatest
caution; it is strictly guarded; it is only of weight when, as it were, a whole
Council of doctors can be cited (39). But in that case no one is entitled to dis
regard it, for the ancient doctors are the 'prophets and teachers' ranked by Paul
next to the Apostles, and described by him as presented to the Church by God.
He who despises them despises God. We must cling to the agreement of the holy
Churches, which are holy because they continue in the communion of the faith (40).

In the so-called second Commonitorium (ch. 41—43) there is first a recapitulation
in which the sufficiency of Scripture as source of truth is once more emphasised.

Besides Holy Scripture, tradition is the source of knowledge of, the authority for, the truth; and tradition is the Church itself, not, as in the West, governed by Rome, as a sovereign, living power, but in its immovable, thousand-year-old doctrines and orders. Even Scripture is to be explained by the tradition which transmits it, although Scripture is itself to some extent the *caput et origo traditionis*. But tradition still really presents itself in two forms as it did among the earliest Alexandrians: there is a perfectly official form—now that of the Councils, and one more profound and indefinite—corresponding to the 'scientific tradition' (παράδοσις γνωστική) of the ancient Alexandrians.

3. *The Church.* [1]

Cyril of Jerusalem in his Catechisms portrays the Church to his disciples as a spiritual communion. But in explaining the predicate 'catholic' [2] he completely identifies this spiritual communion with the empirical Church. It is called Ἐκκλησία, because it summons all men together, and unites them with one another. This it does at God's command; for after God had rejected the first community as the 'synagogue of the wicked',

It is then shown that, at the Council of Ephesus held three years before, no novelty was proposed, but decisions were based on the sayings of the Fathers. The Fathers are named singly whose works were publicly read there (42). Vincentius therefore considered that the authority of the Council consisted wholly in its strict adherence to the testimony of tradition. In the last chapter statements follow to the same effect by the two last Roman Bishops. The authority of the Roman Chair is appended 'that nothing may seem wanting to completeness'. Perhaps the most notable feature in the whole of Vincentius' exposition is that the Bishops as such—apart from the Council—play absolutely no part, and that, in particular, no reference is made to their Apostolic succession as sharing in the proof of doctrine. The ancient "teachers" are the court of appeal. We see that Cyprian's influence was not so far-reaching, even in the West, as one should have supposed. The proof of tradition was not really based on the hierarchy.

[1] Compare the statements of Kattenbusch, l. c., p. 330 ff. The East never arrived at a definite theory of the nature and features of the Church.

[2] On this attribute see Vol. II., p. 75, n. 1. From the middle of the fourth century the clause "καὶ [εἰς] μίαν ἁγίαν καθολικὴν ἐκκλησίαν" must have stood in the Symbols of by far the most of the provincial Churches in the East. The εἰς is to be referred also to the Church.

because they had crucified the Saviour, he built out of the heathen a second Church, on which his favour rests; that is the Church of the living God, pillar and foundation of the truth. To it alone belong the predicates one, holy, and catholic; the communities of the Marcionites, Manichæans, and other heretics are societies of godlessness. The Church, which was formerly barren, is the mother of us all; she is the Bride of Christ. In this second Church God has appointed Apostles, Prophets, and teachers, and miraculous gifts of every kind; he has adorned it with all virtues, proved it to be unconquerable in persecution, and made it an object of veneration even to kings, since its boundaries are wider than those of any secular kingdom. It is called Catholic because it extends over the whole globe, teaches all necessary dogmas to men universally and unceasingly, comprehends and leads to the true worship of God all men without respect of class, is able to cure all sins in soul and body, and possesses in its midst all virtues and all conceivable gifts of grace. [1]

These utterances of Cyril concerning the Church contain the quintessence of all that has ever been said of it by the Greeks. [2] They have adorned it with all conceivable attributes, applying to it all the O. T. passages descriptive of the people of Israel. [3] They glorified it as the communion of faith and virtue, and as a rule clung to this description of it in their catechetical and

---

[1] Cyril, Cat. XVIII., ch. 22—27.

[2] For Western doctrines of the Church see the next book. But they are not so different in theory from those of the East as some suppose.

[3] The Greeks spoke not infrequently of the "state" or "city" of God; Origen had already used the term, and it is common in Eusebius. On the other hand, the fine combination "Christ and the Church (as bride)" or "the Church as the body of Christ", which had been at a very early date reduced to the level of a homiletical or rhetorical view, was either thrust into the background, or superseded by the phrase "Christ and the individual soul." At a later date, the proposition, that Christ is the head of the Church, was often asserted against the Latins; but it was not very effective; for, seeing that the Greeks granted that the Church was a visible body in the common sense of the term, their thesis that this visible Church had none but an invisible head was beset with difficulties. Besides, Origen had been attacked as early as about A.D. 300, because he had explained Adam and Eve as referring to Christ and the Church (Socrates H. E. III. 7), though this allegory was supported by a very ancient tradition. Tychonius repeated it.

homiletical teaching.¹ Indeed, their position was here so far
archaic, that they either did not mention the organisation ot
the Church at all, or—what was even more significant—they
named in this connection the Apostles, Prophets, teachers and
the rest, in brief, the possessors and gifts of the Spirit (see
above in Cyril). We find the same teaching even in John ot
Damascus, who in his great work on dogma has given no
place at all to the Church,² and in the later so-called Symbols
of the Greek Church.³ The difficult question, which Origen
first discussed, and which Augustine considered so thoroughly
in his fight with Donatism—the question about the Church as
corpus verum (the true body) and *corpus permixtum* (the mixed
body)—was hardly touched on in the East.⁴ When we read
Greek statements as to the Church—statements, besides, which
are altogether few in number—we not infrequently believe that
we are living in the second century, nay, before the Gnostic
controversy. We must not perceive in this attitude of the Greek
Fathers any sign of exceptional maturity. It was prescribed to
them, on the one hand, by natural theology, on the other, by
the narrowness of their view of the task of the Church. Redemption through Christ applied in intention to the whole
human race, which meanwhile was always simply conceived as
the sum of all individuals. In its result, it was limited by the
liberty of man to resist salvation through sin. The Church was
really, therefore, nothing but the sum of all individual believers
in heaven and upon earth. The view that the Church was the
mother of believers, a divine creation, the body of Christ, was
not properly carried out in dogma. Even the thought that
Christ had so assumed human nature that all it experienced in
him benefited mankind, was only applied—not to the Church—

---

¹ There are very numerous instances of this, and most of all in the influential
Chrysostom. Epiphanius' contention in the Expos. fid. cathol., ch. 3 is worthy of
notice: Ὁ Θεὸς, ὁ ἐπὶ πάντων, ἡμῖν Θεὸς ὑπάρχει τοῖς ἐκ τῆς ἁγίας ἐκκλησίας
γεννηθεῖσιν. This Jewish Christian regarded the Church as Israel, and its God as
the God of Israel; see what follows.

² Langen, Joh. Damascenus, p. 299 f.

³ Gass, l. c., p. 205 f.

⁴ It is treated in the later Symbols; see Gass, p. 206 f.

but to mankind as it existed, and the Eucharist itself did no
help the Church to a special place in dogmatics. [1]   In spite o
the 'belief in one holy Catholic Church' (πιστεύειν εἰς μίαν
ἁγίαν καθολικὴν ἐκκλησίαν) *the Church was no dogmatic concep
tion* in the strict sense of the term.   It did not form a link i
the chain of the doctrines of redemption.   And that is no
surprising.   Seeing the form given to the blessing of salvation
a *religious* conception of the Church could not be obtained
All was contained in the factors, God, mankind, Christ, th
mysteries, and the individual.

But occasion was given to draw up definitions of the Churc
by (1) the O. T. and the spurious Jewish Church, (2) heres
and the actual organisation of the Church, (3) the administratio
of the mysteries, (4) and the fight against the Roman claims t
the primacy.   As regards the first point, all that was necessar
had been said in the second and third centuries; there was no
thing to add; it was repeated with greater or less animosity t
Judaism, whose history appeared sometimes as the mysteriou
type of the Church, sometimes as its antitype.   As to the secon
and third, there was no doubt that *the Church was the tru
teacher of the truth* [2] *and the legitimate administrator of th
mysteries.* [3]   It transmitted the μάθησις (learning) and it possesse
the mysteries.   Therefore—and of this there was no doubt—i
was essential to her to have the organisation, which was crowne
by Bishops and Councils, and priests who should present th
sacrifices and judge in God's stead. Bishops and Councils w
have spoken of above, the priests and their duties will b
discussed in Chap. X. [4]   It is remarkable, however, that the latte

[1] Cyril of Alexandria frequently connects the Church with the incarnation an
the Eucharist; but even he has not gone beyond the homiletic and. edifying poin
of view.

[2] Religious truth, however, really embraced all philosophy, see Anastasius Sin
Viæ dux (Migne, Patrol., Vol. 89, p. 76 sq.): Ὀρθοδοξία ἐστὶν ἀψευδὴς περὶ Θεο
καὶ κτίσεως ὑπόληψις ἢ ἔννοια περὶ πάντων ἀληθής, ἢ δόξα τῶν ὄντων καθάπερ εἰσίν

[3] Damalas has given a very pregnant summary of the old Patristic conceptio
Ἡ ὀρθόδοξος πίστις (1877) p. 3: ἡ δὲ πίστις αὕτη εἰς τὴν μίαν ἁγίαν καθολικὴν κα
ἀποστολικὴν ἐκκλησίαν ἐστὶ πεποίθησις, ὅτι αὕτη ἐστὶν ὁ φορεὺς τῆς θείας χάριτο
τῆς ἐνδεικνυμένης εἰς δύο τινά, πρῶτον ὅτι αὕτη ἐστὶν ὁ ἀλάνθαστος διδάσκαλος τῆ
χριστιανικῆς ἀληθείας καὶ δεύτερον ὁ γνήσιος τῶν μυστηρίων οἰκονόμος.

[4] See Kattenbusch, l. c., pp. 346 ff., 357 ff., 393 ff.

is brought more to the front than the former. The Pseudo-areopagite was not the first to make his view of the Church depend essentially on the mysteries, and to regard the hierarchy primarily as performers of the sacred rites; he only completed what Ignatius, Clement, the first draft of the Apostolic Consti-tutions, Chrysostom *de sacerdotio*, [1] and many others had developed before or contemporaneously with him. The Church had been entrusted to the Bishops, because they constituted the living representation of God on earth, the vicars of Christ, participators in the activity of the Holy Spirit, and therefore the source of all sacraments. They were much less thought of as successors of the Apostles; the Church was the legacy not of the Apostles, but of Christ, and the dwelling place of the Holy Spirit. [2]

In the polemic against the Roman claims to supremacy, the view was strongly emphasised that Christ is the foundation and sole head of the Church, and this principle was opposed even to an exaggerated estimate of the Apostles in general and Peter in particular.

" He who secedes from the Church, withdraws himself at the same time from the influences of the Holy Spirit, and it is not easy to find a wise man among the heretics "; [3] but on what

---

[1] See Vol. III. 4—6, VI. 4; also the Homily on the day of his ordination as priest, Montfaucon I., p. 436 sq.

[2] Of course the Church was conscious of being, and called itself "apostolic." But it is perhaps not a mere accident that this predicate is not so stereotyped in the Symbols and other official manifestoes as the rest—unity, holiness and catholicity. The otherwise substantially identical expositions by the Greek Fathers of the word "catholic" have been collected by Söder, Der Begriff der Katholicität der Kirche und des Glaubens (1881), pp. 95 ff., 110 ff., 113 f., 115 f. "Catholic" was equivalent to orthodox even before Eusebius, as is shown by the interpolations of the word into the Martyrium Polycarpi. That this word was interpolated I have tried to prove in "The Expositor," 1885, Dec., p. 410 sq. It may be in place here to remark generally that the copyists are least to be trusted in the case of such predicates as were current at a later date—*e.g.*, as regards words like "bearer of God" "Homoousios", "Catholic" etc. The Monophysites especially made great efforts to introduce their catch-words into older writers. Even to-day the Armenians are not to be trusted.

[3] Heretics and Schismatics were more and more identified; see the so-called 6th Canon of Constantinople, A.D. 381 (it really dates from A.D. 382): αἱρετικοὺς λέγομεν τούς τε πάλαι τῆς ἐκκλησίας ἀποκηρυχθέντας καὶ τοὺς μετὰ ταῦτα ὑφ'

points the unity of the Church was based has not been made
clear. It first appears as if faith and virtue were sufficient, but
participation in the mysteries of the Church, and submission
to its organisation and tradition were added: indeed these in
practice took the first place. Yet the organisation of the Church
was not really carried higher than the Bishops, in spite of all
the empty words used about the Patriarchs: the Church was
orthodox and perfect, because it offered a security in its episcopal
and priestly constitution that it was the *ancient institution founded
by Christ*. In this conviction—we can hardly call it a doctrine—
the Church became more and more narrow; it made itself
a holy piece of antiquity. [1]

But after the close of the fifth century it ceased to be the
one Church. Tradition, which had been created to maintain the
unity of the Church, served in the end to split it up, because
national and local traditions, views, and customs had been
received into it to an increasing extent. The great cleavage into
Catholic and Novatian Catholic was not yet determined, or
supported by national considerations. The division into Græco-
Roman Catholicism and Germanic Arianism did owe its duration to opposite national tendencies. On the other hand, the
disruption of the Eastern Church into the Byzantine (Roman)
and the Oriental (Nestorian-Syrian, Jacobitish-Syrian, Coptic, and
Armenian) rested entirely on national antitheses, and, preserved
mainly by the monks who, in spite of all their renunciation of
the world, have always adopted a National Church attitude, has
continued up to the present day. Now, after the schism had
further taken place between the Byzantine (Neo-Roman) and the
Roman branches, the Church was divided into three (four) great
territories distinguished by their nationality: the Germano-Roman

ἡμῶν ἀναθεματισθέντας. πρὸς δὲ τούτοις καὶ τοὺς τὴν πίστιν μὲν τὴν ὑγιῆ προσ-
ποιουμένους ὁμολογεῖν, ἀποσχίσαντας δὲ καὶ ἀντισυνάγοντας τοῖς κανονικοῖς ἡμῶ·
ἐπισκόποις.

[1] The question whether the holiness of Christians was founded on being member
in the Church—initiation into it—or depended on personal virtue was not decidee
in the East, but it was never even definitely put. The cause of this vagueness existee
ultimately in the obscurity which prevailed among the Greeks in reference to the
relation of natural theology and dogma in general; see on this the following
chapters.

West (Rome), the countries on the Ægean sea (Constantinople), and the East split into Nestorianism and Monophysitism. Each had its own peculiar traditions and authorities. The Orientals, though rent asunder and quarrelling with each other, felt that they formed a unity compared with the two other sections, *i.e.*, the "Romans," and could, in reply to the "bragging of the Romans," point to a hundred marks which revealed the superiority of their Churches. They regarded their land as the cradle of the human race, their Church as the primitive home of religion; and if Jerusalem was no longer in their possession, yet they still had the ancient site of Paradise. [1] The Neo-Romans boasted of their Patriarchate, their unchanged faith, and their nation, which took no part in the crucifixion of Christ, in which the Romans and Barbarians had made common cause. The Romans, finally, had the chiefs of the Apostles, Peter and Paul, and the Pope, Peter's successor, with the secular power committed to him by Christ and Constantine. The common foundation of these Churches was not solid enough to resist the elements that were dissolving it. Nationality was stronger than religion.

Literature.—Jacobi, Die kirchliche Lehre von der Tradition u. heil. Schrift., Part I., 1847. Holtzmann, Kanon u. Tradition, 1859 (does not discuss to any extent the Church in antiquity). Söder, Der Begriff der Katholicität der Kirche, 1881. Seeberg, Studien zur Geschichte des Begriffs der Kirche, 1885. Kattenbusch, l. c. There is much material in Schwane, also in the writings which passed between Old Catholics and Roman Catholics after A.D. 1869.

[1] See, *e.g.*, Elias of Nisibis, Proof of the truth of the faith (Ed. by Horst, 1886, p. 112 ff.).

A.—Presuppositions of the Doctrine of Redemption, or Natural Theology.

"Natural Theology" did not pass through any very thorough-going development in the Greek Church; but it reveals differences, according as Aristotelianism or Neoplatonism prevailed. By Natural Theology we are to understand the complex of conceptions that, according to the view then held, formed the self-evident and certain contents of the human mind, which was only held to be more or less darkened (see Chap. II.). These conceptions, however, arose in fact historically, and corresponded to the degree of culture at which the ancient world had arrived, especially through the work of the Greek Philosophers. We can divide them appropriately into doctrines concerning God and concerning man. But changes also took place in proportion to the growing influence exerted on these conceptions by the words of the Bible literally understood. Nevertheless the fundamental features remained in force; yet they were displaced and confused by foreign material during the period from Origen to John of Damascus.

A.—*PRESUPPOSITION OF DOCTRINE OF REDEMPTION OR NATURAL THEOLOGY.*

CHAPTER IV.

PRESUPPOSITIONS AND CONCEPTIONS REGARDING GOD, THE CREATOR, AS DISPENSER OF SALVATION.

§ 1. *The Doctrine of God. Its Method.*

THE main features of the doctrine of God were those familiar from the theology of the Apologists, as they were partly fixed and partly supplemented by the fight with Gnosticism. Speculations on the Deity as a Trinity (τριάς) modified but little the general doctrine of God (yet see attempts in Augustine, De trinitate); for the unity, simplicity, indivisibility, and unchangeableness of God were at the same time maintained most definitely: in other words, the Father alone was almost always regarded as "root of the Deity" (ρίζα τῆς θεότητος), where the Deity, in its essential being, was described in comparison with the world. The ultimate reason of this was that theology counted on a general intelligence for its general doctrine of God, and therefore had recourse to natural religion and theology, *i. e.,* to the results of Greek philosophy. It was indeed admitted by many Fathers (see esp. Athanasius, De incarn.) that men could know the Deity from creation only dimly, if at all; and that therefore the manifestation of God in Christ alone made it possible to recognise the nature of God as the undivided, spiritual and good Lord of the World. But, in fact, it was only a question of more or less as regards the natural knowledge of the spiritual and good God, the Creator. Other Fathers, especially those influenced by Aristotle, declared the knowledge of God in its whole extent to be innate (see Arnobius), or, a knowledge to be constantly tested by the

observation of nature. No difference is here caused by the fact
that some Fathers have described the existence of God and his
distinctive nature as capable of proof, others, as incapable; for
the latter only rejected the proof in so far as God could not
be discovered by means of deduction from a *prius*. The
psychological, cosmological, [1] and natural theological proofs were
not despised by them in meeting Atheism, Polytheism, Manichæism, etc. We already find in Augustine suggestions of an
ontological proof. [2] All these evidences were, indeed, given
subject to the proviso, that all knowledge of God must be
traced back to God himself, that it became indistinct in proportion to man's alienation from God, and that the revelation
of Scripture first rendered everything clear and certain.

Further, it was expressly contended that God, as the infinite
one, was, strictly speaking, incapable of being known, because
his nature could not be described by any predicate. But this
inscrutability, so far as represented in the avowal "whatever
the creature is, that God is not," was held—and with this
the Neoplatonists were agreed—to be the valuable and true
knowledge (Athan. ad monach. 2: "even if it is not possible
to comprehend what God is, it is possible to say what he is
not:" καὶ εἰ μὴ δυνατὸν καταλαβέσθαι τί ἐστι Θεός, ἀλλὰ δυνατὸν
εἰπεῖν, τί οὔκ ἐστιν). [3] The revelation through the Logos only

---

[1] The influence of Aristotle is first conspicuous in Diodore of Tarsus, who reproduced independently the cosmological proof of Aristotle (see Photius, Biblioth.
223). From the sixth century it is evident in the majority of the Fathers, and
especially John of Damascus. See De fide orthod. I. 3 (12): Everything perceptible
by the senses, as also the higher world of spirits, is subject to change; therefore
it must have had a beginning, and been created. There must accordingly exist a
being who created it, and that is God. Two other proofs are found in John of Dam.

[2] Augustine's line of argument was first to demonstrate rules of human thought,
which accordingly transcended it. These rules—logical and ethical—he stated to
be *truths*, their sum being *the truth*. This truth was a living power, accordingly
it existed. Thus the way to the existence of God was given; see esp. De lib. arbitr. II.
3—15, but the thought is also suggested elsewhere in his writings, *e.g.*, the Confessions.

[3] In this the great majority of the Fathers were agreed. Augustine describes (De
doctr. I. 6) the impossibility of declaring God, in a way that coincides word for
word with the tenets of the Basilidians (Hippol., Philos. VII. 20). Augustine writes:
"Diximusne ·aliquid et sonuimus aliquid dignum deo? Immo vero nihil me aliud
quam dicere voluisse sentio; si autem dixi, non hoc est quod dicere volui. Hoc
unde scio, nisi quia deus ineffabilis est, quod autem a me dictum est, si ineffabile

went beyond this in that it established this knowledge regarding the infinite Spirit and his inexpressible nature, and made it possible to perceive him in his likeness. [1] The Fathers influenced by Neoplatonism, however, assumed further that the contemplative ascetic, who was on the way to deification, could gain a direct vision of God in all his splendour, a conception which the Areopagite has combined with a scholastic theory of the knowableness of God by negation, eminence, causality. [2]

---

esset, dictum non esset? Ac per hoc ne ineffabilis quidem dicendus est deus, quia et hoc cum dicitur, aliquid dicitur. Et fit nescio quæ pugna verborum, quoniam si illud est ineffabile, quod dici non potest, non est ineffabile, quod vel ineffabile dici potest." Basilides: Ἔστι γὰρ, φησίν, ἐκεῖνο οὐχ ἁπλῶς ἄρρητον, ὃ ὀνομάζεται· ἄρρητον γοῦν αὐτὸ καλοῦμεν, ἐκεῖνο δὲ οὐδὲ ἄρρητον· καὶ γὰρ τὸ οὐδ᾽ ἄρρητον οὐκ ἄρρητον ὀνομάζεται, ἀλλὰ ἔστι, φησίν, ὑπεράνω παντὸς ὀνόματος ὀνομαζομένου. Men were therefore at the point already reached by Basilides' followers in the second century. Even Catechumens were taught this; see Cyril, Cat. VI., ch. 2: οὐ τὸ τί ἐστι Θεὸς ἐξηγούμεθα... ἐν τοῖς περὶ Θεοῦ μεγάλη γνῶσίς τὸ τὴν ἀγνωσίαν ὁμολογεῖν. Similar teaching is very frequent in Plotinus. In the Vita Plot. of Porphyry, ch. 23, the supreme God is thus defined: ὁ Θεὸς ὁ μήτε μορφὴν μήτε τινὰ ἰδέαν ἔχων, ὑπὲρ δὲ νοῦν καὶ πᾶν τὸ νοητὸν ἱδρύμενος.

[1] The Dogmatics of John of Damascus begin with John I. 18, Matt. XI. 17, and 1 Cor. II. 11.

[2] The striking contention of some disciples of Lucian (according to Philostorgius), and the most extreme Arians, Eunomius and Aëtius, but not Arius himself, that men could know the nature of God as well as God himself did, and as well as they knew themselves, is most closely connected with their Christology and their Aristotelianism. When the orthodox Fathers argued that the indescribable God could only be perceived in the Logos and through his work, and that God therefore would have been unknowable had not the Logos been his image, possessed of a like nature, those Arians had to meet the objection by emphasising even in the course of the christological controversy, the possibility of knowing God directly. In taking up this position they had of course to leave the nature of God out of the question, and to confine themselves to his will, as it had been clearly manifested in creation, and the preaching of the truth by the Logos. But this to them was no limitation; for they only attached importance in the first place to the knowledge of the divine will, and secondly to the renewed submission of men to the sovereignty of the divine will: (not to participation in the divine nature, unless in so far as that was already involved in the original equipment of man; see Socrates IV. 7; Epiph. H. LXXVI. 4, and the counter-observations of the Cappadocians). Their expositions are exceded by the Areopagite's completely Neoplatonic theology, from which, meanwhile, Augustine in one of his lines of thought was not far removed. The Areopagite already adopted the position that ruled for more than a thousand years, in which the contention that God—by reason of his splendour—was absolutely unknowable, was balanced by the mystical assumption of a sensuous, suprasensuous knowableness in virtue of the fusion of the mind of

§ 2. *The Doctrine of God's Nature and Attributes.*

The Being of God was immortal substance and was primarily
defined—as already results from the method of knowing God—
by affirming that he was without beginning or end, that he
was a spirit and the supreme First Cause, all which predicates
were proved in connection with the proofs of his existence.
The deity is the pneumatic Ὄν which, because it is not the
world, is supramundane, simply governing the world, the one,
indivisible, imperishable, unchangeable, supremely good and
impassive being, to which, in the strict sense, a real existence
alone belongs: the Fathers influenced by Aristotelianism
emphasised especially the spiritual power which determined its
own aims and the causality of the deity. God is the intelligible
reality and infinite reason. So far as it is maintained of this
being *(secundum hominem)* that he is good, the predicate
affirms nothing but that he is perfect, *i. e.,* is completely self-
sufficient and possesses blessedness in himself and therefore is
not envious—see esp. Athanasius adv. pagan., also the
Catechisms of Cyril. But the goodness of the Deity was also
established from the fact of the revelation of God, first from
creation, and here meant that God, since he is the gracious
one, willed that creatures should participate in his blessedness,
and carried out his intention under all circumstances.

Augustine broke through this natural conception of the
goodness of God; for he understands by the Deity as *summum
bonum* the power of love which takes hold of man, and leads
him from worldliness and selfishness to peace and felicity. But
even in Augustine this idea is intimately connected with the
natural view.

As regards the divine attributes, the Fathers sought, while
speaking of such, to keep clear of the idea of a plurality in

God with the mind of man. To him also we trace back the theology of affirmation
and negation (kataphatic and apophatic)—the thing had, indeed, been very long
in existence—*i.e.*, the method of making statements about God *via eminentiæ* and
via negationis; see his Letters, the work, De divinis nominibus, and the beginning
of the tractate, De mystica theologia. The importance of John of Damascus consists
for posterity in his having united the Neoplatonic and Aristotelian elements in his
doctrine of God; see De fide orthod. I. 1—4.

God, or conceptions of anything accidental. It is only for
human thought that the absolute, perfect, homogeneous Being
has attributes assigned to him, as varied representations of
him in relation to the finite. The elevation above time and
space presented itself as eternity and omnipresence; the latter
attribute at the same time was the root of omniscience and
omnipotence. Omnipotence was limited by the Fathers by two
thoughts: it was circumscribed by the good will of God, and
it left scope for human liberty.[1] Origen's thesis of the limitation
of omniscience found no supporters in later times.

From the goodness (perfection) of God[2] all conceivable
ethical qualities were deduced. But they did not obtain their
due significance, because the abstract idea that God was the
requiter, i. e., rewarded the good and punished the wicked,
formed, in spite of all Neoplatonic philosophy, the foundation
of the whole conceptions of God, in so far as ethics were taken
into account at all. This view, however, which was considered
the "natural" one, readily became indifferent to the thought
that men as God's creatures are dependent on him, that they
are meant to form an inner unity, and that their life is conducted to a definite goal; in other words, it endangered
the religious view of Christianity. It gave man complete independence in presence of God, and broke mankind up into a
group of disconnected individuals. It descended from Judaism
and the ancient world—the gods are *just*, because they reward
and punish, the two facts being conceived in coördination.
This view, further, was entitled to its place within the narrow

---

[1] Along with all fatalism and astrology the Greek Fathers also unanimously
rejected the idea that God's prescience acted as fate and was the first cause of
human actions, or that prophecy controlled the course of events. It was rather
taught that prescience was consequent to the event perceived beforehand. But
Augustine was not perfectly satisfied with this idea. He deepened it through the
thought that the sum of all that happened was before God in an eternal *now*.

[2] But of this the saying of Gregory of Nyssa is true (περὶ ψυχ. κ. ἀναστασ·
Oehler, p. 92): Παντὸς ἀγαθοῦ ἐπέκεινα ἡ θεία φύσις, τὸ δὲ ἀγαθὸν ἀγαθῷ φίλον
πάντως, διὰ τοῦτο ἑαυτὴν βλέπουσα καὶ ὃ ἔχει θέλει καὶ ὃ θέλει ἔχει οὐδὲν τῶν ἔξωθεν εἰς ἑαυτὸν δεχομένη. Ἔξω δὲ αὐτῆς οὐδέν, ὅτι μὴ ἡ κακία μόνη, ἥτις, κἂν
παράδοξον ᾖ, ἐν τῷ μὴ εἶναι τὸ εἶναι ἔχει. οὐ γὰρ ἄλλη τίς ἐστι κακίας γένεσις, εἰ
μὴ ἡ τοῦ ὄντος στέρησις. Τὸ δὲ κυρίως ὂν ἡ τοῦ ἀγαθοῦ φύσις ἐστίν· ὃ οὖν ἐν τῷ
ὄντι οὐκ ἔστιν, ἐν τῷ μὴ εἶναι πάντως ἐστίν.

horizon of the citizens of ancient communities,[1] but while it could not be omitted from Christianity, it required to be subordinated to a higher thought. Accordingly, significant tendencies to correct the prevalent system of thought were not wanting on the part of the Fathers. Origen had already tried to regard the righteousness of God as a form of his loving discipline; the conception that suffering is always bound up with penal justice, had undoubtedly something to do with this attempt. The continued fight with dualism—Manichæism—constantly made it necessary to demonstrate that power, goodness, wisdom, and justice were combined in the Deity.[2] But in almost all the Fathers the attributes of goodness and justice stood asunder. We can see the reason of this in the fact that up to Augustine no serious effort was made to understand the goodness of God as moral holiness, and this failure was in turn due to the characteristic method of obtaining a knowledge of God, the attempt to rise to the Deity from the notion of the finite by means of sublimations.[3] The theory of God was beset at this most important point with uncertainties, nay, inconsistencies. He was at once the impassive Being ("Ov) and the Judge who requited actions[4]—the latter conception, further, not only including the coördination of goodness and justice, but also the superiority of the former to the latter. The Alexandrians had grasped at the expedient, following Philo,[5] of representing God as absolutely benevolent, but the Logos as the Just; this, however, was to confess despair of solving the problem, showing once more very clearly that men could not think without compunction (*affectiones humanæ*) of the (penal) justice

---

[1] See Leopold Schmidt, Die Ethik der alten Griechen, 2 Vols., 1882; further, Ritschl in the Th. L. Z. 1883, Col. 6 f.

[2] These four attributes Gregory of Nyssa has particularised and sought to harmonise in his great Catechism.

[3] This method, however, was by no means despised by Augustine himself.

[4] The doctrine of God came in this form to the theologians of the middle ages. The nuances and inconsistencies of scholastic theology were caused by the necessity of alternating between the two ideas of God as the intelligible "Ov and the Requiter. Some emphasised the one, others the other, more strongly. In certain doctrines only the former, in others only the latter conception, could be used.

[5] See Bigg, The Christian Platonists of Alex. (1886), p. 12 f.

of which at most the Logos was capable; and it is interesting as a counterpart to the opposite idea adopted in later times.[1] But we see even here, why the doctrine of redemption could not become one of atonement in the ancient Church. If the distinctive form in which redemption was accomplished was to be justified, and its intrinsic necessity to be proved, then there must not only exist, but speculation must be founded on, the conviction that God's saving purpose transcended the thought of requital, and that he was morally holy. But that is out of the question where the Fathers are concerned.[2]

§ 3. *The Cosmology.*

The Cosmological and allied anthropological problems were treated by the Fathers—who formally used Gen. I.—III. as their text—with the whole apparatus of contemporary philosophy, in this way satisfying their scientific craving for a rational conception of the world. The systems are therefore very different in details; but on the whole they existed peaceably side by side, showing that the differences presupposed a measure of agreement, sufficient for the solidarity of the doctrinal structure.

[1] In this view—in the Middle Ages—God appears rather as the strictly Just, Christ as the "good"; but the idea of goodness had changed.

[2] In the lower ranks of the communities, and among a few Oriental sects (Audians), anthropomorphic conceptions of God, the belief that he had a human shape, a body etc., held their ground. But they were retained also in some circles of monks (*e.g.*, those of the Scetian Desert), and even by a few Bishops. From the close of the fourth century, with the hostility to Origen's spiritualism was combined active resistance to this opposite view (Sozom. VIII. 11). The Stoic notion of God's corporeality had scarcely a defender after Tertullian ; for Lactantius' view of the "figura" and "affectus" of God is not Stoic, but belongs to popular realism. In general, much that was anthropomorphic was retained in Western theology along with the realistic eschatology, and that by theologians who cherished a colourless eclectic moralism. Very instructive is Augustine's confession (Confess. V. *fin.*; VI. 3) that it was the sermons of Ambrose that first delivered him from the prejudice that the Catholic Church taught that the Deity was fashioned like man. If we reflect how much Augustine had mingled with Catholic Christians before his conversion, and how much he had heard of the Church, we cannot suppose he was the only one guilty of this prejudice. We need only recall the "apocryphal" writings of the Byzantine age, which were read to an extraordinary extent, to see how strong were anthropomorphism and the conceptions of a magic God.

These differences were slightest in the Cosmology proper. The task set the theologians of the fourth century was to bring Origen's cosmology more into harmony with the demands of the rule of faith, to adapt it more closely to the account given in Gen. I., and to defeat the Manichæan Cosmology. After the last decades of the fourth century, the slow course of development was hastened by violent opposition to Origen's cosmology, and the view of the Church, held before Origen, was substantially restored, though now as a scientific theory.[1] Yet the conception of an upper world of spirits, related to the present world as its ideal and type, continued to exist, and ever threw its shadow on the latter.[2] On the other hand, the Trinitarian

[1] See Justinian's edict against Origen, and the fifth Synod of Constantinople, Hefele, Concil. Gesch. II. 2, p. 780—797; at an earlier date, the attacks of Theophilus and Jerome on Origen.

[2] Origen held that the present world was only a place of punishment and purification. This view, which approximated very closely to the old Gnostic idea, was rejected; but the conception remained of an upper world of spirits, of which our world was the materialised copy. Where this conception was potent, a considerable part of the feeling which possessed Origen (after Plato) as he looked at our world must have endured. It was never wanting among the orthodox Fathers, and the Greeks of to-day have not lost it. "The world is a whole, but divided into two spheres of which the higher is the necessary *prius* and type of the lower": that is still the Greek view (see Gass, Symbolik, p. 143 f.). "God first and by his mere thought evoked out of non-existence all heavenly powers to exhibit his glory, and this intelligible world (κόσμος νοερός) is the expression of undisturbed harmony and obedient service." Man belongs to both worlds. The conception, as expounded by the Areopagite and established by John of Damascus (De fide orthod. II 2—12), that the world was created in successive stages, has not the importance of a dogma, but it has that of a wide-spread theologoumenon. It is Neoplatonic and Gnostic, and its publication and recognition show that the dissatisfaction felt by Origen with the account of the creation in Gen. I. was constantly shared by others. Men felt a living interest, not in the way plants, fishes, and birds came into being, but in the emanation of the spiritual from the Deity at the head of creation down to man. Therefore we have the κόσμος νοερός, the intelligible world, whose most characteristic feature consisted in its (3) gradations (διακοσμήσεις), which again fell into (three) orders, down to archangels and angels. (See Dionys. De divina hierarch. 6 sq., and John of Damascus, l.c., ch. III: πᾶσα ἡ θεολογία τὰς οὐρανίους οὐσίας ἐννέα κέκληκε. ταύτας ὁ Θεῖος ἱεροτελέστης εἰς τρεῖς ἀφορίζει τριαδικὰς διακοσμήσεις, Seraphim, Cherubim, thrones, dominions, powers, forces, principalities, archangels, and angels. We find a step in this direction as early as the App. Constit. VII. 35). In the creation, the system of spiritual powers was built from above downwards; while in sanctification by the mysteries, it was necessary to ascend the same series. The significant point was the union of the

conflicts led to a precise distinction being drawn between creating, making, begetting, and emanating, and thus the notion of creation out of nothing now first received its strict impress. But Neoplatonic ideas of the origin of the world lasted till after the beginning of the fifth century, even in the case of some Bishops, and side by side with it the Manichæan conception of the world spread secretly and found adherents among the clergy themselves up to the middle of it. The following proposition may be regarded as containing the quintessence of the orthodox Fathers from the fifth century, and at the same time as the presupposition that gave scope to all their further speculations. It can be stated thus: God from eternity bore in his own mind the idea of the world. In free self-determination he, in order to prove his goodness, created by the Logos, who embraces all ideas, this world, which has had a beginning and will have an end, in six days out of nothing, in accordance with the pattern of an upper world created by him.

The justification of divine providence and the production of Theodicies were called for by Manichæism and fatalism on the one hand, and the great political catastrophes and calamities on the other. It was taught that God constantly remained close to his creation, preserving and governing it. With this, rational beings were looked upon in their numerical sum total as the peculiar objects of divine providence. Providence was also defended in opposition to the loose and unstable form in which earlier and contemporary monotheistic philosophers had avowed it; it was recognised in principle to be a power pro-

conception of creation with the system of the cultus, or, better, the scheme which embodied the idea of creation in accordance with the line of progress laid down for asceticism and sanctification. This was retained by Greek theology in spite of all its disavowal of Origen, Neoplatonism, and Gnosticism. But even in the region of the material, incomparably greater interest was taken in warmth, cold, moisture, drought, in fire, air, earth, and water, in the four vital humours, than in the childish elements which the O. T. narrative of creation takes into account. Yet the whole was included under the title of the 'work of the six days', and the allegories of Origen were, in theory, rejected. The exegesis of Gen. I. became the doctoral problem proper among the Greek Fathers. The most important wrote works on the Hexaëmeron; among them that of Johannes Philoponus is scientifically the most advanced (περὶ κοσμοποιίας); it is dependent, not on Platonism, but on Aristotle, though it also opposes the latter.

tecting also the individual creature. Yet here Christian theologians themselves did not arrive at complete certainty. It was
admitted that providence was above human freedom in so far
as it was maintained that neither that freedom nor the evil
proceeding from it could hinder the divine intentions. But the
belief in providence was not definitely connected with redemption by Christ or with the Church, for it was considered a self-
evident presupposition of redemption and a piece of Natural
Theology. Therefore it was also destitute of any strict object.
The uncertainty of the ancient world as to the extent and
method of providence had left its influence, [1] and empirical
reflections on the objectlessness of certain institutions, or
phenomena in the world—*e. g.,* of vermin—could not be
defeated by a view which had itself a naturalistic basis. Yet
in proportion as the sure and real knowledge of God was only
derived from the Christian religion, it was also recognised that
faith in providence was first made certain through Christ, and
that Christians were under the particular providence of God. [2]
The problem of the theodicy was solved (1) by proving that the
freedom of the creature was something appropriate and good,
the possibility of wickedness and evil, however, being necessarily combined with it; (2) by denying to wickedness any
reality in the higher sense of the term, since wickedness as it
was separated from God, the principle of all being, was held
to be not—being; [3] (3) by defending the *mala pœnœ* or evil as
fitting means of purification; and finally, (4) by representing
temporal sufferings as indifferent to the soul. Some older
Fathers, *e. g.,* Lactantius, emphasised, besides, even the necessity of wickedness in the interest of moralism: without it
virtue would be impossible. [4] But such opinions died out in the
fight with Manichæism. [5]

[1] For this reason a startling casuistry is to be noticed here and there, and
exceptions are laid down.

[2] Degrees of providence were generally distinguished.

[3] After Origen this Platonic proposition enjoyed the widest circulation; see esp.
Athanasius and the Cappadocians; but the Antiochians held no other view. Augustine
made use of it in a peculiar and characteristic way.

[4] Lactant. Instit. div. II., ch. 8, 12; V., ch. 7.

[5] See Vol. V., for the extent and form in which Augustine held such views.

In reference to the heavenly spirits which belonged to, and indeed formed, the upper world, the recognised Fathers were convinced of the following points. (1) They were created by God (see the Symb. Nic.). (2) They were endowed with freedom, but had no material bodies (ἐγγύτατα τοῦ ἀσωμάτου). (3) They had passed through a crisis after which a section had remained true to the good, while another had revolted. (4) The good spirits were instruments of the divine government of the world, their activity being useful and beneficial to men, even entering into the sacramental system by which grace was imparted. (5) The reality of wickedness in the world was to be attributed to the bad spirits, and especially to their head, the devil; they exercised an almost unbounded power on earth, not being able indeed to compel man, but only to induce him, to sin; they could also be scared away without fail by the name of Christ, the sign of the cross, and the Sacraments. [1] As regards the relation of the good angels to men, their superiority to men—in the

---

[1] No doubt existed of the necessity of believing in heavenly spiritual beings. Origen counted this belief a doctrine of the Church (De princip. præf. 10). The points numbered in the text may be regarded as the quintessence of what obtained generally. But such an agreement only made its appearance in the sixth century. Until then this point was a centre of contention between a form of Biblical "realism," and the Origenistic, i.e., the Greek philosophical, view as to the world of spirits. The treatment of the question by the Areopagite, and its approval by the Church, constituted a triumph of Neoplatonic mysticism over Biblicism. But that tendencies which went still farther in this direction had not been wholly destroyed, was shown by the Hesychastic controversy of the fourteenth century, or the assumption of an uncreated divine light, which was not the nature of God, but a specific energy, different from himself, and which could be seen. (See Engelhardt in Illgen's Ztschr., 1838, Part I., p. 68 ff.; Gass, Die Mystik des Nik. Kabasilas, 1849, p. 1 ff., and in Herzog's R.-E., 2nd Ed.). The Logos, accordingly, no longer satisfied, or rather, as Scholasticism had placed the Logos under an embargo, piety sought for a new mediator. He was to accomplish what the Logos no longer did: he was to be a visible revelation of God, himself and yet not himself; for God himself was simply quiescent being; accordingly he himself was conceived and realised in the form of an energy that could be traced. The theory of the Areopagite was, however, not satisfactory in this respect; for while the spirits might doctrinally be regarded as created beings, they were perceived as divine forces, emanations, rays of the perfect light, conceivable by degrees by man, and bringing him nearer to the deity. We have here a great difference from the western conception; in the East the Platonic and Gnostic doctrine of Æons had never been entirely abolished. In the West, while the gradation of angelic powers had been accepted, the pious impulse from which it originated had not.

present condition of the latter—was emphasised, but it was also taught on the other hand, that man after he was made perfect would be at least equal to them. The former position gave rise to a sort of angel-worship, which nevertheless in earlier times was no proper part of religion. The Synod of Laodicea, about A.D. 360, declared it in its thirty-fifth Canon to be idolatry.[1] And it was kept in check by the idea that Christ's work possessed also a mysterious significance for the upper world. But the polytheistic cravings of man constantly influenced religious ideas, and as the Deity was farther and farther removed from ordinary Christian people by speculation, there gradually arose, along with the thought of the intercession of the angels,[2] a worshipping of them, which was indeed only settled ecclesiastically at the seventh Œcumenical Synod (A.D. 787). There it was defined as adoration (προσκύνησις) in distinction from service (λατρεία).[3] Even Gregory I. had assigned the service of angels to the pre-christian stage of religion. The points of doctrine which we have above grouped together became the bases of a great number of very different conceptions, which grew up in opposition to Origen's doctrine, or under its influence, or in dependence on exegesis (esp. of Gen. VI.), or, lastly, as a result of reminiscences of Greek folk-lore and philosophy. Men speculated on the date of the creation of angels, and the method by which they were created, on their spirituality or higher corporeality, their functions—as guardian angels and genii, the manner in which the wicked angels fell,[4] the orders and

---

[1] There undoubtedly existed, even in the earliest time, a view which conjoined the angels with God, and thus made them also objects of worship, or, included them in the *fides, quæ creditur*. We may here perhaps recall even 1 Tim. V. 21: διαμαρτύρομαι ἐνώπιον τοῦ Θεοῦ καὶ Χριστοῦ Ἰησοῦ καὶ τῶν ἐκλεκτῶν ἀγγέλων. We can at any rate refer to Justin., Apol I. 6: (We worship God) καὶ τὸν παρ' αὐτοῦ υἱόν... καὶ τὸν τῶν ἄλλων ἑπομένων καὶ ἐξομοιουμένων ἀγαθῶν ἀγγέλων στρατόν. Athenag. Suppl. 10, 24.

[2] This thought is undoubtedly extremely ancient, but at the earlier date it only existed in the outer circle of the faith.

[3] It had long—as early as the fourth century—been on the way; see the miraculous oratories of St. Michael; Sozom. II. 3, Theodoret on Coloss. T. III., p. 355 ff.

[4] On the devil, "the prince of the ranks encircling the earth," see the exposition by John of Dam., De fide orthod. II. 4. The devil and the demons of their own free will turned away unnaturally from God.

divisions of angels, and much else. Here also the doctrine of Origen, which culminated in the restoration of the revolted spirits, was in the end expressly disowned. On the other hand, the Neoplatonic conception of spirits and their orders, or the Gnostic idea of the Æons as interpreters of the divine, was more and more legitimised in the Church doctrine of angels, and was combined by the Areopagite with the mystic system of the illumination of the world, and the communication of the divine to the creaturely. It was a very old idea—see Hebrews and First Clement—that Christ was in Heaven the High Priest and head (προστάτης) of believers in the presence of God. Clement of Alex. had already worked out this conception, following Philo's model, to the effect that Christ, in conjunction with the angelic powers subject to him, conveyed to men the energies of the heavenly sphere; that he ever offered himself for men to the Father as a sacrifice without fire (θῦμα ἄπυρον); that the Holy Spirit along with the angels kept the heavenly and the earthly Church in constant contact. In short, the thought of a graded hierarchy in heaven, with heavenly sacrifices, intercessions, etc., as it also occurs among the Valentinians, lay on the confines of the Alexandrian's speculation. These thoughts are more fully matured in Origen: the sacrifice of Christ applied also to the celestials, and the upper world, brought into harmony, contributed to the redemption of the lower. They were confirmed by the Neoplatonic philosophy of religion. On the other hand, Ignatius conceived the governing body of the Church on earth as a hierarchy which represented the heavenly order, and put it in operation. The two ideas—the Son, the Holy Ghost and the angelic hosts on the one hand, and the earthly priesthood, on the other—only needed to be combined, and a new stage of ecclesiastical theosophy was reached. The Pseudo-areopagite was the first to gain it— after, indeed, it had been already suggested clearly enough by Clement of Alex.; see Strom. VI. 13, 107, and other passages. Clement makes three dwellings in heaven correspond on one side to the divisions of angels, and, again, to the threefold hierarchy on earth. On the spread of this form of theosophy among the Syrian Monophysite monks, see Frothingham, Stephen bar Sudaili, 1886.

This whole conception was after all, indeed, nothing but a timid expression of the thought that the plan of creation itself, extending down from the deity to man, included the means of redemption, and that, as alienation from the deity was due to the existence of graduated creations, so, at the same time, was the restoration to God. This conception, which contrasts abruptly with that of the Old Testament and Christianity, was compatible in principle neither with the idea of the creation, nor with the one historical redemption that took place once for all. It was Gnostic and Neoplatonic, *i. e.*, pagan. This its character was simply disguised by the retention of the creation so far as words went, and by the substitution for the Æons of Jesus Christ, the Holy Ghost, and angelic powers with Biblical names; and, further, of sacraments, sacrifices, and priests, whose existence and operations were derived from the work of Christ.

The root of this whole conception is ultimately found in the notion that the Logos, who was identified with the Son of God, continued to be conceived as the abode and bearer of all the ideas from which the world was evolved. Even Athanasius was not in a position thoroughly to correct this view,— see Atzberger, Die Logoslehre des heiligen Athanasius, 1880, p. 138 ff. Consequently, even the most clear-sighted of the Fathers were helpless against speculations which deduced redemption from the Cosmology. And thus a new Church Theosophy arose. A fantastic pantheism was introduced which had been created by the barbarous theosophy of expiring antiquity. It harmonised excellently with the religious barbarism which satisfied itself in the crudest and most daring myths and legends; nay, it kindled into fresh life with it. The living God, apart from whom the Soul possesses nothing, and the fervour of the saint threatened meanwhile to disappear. And side by side, nay, in cordial agreement, with these fantastic speculations, there existed a prosaic worship of the letter.

Literature.—See Nitzsch's account, here especially thorough, Dogmengesch. I. pp. 268—287, 328—347, and Schwane, Vol. II. pp. 15—108, 272—328.

CHAPTER V.

PRESUPPOSITIONS AND CONCEPTIONS REGARDING MAN AS THE RECIPIENT OF SALVATION.

§ 1. *Introductory.*

ACCORDING to the ideas of the Fathers, the doctrines of the condition and destiny of man belonged to Natural Theology. This appears from the fact that, starting from their Cosmology, they all strove to ascertain, from the original state of man, the nature of Christian redemption, in other words, the state of perfection. At the same time the reservation held good, that we should receive more than we could think or expect, and, in fact, that which was expected, and was deduced from the religious and ethical value which man had come to put upon himself in the course of history, was only carried back into his original state. The following propositions contain everything that can be stated as embodying a common conviction and common presupposition of all further conceptions, which in this matter turned out very different, in accordance with the speculative and empirical studies of the Fathers, and the object of their investigations for the time. *Man made in the image of God is a free self-determining being. He was endowed with reason by God, that he might decide for the good, and enjoy immortality. He has fallen short of this destiny by having voluntarily yielded and continuing to yield himself—under temptation, but not under compulsion—to sin, yet without having lost the possibility and power of a virtuous life, or the capacity for immortality. The possibility was strengthened and immortality restored and offered by the Christian revelation which came to the aid of the darkened reason with complete know-*

*ledge of God. Accordingly, knowledge decides between good and
evil. Strictly taken, the will is morally nothing.*. On this basis very
different views were possible. It was asked, first, what was
original endowment, and what destiny, in the case of man;
secondly, in connection with this, how much was to be claimed
as human *nature*, and how much as *a gift of grace* originally
bestowed; and thirdly, in keeping with the above, how far
and how deep the consequences of sin extended. The question
was put, in the fourth place, whether bare freedom constituted
man's character, or whether it did not correspond to his *nature*
to be good. Fifthly, the philosophical question as to the constitution of man was here introduced and answered in various
ways [dichotomically, trichotomically, the extent and scope of
the flesh (σάρξ) in human nature, in its relation to the spirit
(πνεῦμα) and to sin]. Sixthly, the relation of the creaturely
spirit (πνεῦμα) to the divine, in other words, the origin of the
human spirit, was discussed. Seventhly, lastly, and above all,
men possessed two sources of knowledge: the account in
Genesis with a realistic exposition, which seemed to pour scorn
on all "spiritual" conceptions, but had nevertheless to be
respected; and the relative section from Origen's theology,
which was felt to an increasing extent to be intolerable to the
Church, and which yet expressed the scientific, religious conviction of the Fathers, in so far as their thought was scientific.
Under such circumstances different conceptions, compromises of
all sorts, necessarily arose; but hardly anywhere was an
advance made in the end on the views already presented by
Irenæus. In the latest results, as they are to be found in the
Dogmatics of John of Damascus, there is much that is more
realistic than in Irenæus, but on the whole a type of doctrine
is obtained which is more inadequate and confused, and less
valuable. In what follows we intend to enter in detail only
into the most important points.

§ 2. *The Anthropology.*

Since the end of the creation of the world was held to
consist in the creation of rational beings, who could exhibit

the image of God and share in his blessedness, it followed that the power of free self-determination and the capacity for immortality belonged to the notion of man, and that they were therefore regarded as inalienable. All the doctors of the Church, however, comprehended, in the idea of innate freedom, the conceptions of the rational and moral plan of man's nature as a whole, and they defined this natural disposition to be the power to know God's will accurately, to follow it, and thus to rise above nature. While it was left in doubt whether this whole natural plan implied that man possessed bare freedom or freedom directed to the good, it certainly characterised man as a spiritual being, and for that very reason as an image of God. Being such, man was independent as regards God. In other words, the fact that he was an "image" did not directly establish a lasting dependence on God, nor did it find expression in such a dependence. On the contrary, it established his freedom in relation to God, so that man, being independent, was now only subject to *the law of God*, *i.e.*, to that dispensation in virtue of which he was either rewarded or punished according as he behaved. The connection with God was thus exhausted in the noble constitution of man fixed once for all, but was supremely valued and acutely felt as a gift of divine grace, in the comparison with irrational animals. Meanwhile, the Fathers differed from one another. Some—like Athanasius, see even Tatian—assigned to human nature, in the strictest sense of the term, only the creaturely and sensuous state of being, in respect of which man is perishable, and they described everything else as a gift of divine grace inherent in human nature. Others embraced in this nature the moral capacity, endowment of reason, and knowledge of God;—so the majority; and very strenuously John of Damascus who repeatedly characterises the good as the natural: see De fide orthod. II. 30, III. 14. The third class, finally, included even immortality, as a possession and not merely as a destiny, among the natural attributes of the human soul. These distinctions, which, however, are not particularly important for dogmatics, since all ultimately held nature to be a gift of grace, and the gift of grace to be a natural provision, were due partly to the different psychological conceptions of the Fathers, partly to the standpoint from which they investigated the problems; they might —as *e.g.*, Athanasius—start from the doctrine of redemption or depend on moral, or empirical philosophical considerations. In psychology, the only point settled was that the fundamental form of human nature was twofold, spiritual and corporeal. This conception existed even where the soul itself was represented as something corporeal, or as only "as nearly as possible incorporeal" (ἐγγύτατα τοῦ ἀσωμάτου). Very many Greek Fathers, however, followed the view of Plato and Origen, according to which man consists of spirit, body, and soul—the soul uniting the other two. Consistently carried out, this opinion constantly led them back to the conception of Origen (Philo) that the spirit in man alone constituted his true nature, that it had its own, even a pretemporal, history, that in itself it belonged to the supernatural and divine sphere, and that the body was only a prison which had to be stripped off before the spirit could present itself in its true being. In order to escape these consequences, which were already discredited in the controversy with Neoplatonism and Manichæism, different methods were adopted. Among these occurred that already alluded to above, the conception of the spirit solely as a "super-added gift" (donum superadditum), a religious principle, to be found exclusively in the pious. But this expedient was seldom chosen; the whole question, so important and crucial, was rather stifled in a hundred questions of detail, tortured out of, or read into, the account in Genesis. The ever increasing restriction of the allegorical and spiritualising method of interpreting Gen. I. ff., led the Fathers *nolens-volens* to opinions remote from their scientific thought on religion The only passage in that account, moreover, which seemed to support the spiritualistic conception —"God breathed his own breath into man"—proved too much, and had therefore to be let alone. [1] Origen's idea, that the

---

[1] Augustine's exposition in Ep. CCV. 19, was ultimately the opinion of most of the Greek Fathers, so far as they were not completely devoted to Neoplatonism. "Vis etiam per me scire, utrum dei flatus ille in Adam idem ipse sit anima. Breviter respondeo, aut ipse est aut ipso anima facta est. *Sed si ipse est, factus est . . .* In hac enim quæstione maxime cavendum est, ne anima non a deo facta natura,

body was a prison of the soul, was contrasted with the other, also ancient, that man was rather a microcosm, having received parts from the two created worlds, the upper and under.[1] But this conception, the only one which contained a coherent theory of equal value formally with the doctrine of Origen, could not fail to remain a mere theory, for the ethics corresponding to it, or its ethical ideal, were not supported by the final aims of the dominant theology. When anthropological questions or the Biblical narrative were not directly taken into account, it becomes everywhere obvious, that the old Platonic antithesis of spirit and body was regarded by the Fathers as the antithesis between that which was precious and that which was to be mortified, and that the earthly and creaturely in man was felt to be a hampering barrier which was to be surmounted. Monachism and the eschatological prospect of deification are examples which show how thoroughly practical ideas and hopes were determined by the dualistic view, though its point had been blunted by the tenet of the resurrection of the body. Meanwhile the theoretical doctrines as to the nature of man continued to be beset by a profound inconsistency, and ultimately, in consequence of Biblicism, became aimless and barren.[2]

Supplement.—The different psychological views of the Fathers are reflected in the various theories as to the origin of individual souls. The oldest of these was the *traducian* theory of Tertullian, which was also represented by a few Greeks—Gregory of Nyssa, Anastasius Sinaita. According to

---

sed ipsius dei substantia tamquam unigenitus filius, quod est verbum eius, aut aliqua eius particula esse credatur, tamquam illa natura atque substantia, qua deus est quidquid est, commutabilis esse possit: quod esse animam nemo non sentit, qui se animam habere sentit." But the thought which underlay the last saying of the dying Plotinus (Porphyr., Vita Plot., ch. 2): πειρῶμαι τὸ ἐν ἡμῖν θεῖον ἀνάγειν πρὸς τὸ ἐν τῷ παντὶ θεῖον, was not entirely surmounted by many Greek Fathers.

1 Therefore the great controversy lasting for centuries, whether the skins with which God clothed Adam and Eve were real skins, or bodies. He who agreed with Origen taught the latter; he who looked on man as a microcosm, the former. Yet here also there were composite forms: *e.g.*, the skin meant only the fleshly body.

2 Scriptural proofs in support of the pre-existence of souls were not wanting: see John IX. 2. Jerome held to the doctrine for a time. Even Augustine was uncertain, and up to the time of Gregory the Great its flat rejection had not been determined on in the West (see Ep. VII. 53).

it the soul was begotten along with the body. Its extreme opposite was Origen's idea of *pre-existence* which had still many adherents in the fourth century, but fell more and more into discredit, until, finally, it was expressly condemned at the Synod of Constantinople, A. D. 553. According to this doctrine, all souls were created at once by God along with the upper world, and fell successively into the lower world, and into their bodies. The middle view—an expedient of perplexity—was the *creatian* which gradually gained ground all through the fourth century, and can be characterised as the most wide-spread, at least in the West, from the beginning of the fifth. It taught that God was ever creating souls and planting them in the embryos. The East contented itself with disowning Origen's theory. Augustine, the greatest theologian of the West, was unable to come to any fixed view regarding the origin of the soul.

The different views of the Fathers are further reflected in the different conceptions of the image of God in man. Religious and moral speculation were to be harmonised at this point; for the former was, indeed, never wholly wanting. Apart from such theologians as saw the image of God, somehow or other, even in the human figure, almost all were convinced that it consisted in reason and freedom. But with this it was impossible to remain perfectly satisfied, since man was still able to break away from God, so as in fact to become unlike him, and to die. On the other hand, theologians were certain that goodness and moral purity never could be innate. In order to solve the problem, different methods were adopted. Some abandoned the premise that the possession of the divine image was inalienable, and maintained that as it resided in the spirit that had been bestowed it could be completely lost through sinful sensuousness. The spirit returned to God, and the man relapsed to the level of the beasts. But this solution seemed unsatisfactory, because it was necessary, in spite of it, to retain the freedom that still, under all circumstances, existed to choose the good. Accordingly, it was impossible to treat this theory with any real seriousness.. Others saw the possession of the Divine image, resting on reason and freedom, in the destiny of man to virtue and immortality, yet without stating what change in that case was actually made by falling short of this destiny. The third section, finally, distinguished, after the example of Origen, between "image" (εἰκών) and "likeness" (ὁμοίωσις), and saw the former in the inalienable spiritual plan of man, the latter in moral similarity to God, which was, indeed, one always to be gained on the basis of natural endowments. The Fathers were unwilling, as this review shows, to rest content with the thought that the inalienable spiritual natural endowment of man constituted the divine image, but they found no means of getting beyond it. Their conception of moral goodness as the product of human freedom hindered them. All the more strongly did they emphasise and praise, as a kind of set-off, the goodness of God as Creator revealed in the natural constitution of man.

The different views of the Fathers are finally reflected in their conception of the primitive state. Christianity restores man to his state of ideal perfection. This state must, however, have already existed in some form at the beginning, since God's creation is perfect, and Genesis teaches, that man when created was good, and in a condition of blessedness (Paradise). On the other hand, it could not have been perfect, since man's perfection could not be attained except through freedom. The problem resolves itself into a complete contradiction, which, indeed, was already clearly to be found in Irenæus: the original condition of man must coincide with the state of perfection, and yet it must only have been preliminary. The Fathers tried various ways of solving this crucial and insoluble difficulty, in which again the empirical and moral philosophical conception combined with a religious one. An attempt was made by very many Fathers to limit somewhat the blessedness of the Paradisaical state, or to give a form to their conceptions of it different in quality—fanciful and material—from that of their ideas of the final perfection; accordingly, it was explained —by Gregory of Nyssa—that God himself, looking to the Fall, had not ordained the Paradisaical state to be perfect. By some, again, the inconsistencies were glossed over, while others determined, following Origen, wholly to abandon the historical interpretation of the state in Paradise, and to construct independently a primitive state for themselves. The last method had the advantage, in combination with the assumption of the pre-existence of souls, that it could transfer *all* men mystically into the original state. However, this radical solution conflicted too strongly with the letter of revelation, and the spirit of the Church tradition. It was rejected, and thus the problem remained in its obscurity. Therefore men contented themselves more and more with disregarding the main question: they set down incongruities side by side, and extracted separate points from the account in Genesis. To the latter belonged especially those which were believed to recommend virginity and asceticism, and to prove that these formed the mode of life *(habitus)* which corresponded to the true nature of man. Nor were opinions wanting that characterised asceticism as a salutary means of correcting the deterioration of the human state. "Asceticism and its toils were not invented to procure the virtue that comes from without, but to remove superinduced and unnatural vileness, just as we restore the natural brightness of iron by carefully removing the rust, which is not natural, but has come to it through negligence" (John of Damascus, De fide orth. III. 14).

The principles of ethics were, as a rule, discussed in connection with the original state of man. But even in reference to the blessedness enjoyed in that state no clear conception was reached; for if man's distinctive nature was based on bare freedom, what sort of blessedness could there be for him? What could be bestowed on him which he did not possess already, or which, if bestowed, did not once more call in question the original possession? What could fall to his lot except an arbitrarily chosen reward? Again, as regards ethics, nothing certain could be established. While negative morality, asceticism, was conceived, as a rule, to be the natural and destined condition of man, yet an effort was made to construct an ideal of positive morality, in which the virtues of philosophy appeared in a rather superficial connection with those of religion. [1] Negative and positive morality each looked up, after

---

[1] See here even the Latins. Ambrosius learned the combination, as carried out by him in his De officiis, from the Cappadocians; see also the remarkable opening

all, to a different supreme good, in the one case immortality, in the other the loftiest virtue. Therefore they could not be combined. The assumption of works of supererogation, which the Christian could accomplish while remaining in the world, formed the bridge between the two ethical ideals, but one which it must be admitted, contributed to flight from the one sphere to the other, rather than their connection. All attacks on the theory that ascetic achievements were especially valuable and meritorious were regarded as the outcome of moral laxity, and it is certain that in many cases they actually were.

§ 3. Ethics. Sin.

It was recognised by all the Fathers that the human race had turned from the good and thus degenerated from its origin, *i.e.,*—according to the view of the majority—from Adam. This universality of sin was throughout explained, not from an innate wicked power in man impelling him necessarily to sin, nor from matter in itself, still less from complicity on the part of the Deity. [1] Nor, on the other hand, was it as a rule ascribed to a direct inheritance of Adam's sin, for inherited sin is a contradiction in itself; Adam was the type, but not the ancestor, of sinners. The true explanation was found in the misuse of freedom, caused by the seductions of wicked demons, and the transmission of wicked customs. Along with this, the majority undoubtedly cherished the secret idea, which was not surmounted, that the incentive to revolt from God [2] came to a certain extent

of his work De pœnit. I. 1: "If the final and supreme aim of all virtue is to minister as far as possible to the spiritual benefit of our fellow-man, we may characterise benevolent moderation as one of the finest virtues." For the popular conceptions of Greek Christians, see Socr. H. E. III. 16, in connection with Rom. I. On the other hand, Augustine attempted to derive the philosophic virtues from man's dependence on God, from love; see, above all, the splendid exposition, Ep. CLV., ch. 12.

[1] Even the subtle way in which Origen justified evil as an element in the best possible world (see Vol. II., p. 343 f.) was seldom repeated. Yet see Augustine, De ordine II. 11 sq. (one of his oldest writings): "mala in ordinem redacta faciunt decorem universi."

[2] Sin was described as something negative not only by Augustine, but by all thinking Greeks before him. Their conception was undoubtedly based on a philo-

necessarily from the sensuous nature and creaturely infirmity of man, and resulted from his composite constitution, and his liability to death, whether that was acquired naturally or by transgression, or inherited. Decay and death were especially held to constitute an inducement to and cause of continuance in sin. With natural sensuousness the fate of death was conjoined. Both drove man from God. But in spite of this view the assumption was retained of unaltered freedom. If on the one hand stress was laid on sensuousness being a natural endowment of man, the unnaturalness of wickedness was emphasised on the other, and thus bare freedom received a closer relation to goodness, which, of course, was conceived as repressed by sin. The good was the natural, but, again, in view of man's sensuousness, unnatural evil was also natural to him. The essence of sin, since wickedness was held to be something purely negative, was universally seen in alienation from God, being and goodness; but all that this meant positively was that man had subordinated his will to his sensuousness, and thereby lost the feeling, desire, and knowledge of the divine. The consequences of sin were held to be the following: First, by the majority, the universal mortality which had prevailed from Adam, or the loss of the true life;[1] secondly, the obscuration of the knowledge of God, and with it of religion in general. This darkening made it possible for the demons to seduce man from the true God, to gain him to their own service, and the idolatry of the creature, in the form of polytheism, and so even to exercise an almost complete dominion over him, and the earth associated with humanity. A third consequence of sin was found in a certain weakening of freedom, which, though still existing, yet only in rare cases succeeded, without new divine influences, in reaching a morally good, perfect life.

sophical view that God was not only the originator of being, but really the sole being. On the other hand, a distinction was made between the eternal being and the creaturely, which came from God.

[1] The Antiochenes thought differently (see under), and so did the author of the App. Const., who is exceedingly lax in his views; see, *e.g.*, V. 7, p. 132 (Ed. Lagarde). The latter regards death as an original divine institution, which makes it possible for God to punish or reward. The resurrection was due to the rational soul from God.

Supplement.—The view taken by Irenæus and Tertullian of the fundamental importance of the first Fall for the whole future race, was imperilled by Origen's theory of a fall on the part of spirits in their preëxistent state. It once more gradually won acceptance as an authoritative Biblical doctrine, but it never obtained the same certainty, clearness, or importance among the Greek Fathers as among the Latin (*i.e.*, after Ambrose); see Book II. of our description. The explanation which the theory of original sin furnished for the phenomenon of universal sinfulness was in form similar to Origen's, but was inferior to it in intelligibility, and was never unreservedly accepted by the Orientals. The later Greeks indeed, doubtless under the influence of the West, recognised original sin, but this only resulted in a contradiction; for the thought that each man was born *in puris naturalibus*, was, while no longer strictly formulated, never actually condemned. The old dilemma remained, that each man sinned either from a necessity of his nature or in virtue of his freedom; and the former opinion was at all times held in the East to be Manichæan. Inherited death, due to Adam, was taught as a rule; yet even in this matter certain views were never wholly obliterated which are only intelligible if death was regarded as something natural. From the point of view of the doctrine of redemption especially, it could seem more pertinent to hold death to be the natural destiny of man, from which, however, redemption delivered him. Accordingly, after Origen's theory had been abandoned on account of its want of Biblical support, all that was got in exchange for it was a contradiction: death was something natural and again unnatural. We cannot wonder at this contradiction; in the same way, no one really held the immortality assigned to the primitive state to be something indisputably natural, but neither was it regarded as absolutely supernatural.

§ 4. *The Fall and Original Sin. Doctrine of Redemption.*

This is the place to define more precisely the influence which this Natural Theology gained on Dogmatics, *i.e.*, on the conceptions of redemption through Jesus Christ. In so doing we

must keep firmly in mind, that, in spite of this influence, the
feeling remained uppermost that redemption was something
superlatively exalted, something unmerited, a pure gift of God
to humanity. This feeling was, however, more and more encouraged also by the fact that the simple tenets of Natural
Theology fell into confusion and became less impressive through
the enjoined and ever increasing attention to Biblical texts re-
alistically interpreted, and the necessity of repelling the system
of Origen. To this was added the constantly growing reluctance
to reflect independently at all, as well as the grand impressions
made by the divine dispensation which culminated in the incarnation of the Son of God, and was brought to view in the
mysteries.

In the first place, the conviction of the lofty and, at bottom,
inalienable dignity of man roused the idea that man receives
through redemption that which corresponds to his nature. If
adoption to the sonship of God and participation in the divine
nature appeared on the one hand as a gift above all reason
and expectation, yet it was looked at on the other as corresponding to the nature of man already fixed in his creation.
For man *is* God's image, and exalted as he is above the lower
animals by his constitution, rises as a spiritual being into the
heavenly sphere.

Secondly, the last word that Natural Theology has to say
of man is that he is a free and rational being, introduced into
the opposition of good and evil. Such a being has really to
do with God only in his capacity of *creator* and *rewarder*.
All other points of contact must necessarily always resolve into
that. Again, for such a being there can only exist one good,
that is knowledge, which includes virtue, and besides this certain rewards alone find a place; for his nature requires that he
should be independent in all his movements, nay, these only
possess any value through such independence. The Deity stands
at the beginning and the close of the history of free men as
the power that creates and rewards. But the intervening space
is not occupied by the Deity himself in order to govern man
and to preserve his allegiance. On the contrary, man has to
deal solely with divine knowledge and rules in accordance with

which his freedom is meant to evince itself; for this freedom, while in itself a liberty of choice, was given to him that he might achieve, in a zealous pursuit of virtue based on rational knowledge, the moral perfection possessed by the Deity Himself.

This whole view, which is familiar to us from the Apologists, was never completely lost by the Greek Fathers. Its first consequence was that henceforth the whole of religion could be,—as already in the case of the Apologists—and was, looked at from the point of view of *knowledge* and *law*. It appeared as a morality based on pure knowledge of God and the world, one to which nothing could be added. Along with freedom, the natural moral law was implanted in man, that is, the sure consciousness of the rules, by which he had to prove what was in him. The rules corresponded ultimately to the laws of the universe set in operation and maintained by God as supreme First Cause. This natural law, when it had been obscured in the mind of man, was repeated in the Decalogue by an external legislation, and, on account of the hard-heartedness of the Jews, was supplemented with burdens, temporary commandments; and it was finally reduced by Jesus Christ to the simplest of formulas, set in operation by the impressive preaching of rewards and punishments, and perfectly fulfilled by Jesus. He revealed the perfect knowledge of God, and restored the natural moral law—these two statements being really identical, for in both God appears as the supreme cause. [1] In this state-

---

[1] We perceive the Greek conception most clearly from the law in Apost. Const. VI. 19—24. The section begins with the words : γνόντες γὰρ Θεὸν διὰ Ἰησοῦ Χριστοῦ καὶ τὴν σύμπασαν αὐτοῦ οἰκονομίαν ἀρχῆθεν γεγενημένην, ὅτι δέδωκε νόμον ἁπλοῦν εἰς βοήθειαν τοῦ φυσικοῦ καθαρόν, σωτήριον, ἅγιον, ἐν ᾧ καὶ τὸ ἴδιον ὄνομα ἐγκατέθετο. The Decalogue is meant; it was given to the nation before its revolt, and God had no intention of adding sacrificial regulations, but tolerated sacrifices. After the revolt (of the golden calf) he himself, however, gave the ceremonial law: "He bound the people with irremovable fetters, and imposed heavy burdens and a hard yoke upon them, that they might abandon idolatry and turn again to that law which God had implanted by nature in all men" (ch. XX.). These "branding irons, lancets, and medicines" were, however, only for the sick. Christians who voluntarily believed in one God were delivered by him, above all, from the sacrificial service. Christ has fulfilled (κυρώσας) the law, but removed the additions, "if not all, yet the more irksome"; this is the opposite of Tertullian's opinion. He restored man's right of self-determination, and in doing so confirmed the natural law (τὸν φυσικὸν νόμον ἐβεβαίωσεν). More rigorous conditions are only

ment we have already mentioned the second consequence of the
speculation : all grace can only possess the character of a support, of a rectification of knowledge. The whole of the operations of God's grace are in the end, crutches offered to feeble
man. In offering them, God reveals a goodness which, after
what he has already done in creation, is without any fixed
limit. Grace is therefore not absolutely necessary for every man. [1]
God, again, by no means reveals himself in it even as the
blessing which man requires, but he simply imparts complete
knowledge, and thus explains, and strengthens the motives for
observing, the rules of conduct which man had long possessed.
But in the third place, it follows from the speculation, that sin
is nothing but the transgression, induced by imperfect knowledge,
of those rules, whose observance does not exhibit man's dependence on God, but his independence and freedom. Sin subjects
man to the judgment of God. Punishment is the gravest result
of sin. But God would not be just, if he were not an indulgent judge. His goodness which supports man, has its counterpart in the indulgence which overlooks the time of ignorance
of the individual, and leaves unpunished the sins of men whenever they feel penitent. [2] Since it is impossible in this whole

---

apparent. Just vengeance is even yet permitted, toleration is only better: οὐ τὰ
φυσικὰ πάθη ἐκκόπτειν ἐνομοθέτησεν ἀλλὰ τὴν τούτων ἀμετρίαν (This is not the
usual Greek view, but a conception peculiar to this lax author). But Christ himself
abolished what had been "added" solely by fulfilling it first in his life and death,
or by transforming the ceremonies into spiritual rites. The respect which Irenæus,
as distinguished from the older teachers, had already entertained for the ceremonial
law is shown even more clearly here.

[1] Yet see what is said below on Macarius.

[2] Forgiveness of sins was a conception which in this connection could hardly
be carried out by the Fathers. The passing over of the time of ignorance and the
acceptance of the reparation involved in penitence constituted forgiveness. Hardly
another teacher from and after the fourth century, has expressed it so clearly as
Clemens Alex.: τῶν προγεγενημένων Θεὸς δίδωσιν ἄφεσιν, τῶν δὲ ἐπιόντων αὐτὸς
ἕκαστος ἑαυτῷ (Quis div. salv. 40, cf. Strom. II. 14, 58, and elsewhere); but the
statement as to Christ in Pædag. I. 3, 7: τὰ μὲν ἁμαρτήματα ὡς Θεὸς ἀφιείς, εἰς
δὲ τὸ μὴ ἐξαμαρτάνειν παιδαγωγῶν ὡς ἄνθρωπος, formed a part of the fundamental
view of the following age. We cannot wonder at this. Between mechanical ex-
piations and penitence there is in fact no third term, as soon as the forgiveness
of sins is applied to individual cases. Only where faith in forgiveness is *the* faith
itself, is it more than a word, and yet not magical.

question that there can be any suggestion of a restoration of
man to that communion with God which he had forsaken,
since on the contrary, the sole point was that man, to whom
it was always possible to return, should not be impeded while
striving and yet stumbling, the view was, in fact, inevitable
that God remits punishment to every penitent. God would not
appear just, but harsh and unloving, if he did not accept sincere
penitence as an equivalent for transgressions. It was accordingly agreed that, although men are sinners, they become just
in the sight of God through virtue and penitence, and redemption to eternal life through Christ can only benefit such as have
acquired this righteousness through their independent efforts.
The sacraments initiated men into this effort to obtain virtue,
and they had also an indescribable influence upon it. But
personal fulfilment of the law was still something thoroughly
independent. Finally, it followed from this moral view, that it
was impossible to gain a clear idea of the state of perfection.
A state of freedom and a perfect virtue based on perfect
knowledge cannot be raised higher than they are, and that
which is given to reward the latter can never be intrinsically
connected with it. The complete vacuity of the conceptions
held of the final state, apart from the effect of the hope of an
ever increasing knowledge, i.e., vision of God, was accordingly
also the natural consequence of the conviction that man,
because he is free, is dependent on no one, and that he is
always at the goal when he fulfils the law of God.

Thirdly, the rationalistic exposition of the doctrine of God
and creation could not fail to impel apologists to expound the
reasonableness of the doctrines of the Trinity, the resurrection
of the body, etc. As a matter of fact the attempt was
even made to prove the existence of a general agreement,
a "common sense", as to the doctrine of the Trinity, and
references were especially made to heathen philosophers,
though, on the other hand, when it seemed expedient, the
Greeks were denied any knowledge of the Trinity. Such
references were all the more natural, since Neoplatonic philosophers, and at an earlier date Numenius, had constructed
a kind of trinity. Cyril, again, in his Catechisms, supported

the resurrection of the body to a very large extent on rational grounds, and others followed his example. For the extent to which even the doctrine of the Incarnation was included in Natural Theology, see following chapter.

Fourthly, from all this it followed, that man could ultimately receive nothing from history which he could not, nay, had not to, wrest for himself. But the Logos in the flesh (λόγος ἔνσαρκος) belonged to history. Accordingly, it was impossible wholly to get rid of the view that there was a standpoint for which the historical Christ, since he was merely the edifying teacher, meant nothing. This view was, as we know, expressed perfectly plainly by Origen (see Vol. II., p. 342, n. 1); and in this he by no means stood alone. It was not only repeated by half-heathen theologians, like Synesius, but it runs like a hidden thread through the conceptions of all Greek theologians, as long as they continued to think independently. It is the negative complement of the idea that the knowledge accompanied by virtue, which transcends all that is visible, and therefore all that is historical, includes blessedness in itself, and moreover, that it can be achieved from our own resources through a direct *afflatus divinus*. But still further: even in Augustine this view was not wholly surmounted. The man, who perceived the Deity, and had gained faith, love, and hope, stood beside the throne of God, and was with the Father of light and his essential Word; the historical Christ lay beneath him. [1] Further, even opponents of Origen, like Methodius and his successors, the mystics, had arrived at the same conception (see Vol. III., p. 110). For the ascetic mystic history passed away along with the world; he might cast aside all crutches, traversing independently the long, mysterious path from the extreme outside to the inmost recess of the spiritual. At the end of this path there stood, not Jesus Christ, but the unembodied Logos (λόγος ἄσαρκος), since he was pure truth and pure life. An incarnate Christ (ἔνσαρκος) was born in each who traversed this path. He in whom Christ was born, however, no longer needed the historical Christ. [2]

[1] Augustine, De doctr. I. 34.
[2] See even Augustine, on John, tract. 21, n. 8: "Gratulemur et gratias agamus

Rationalism, or Christianity as the moral law which is freely fulfilled, and mysticism are regarded as opposites, and so they are before the tribunal of philosophy. But before that of positive religion they are not, they are rather akin, at least in the form in which they confront us in antiquity.[1] Mysticism of course embraces germs which when unfolded will resist rationalism. But at first it is nothing but rationalism applied to a sphere above reason (ratio). The admission that there was such a sphere formed the difference. It was mysticism as much as rationalistic moralism which secretly formed an opposition to the Christianity proclaimed by Jesus Christ to be *the way and the truth for all men and for every grade.* The most vital piety of the Greek Fathers, and the strenuous effort to make themselves at home in religion, insured them at least against losing the historical Christ.

But it was only a danger that here threatened. We may not say more. The Deity had come down to earth, God had become man, and that in the historical Jesus—faith in this stupendous fact, "the newest of the new, nay, the only new thing under the sun," limited all rationalism. It imperatively demanded the investigation, on the one hand, of the ground and cause, on the other, of the fruit and blessing, of this divine dispensation. It was necessary to find the relation of the latter to the mystery and horror of death. It was indeed impossible to make the "naturalness" of death credible; for all nature, higher and lower, rebelled against it. And the consciousness of a capacity for perfect knowledge and goodness underlay in practical life the sense of incapacity. Hence the conviction that man must be redeemed, and through Jesus Christ is redeemed. The doctrines of innate freedom, the law, and the independent achievement of virtue were not abandoned;

non solum nos Christianos factos esse, sed Christum . . . admiramini gaudete: Christus facti sumus."

[1] Bigg (The Christian Platonists of Alex., 1886, p. 51 f.) has also correctly perceived this; he is speaking of the attitude of Clement and of the Alexandrians generally: "On one side Rationalist, on another Mystic." "Though there is in them a strong vein of Common Sense or Rationalism, they were not less sensible of the mystic supernatural side of the religious life than Irenæus. *The difference is that with them the mystical grows out of the rational."*

but they were counterbalanced by faith in the necessity and reality of redemption. And this combination, unsatisfactory as it seems to us, was yet capable of forming men of Christian character. Such men were never wanting in any century of the older Greek Church after Athanasius and Chrysostom, although their theology lacked the confession of the Psalmist: "It is good for me to cleave to God" (Mihi adhærere deo bonum est). [1]

Instead of multiplying details we may here give the views on freedom, sin, and grace, of four eminent Greek Fathers, Athanasius, Gregory of Nyssa, Theodore of Mopsuestia, and John of Damascus.

(1) Athanasius.—The conceptions formed by Athanasius of the original state of man, of sin and grace, show especially his inability to distinguish between nature and grace. In his work "De incarnatione" [2] he strove to prove that the incarnation was a necessity on the part of God. Therefore he emphasises strongly the destiny of man, and distinguishes it sharply from his empirical condition; for this destiny sets God a task which he must carry out under all circumstances, if his goodness (ἀγαθότης) is to remain in force. Therefore, in many of the arguments of this work, human nature appears as the creaturely and sensuous constitution, while everything else, including the endowment of reason, takes the form of a *donum superadditum*, potentially given in the original state, and binding on God himself, a gift of grace, which was meant to rise to complete

[1] The text is indeed quoted by Macarius (Ep. I. *fin*) as the sum of all knowledge. But even to this theologian, who came nearest Western thought in some paraenetic remarks, and frequently drew the sharpest contrast between nature and grace (see Hom. I. 10, IV. 7—9), the "cleaving to God" meant nothing but the independent decision for God. The following passage (Hom. IV. 5) proves how remote Macarius was from Augustine: "How should God treat a man who, in the exercise of free will, devotes himself to the world, lets himself be seduced by its pleasures, or revels in dissipations? God only sends his help to him who renounces worldly pleasures, and preserves himself completely from the snares and traps of the sensuous world," etc. Here we see that the contrast between nature and grace was not so seriously meant. The same is the case with "law and gospel." No Greek Father was able to regard these as contrasted in the same way as we see them in the writings of Paul and Augustine.

[2] On its authenticity, see the next chapter.

knowledge of God through the free moral development of man
—for that was the goal. [Athanasius uses very different expressions for this in his writings: φαντασία περὶ Θεοῦ (power
of conceiving God), γνῶσις (knowledge) κατανόησις (perception)
κατάληψις (comprehension) θεωρία τῶν θείων (theory of divine
things) θεωρία τῶν νοητῶν (—of the intelligible) θεωρία περὶ τοῦ
Θεοῦ (science of God) ἔννοια τῆς εἰς πατέρα γνώσεως (concept
of knowledge as to the Father)]. The change which took place
in man through sin, or through death, is accordingly conceived
as a loss of the divine. God is at the same time supremely
interested in preventing man, once destined to obtain perfect
divine knowledge, from becoming a prey to his lower nature,
and being destroyed.[1]

But even in the De incarn., and to a still greater extent
in his later anti-Arian writings, Athanasius defends the idea that
the rational spirit (ψυχὴ λογική—Athanasius being a dichotomist)
belongs to man's constitution, is immortal, and at bottom also
inalienable. This ψυχὴ λογική can gradually recognise the Logos
and God from creation; it is, accordingly, not only an inalienable religious *talent*, but also an inalienable religious *factor*.
Its power extends so far that there have been holy men in all
ages (c. gent. 2; c. Arian. III. 33: πολλοὶ γὰρ οὖν ἅγιοι γεγόνασι
καθαροὶ πάσης ἁμαρτίας). The reconciliation of the two contradictory statements, that the higher endowment appears first as
grace, then as nature, is to be found in the following points.
(1) The ψυχὴ λογική is only rational (logical) because it parti-
cipates in the Logos, is his image, possesses a shadow of him
(De incarn. 3), and retains its power only when steadfastly connected with him. For this reason it can be termed, although a
natural provision, an "external" (c. Arian. II. 68: "Adam was
outside before his transgression, having received grace and not
having had it adapted to his body"; ὁ Ἀδὰμ πρὸ τῆς παραβάσεως ἔξωθεν ἦν, λαβὼν τὴν χάριν καὶ μὴ συνηρμοσμένην ἔχων
αὐτὴν τῷ σώματι). (2) It is only in the apologetic arguments
of the treatise De incarn. that Adam's fall and its consequence
appear as forming a tremendous cleavage, and the state before

---

[1] De incarn. IV.: ἡ παράβασις τῆς ἐντολῆς εἰς τὸ κατὰ φύσιν αὐτοὺς ἐπέστρεψεν.
Accordingly, everything is supernatural which raises man above the level of nature.

and after the fall as a contrast. That was not the characteristic view of Athanasius, [1] as is shown by other arguments in the same writing, and the rest of the tractates. He contemplates not a loss once for all, but a gradual enfeeblement. Mankind has more and more lost, from generation to generation, the consciousness of God, *i.e.*, through the darkening of his mind. That which above all burdened humanity, however, was not sin, but the sentence of death pronounced by God on the sinner— see next chapter. The faculties for knowing God, and thus for attaining the goal, remained, but there was no corresponding power actually to reach the goal. A Catholic investigator has expressed this as follows: [2] "Sinful man gradually lost, according to Athanasius, what was supernatural in his prerogatives, and retained only what was natural. Supernatural were moral goodness on the one hand, the correct consciousness and due use of rationality and immortality on the other; while rationality and immortality generally were natural." The intrusion here of the modern Catholic categories of "natural and "supernatural" is incorrect; for the spiritual nature of man was held by all the Fathers to be supernatural. But the idea is correct. But we must go further. The difference here is exclusively quantitative; it is only qualitative from the fact that what remains of higher powers is as a rule of less than its initial value, *i.e.*, is no longer capable of reaching the goal. The same Catholic scholar is therefore perfectly correct, when —expressing himself with due caution—he finds (p. 159 f.) that Athanasius "does not seem to treat" the punishment of sin—better, sin — "with sufficient gravity". "He teaches, indeed, that the spiritual gifts of man were lost through sin, but he conceives this ruin as gradual in time and degree, depending on the extent to which men had turned from the contemplation of the spiritual and to the sensuous"; *i.e.*, Athanasius simply follows an empirical and natural line of thought, in virtue of which he finds in mankind very different grades of moral and intellectual position. That this was a consequence of human freedom con-

---

[1] Against Wendt, "Die christl. Lehre von der menschlichen Volkommenheit (1880), p. 47 f.

[2] Atzberger, Die Logoslehre des h. Athanasius. (1880), p. 156.

stituted a sufficient explanation in itself and freed the Deity of
all blame. But it did not explain the universality of death,
and left out of account Gen. I.—III. The above empirical view,
which ultimately, indeed, cast a certain shadow on the Deity,
and these chapters of the Bible compelled him to secure, somehow or other, a historical beginning for the present condition
and therewith an original state of man. But the relations of
the present to that beginning are really exhausted in the continuance of the once pronounced sentence of death; [1] and the
primitive state, which is clearly enough described (c. gentes 2,
De incarn. 3, 4) as a destiny—Adam himself having not yet
attained what his endowments fitted him for, continued in this
sense; nay, it ultimately embraced the idea that God was under
the necessity of bringing the sentence of death to an end.

However, Athanasius did arrive at positive conclusions as to
the specific grace bestowed in the Christian redemption, in his
polemic against the Arians. It is not to be wondered at that
the discussion of grace in connection with creation and the
natural endowments of man only resulted, on the premises
stated by the Fathers, in tautologies. But against the Arians,
where Athanasius was not interested in cosmology, he shows
that we have received from grace what was by nature peculiar
to the Son, and he definitely distinguishes between grace in
creation and in redemption. Deut. XXXII. 6, 7, 18, where it
is said that God created and begot men, he interprets as follows:
"By creating, Moses describes the natural state of men, for
they are works and beings made; by begetting, he lets us see
the love of God to them after their creation" (c. Arian. II. 58).
Similarly on John I. 12, 13: "John makes use of the words
'to become' because they are called sons, not by nature, but
by adoption; but he has employed the word 'begotten', because
they in any case have received the name of son... The goodness of God consists in this, that he afterwards becomes, by
grace, the father of those whose creator he already is. He
becomes their father, however, when—as the Apostle says—
the men who have been created receive into their hearts the
Spirit of his Son, which calls, 'Abba, Father.' But the latter

[1] All men were lost in Adam's transgression," c. Arian. II. 61.

consist of all who have received the Word and have obtained power from him to become children of God. For since by nature they are creatures, they can only become sons by receiving the spirit of the natural and true Son. In order that this may happen the Word became flesh, that men might be made capable of receiving the Deity. This conception can also be found in the Prophet Malachi, who says: 'Did not one God create you? Have you not all one Father?' For here again he says in the first place 'created', and in the second 'father', in order similarly to show that we are first, and by nature, creatures, but afterwards are adopted as sons, God the creator becoming also our father," etc. (c. Arian. II. 59). These expositions are certainly worth noting, but we must not overestimate them; for in the same discourses against the Arians they are modified to the effect that our sonship depends on the Logos dwelling in us, *i.e.*, it receives a cosmological basis (see c. Arian. III. 10). In some passages it indeed looks as if the Logos only dwelt in us in consequence of the incarnation (see above and l. c. IV. 22); but it is quite clear in others that Athanasius thought of an indwelling before the incarnation, an indwelling wholly independent of it. With the recollection that there were sons of God in the O. T., Athanasius proves that the Logos was eternal. Accordingly, it is with him as with Clement of Alexandria: when the Fathers are not dealing with apologetic theology, and disregard the O. T., they are able to comprehend and describe the grace due to the historical Christ in its specific significance; but when they reason connectedly everything ultimately resolves into the natural endowment fixed once for all.

Literature.—See, besides the works quoted of Atzberger and Wendt, Möhler, Athanasius, I. p. 136 ff. Voigt, Athanasius, p. 104 ff., and Ritschl, Rechtfertigung und Versöhnung, 2 Ed. Vol. I. p. 8 ff.

(2) Gregory of Nyssa.—Gregory's theories also appear to be hampered by a contradiction because they are sketched from two different points of view. On the one hand he regards the nature of man in spirit and body as constituting his true being. To him, as opposed to Origen, the whole earthly world is

good, a mirror of divine wisdom and power, a place meant to be pervaded by the divine. Before this could be possible "it was necessary that a union should be effected between its essential elements and the higher spiritual and divine nature, whereby first the divine shone as through a glass into the earthly world, after which the earthly, elevated with the divine, could be freed from liability to decay, and be transfigured. This central significance, this part of constituting a bond between two worlds in themselves opposed, was assigned to man, who stood at the head of the ascending scale of earthly creatures, which he comprehended like a microcosm, while he also as λογικὸν ζῶον (a rational being) projected into the invisible world, in virtue of his nature made in the image of God, *i.e.*, spiritual and moral, and, especially, ethically free. This nature of man, besides, being created, possessed nothing of itself, but only like the sun-loving eye turned ever of its own accord to the eternal light, living on it, and interpreting it to the earthly world to which it essentially belonged." [1]   But on the other hand, though Gregory rejected Origen's theories of the pre-existence of souls, the pre-temporal fall, and the world as a place of punishment (περὶ κατασκευῆς ἀνθρώπων, ch. 28, 29), regarding them as Hellenic dogmas and therefore mythological, yet he was dominated by the fundamental thought which led Origen to the above view. The spiritual and the earthly and sensuous resisted each other. If man was, as Scripture says, created in the image of God, [2] then he was a spiritual being, and his being so constituted his nature (see l.c. ch. 16—18). Man was a self-determining, but, because created, a changeable spirit, meant to share in all the blessings of God. So far as he had a sensuous side, and was mortal, he was not an

---

[1] See Catech. mag. 5, 6, and the work, περὶ ψυχ. κ. ἀναστας., as also περὶ κατασκ. ἀνθρωπ. 2 ff. 16. Möller in Herzog R.-E., 2 Ed. Vol. V., p. 401, and his work, Gregorii Nyss. de natura hom. doctr. illustr. et cum Origeniana comparata, 1854.

[2] Orat. I. T. I., p. 150: Κατ᾽ εἰκόνα ἔχω τὸ λογικὸς εἶναι καθ᾽ ὁμοίωσιν δὲ γίνομαι ἐν τῷ Χριστιανὸς γενέσθαι. The "image" cannot consist in the bodily. The latter is at most a copy of the "image," see περὶ κατασκ. ἀνθρωπ. 8, 12. But the "image" itself implies that it can only really be completely produced by free self-determination on the part of man. "If any compulsion obtained, the image would not be realised," (Catech. mag. 5).

image of God. Gregory now laid stress on man (homo)—as he conceived it, humanity—having been first created, and then having been fashioned into male and female. He concluded from this that the earthly and sensuous side of man was ἐπιγεννηματική, a subsequent creation, that, accordingly, the spiritual in man was conceptually the primary, and his sensuous and bodily nature the secondary, part of him. [1] He further concluded that man was originally designed to live a sexless life like the angels, that God would have multiplied men as he did the angels by his power "in a noble fashion" (περὶ κατασκ., 17), and that the proper and natural dwelling-place of men was the pure and incorporeal future state.

But near as he was to consequences drawn by Origen, [2] Gregory rejected them. The destiny of man sketched above was an ideal one. In other words, God, looking to the Fall, at once created and added the earthly and sensuous nature of man; nay, this was not merely due to the Fall, but, as is shown by the first line of thought given above, the earthly nature of man had also, since it was possessed by divine energies and transfigured, a lasting significance. But the Paradisaical state in which men lived before the Fall, was not the highest; for the body was not transfigured, though it had not yet been stained by sexual intercourse. The highest state, in so far as it was brought about by the resurrection (εἰς τὸ ἀρχαῖον τῆς φύσεως ἡμῶν ἀποκατάστασις), was that which notionally preceded the life in Paradise, but had never till now been concretely realised. It was life in its incorporeal abode after the fashion of the angels. [3] The incarnation of God had procured this state

---

[1] We have, however, to make a distinction here. As a creaturely spirit man necessarily has a body, just as every picture has a material foundation, and every mirror a back. This body, therefore, belonged, according to Gregory, to the notion of man's nature; it was the phenomenon of the soul as the latter was the noumenon of the body. But Gregory distinguishes this body from the sensuous and sexually differentiated one.

[2] Gregory borders very closely upon them, not only in περὶ κατασκ., but also in other writings. The fall does not, indeed, take the form of an event in the experience of individual men actually to be found in a pre-existent state, but of a kind of "intelligible collective deed of all humanity."

[3] See περὶ κατασκ. ἀνθρωπ. 16—18.

for all who, in virtue of their freedom, led a holy life, *i.e.*, who lived as man did in Paradise before the Fall; for that was possible to man even when on earth. In all this we must remember that Gregory's hold on the traditional dependence on Gen. I.—III. was very loose: he does not speak of Adam, but always of us. All men had the same freedom as Adam. [1] All souls really passed through Adam's history. Above all, no transference of sin took place, although Gregory is a Traducian (see περὶ κατ. ανθρ. ch. 29); every man sinned, because in virtue of his freedom he could sin, and by his sensuous nature (πάθη) was induced to sin. By this means a state of depravity and death was introduced—sin also being death—from which man in fact could not deliver himself. Nothing but the union of God with humanity procured redemption. Redemption was, in harmony with the speculations as to Adam, strictly objective, and the question as to its appropriation was therefore, at bottom, no question. A new condition was revealed for all men without any co-operation on their part, but it became real only to those who led a holy life, *i.e.*, who abstained entirely from sin.

Literature.—See, besides Möller's work, Wendt, l.c., p. 49 f.; Herrmann, Gregorii Nyss. sententiæ de salute adipiscenda, 1875; Bergades, De universo et de anima hominis doctrina Gregorii Nyss., Thessalonich, 1876; Stigler, Die Psychologie des hl. Gregor von Nyssa, Regensburg, 1857; Ritschl., l.c. Vol. I. p. 12 ff.; Hilt, Des hl. Gregor von Nyssa Lehre vom Menschen, Köln, 1890.

(3) Theodore.—Even in Irenæus [2] two inconsistent conceptions of the result of redemption stood side by side. It was held, on the one hand, to restore man to the original state from which he had fallen, and, on the other, to raise him from the primitive natural state of childhood to a higher stage. The

---

[1] Gregory here carries his speculation still further: God did not first create a single man, but the whole race in a previously fixed number; these collectively composed only one nature. They were really *one* man, divided into a multiplicity. Adam—that means all (περὶ κατασκ. 16, 17, 22). In God's prescience the whole of humanity was comprised in the first preparation.

[2] See Vol. II., p. 267 ff.

majority of the Greek Fathers were not in a position to decide bluntly for either of these ideas; yet the former, under the influence of Origen, prevailed. It was only in the school of Antioch that it was really rejected, that the other view was emphatically avowed, and thus the most decided attitude adopted of opposition to Origen's theology.[1] The view of the Antiochenes was teleological—but there was an entire absence of any religious view of sin. In this respect it was directly opposed to Augustine's system.

According to Theodore,[2] God's plan included from the beginning two epochs ("$K\alpha\tau\alpha\sigma\tau\acute{\alpha}\sigma\epsilon\iota\varsigma$"), the present and future states of the world. The former was characterised by change-ableness, temptation, and mortality, the latter by perfection, immutability, and immortality. The new age only began with the resurrection of the dead, its original starting-point being the incarnation of the Son of God. Further, there was a spiritual and a sensuous. Man was composed of both, the body having been created first, and the soul having then been breathed into it. This is the opposite of Gregory of Nyssa's view. Man was the connecting link between the two spheres; he was designed to reveal the image of God in this world. "Like a king, who, after building a great city and adorning it with works of every kind, causes, when the whole is completed, a fine statue of himself to be erected, in which all the inhabitants may gratefully revere the constructor, so the Creator of the world, after he had elaborated his work, finally produced man to be his own image, and all creatures find in him their centre, and thus contribute to the due glorification of God." Now although man is equipped with all the powers of reason and of will, *yet, from the very nature of his present condition, he is changeable, is defeated in the conflict, and is mortal.* Not till the new principle of life was imparted by means of Christ

---

[1] It is instructive that Marcellus also thinks of a glory presented through redemption, which is $\dot{\upsilon}\pi\grave{\epsilon}\rho$ $\check{\alpha}\nu\theta\rho\omega\pi o\nu$.

[2] See Kihn, Theodor von Mops., p. 171 ff. Also the examples partly taken from Theodore's commentaries on Genesis, Job, and Paul's epistles (see Swete, Theodori in epp. Pauli comment. 1880, 1881), partly from fragments of other writings of Theodore; cf. also Dorner, Theodori de imagine dei doctrina, 1844.

could the changeable nature be raised to immutability. Till then, accordingly, man was exposed to temptation, and as a being made up of spirit and body was *necessarily mortal*. The threat of death in Paradise did not mean that death was the consequence of sin—it was rather natural; but it was designed to inspire man with as great a hatred of sin, as if the latter were punished by death. Death, natural in itself, was a divine means of education, and accordingly salutary. "God knew that mortality would be beneficial to Adam, for if they had been invested with immortality, men, when they sinned, would have been exposed to eternal destruction." But even the permission of sin was salutary, and formed part of the divine plan of education. God gave a command, and thereby elicited sin, in order that he might, like a loving Father, teach man his freedom of choice and weakness. "Man was to learn that while he was in a state of moral changeableness, he would not be capable of sustaining an immortal existence. Therefore death was announced to him as the penalty of disobedience, although mortality was from the beginning an attribute of human nature." [1] No sin without a command, but also no knowledge of good and evil, of the possession of spiritual faculties, finally, no conflict. Accordingly, God gave the command in order to raise Adam above the stage of childhood, and it necessarily provoked conflict and defeat.

Adam is, however, to be thought of here, not as the ancestor, but as the type, of the human race. The law was given with the same object to all his descendants, to teach them to distinguish between good and evil, and to know their own powers and weakness. In the history of Adam we become acquainted with our own natural disposition. "In keeping with this we are under the necessity in our present life of rendering obedience to laws by which our natural power of making distinctions is awakened, we, meanwhile, being taught from what we ought to abstain and what to do, that the principles of reason may be active in us. Only when we find ourselves in the future state (Katastasis) will we be able with slight effort to perform what we recognise as good. Without law, therefore,

[1] Kihn, l. c., p. 174.

we would have had no distinction between good and evil, and no knowledge of sin, and like irrational animals we would have done whatever occurred to us." In this state knowledge and fighting are required to obtain the victory, but we are constantly hampered by the body, the source of temptations. Christ first gave us redemption from death, an immortal nature, which, therefore, will obtain 'the victory without effort (on Rom. V. 18).

Theodore was able to explain away the Pauline passages which support a transmission of the death worked by sin, just as he ignored the life of the first man in Paradise before the Fall. All men died because of their own sinful actions; but even this was meant figuratively. They died because of their natural constitution, in which sin was latent. He opposed Augustine's and Jerome's doctrine of original sin in an indepen-dent work, fragments of which have been preserved by Marius Mercator. "Adam was created mortal whether he sinned or not. For God did not say, 'Ye will be mortal,' but 'Ye will die.'" Theodore quoted Ps. CIII. 15, and Rome. II. 6. Against original sin he appealed to the case of saints like Noah, Abraham, and Moses. If God had passed sentence of death. on all as the punishment of sin, he would not have made Enoch immortal. Accordingly, Baptism did not, according to Theodore, remove inherited sin, but initiated the believer into sinless discipleship of Christ, and at the same time blotted out the sins he had himself committed. In the former sense it had its use even for children; for Baptism, like all grace emanating from the incarnation, raised man to a new stage, elevated him above his present nature, and prepared him for the future state (Katastasis). This is most strongly emphasised by Theodore, and here his teaching is distinguished from the doctrines of Pelagius and Julian of Eclanum, [1] who subordinated redemption through Christ completely to the rationalistic theory. That Theodore did not do. While he was thoroughly convinced, with Pelagius, that in the present state everything turned on men's own actions which rested on knowledge, freedom, effort, and heroic fighting, yet he was equally certain on the other hand,

[1] See Kihn, l. c., p. 179 f.

that human nature did not attain immutability, immortality, and sinlessness through this conflict—it was merely a condition—but only through redemption. For this reason Christ came. He did not restore, but produced a new, a higher state. He did not heal, but transfigured.[1]

Theodore's doctrine of man was strictly rationalistic and Aristotelian; it surpassed the theories of all the rest of the Greek Fathers in intelligibility and consistency. But for that very reason it did not correspond to all the ideas and desires embraced in the tradition of the Church.

(4) John of Damascus.—The doctrines taught by this dogmatist became final in the Greek Church, the later Symbols being substantially at one with them,[2] because he combined the conceptions of the Cappadocians with the Antiochene tradition, in the modified form assumed by the latter in Chrysostom, and at the same time did justice to the constantly increasing tendency to refrain as much as possible from allegorising Gen. I. ff. Briefly, John taught as follows:[3]—

Since God, "overflowing with goodness", was not satisfied with the contemplation of himself, but desired to have some one to whom he could do good, he created the universe, angels, and men. Even the angels were immortal, not by nature, but by grace; for everything which has a beginning has necessarily an end. But immortality being a gift became natural to spiritual beings, and therefore also to men. Men were created by God from nature, visible and invisible, in his own image, to be kings and rulers of the whole earth. Before their creation God had prepared Paradise for them to be as it were a royal castle, "set by his hands in Eden, a store-house of all joy and delight, situated to the East, and higher than the whole earth, but

---

[1] Chrysostom agrees entirely with Theodore in the opinion that man's free will takes the first step, which is then seconded by God with his power, in the appropriation of the good; see his notes on Rom. IX. 16, in Hom. 16; in ep. ad Heb., Hom. 12; in Ev. Joh., Hom. 17, etc. The passages are reproduced in Münscher, Lehrbuch der Dogmengeschichte (1832), p. 363 ff.

[2] See Gass, Symbolik d. griech. Kirche, p. 150 ff.

[3] De fide orthod. II. 2 ff., 11 ff. 24—30; III. 1, 14, 20; IV. 4, 11, 19—22, and the Homily in "ficum arefactum," as also the Dialogue against the Manichæans. Langen, l. c., p. 289 ff.; Wendt, l. c., p. 59 ff.

tempered and illumined by the finest and purest air, planted
with ever blossoming flowers, filled with perfume, full of light,
surpassing every idea of earthly grace and beauty, a truly
divine place." ¹ But it was only with his body that man was
supposed to live in this material Paradise; he inhabited with
his spirit at the same time the "spiritual" Paradise, which is
indicated by the tree of life. ² Of the tree of knowledge he
was not at first to eat; for knowledge, while good for the
perfect, is bad for the imperfect. The result of knowledge in
the case of the imperfect was to make man, instead of devot-
ing himself to the contemplation and praise of God, think of
himself: Adam, immediately after eating, noticed that he was
naked. "God intended that we should be free from desire and
care, and occupied solely with luxuriating in the contemplation
of himself." The eating "of all the trees" denoted the knowledge of God from the works of nature. In created man—the
union of visible and invisible nature—the *image* of God consisted in power of thought and freedom of will, *likeness* to him
in similarity in virtue, so far as that was possible. Soul and
body (as against Origen) were created together. Man was
originally innocent, upright, and adorned with all virtues; ³ his
being so was a gift of grace; but so also was the fact that he
was spiritual. He was spiritual that he might endure and
praise his benefactor; corporeal, that he might be disciplined
by suffering and the recollection of suffering; he was too proud
of his greatness. Man was created a being who ruled in this
present life, and was transferred to another. ⁴ He was finally
to be made divine by submission to God: his deification

---

¹ Accordingly we have here a recrudescence to some extent of what the older
Greek Fathers called "Judaism" or "earthly conceptions," cf. Peter's Apocalypse.

² Two traditional, inconsistent ideas are combined here: John was not quite
clear as to the tree of life. He gives different explanations of it in De fide II. 11
and IV. 11.

³ This is strongly emphasised by John (II. 12, IV. 4); but he has carefully
avoided stating how God could on his part adorn men with virtues. It cannot be
proved that this is to be attributed to the influence of the West. Such an assumption is not necessary, for we also find in the older Greek Fathers rhetorical
glorifications of the primitive state which do not harmonise with the system of
doctrine.

⁴ These are the two states (katastaseis) of the Antiochenes.

consisting in participation in the divine glory, not in a transformation into the divine essence.

Actually, *i.e.*, according to the logical development of the
system, the innocence of primitive man consisted in his power
to be innocent, and, with the support of divine grace, to abide
by and advance in goodness. A necessary converse of this was
the power to revolt; "for it is no virtue which is done under compulsion". Man, "that little world", retained, however, along with
his spiritual attributes, those of irrational nature; even in his soul
there was an irrational part, which was partly capable of sub-
mitting to the rational, but was partly independent of it (the
vital functions). The former embraced the desires, some of which
were within limits permitted, while the others were not. But,
the vital functions apart, over all was placed free will. It is in
our power to choose, and man decides on his own actions.
His origin alone is God's affair. "But error was produced by
our wickedness for our punishment and benefit For God did
not make death, nor did he delight in the ruin of the living; on
the contrary, death was due to man, *i.e.*, to Adam's transgression, and so also were the other penalties."[1] It was not right
to attribute everything to divine providence; "for that which
is in our power is not the affair of providence, but of our own
free will." God, certainly, in virtue of his omniscience, knows
everything from all eternity; he therefore assists by his grace
those who, he knows, will avail themselves of it. They alone
are also predestinated; their decision to be and do good is
known to God. Those are damned to whom all the supports
of grace are in vain.[2] With all this it remains true that all
virtue comes from God; for by him it was implanted in nature,
and by his support alone it is maintained. Accordingly, we
have once more the principle that nature, rational and free, is
a gift of grace; to be natural is to be virtuous, and conversion
is the return from the unnatural.[3]

---

[1] The significance of Adam's fall for his posterity is recognised (II. 28), but it
is noteworthy, only cursorily. John has no separate chapter on the Fall in his
great work. Even II. 30, only discusses it under a more general heading.

[2] See, l. c., II. 29, 30; IV. 22.

[3] II. 30.

Man was created male. Woman was formed merely because God foresaw the Fall, and in order that the race might be preserved in spite of death. [1] Man did not allow reason to triumph; he mistook the path of honour, and preferred his lusts. Consequently, instead of living for ever, he fell a prey to death and became subject to tribulation and a miserable life. For it was not good that he should enjoy immortality untempted and unproved, lest he should share the pride and condemnation of the devil. "Accordingly, man was first to attest himself, and, made perfect by observance of the commandment when tempted, was then to obtain immortality as the reward of virtue. For, placed between God and matter, he was to acquire steadfastness in goodness, after he had abandoned his natural relation to things, and become habitually united to God." But, seduced by the devil who enviously grudged man the possession which he had himself lost, man turned to matter, and so, severed from God, his First Cause, became subject to suffering, and mortal, and required sexual intercourse. (The fig-leaves denote the tribulations of life, and the skins the mortal body). Death, come into the world through sin, henceforth, like a hideous wild beast, made havoc of human life, although the liberty to choose good as well as evil was never destroyed. [2] But God did not leave himself without a witness, and at last sent his own Son, who was to strengthen nature, and to renew and show and teach by his action the way of virtue which led from destruction to eternal life. The union of Deity with humanity was "the newest of the new, the only new thing under the sun." [3] It applied, moreover, to the whole of human nature in order to bestow salvation on the whole. [4]. This union resulted in the *restitutio* to the original state, which was perfect in so far as man, though not yet tested, was adorned with virtues. Christ participated in the worst part of our nature in order, by and in himself, to restore the form of the image and likeness, and to teach us further by virtuous conduct, which by his aid

---

[1] L. c., see Gregory of Nyssa.

[2] II. 26 ff.

[3] III. 1.

[4] III. 6.

he made light for us. Then he overcame death, becoming the
first-fruits of our resurrection, and renewing the worn-out and
cast-off vessel. [1]

It has been pointed out above (p. 240) that natural theology
underwent no development in the Greek Church. We must
premise, however, that the course of the history of philosophy
is of greater moment for the development of the system, or
for systematic monographs. Without anticipating we may here
make the following remark. The Fathers of orthodox *dogma*
in the fourth and fifth centuries were Platonists. Aristotelianism
always led in this period to a heterodox form of dogma—
Lucian, the Arians, the Antiochenes, etc. But a theological
system constructed by the aid of Platonism could not fail at
that time to become equally heterodox. After Platonism had
done its work on dogma, and certain notions and conceptions
were generally fixed, an orthodox system could only be created
by means of Aristotelianism. Any further use of Platonism led
to questionable propositions.

[1] IV. 4, II. 12.

B.—*THE DOCTRINE OF REDEMPTION IN THE PERSON OF THE GOD-MAN IN ITS HISTORICAL DEVELOPMENT.*

CHAPTER VI.

THE DOCTRINE OF THE NECESSITY AND REALITY OF REDEMPTION THROUGH THE INCARNATION OF THE SON OF GOD.

NATURAL theology was so wide in its scope as understood by the Greek Church, that, as indications in the preceding chapter will have already shown, only a historical fact absolutely unparallelled could make headway against it. The Greek Fathers knew of such a fact—"the newest of the new, yea, the only new thing under the sun"; it was the Incarnation of the Son of God. It alone balanced the whole system of natural theology, so far as it was balanced, and exerted a decisive influence upon it. But the incarnation could only be attached with complete perspicuity to that point in the natural system which seemed the more irrational, the more highly the value of human nature was rated—this point of contact being death. The dreadful paradox of death was destroyed by the most paradoxical fact conceivable, the incarnation of the Deity.

This at once implied that the fact could not but be capable of a *subsequent* explanation, nay, even of a kind of *a priori* deduction. But its glory, as an expression of the unfathomable goodness of God, was not thereby to be diminished. The necessity of redemption, whether that consisted in the restoration or the perfection of the human race, was based by the Fathers, as a rule, on the actual state of wretchedness of mankind under the dominion of death and sin. So far, however, as this condition was compared with the original state or destiny of man, redemption was already thought of as intrinsically necessary,

and was no longer merely regarded as a postulate of man's
need of salvation. In this connection the Fathers often lost
sight of the capacity left to man of being and doing good.
In innumerable passages they speak of the helplessness and
irredeemableness of mankind, using expressions which could
without difficulty be inserted in Augustine's doctrine of sin.
But just as often a phrase occurs which betrays the fact that
the whole view is nevertheless quite different; in other words,
that the outward condition characterised by feebleness and
death, and the sensuousness of corruptible human nature are
thought of as the source of all evil and all sin. This state is
accompanied by a darkening of knowledge which could not
fail to subject man to the influence of the demons and lead
him into idolatry.

The divine act of grace in Christ applied to death, the
demonic rule, sin, and error. In Homilies, Biblical commentaries, and devotional writings, these points of view interchange,
or are apparently regarded as equivalent. [1] But since natural
theology formed the background of their conceptions, the
absolute necessity of the form assumed by the act of grace in
the incarnation could be demonstrated neither in relation to
sin nor to error. The whole question turned here on support,
example, and illumination, or, if this line was crossed, theology
ceased to be systematic and consistent. The importance of
Athanasius and the Cappadocians consisted in the strenuous
emphasis laid by them on the impressive connection existing
between the incarnation and the restoration of the human race

---

[1] Perhaps the most comprehensive passage is Eusebius, Demonstr. ev. IV. 12.
But it also shows how far Eusebius still was from the thorough-going view of
Athanasius: Τῆς οἰκονομίας οὐ μίαν αἰτίαν ἀλλὰ καὶ πλείους εὕροι ἄν τις ἐθελήσας
ζητεῖν, πρώτην μὲν γὰρ ὁ λόγος διδάσκει, ἵνα καὶ νεκρῶν καὶ ζώντων κυριεύσῃ· δευτέραν δὲ ὅπως τὰς ἡμετέρας ἀπομάξοιτο ἁμαρτίας, ὑπὲρ ἡμῶν τρωθεὶς καὶ γενόμενος
ὑπὲρ ἡμῶν κατάρα· τρίτην ὡς ἂν ἱερεῖον Θεοῦ καὶ μεγάλη θυσία ὑπὲρ σύμπαντος
κόσμου προσαχθείη τῷ ἐπὶ πάντων Θεῷ· τετάρτην ὡς ἂν αὐτὸς τῆς πολυπλανοῦς καὶ
δαιμονικῆς ἐνεργείας ἀπορρήτοις λόγοις καθαίρεσιν ἀπεργάσαιτο· πέμπτην ἐπὶ ταύτῃ,
ὡς ἂν τοῖς αὐτοῦ γνωρίμοις καὶ μαθηταῖς τῆς κατὰ τὸν θάνατον παρὰ Θεῷ ζωῆς τὴν
ἐλπίδα μὴ λόγοις μηδὲ ῥήμασιν καὶ φωναῖς ἀλλὰ αὐτοῖς ἔργοις παραστήσας, ὀφθαλ-
μοῖς δὲ παραδοὺς τὴν διὰ τῶν λόγων ἐπαγγελίαν, εὐθαρσεῖς αὐτοὺς καὶ προθυμοτέρους
ἀπεργάσαιτο καὶ πᾶσιν Ἕλλησιν ὁμοῦ καὶ βαρβάροις τὴν πρὸς αὐτοῦ καταβληθεῖσαν
εὐσεβῆ πολιτείαν κηρύξαι.

to the divine life, and in their consequent escape to some extent
from the rationalistic scheme of doctrine; for the reference of
the incarnation to sin did not carry the Greeks beyond it.
The above combination had been made in the Church long
before this (see Irenæus), but in the theology of Origen it had
been subordinated to, and obscured by, complicated presuppositions.

Athanasius wrote a treatise "Concerning the incarnation of
the Logos" (περὶ ἐνανθρωπήσεως τοῦ λόγου), an early writing whose
value is so great because it dates before the outbreak of the
Arian controversy.[1] In this work he went a step further: for
he strove to prove that the redemption was a necessity on the
part of God. He based this necessity on the goodness (ἀγαθότης)
of God. This goodness, i.e., God's consistency and honour,
involved as they were in his goodness, were necessarily expressed in the maintenance and execution of decrees once formed
by him. His decrees, however, consisted, on the one hand, in
his appointment of rational creatures to share in the divine
life, and, on the other, in the sentence of death on transgressions. Both of these had to be established. God's intention
could not be allowed to suffer shipwreck through the wickedness of the devil and the sad choice of humanity. If it were,
God would seem weak, and it would have been better if he
had never created man at all. Then the transgression occurred.
"What was God now to do? Ought he to have demanded
penitence on the part of man? For one could have deemed
that worthy of God and said, that as men had become mortal
through the transgression, they should in like manner recover
immortality through repentance (change of mind). But repentance (in itself) did not retain the true knowledge as regards
God; God accordingly would in his turn have shown himself

---

[1] Draescke has attempted to show in a full discussion (Athanasiana i. d. Stud.
u. Krit., 1893, pp. 251—315 that the writings "Against the Greeks" and the "Incarnation of the Logos" belong, not to Athanasius, but to Eusebius of Emesa, and
were written A.D. 350. But after a close examination of his numerous arguments
I find none of them convincing, and I am rather confirmed in my belief
that no important objection can be raised against the authenticity of the two
tractates. An accurate analysis of "De incarn." is given by Kattenbusch, l. c. I.,
p. 297 ff.

untruthful, if death had not compelled men ; [1] *nor did repentance deliver from the physical, but only put an end to sins. Therefore, if the transgression had alone existed, and not its consequence, mortality, repentance would have been all very well.* But when, the transgression having occurred, men were fettered to the mortality that had become natural to them, and were robbed of the grace which corresponded to their creation in the divine image, what else should have happened? Or what was needed for this grace and renewal except (the coming of) him who also in the beginning made all things of nothing, the Logos of God? For it was his part once more to restore the corruptible to incorruption." [2]

Athanasius shows that the Logos who originally created all things from nothing required to assume a body and thus to secure the restoration of man from corruptibility to incorruption (ἀφθαρσία). How this happened Athanasius discusses in various, to some extent inconsistent, lines of thought, in which he speaks especially of a removal of men's guilt through the death of Christ, as well as of an exhaustion of the sentence of death in the sacrifice of his body presented by the Logos. From these premises it follows that Athanasius had the death of Christ in view, whenever he thought of the incarnation of the Logos. "The Logos could not suffer τὴν τοῦ θανάτου κράτησιν ('the power of death' in mankind), and therefore took up the

---

[1] This sentence does not seem to me quite clear; the meaning is probably: since repentance does not convey the true knowledge of God, but death resulted from loss of the latter, God would have broken his word if he had abolished death in consequence of mere repentance.

[2] De incarn. 7: Τί οὖν ἔδει καὶ περὶ τούτου γενέσθαι ἢ ποιῆσαι τὸν Θεόν; μετάνοιαν ἐπὶ τῇ παραβάσει τοὺς ἀνθρώπους ἀπαιτῆσαι; τοῦτο γὰρ ἄν τις ἄξιον φήσειεν Θεοῦ, λέγων, ὅτι ὥσπερ ἐκ τῆς παραβάσεως εἰς φθορὰν γεγόνασιν, οὕτως ἐκ τῆς μετανοίας γένοιντο πάλιν ἂν εἰς ἀφθαρσίαν. Ἀλλ' ἡ μετάνοια οὔτε τὸ εὔλογον τὸ πρὸς τὸν Θεὸν ἐφύλαττεν· ἔμενε γὰρ πάλιν οὐκ ἀληθής, μὴ κρατουμένων ἐν τῷ θανάτῳ τῶν ἀνθρώπων· οὔτε δὲ ἡ μετάνοια ἀπὸ τῶν κατὰ φύσιν ἀποκαλεῖται, ἀλλὰ μόνον παύει τῶν ἁμαρτημάτων. Εἰ μὲν οὖν μόνον ἦν πλημμέλημα καὶ μὴ φθορᾶς ἐπακολούθησις, καλῶς ἂν ἦν ἡ μετάνοια· εἰ δὲ ἅπαξ προλαβούσης τῆς παραβάσεως, εἰς τὴν κατὰ φύσιν φθορὰν ἐκρατοῦντο οἱ ἄνθρωποι, καὶ τὴν τοῦ κατ' εἰκόνα χάριν ἀφαιρεθέντες ἦσαν, τί ἄλλο ἔδει γενέσθαι; ἢ τίνος ἦν χρεία πρὸς τὴν τοιαύτην χάριν καὶ ἀνάκλησιν, ἢ τοῦ καὶ κατὰ τὴν ἀρχὴν ἐκ τοῦ μὴ ὄντος πεποιηκότος τὰ ὅλα τοῦ Θεοῦ λόγου; αὐτοῦ γὰρ ἦν πάλιν καὶ τὸ φθαρτὸν εἰς ἀφθαρσίαν ἐνεγκεῖν καὶ τὸ ὑπὲρ πάντων εὔλογον ἀποσῶσαι πρὸς τὸν πατέρα. Compare Orat. c. Arian. II. 68.

fight with death. He assumed a body and so became mortal.
This body he surrendered to death on behalf of all. His body
could not be really overcome, 'kept', by death. In it all
died, and for this very reason the law of death (νόμος τοῦ
Θανάτου) is now abrogated; its power was exhausted on the
body of the Lord (κυριακὸν σῶμα); it had no further claim on
his fellow-men (κατὰ τῶν ὁμοίων ἀνθρώπων) ... The body assumed
by the Logos came to share in the universal meaning of the
Logos. The resurrection of the body and of the Logos guaranteed
the general resurrection and incorruption (ἀφθαρσία)." [1] Here
follows the place assigned to the sacrifice. It presented that
which was due (ὀφειλόμενον) to God in place of death. But
the pervading and prominent thought of Athanasius is that the
incarnation itself involved the Christian's passage from the fate of
death to incorruption (ἀφθαρσία), since the physical union of the
human with the divine nature in the midst of mankind raised the
latter to the region of divine rest and blessedness. [2] The result
of the incarnation consisted accordingly, first, in the eradication
of corruption (φθορά)—by the existence of the divine in its
midst, but, finally, by the death of Christ, in which the truth-
fulness of God was justified—and in the corresponding transformation into incorruptibility—renewal, or completion of the
divine image by participation in the nature, free from all suffering, of the Deity. [3] But, secondly, the incarnation also resulted,

---

[1] Kattenbusch, p. 298.

[2] L. c., ch. IX.: "Ὥσπερ μεγάλου βασιλέως εἰσελθόντος εἴς τινα πόλιν μεγάλην,
καί οἰκήσαντος εἰς μίαν τῶν ἐν αὐτῇ οἰκιῶν, πάντως ἡ τοιαύτη πόλις τιμῆς πολλῆς
καταξιοῦται, καὶ οὐκέτι τις ἐχθρὸς αὐτὴν οὔτε λῃστὴς ἐπιβαίνων καταστρέφει, πάσης
δὲ μᾶλλον ἐπιμελείας ἀξιοῦται διὰ τὸν εἰς μίαν αὐτῆς οἰκίαν οἰκήσαντα βασιλέα·
οὕτως καὶ ἐπὶ τοῦ πάντων βασιλέως γέγονεν. Ἐλθόντος γὰρ αὐτοῦ ἐπὶ τὴν ἡμετέραν
χώραν καὶ οἰκήσαντος εἰς ἓν τῶν ὁμοίων σῶμα, λοιπὸν πᾶσα ἡ κατὰ τῶν ἀνθρώπων
παρὰ τῶν ἐχθρῶν ἐπιβουλὴ πέπαυται, καὶ ἡ τοῦ θανάτου ἠφάνισται φθορὰ ἡ πάλαι
κατ᾽ αὐτῶν ἰσχύουσα. Kattenbusch is right in considering Ritschl (l. c., I., p. 10,
11) to have gone too far in his assertion that "Athanasius' interpretation of the
death and resurrection of Christ is a particular instance of the main thought that
the Logos of God guarantees all redemptive work, using the human body in which
he dwells as the means." Athanasius certainly did not regard the death and resurrection as merely particular instances. They formed the object of the incarnation;
not that they were added or supplementary to it; they were bound up with it.

[3] Yet the view of Athanasius was not simply naturalistic; incorruptibleness
rather included the elements of goodness, love, and wisdom; a renewal affecting

as indeed had been long before held by the Apologists, in the restoration of the correct knowledge of God, which embraced the power of living rightly, through the incarnate Logos. But while Athanasius kept firmly in view this restoration of the knowledge of God through the Logos, he was not thinking merely of the new law, *i.e.*, the preaching of Christ; he held it to have been given in the contemplation of the Person of Christ. In his work, that of a man, God came down to us. The dullest eye was now in a position to perceive the one true God—viz., in Christ—and to escape from the error of demon-worship. This thought is very significant; it had already been expressed by Clement and Origen, having received a deeper meaning from the latter, though he had not yet given it so central a place in his system. Athanasius expressly notes that creation was not sufficient to let us perceive the Creator and Father; we needed a man to live and work among us before we could see clearly and certainly the God and Father of all. [1]

the inner nature of man was also involved. But it was not possible for Athanasius to expound this systematically; therefore Schultz seems to me to have asserted too much (Gottheit Christi, p. 80).

[1] The chief passages occur l. c., XIV—XVI., chap. XIV. *fin*: One might suppose that the fitting way to know God was to recover our knowledge of him from the works of creation. It is not so, for men are no longer capable of directing their gaze upward; they look down. "Therefore, when he seeks to benefit men, he takes up his dwelling among us as man, and assumes a body like the human one, and instructs men within their own lower sphere, *i.e.*, through the works of the body, that those who would not perceive him from his care for all and his rule might at least from the works of the body itself know the Logos of God in the body, and through him the Father." C. 15: Ἐπειδὴ οἱ ἄνθρωποι ἀποστραφέντες τὴν πρὸς τὸν Θεὸν θεωρίαν, καὶ ὡς ἐν βύθῳ βυθισθέντες κάτω τοὺς ὀφθαλμοὺς ἔχοντες, ἐν γενέσει καὶ τοῖς αἰσθητοῖς τὸν Θεὸν ἀνεζήτουν, ἀνθρώπους θνητοὺς καὶ δαίμονας ἑαυτοῖς θεοὺς ἀνατυπούμενοι· τούτου ἕνεκα ὁ φιλάνθρωπος καὶ κοινὸς πάντων σωτήρ, ὁ τοῦ Θεοῦ λόγος, λαμβάνει ἑαυτῷ σῶμα καὶ ὡς ἄνθρωπος ἐν ἀνθρώποις ἀναστέφεται καὶ τὰς αἰσθήσεις πάντων ἀνθρώπων προσλαμβάνει, ἵνα οἱ ἐν σωματικοῖς νοοῦντες εἶναι τὸν Θεόν, αφ' ὧν ὁ κύριος ἐργάζεται διὰ τῶν τοῦ σώματος ἔργων, ἀπ' αὐτῶν νοήσωσι τὴν ἀλήθειαν, καὶ δι' αὐτοῦ τὸν πατέρα λογίσωνται. The sequel shows, indeed, that Athanasius thought above all of Jesus' miraculous works. He has summarised his whole conception of the result of redemption in the pregnant sentence (ch. XVI.): Ἀμφότερα γὰρ ἐφιλανθρωπεύετο ὁ σωτὴρ διὰ τῆς ἐνανθρωπήσεως, ὅτι καὶ τὸν θάνατον ἐξ ἡμῶν ἠφάνιζε καὶ ἀνεκαίνιζεν ἡμᾶς· καὶ ὅτι ἀφανὴς ὢν καὶ ἀόρατος διὰ τῶν ἔργων ἐνέφαινε καὶ ἐγνώριζεν ἑαυτὸν εἶναι τὸν λόγον τοῦ πατρός, τὸν τοῦ παντὸς ἡγεμόνα καὶ βασιλέα. Origen had already laid stress on the perception of God in Christ, and set it above philosophical knowledge (analytic, synthetic, and analogical, against

When Athanasius placed the knowledge of God side by side
with the deliverance from death, the transition was obtained
from the fact of redemption to the doctrine of the appropriation,
and to the explanation of the particular result, of the work of
love done by the Logos. This only benefited those who
voluntarily appropriated the divine knowledge made accessible
by the incarnate Logos, and who regulated their conduct by
the standards and with the power thus given them.[1] In any
case the transformation of the corruptible into the incorruptible
(the Theopoiesis) remained under this conception the ultimate
and proper result of the work of the Logos, being ranked
higher than the other, the knowledge of God.[2] But here we
find the greatest difference between Athanasius and like-minded
theologians on the one hand, and Arius, the Eusebians, etc.,
on the other. The elements contained in their views are the
same; but the order is different. For these "conservative"
theologians saw the work of the Logos primarily in the communication of the true and complete knowledge which should
be followed by a state of perfection. But Athanasius made every-

---

Alcinous, Maximus of Tyre, and Celsus): see c. Cels. VII. 42, 44; De princip. I. 1.
For Clement see Protrept. I. 8: ὁ λόγος ὁ τοῦ Θεοῦ ἄνθρωπος γενόμενος, ἵνα δὴ καὶ
σὺ παρὰ ἀνθρώπου μάθῃς, πῇ ποτὲ ἄρα ἄνθρωπος γένηται Θεός.

[1] Parallel with this view and intertwined with it we undoubtedly have the other,
that eternal life is mystically appropriated by means of sacred rites and the holy
food. In this conception, which is extremely ancient, Christianity seems degraded
to the level of the nature-religions of the East or the Græco-oriental mysteries
(see Schultz, Gottheit Christi, p. 69). But as even the earliest Alexandrians (also
Ignatius) constantly resolved the naturalistic view into a spiritual and moral one,
so also hardly any one of the theologians of the following centuries can be named
who would have purely and simply defended the former.

[2] See esp. Orat. c. Arian. II. 67—70, where the final designs of Athanasius'
Christianity are revealed. It is at the same time to be noted that while redemption
meant restoration, it was the transference into a still higher grace. We experience
all that was done to the body of Christ. We are baptised, as Christ was in Jordan,
we next received the Holy Spirit, and so also our flesh has died, and been renewed,
sanctified and raised to eternal life in his resurrection. Accordingly, Athanasius
sums up at the close of his work, ch. 54: Αὐτὸς γὰρ ἐνηνθρώπησεν, ἵνα ἡμεῖς θεο-
ποιηθῶμεν· καὶ αὐτὸς ἐφανέρωσεν ἑαυτὸν διὰ σώματος, ἵνα ἡμεῖς τοῦ ἀοράτου πατρὸς
ἔννοιαν λάβωμεν· καὶ αὐτὸς ὑπέμεινε τὴν παρ᾽ ἀνθρώπων ὕβριν, ἵνα ἡμεῖς ἀθανασίαν
κληρονομήσωμεν. ἐβλάπτετο μὲν γὰρ αὐτὸς οὐδέν, ἀπαθὴς καὶ ἄφθαρτος καὶ αὐτολόγος
ὢν καὶ Θεός· τοὺς δὲ πάσχοντας ἀνθρώπους, δι᾽ οὓς καὶ ταῦτα ὑπέμεινεν, ἐν τῇ ἑαυτοῦ
ἀπαθείᾳ ἐτήρει καὶ διέσωζε.

thing tend to this consummation as the restoration and the communication of the divine nature. Accordingly, it was to him a vital theological question how the incorruptible was constituted which was represented in the Logos, and what kind of union it had formed with the corruptible. But while he put the question he was sure of the answer. His opponents, however, could not at all share in his interest in this point, since their interest in Christ as the supreme teacher did not lead them directly to define more precisely the kind of heavenly manifestation which he represented even for them. When they did give such definitions, they were influenced by theoretical, or exegetical considerations, or were engaged in refuting the propositions of their opponents by setting up others.

The Trinitarian and Christological problems which had occupied the ancient Church for more than three centuries here rise before us. That their decision was so long delayed, and only slowly found a more general acceptance, was not merely due to outward circumstances, such as the absence of a clearly marked tradition, the letter of the Bible, or the politics of Bishops and Emperors. It was, on the contrary, owing chiefly to the fact that large circles in the Church felt the need of subordinating even the doctrine of redemption to rational theology, or of keeping it within the framework of moralism. The opposite conviction, that nature was transformed through the incarnate Logos, resulted here and there in a chaotic pantheism;[1] but that was the least danger. The gravest hindrance to the acceptance of the view of Athanasius consisted in the paradoxical tenets which arose regarding the Deity and Jesus Christ. Here his opponents found their strength; they were more strongly supported by the letter of Scripture and tradition, as well as by reason.

Supplement I.—No subsequent Greek theologian answered the question, why God became man, so decidedly and clearly as Athanasius. But all Fathers of unimpeached orthodoxy followed in his footsteps, and at the same time showed that his doctrinal

---

[1] Not in Athanasius himself—Kattenbusch says rightly (p. 299): The θεοποίησις is for A. an enhancement of human life physically and morally; his idea of it does not look forward to man being pantheistically merged in God, but to the renewal of man after his original type.

ideas could only be held on the basis of Platonism. This is at
once clear in the case of Gregory of Nyssa, who in some points
strengthened the expositions given by Athanasius.   Yet his
model was Methodius rather than Athanasius. [1]

Gregory sought, in the first place, to give a more elaborate
defence of the method of redemption—by means of the incarnation,—but in doing so he obscured Athanasius' simple combination of the incarnation and its effect.   According to Gregory,
God is boundless might, but his might was never divorced
from goodness, wisdom, and righteousness.   He next shows in
detail (Catech. magn. 17—26) against Jews and heathens — as
Anselm did afterwards — that the incarnation was the *best* form
of redemption, because the above four fundamental attributes
of God came clearly to light in it.   Especially interesting in
these arguments is the emphasis laid on God's treatment of
those who had passed over to his enemies, his respect for their
freedom in everything, and his redemption of men without
wronging the devil, their master, who possessed a certain claim
upon them.   This account of the matter indeed had strictly an
apologetic purpose. [2] In the second place, Gregory, while following Athanasius, still more strongly identified the state from
which God has delivered us with death.   The state of sin was
death.   He taught, with the Neoplatonists, that God alone was
Being.   Therefore all revolt from God to the sensuous, *i.e.*, to
not-being, was death.   Natural death was not the only death;
it might rather mean deliverance from the bonds of the body
become brutal (l. c., ch. 8).   Sensuousness was death.   In the
third place, although he also saw the redemption in the act of
incarnation, Gregory held that it was not perfected until the
resurrection of Jesus.   That is, he was more thoroughly influenced than Athanasius by the conviction that the actual redemption presupposed renunciation of the body.   We are first

---

[1] See Vol. III., p. 104 ff.

[2] The Apologetic argument also includes the treatment of the question, why the
redemption was not accomplished sooner. Apologists from Justin to Eusebius and
Athanasius had put it and attempted to answer it.   Gregory also got rid of it by
referring to the physician who waits till illness has fully developed before he
interferes (Catech. magn., ch. 29 ff.).

redeemed, when we share in the resurrection which the human
nature assumed by Christ experienced through the resurrection
(l. c., ch. 16). The mystery of the incarnation only becomes
clear in this resurrection. The Deity assumed human nature,
in order by this union to exhaust, until it had wholly disappeared, that which was liable to death in this nature, viz., evil.
This result was only perfected in the resurrection of the human
nature of Christ; for in it that nature was first shown completely
purified and rendered capable of being possessed of eternal life. [1]
In the fourth place, Gregory was able to demonstrate the application of the incarnation more definitely than Athanasius could
with his figure of the king and the city. But he does so by
the aid of a thoroughly Platonic idea which is only slightly
suggested in Athanasius, and is not really covered by a Biblical
reference (to the two Adams; see Irenæus). Christ did not
assume the human nature of an individual person, but human
nature. Accordingly, all that was human was intertwined with
the Deity; the whole of human nature became divine by intermixture with the Divine. Gregory conceives this as a strictly
physical process: the leaven of the Deity has pervaded the whole
dough of humanity, through and in Christ; for Christ united with
himself the whole of human nature with all its characteristics. [2]
This conception, which was based on the Platonic universal

---

[1] L. c., ch. 16. For, since our nature in its regular course changed also in him
into the separation of body and soul, he reunited that which had been divided by
his divine power as if by a kind of cement, and rejoined in an indissoluble union
the severed parts (comp. Irenæus and Methodius). And that was the resurrection,
viz., the return after dissolution and division of the allies to an indissoluble union,
both being so bound together, that man's original state of grace was recalled, and
we return to eternal life, after the evil mingled with our nature has been removed
by our dissolution (!); just as it happens with liquids, which, the vessel being
broken, escape and are lost, because there is nothing now to hold them. But as
death began in one man and from him passed to the whole of nature and the
human race, in the same way the beginning of the resurrection extended through
one man to the whole of humanity."

[2] See conclusion of the preceding note, and Herrmann, Gregorii Nyss. sententias
de salute adipis., p. 16 ff. Underlying all the arguments of the "Great Catechism"
we have the thought that the incarnation was an actus medicinalis which is to be
thought of as strictly natural, and that extends to all mankind. See Dorner (Entwick.-
Gesch. d. L. v. d. Person Christi, I., p. 958 f.), who, besides, regards Gregory's
whole conception as strictly ethical.

notion "humanity", differed from that of Origen; but it also led to the doctrine of Apokatastasis (universalism), which Gregory adopted. Meanwhile, in order to counterbalance this whole "mystical", *i.e.*, physical, conception, he emphasised the personal and spontaneous fulfilment of the law as a condition, in the same way as the later Antiochenes. The perfect fulfilment of the law was, however, according to Gregory, only possible to ascetics. [1]

In the fifth place, Gregory set the sacraments in the closest relation to the incarnation, recognising (l. c., ch. 33—40) Baptism and the Lord's Supper as the only means by which mortal man was renewed and became immortal. It undoubtedly appears superfluous to a rigorous thinker to require that something special should happen to the individual when all mankind has been deified in the humanity assumed by Christ. But the form given to his ideas by Gregory was in keeping with the thought of his time, when mysterious rites were held to portray and represent that which was inconceivable. Sixthly, and lastly, Gregory gave a turn to the thought of the incarnation in which justice was done to the boldest conception of Origen, and "the newest of the new" was subordinated to a cosmological and more general view. Origen had already, following the Gnostics, taught—in connection with Philipp. II. 10 and other texts—that the incarnation and sacrificial death of Christ had an importance that went beyond mankind. The work of Christ extended to wherever there were spiritual creatures; wherever there was alienation from God, there was restoration through Christ. He offered himself to the Father for angels and æons (see Valentine). To all orders of spiritual beings he appeared in their own shape. He restored harmony to the whole universe. Nay, Christ's blood was not only shed on earth at Jerusalem "for sin" (pro peccato); but also "for a gift on the high altar which is in the heavens" (pro munere in superno altari quod est in cœlis).[2] Gregory took up this thought. The reconciliation and restitution extend to all rational creation.[3] Christ came down to all spiritual crea-

---

[1] See Herrmann, l. c., p. 2 sq.

[2] Passages in Bigg, l. c., p. 212 f.

[3] See περὶ ψυχ. κ. ἀναστάσ., p. 66 sq., ed. Oehler. Orat. cat. 26.

tures, and adopted the forms in which they lived, in order to bring them into harmony with God: οὐ μόνον ἐν ἀνθρώποις ἄνθρω-πος γίνεται, ἀλλὰ κατὰ τὸ ἀκόλουθον πάντως καὶ ἐν ἀγγέλοις γινόμενος πρὸς τὴν ἐκείνων φύσιν ἑαυτὸν συγκατάγει. [1] This thought, far from enriching the work of the historical Christ, served only, as in the case of the Gnostics, to dissipate it. And, in fact, it was only as an apologist of Catholic Christianity that Gregory held closely to the historical personality of Christ. When he philosophised and took his own way, he said little or nothing of the Christ of history. [2] It is almost with him as with Origen. He also reveals a supreme view of the world, according to which that which alienates the Kosmos from God forms part of its plan as much as that which restores it to him, the Kosmos being, from its creation, full of God, and, because it *is*, existing in God. The incarnation is only a particular instance of the universal presence of the divine in crea-tion. Gregory contributed to transmit to posterity the pantheistic conception, which be himself never thought out abstractly, or apart from history. A real affinity existed between him and the pantheistic Monophysites, the Areopagite, and Scotus Erigena, and even modern "liberal" theology of the Hegelian shade may appeal to him. In the "Great Catechism" (ch. XXV.), which was meant to defend the historical act of the incarnation, he has an argument which is in this respect extremely signi-ficant. [3] "The assumption of our nature by the deity should, however, excite no well-founded surprise on the part of those who view things (τὰ ὄντα) with any breadth of mind, (not too

---

[1] Orat. in ascens. Christi in Migne T. XLVI., p. 693; on the other hand, Di-dymus (De trinit. II. 7, ed. Mingarelli, p. 200): ὁ Θεὸς λόγος οὐ διὰ τοὺς ἁμαρτή-σαντας ἀγγέλους ἄγγελος· ἀλλὰ διὰ τοὺς ἐν ἁμαρτίᾳ ἀνθρώπους ἄνθρωπος ἀτρέπτως, ἀσυγχύτως, ἀναμαρτήτως, ἀφράστως. Yet in other places he has expressed himself like Origen. The latter was attacked by Jerome and Theophilus on account of this doctrine. The Synod of Constantinople condemned it.

[2] Compare the whole dialogue with Macrina on the soul and the resurrection, where the historical Christ is quite overlooked.

[3] To Athanasius also it was not unknown; see De incarn. 41: τὸν κόσμον σῶμα λέγα φασὶν εἶναι οἱ τῶν Ἑλλήνων φιλόσοφοι καὶ ἀληθεύουσι λέγοντες. Ὁρῶμεν γὰρ αὐτὸν καὶ τὰ τούτου μέρη ταῖς αἰσθήσεσι ὑποπίπτοντα. Εἰ τοίνυν ἐν τῷ κόσμῳ σώματι ὄντι ὁ τοῦ Θεοῦ λόγος ἐστί, καὶ ἐν ὅλοις καὶ τοῖς κατὰ μέρος αὐτῶν πᾶσιν ἐπιβέβηκε. τί θαυμαστὸν ἢ τί ἄτοπον εἰ καὶ ἐν ἀνθρώπῳ φαμὲν αὐτὸν ἐπιβεβηκέναι κ.τ.λ., c. 42.

μικροψύχως). For who is so weak in mind as not to believe
when he looks at the universe that the divine is in everything,
pervading and embracing it, and dwelling in it? For everything depends on the existent, and it is impossible that there
should be anything not having its existence in that which is.
Now, if all is in it and it in all, why do they take offence at
the dispensation of the mystery taught by the incarnation of
God, of him who, we are convinced, is not even now outside
of mankind? For if the form of the divine presence is not now
the same, yet we are as much agreed that God is among us
to-day as that he was in the world then. Now he is united
with us as the one who embraces nature in his being, but then
he had united himself with our being, that our nature, snatched
from death, and delivered from the tyranny of the Adversary,
might become divine through intermixture with the divine. For
his return from death was for the mortal race the beginning
of return to eternal life." The pantheistic theory of redemption appeared in after times in two forms. In one of these the
work of the historical Christ was regarded as a particular
instance, or symbol, of the universal, purifying and sanctifying operations continuously carried out through sanctifying
media—the sacraments—by the Logos in combination with, as
in their turn on behalf of, the graded orders of supersensuous
creatures; this was the view of Dionysius the Areopagite. The
other form of the theory included in the very idea of the
incarnation the union of the Logos with those individual believing souls in whom he was well pleased. The latter conception
which was already prominent in Methodius is especially marked
in Macarius. In Homily IV. *e.g.*, (ch. 8, 9), his first words
lead us to expect an exposition of the one historical incarnation.
Instead of that we read: "Thus in his love the infinite, inscrut-
able God humbled himself and assumed the members of our bodily
nature ... and transformed in love and benevolence to men he
incorporates and unites himself with the holy and faithful souls
in whom he is well pleased, etc." In each a Christ is born. [1]

---

[1] A third form of the pantheistic conception of the incarnation can be perceived
in the thesis, that the humanity of Christ was heavenly; in other words, that the
Logos had always borne humanity in himself, so that his body was not of later

The thought that Christ assumed the general concept of humanity occurs, though mingled with distinctive ideas, in Hilary, who was dependent on Gregory.[1] We find it also in Basil,[2] Ephræm,[3] Apollinaris,[4] Cyril of Alexandria, etc. Throughout these writers the conception is clearly marked that in Christ our nature is sanctified and rendered divine, that what it has experienced benefits us, as a matter of course, in our

origin than his divinity. This Gnostic view, which, however, is not necessarily pantheistic, had supporters, e.g., in Corinth in the time of Athanasius, who himself opposed it. (Ep. ad Epictetum Corinth.: see Epiphan.. p. 77, c. Dimoeritas). They said that the body born of Mary was ὁμοούσιον τῇ τοῦ λόγου θεότητι, συναΐδιον αὐτῷ διὰ παντὸς γεγενῆσθαι, ἐπειδὴ ἐκ τῆς οὐσίας τῆς Σοφίας συνέστη. They taught, accordingly, that humanity itself sprang from the Logos; he had for the purpose of his manifestation formed for himself by metamorphosis a body capable of suffering. He had, therefore, on one side of his being given up his immutability, departed from his own nature (ἠλλάγη τῆς ἰδίας φύσεως) and transformed himself into a sensuous man. The point of interest here was the perfect unity of Christ. Those whom Hilary opposed (De trinit. X. 15 sq.) did not maintain the heavenly and eternal humanity of the Logos. On the other hand, this thesis occurs in Apollinaris, in whom, however, it is not to be explained pantheistically, although pantheistic inferences can hardly be averted. The heavenly humanity of Christ is also opposed by Basil in Ep. ad Sozopol. (65); it re-emerged in the circles of the most extreme Monophysites; but it was at the same time openly affirmed there by Stephen Bar Sudaili: "everything is of one nature with God"; "all nature is consubstantial with the divine essence" (Assem., Biblioth. II. 30, 291); see Dorner, l. c., II., p. 162 f., and Frothingham, Stephen Bar Sudaili (1886) who has printed, p. 28 sq., the letter of Xenaias which warns against the heresy "that assimilates the creation to God." Finally, a kind of subtilised form of this phenomenon is found in the old-catholic conception, that the Son of God came down to men immediately after the Fall, that he repeatedly dwelt among them, and thus accustomed himself to his future manifestation (see Irenæus' conception, Vol. II., p. 236). In the later Fathers, when they were not writing apologetically, this old conception does not, so far as I know, occur often, or, it is very strictly distinguished from the incarnation; see, e.g., Athan., Orat. III. 30.

[1] See, e.g., Hilary, Tract. in Ps. LI, ch. 16: "Ut et filius hominis esset filius dei, naturam in se universæ carnis assumpsit, per quam effectus vera vitis genus in se universæ propaginis tenet." Ps. LIV. ch. 9: "Universitatis nostræ caro est factus." Other passages are given in Dorner, Entw-Gesch. der Lehre v. d. Person Christi, I., p. 1067, and Ritschl, l. c., I. p. 15.

[2] Hom. 25, T. I., p. 504 sq. This exposition coincides completely with Gregory's thought.

[3] Dorner, l. c., p. 961.

Dorner, l. c., the κατὰ μέρος πίστις. See besides the passage given in Vol. II., p. 223, n. 1.

individual capacity, and that we in a very real way have risen
with Christ.

Even in the Antiochenes passages occur which are thus to be
interpreted—exegesis led them to this view; [1] but they exist, so
far as I know, even in Chrysostom, [2] and they are so phrased
in general as to show that according to them this suffering and
dying with Christ, as an independent fact, was not merely a
supplementary condition of the actual union with Christ, but
the only form in which it was accomplished. In them the
general concept of humanity does not occur; accordingly, the
humanity of Christ is conceived much more concretely. He is
really a fighting, striving man who reaches victory through
free-will. [3] As this man himself is united morally with the
deity, the moral element must never be left out of account in
our union with him. But in so far as the incarnation of Christ
produces a new state (Katastasis), one not included in the plan
of humanity, it undoubtedly results in our glorification, a state
not involved in the moral element *per se*.

When we come to John of Damascus we no longer find any
definitive conception of the incarnation. The clear intention
assigned to it by Athanasius has escaped him; even of the ideas
of Gregory of Nyssa only a part, and that the apologetic part,
are reproduced (De fide Orth. III. 1, 6). At this point also
the attempt to unite the Aristotelian tradition of the school of
Antioch with the Alexandrian only led to a combination of
fragments. Yet the sentence, "Christ did not come to this or
that one, but to our common nature", [4] never wholly became
a dead letter in the Greek Church. But everything taught in
that Church as to the incarnation is already to be found either
developed, or in germ, in Irenæus; not the simple exposition
of Athanasius, but a mixture of the thought of the historical

---

1 See Theodore on Rom. VI. 6: τῷ Χριστῷ, φησίν, ἐσταυρωμένῳ ὥσπερ ἅπασα
ἡμῶν ἡ ὑπὸ τὴν θνητότητα κειμένη φύσις συνεσταυρώθη, ἐπειδὴ καὶ πᾶσα αὐτῷ συναν
ἔστη, πάντων ἀνθρώπων αὐτῷ συμμετασχεῖν ἐλπιζόντων τῆς ἀναστάσεως· ὡς ἐντεῦθεν συναφανισθῆναι μὲν τὴν περὶ τὸ ἁμαρτάνειν ἡμῶν εὐκολίαν, διὰ τῆς ἐπὶ τὴν ἀθανασίαν τοῦ σώματος μεταστάσεως.

2 Förster, Chrysostomus, p. 126 ff.

3 See Kihn, Theodor., p. 180 ff.

4 Χριστὸς οὐ πρὸς ἕνα καὶ δεύτερον ἦλθεν, ἀλλὰ πρὸς τὴν κοινὴν φύσιν.

with that of the mystical redemption, is to be traced in the majority of the Fathers. It is the Christ in us, the cosmical Christ, as we already saw in Methodius.

Supplement II.—Those Fathers, and they were in the majority, who found the cause of the incarnation in the intention of God to rehabilitate the human race, knew of no necessity for the incarnation apart from the entrance of sin. While they almost all explained that what Christ conferred was more and greater than what man had lost, yet they did not use this idea in their speculations, and they attached as a rule no special significance to it. But even Irenæus had also looked at the incarnation as the final and supreme means of the divine economy by which God gradually brought the original creation, at first necessarily imperfect, to completion. [1] Where this idea occurred, it also involved the other, that Christ would have come even if there had been no sin. Accordingly, those Fathers who laid no special stress on sin, seeing it appeared to them to be more or less natural, and who conceived redemption rather as a perfecting than restitution, maintained the necessity of the incarnation even apart from sin: so Theodore of Mopsuestia, Pelagius and others. [2] The incarnation was regarded by them as forming the basis of the life in which man is raised above his nature and common virtue, that is, the ascetic and angelic life. Clement of Alex., starting from quite different premises, expressed the same thought. Abstinence from evil was the perfection that had been attained even by Greeks and Jews; on the other hand, the perfect Gnostic, only possible after the complete revelation of the Logos, found perfection in the ascetic life of intuition, a life resting on faith, hope, and love. [3] Therefore in order to institute this life, the complete revelation of the Logos was required; it was unnecessary to bring sin into the question. However, the proposition that Christ would have come even if Adam had not sinned was, so far as I know, bluntly asserted by no Greek theologian; the combination of Adam and Christ in the Bible stood in the way.

Supplement III.—On the ground of Biblical texts like Matt.

---

[1] See Vol. II., p. 272, 307; the thought is not wanting in Tertullian.
[2] See Dorner, l. c. II., p. 432 ff. Kihn, Theodor., p. 179 f.
[3] Strom. VI. 7, 60.

XXV. 24, Eph. I. 3—5, 11, II. Tim. I. 8—10, the Greeks have
also spoken (*e.g.*, Athan. c. Arian. II. 75—77) of an election
of believers in Christ before the foundation of the world, and
of the decree of redemption framed by God, with reference
already to sin, before the creation.   Athanasius even says that
our future eternal life in Christ is conditioned by the fact that
our life was founded on Christ even before time was.   But the
idea of predestination, like the thought that Christ is the head
of his Church, is confined to the lines of a Biblical doctrine,
which for that very reason is true. Neither the doctrine of the
work of Christ, nor of the appropriation of his work, is influenced
by those conceptions. As a rule, however, the idea of predestination takes the form that God having foreseen men's attainments
in virtue elected them.   This version is especially clear in the
school of Antioch, and even enters into their Christology; but
it is the opposite of what Paul meant.

APPENDIX TO CHAPTER VI.

THE IDEAS OF REDEMPTION FROM THE DEVIL, AND OF ATONE-MENT THROUGH THE WORK OF THE GOD-MAN.

§ 1. *Christ's Death as Ransom and Sacrifice.*

THE Greek Fathers did not go beyond, nor could they give a more consistent form to, the views on this subject already expounded by Irenæus and Origen.[1] The fact of the incarnation was so closely and exclusively connected, at least in the East, with the conception of the *result* of redemption, that everything else had to yield in importance to the latter. Of course at all times and in all directions the attempt was made, after the example of Irenæus and the indications of Holy Scripture, to insert the facts of Jesus' history in the work of redemption. This can be seen especially in Athanasius and the two Cyrils—"Whatever happened to his humanity has happened to us." Again, the death of Christ was frequently recalled when the forgiveness of sins was taken into account; but it is difficult here to draw the line between exegesis, rhetoric, and dogmatics. As a rule, we obtain the impression that theology could have dispensed with all the facts of Christ's life.[2] On the other hand, the death of Christ always appeared so tragic and wonderful an event, that men were compelled to attribute a special

[1] See Vol. II., pp. 286 ff., 365 ff.

[2] The two Cappadocians doubted, not without reserve, the necessity of Christ's death. G. of Nazianzus says that the divine Logos could also have redeemed us θελήματι μόνον, and G. of Nyssa (Orat. cat. 17) thought that the method of redemption was to be considered as arbitrary as the remedies of physicians. In other places, indeed, they expressed themselves differently, and Athanasius connected the death of Christ closely with the incarnation (see above).

saving value to it. But just as it was not represented in art
up to the fifth century, so the majority of the Greeks really
regarded it, along with Christ's whole passion, as a sacred mystery, and that not only in the intellectual sense. Here thought
yielded to emotion, and imposed silence on itself. Goethe said
towards the close of his life, "We draw a veil over the sufferings of Christ simply because we revere them so deeply; we
hold it to be reprehensible presumption to play and trifle with
and embellish those profound mysteries in which the divine
depths of suffering lie hidden, never to rest until even the
noblest seems mean and tasteless." That exactly represents the
Greek feeling. It also gives the key to the saying of Gregory
of Nazianzus (Orat. XXVII. 10) that the appreciation of the
sufferings of Christ was one of those points on which it was
possible to make a mistake with impunity (cf. Iren. I. 10). By
this he meant, not only that the specific result of the passion
was uncertain, but also that it was inexpressible. [1] It was reserved for the Middle Ages and our modern times to cast off
all modesty and reverence here.

Yet a few theologians and exegetes could not refrain from
speculating about the death of Christ, though they did not yet
use frivolous arithmetical sums. The death of Christ was, in
the first place, connected, following Rom. VIII. 3, with the
condemnation of sin—death—in the flesh ($\varkappa\alpha\tau\alpha\varkappa\rho\iota\nu\epsilon\iota\nu$ $\tau\dot\eta\nu$ $\dot\alpha\mu\alpha\rho$-
$\tau\iota\alpha\nu$ ($\tau\dot o\nu$ $\theta\dot\alpha\nu\alpha\tau o\nu$) $\dot\epsilon\nu$ $\tau\tilde\eta$ $\sigma\alpha\rho\varkappa\iota$). That constituted the strongest
connection of Ensarkosis (embodiment in the flesh), death, resur-
rection, and redemption, reached within the Greek Church. In
Christ's final agony *the Ensarkosis first came to some extent to
its end,* for by death the flesh was purified from sin and mortality, and was presented in Christ's resurrection pure, holy,
and incorruptible. This thought was worked out in various
ways by Athanasius, Gregory of Nyssa, and Cyril of Jerusalem,
as well as, especially, by Apollinaris. [2] But in later times the
conception of the complete hypostatic union forbade the vanquish-

---

[1] See the great importance laid already by Justin on the Cross, an importance
which it still has for the piety of the Greek Church.

[2] Apollinaris who was the strictest dogmatist of the fourth century, substantially
limited the significance of Christ's death, so far as I know, to this effect.

ing of corruption (Φθορά) and death being dated a moment later than the assumption of human nature. Therefore it was held that Christ had even at the incarnation destroyed corruption and death (the penalty of sin) from the flesh; but his death was wholly voluntary and *economic*.

In the second place Irenæus had already, in a connected argument, emphasised the necessity of tracing the incarnation of the Logos and his passion to the goodness and righteousness of God, and he further insisted that Christ had delivered us not from a state of infirmity, but from the power of the devil, redeeming those estranged from God, and unnaturally imprisoned, not by force, but with due regard to justice. Origen, however, was the first to explain the passion and death of Christ with logical precision under the points of view of *ransom* and *sacrifice*. With regard to the former he was the first to set up the theory that the devil had acquired a legal claim on men, and therefore to regard the death of Christ (or his soul) as a ransom paid to the devil. This Marcionite doctrine of price and barter was already supplemented by Origen with the assumption of an act of deceit on the part of God. It was, in spite of an energetic protest, taken up by his disciples, and afterwards carried out still more offensively. It occurs in Gregory of Nyssa who (Catech. 15—27), in dealing with the notion of God, treats it broadly and repulsively. We find it in Ambrose, who speaks of the *pia fraus*, in Augustine and Leo I. It assumes its worst form in Gregory I.: the humanity of Christ was the bait; the fish, the devil, snapped at it, and was left hanging on the invisible hook, Christ's divinity. It proves that the Fathers had gradually lost any fixed conception of the holiness and righteousness of God; but on the other hand, it expresses the belief that the devil's power will not first be broken by the future appearing of Christ, but has been already shattered by his death. In this sense it is the epitaph of the old dogmatics which turned on eschatology.[1] For the rest, Gregory of Nazi-

---

[1] Irenæus held that men were God's debtors, but in the power (unjustly) of the devil. Origen held a different view. The devil had a claim on men, and Christ paid him his soul as the price, but the devil could not keep it. The devil acted unjustly to Christ, he was not entitled to take possession of one who was sinless;

anzus [1] and John of Damascus felt scruples about admitting God
and the devil to have been partners in a legal transaction.

With reference to the sacrifice of Christ, Origen was of
epoch-making importance. On the one hand, he started from
Rom. III. 25 and similar texts, on the other, he was strongly
influenced by the Græco-oriental expiatory mysteries, and was
the first to introduce into the Church, following the precedent
set by the Gnostics, a theology of sacrifice or propitiation
based on the death of Christ. He thereby enriched, but at the
same time confused, Greek theology. He taught that all sins
required a holy and pure sacrifice in order to be atoned for,
in other words, to be forgiven by God ; this sacrifice was the
body of Christ, presented to the Father. This thought which,
as expounded, approximates to the idea of a vicarious suffering
of punishment, was adopted by Athanasius who combined it
with the other ideas that God's veracity required the threat of
death to be carried out, and that death accordingly was accepted
by Christ on behalf of all, and by him was destroyed. [2] The
idea that only the sacrificial death of God could vanquish death
which was decreed by him, and thus conciliate God, occurs also

see passages given in Münscher, p. 428 ff. Leo I, following Ambrose, gives the
deception theory in a crude form.

[1] See Ullman, Gregor, p. 318 f.

[2] De incarnat. 9: Συνιδὼν γὰρ ὁ λόγος, ὅτι ἄλλως οὐκ ἂν λυθείη τῶν ἀνθρώπων
ἡ φθορά, εἰ μὴ διὰ τοῦ πάντως ἀποθανεῖν, οὐχ οἷόν τε δὲ ἦν τὸν λόγον ἀποθανεῖν,
ἀθάνατον ὄντα καὶ τοῦ πατρὸς υἱόν, τούτου ἕνεκεν τό δυνάμενον ἀποθανεῖν ἑαυτῷ
λαμβάνει σῶμα, ἵνα τοῦτο τοῦ ἐπὶ πάντων λόγου μεταλαβόν, ἀντὶ πάντων ἱκανὸν
γένηται τῷ θανάτῳ καὶ διὰ τὸν ἐνοικήσαντα λόγον ἄφθαρτον διαμείνῃ, καὶ λοιπὸν ἀπὸ
πάντων ἡ φθορὰ παύσηται τῇ τῆς ἀναστάσεως χάριτι· ὅθεν ὡς ἱερεῖον καὶ θῦμα
παντός ἐλεύθερον σπίλου, ὃ αὐτὸς ἑαυτῷ ἔλαβε σῶμα προσάγων εἰς θάνατον, ἀπὸ
πάντων εὐθὺς τῶν ὁμοίων ἠφάνιζε τὸν θάνατον τῇ προσφορᾷ τοῦ καταλλήλου. We
see how the conceptions of the vicarious endurance of punishment, and of a sacrifice, meet here; indeed, generally speaking. it was difficult to keep them apart.
Athanasius throughout lays greater stress on the former; Origen, as a Hellenist,
on the latter; see Athan., l. c., 6—10, but esp. Ch. XX: ὠφείλετο πάντας
ἀποθανεῖν... ὑπὲρ πάντων τὴν θυσίαν ἀνέφερεν, ἀντὶ πάντων τὸν ἑαυτοῦ ναὸν εἰς
θάνατον παραδιδούς, ἵνα τοὺς μὲν πάντας ἀνυπευθύνους καὶ ἐλευθέρους τῆς ἀρχαίας
παραβάσεως ποιήσῃ... ὁ πάντων θάνατος ἐν τῷ κυριακῷ σώματι ἐπληροῦτο καὶ ὁ
θάνατος καὶ ἡ φθορὰ διὰ τὸν συνόντα λόγον ἐξηφανίζετο. θανάτου γὰρ ἦν χρεία, καὶ
θάνατον ὑπὲρ πάντων ἔδει γενέσθαι, ἵνα τὸ παρὰ πάντων ὀφειλόμενον γένηται; c.
Arian. I. 60, II. 7, 66 sq.

in other Greek Fathers of the fourth century.[1] Following the estimate formed of the infinite value of the final passion of the God-man,[2] we constantly find in them also traces, sometimes more, sometimes less, distinct, of the thought of substitution in connection with satisfaction; but it remains obscure,[3] nay, it is frequently again withdrawn. In other words, it was sometimes twisted, as already in Irenæus, into the idea of example pure and simple. Thus the Antiochene school especially, who held his death to have been a natural event, considered that Christ's final passion influenced our freely-formed resolutions, but this version is not entirely wanting in any Greek Father. Others, *e.g.*, Gregory of Nazianzus, explained that God did not demand the sacrifice—or ransom—but received it δι' οἰκονομίαν.[4] In this case, as much as in earlier times, δι' οἰκονομίαν meant "that the Scriptures might be fulfilled"; that is, it was tantamount to abandoning a direct explanation of the fact itself. In any case Cyril of Alexandria shows most clearly the vicarious idea of the passion and death of the God-man in connection with the whole Christological conception.[5] Eusebius'

---

[1] See esp. Cyril, Catech. XIII. 33, but also the Cappadocians; cf. Ullmann, l. c., p. 316 ff.

[2] Even Cyril of Jerusalem says, l. c.: οὐ τοσαύτη ἦν τῶν ἁμαρτωλῶν ἡ ἀνομία, ὅση τοῦ ὑπεραποθνήσκοντος ἡ δικαιοσύνη. οὐ τοσοῦτον ἡμάρτομεν, ὅσον ἐδικαιοπράγησεν ὁ τὴν ψυχὴν ὑπὲρ ἡμῶν τεθεικώς. Similarly Chrysostom in the Ep. ad Rom., Hom. 10, T. X., p. 121. But the idea is emotional, and not the starting-point of a philosophical theory. It is different with the Westerns.

[3] The expiation of our guilt is more infrequently thought of than the taking over of sin's punishment; that is, guilt is only indirectly referred to.

[4] See Ullmann, l. c., p. 319.

[5] The idea of sacrifice falls into the background, which was only to be expected in the case of this energetic spokesman of genuine Greek Christian theology. Substitution passed naturally into, or rather grew out of, the idea of mystical mediation. Because all human nature was purified and transfigured really and physically in Christ, he could, *regarded as an individual*, be conceived as substitute or ἀντίλυτρον; see Cyril on John I. 29 and Gal. III. 13 Meanwhile Cyril also says that Christ outweighed all in merit. For the rest, he does not venture to affirm that Christ became a curse, but explains that he endured what one burdened with a curse must suffer. Compare also the exposition in the Orat. de recta fide ad reginas Mansi IV., p. 809). The points of *voluntariness* and *substitution* were emphasised more strongly by orthodox theologians after Cyril, in order not to compromise the perfectly hypostatic deification—from the moment of the incarnation—of Christ's human nature

method of formulating the idea comes nearest Paul's, but it is only a paraphrase; [1] and the inability of theologians to recognise, expose and dispute the differences in their divergent conceptions is the strongest proof that they were not clearly aware of the bearing and weight of their own propositions.

§ 2. *Christ as man the Mediator.*

The West, which had a scheme of its own in Christology, (see below) also possessed characteristic features in its conception of the work of Christ. [2] Here, as in almost all departments of activity in the Latin Church, it was of the highest moment that Tertullian, the jurist, and Cyprian, the ecclesiastical ruler, were the first Latin theologians. Disinclined for philosophical and strictly religious speculation, and dominated by a prosaic but powerful moralism, the Latins were possessed from the first of an impulse to carry religion into the legal sphere. The sacred authorities, or the Symbol, were regarded as the "law" (*lex*) of God; divine service was the place where the censure of God was pronounced; the deity was thought of as judge. Father, Son, and Spirit were held to be *"personæ"* who possessed a common property *("substantia"* not *"natura").* Christ as the *"persona"* who controlled a two-fold "property," one inherited from his Father (his divinity) and one from his mother (his humanity). Christ required to be obedient to God, and—as Tertullian first said [3] and Cyprian repeated—had to satisfy God *(deo satisfacere).* [4] In this phrase everything was comprised: man—the Christian—was to give God that which he owed him, *i.e.*, he was to satisfy God's legal claims. After this came the "promereri deum", *i. e.*, rendering services to God, gaining God's favour by our merits. But in Tertullian

---

[1] Demonstr. X. 1: ὑπὲρ ἡμῶν κολασθεὶς καὶ τιμωρίαν ὑποσχών, ἣν αὐτὸς μὲν οὐκ ὤφειλεν, ἀλλ᾿ ἡμεῖς τοῦ πλήθους ἕνεκεν τῶν πεπλημμελημένων, ἡμῖν αἴτιος τῆς τῶν ἁμαρτημάτων ἀφέσεως κατέστη... τὴν ἡμῖν προστετιμημένην κατάραν ἐφ᾿ ἑαυτὸν ἑλκύσας, γενόμενος ὑπὲρ ἡμῶν κατάρα.

[2] See fuller details in next book. Here we only give a sketch. Comp. Wirth, Der verdienstbegriff bei Tertullian, 1892.

[3] See Vol. II., p. 294.

[4] This notion was afterwards one of the most common in the West.

and Cyprian "satisfacere deo" meant more precisely to atone for wrongs inflicted on God by acts of penitence, and to appease him *(placare deum, satisfacere deo per hostias*: Arnobius). Further *"promereri"* was applied above all to *bona opera,* works (fasting) and alms-giving (Cypr., De oper. et eleemos.). Even from the middle of the third century an ecclesiastical system was drawn out in the Latin West of works to be rendered to God (order of penance); [1] and this system gradually took in, like a net, all man's relations to God. It was throughout governed by the idea that the magnitude of transgressions and that of the works rendered to God, the penitential offerings, were to have a strictly legal relation, and, similarly, that what a man's merits entitled him to from God had a fixed and regulated value. It is not the case, as has been supposed, that this idea first arose in the Church in the Romano-German period, and is therefore to be described as a result of German criminal law. On the contrary, the idea of *satisfactiones* and *merita* already belonged in its entirety to the Roman age, and during it was strictly worked out. From the days of Tertullian and Cyprian the Latins were familiar with the notion that the Christian had to propitiate God, that cries of pain, sufferings, and deprivations were means, sacrificial means, of expiation, that God took strict account of the *quantity* of the atonement, and that, where there was no guilt to be blotted out, those very means were represented as *merits*. All those trivial definitions, which betray a low state of legal and moral views, and which one would gladly attribute to barbarous nations, had become the property of the Church before the incursion of the Germans; and Anselm's principle, "Every sin must be followed either by satisfaction or punishment",[2] can be already shown in Sulpicius Severus, [3] and corresponds to the thought of Cyprian and his successors. [4]

---

[1] It occurs already in Tertullian; but we do not yet perceive its full extent in the Church in his time; it has not even the full significance that it possesses in Cyprian.

[2] Necesse est ut omne peccatum satisfactio aut poena sequatur.

[3] See Sulp. Sev., Dial. II. 10: Fornicatio deputetur ad poenam, nisi satisfactione purgetur.

[4] For fuller details see a later Vol.

But Cyprian also applied the "*satisfacere deo*" to Christ himself. As in the Middle Ages the most questionable consequences of the theory and practice of penance reacted on the conception of Christ's work, so from the time of Cyprian the latter was influenced by the view taken of human acts of penitence. His suffering and death constituted a sacrifice presented by Christ to God in order to propitiate, him. This thought, started by Cyprian, was never afterwards lost sight of in the West. The angry God whom it was necessary to propitiate and of whom the Greeks knew so little, became more and more familiar in the West. Jewish and Pauline traditions here joined with those of Roman law. Hilary is especially clear in combining the sacrifice of Christ with the removal of guilt and of punishment. [1] This combination was repeated by Ambrose, [2] Augustine, and the great popes of antiquity; [3] least certainly, perhaps, by August-

---

[1] On Ps. LIII. 12: " passio suscepta voluntarie est, officio ipsa satisfactura pœnali"; Ch. 13: "maledictorum se obtulit morti, ut maledictionem legis solveret, hostiam se ipsum voluntarie offerendo." Along with this Hilary has the mystical realistic theory of the Greeks.

[2] A few passages are given in Förster, Ambrosius, pp. 136 ff., 297 f. The "*redimere a culpa*" is for Ambrose the decisive point. In his work De incarn. dom. he is never tired of answering the question as to the motive of the incarnation with the phrase: "*ut caro, quæ peccaverat, redimeretur,*" frequently adding "*a culpa.*" He also uses very often the word "*offerre*" (applied to the death of Christ). In Ps. XLVIII., exp. 17, we read: "quæ maior misericordia quam quod pro nostris flagitiis se præbuit immolandum, ut sanguine suo mundum levaret, cuius peccatum nullo alio modo potuisset aboleri." See Deutsch, Des Ambrosius Lehre von der Sünde und Sündentilgung, 1867.

[3] There are many striking passages in Leo I. in which death is described as an expiatory sacrifice which blots out guilt. See, further, Gregory I., Moral. XVII. 46: "delenda erat culpa, sed nisi per sacrificium deleri non poterat. Quærendum erat sacrificium, sed quale sacrificium poterat pro absolvendis hominibus inveniri? Neque etenim iustum fuit, ut pro rationali homine brutorum animalium victimæ cæderentur... Ergo requirendus erat homo... qui pro hominibus offerri debuisset, ut pro rationali creatura rationalis hostia mactaretur. Sed quid quod homo sine peccato inveniri non poterat, et oblata pro nobis hostia quando nos a peccato mundare potuisset, si ipsa hostia peccati contagio non careret? Ergo ut rationalis esset hostia, homo fuerat offerendus: ut vero a peccatis mundaret hominem, homo et sine peccato. Sed quis esset sine peccato homo, si ex peccati commixtione descenderet. Proinde venit propter nos in uterum virginis filius dei, ibi pro nobis factus est homo. Sumpta est ab illo natura, non culpa. Fecit pro nobis sacrificium, corpus suum exhibuit pro peccatoribus, victimam sine peccato, quæ et humanitate mori et iustitia mundare potuisset."

ine, who being a Neoplatonic philosopher and profound Christian
thinker, was also familiar with other and more productive points
of view. [1] The distinctive nature, however, of this Latin view
of the work of Christ, as the propitiation of an angry God by
a sacrificial death, was characteristically expressed in the firmly
established thought that Christ performed it as man, therefore,
by means, not of his divine, but of his human attributes.[2] The
Latins were shut up to this conclusion. Their views regarding
the work of Christ had been influenced by the works of
penance enjoined by the Church, and on the other hand, the
latter owed their value to the voluntary acceptance of suffering.
Again, "sacrifices" in general were something human—God
does not render, but receives sacrifices. Finally, mankind was
in God's debt. From all this it necessarily followed that Christ
in presenting himself as a sacrifice did so as *man*. But with this
conclusion the Latins severed themselves from the supreme and
final interests of Greek piety—for this rather required that the
deity should have assumed with human nature all the "*passiones*"
of the latter and made them its own. If the rigid Greek con-

---

[1] Whatever occurs in Ambrose is to be found also in Augustine; for the latter
has not, so far as I know, omitted to use a single thought of the former; he only
adds something new.

[2] See Ambrose, De fide III. 5: "Idem igitur sacerdos, idem et hostia, et sacer-
dotium tamen et sacrificium humanæ condicionis officium est. Nam et agnus ad
immolandum ductus est et sacerdos erat secundum ordinem Melchisedech." This
thought recalls Cyprian, although Ambrose has hardly taken it from him; Cypr.
Ep. LXIII. 14: "Christus Iesus dominus et deus noster ipse est summus sacerdos dei
patris et sacrificium patri se ipsum obtulit." The same idea is repeated in contents
and form, but rendered more profound, by Augustine (Confess. X. 68, 69, see
Ritschl, l. c., I., p. 38): "In quantum enim homo, in tantum mediator; in quantum
autem verbum, non medius, quia æqualis deo . . . pro nobis deo victor et victor et victima,
et ideo victor quia victima; pro nobis deo sacerdos et sacrificium; et ideo sacerdos
quia sacrificium;" see De civit. dei IX. 15: "Nec tamen ab hoc mediator est, quia
verbum, maxime quippe immortale et maxime beatum verbum ionge est a mor-
talibus miseris; sed mediator per quod homo." Accordingly, not only was that which
Christ presented in sacrifice human—Ambrose, De incarn. VI.: " ex nobis accepit
quod proprium offeret pro nobis . . . sacrificium de nostro obtulit"; but Christ as
priest and mediator was man. He had to represent man, and that again only a man
could do. Very pregnant is the sentence of Ambrose (in Luc. exp. IV. 7) "ut quia
solvi non queunt divina decreta, persona magis quam sententia mutaretur." That
is the genuine idea of substitution. Ambrose does not even shrink from saying
"quia peccata nostra suscepit, peccatum dictus est" (Expos. in Ps. CXIX., X. 14).

ception, which, indeed, in after times was full of gaps and inconsistencies, represented Christ's sufferings as a whole to be not voluntary, but the complete acceptance of the Ensarkosis (life in the flesh), yet God is always the subject. [1]   On the whole, therefore, the conception of sacrifice is really alien in the view of the Greeks to the strict theory of Christ's significance.   It found its way in through exegesis and the mysteries, and threatened the compactness of the dogmatic conception, according to which everything that Christ did was summed up in the *complete assumptio carnis* (assumption of the flesh). Nor was the alien view able to shake the fundamental conception that the God-Logos was the *subject* in all that pertained to Christ. Among the Latins, on the other hand, the idea of the atoning sacrifice *plus* substitution is genuine, and has no general theory

---

[1] The subtle distinction between East and West is accordingly to be defined as follows. Both held that the human nature of Christ suffered, for the divine was incapable of suffering; but the East taught that the deity suffered through the human nature which he had made his own, the West that the man suffered and presented his human nature as a sacrifice in death; the latter, however, obtained an infinite value, for the deity was associated with it. From this we have two consequences. First, the idea of substitution could take root on Greek ground only superficially, and in an indefinite form; for the dying *God*-man really represented no one, but rather received all really into the plenitude of his divinity; it was different in the West. Secondly, the method of computing the value of Christ's mortal agony could similarly find no footing in the East; for the deity was the subject of the transaction, and precluded all questioning and computing. The striking utterances of Orientals as to the supreme value of Christ's work are really therefore only rhetorical (see above). If, on the other hand, the means of atonement under discussion, and the substitution are human, the question, of course, arises what value these possess, or what value is lent them by the divinity that is behind this sacrifice and this priest. We must take the statements of the Latin Fathers more literally. Ambrose confesses "Felix ruina quæ reparatur in melius" and "Amplius nobis profuit culpa quam nocuit: in quo redemptio quidem nostra divinum munus invenit. Facta est mihi culpa mea merces redemptionis, per quam mihi Christus advenit . . . Fructuosior culpa quam innocentia; innocentia arrogantem me fecerat— and here indeed the paradox becomes nonsensical—culpa subjectum reddidit." (Numerous passages are given in Deutsch, l. c., see also Förster, l. c., pp. 136, 297). Augustine often repeats and varies this thought, and other Western writers reproduce it from him. "Felix culpa quæ tantum et talem meruit habere redemptorem." Lastly, Leo I. preaches (Serm. LXI. 3): "validius donum factum est libertatis, quam debitum servitutis." Sayings like these, apart from the special pleading in which Western writers have always delighted since Tertullian, are to be taken much more seriously than if they had come from the East. And in fact momentous speculations were certainly instituted by them.

against it; for they never were able to rise perfectly to the contemplation of Christ's work as the *assumptio carnis*, an expression of the loftiest piety among the Greeks. Those of the latter who, like the Antiochenes, either did not share or only imperfectly shared the realistic idea of redemption, referred, it is worth remarking, the work of Christ, like the Latins, to the human side of his personality. [1]

Great as are the distinctions here—the West did not possess in antiquity a definite dogmatic theory as to the atoning work of Christ. Greek views exerted their influence; [2] and, besides, Western Christians were not yet disposed, with a very few exceptions, to trouble themselves with thoughts that had no bearing on practical life.

[1] An affinity exists between the theology of the Antiochenes and Latins— esp. pre-Augustinian; but it is greater to a superficial than to a more exact observer. The Antiochene conception always had the Alexandrian for a foil; it never emancipated itself sufficiently from the latter to set up a perfectly compact counter-theology; it was in a sense Greek piety and Greek theology *watered down*. The Latins did not possess this foil. Their theology must not be gauged by Origen and Neoplatonism as if they furnished its starting-point.

[2] So from Hilary down to Augustine. The most important of the Western Fathers accepted the Greek idea of the purchase from the devil, although it flatly contradicted their own doctrine of the atonement; and this proves how uncertain they were. The grotesque conception of the role played by the devil at the death of Christ, had nevertheless something good about it. It reminded men that every knave is a stupid devil, and that the devil is always a stupid knave.

APPENDIX ON MANICHÆISM.

THREE great religious systems confronted each other in Western Asia and Southern Europe from the close of the third century: Neoplatonism, Catholicism and Manichæism. All three may be characterised as the final results of a history, lasting for more than a thousand years, of the religious development of the civilised peoples from Persia to Italy. In all three the old national and particular character of religions was laid aside; they were world-religions of the most universal tendency, and making demands which in their consequences transformed the whole of human life, public and private. For the national cultus they substituted a system which aspired to be theology, theory of the universe and science of history, and at the same time embraced a definite ethics, and a ritual of divine service. Formally, therefore, the three religions were alike, and they were also similar in that each had appropriated the elements of different older religions. Further, they showed their similarity in bringing to the front the ideas of revelation, redemption, ascetic virtue, and immortality. But Neoplatonism was natural religion spiritualised, the polytheism of Greece transfigured by Oriental influences and developed into pantheism. Catholicism was the monotheistic world-religion based on the O. T. and the Gospel, but constructed by the aid of Hellenic speculation and ethics. Manichæism was the dualistic world-religion resting on Chaldæism,[1] but interspersed with Christian, Parsi, and perhaps Buddhist thoughts. To Manichæism the Hellenic element was wanting, to Catholicism the Chaldee and Persian. These three world-religions

[1] See Brandt, Die mandäische Religion, 1889 (further, Wellhausen in the deutsch. Litt.-Ztg., 1890, No. 41).

developed in the course of two centuries (c. A.D. 50—250), Catholicism coming first and Manichæism last. Catholicism and Manichæism were superior to Neoplatonism for the very reason that the latter possessed no founder; it, therefore, developed no elemental force, and never lost the character of being an artificial creation. Attempts which were made to invent a founder for it naturally failed. But, even apart from the contents of its religion, Catholicism was superior to Manichæism, because its founder was venerated not merely as the bearer of revelation, but as the Redeemer in person and the Son of God. The fight waged by Catholicism with Neoplatonism had been already decided about the middle of the fourth century, although the latter continued to hold its ground in the Greek Empire for almost two centuries longer. As against Manichæism the Catholic Church was certain of victory from the beginning; for at the moment when Manichæism disputed its supremacy, it became the privileged State Church. But its opponent did not suffer itself to be annihilated; it lasted till far into the Middle Ages in East and West, though in various modifications and forms.

Authorities—(a) Oriental.

1. **Mohammedan.**—Among our sources for the history of Manichæism the Oriental are the most important; of these the Mohammedan, though comparatively late, are distinguished by the excellence of the tradition and their impartiality, and must be given the first place, since in them old Manichæan writings are employed, and we possess no other originals of this sort belonging to the third century, except a few short and rather unimportant fragments. At the head stands Abulfaragius, Fihrist (c. 980), see the edition by Flügel and the work of the latter: "Mani, seine Lehre und seine Schriften," 1862; further, Shahrastâni, Kitâb al-milal wan-nuhal (12th century), see edition by Cureton and German translation by Haarbrücker, 1851; some notes and extracts in Tabari (10th century), al-Birunî (11th century), Ibn al-Murtada (see Kessler, Mani, I., p. 346 ff.), and other Arabian and Persian historians.

2. **Christian.**—Of Eastern Christians we learn most from

Ephraem Syrus (+373) in various writings, and in a tractate on
the subject edited by Overbeck; from Esnîk, the Armenian (see
Zeitschr. f. d. hist. Theol., 1840, II.; Langlois, Collection, etc.,
II., p. 395 sq.), who wrote in the fifth century against Marcion
and Mani; and from the Alexandrian Patriarch Eutychius (+916)
who composed a chronicle (ed. by Pococke, 1628). Besides this,
separate pieces of information occur in Aphraates (4th century),
Barhebraeus (Arab. and Syr. 13th century) and others.

(b) Greek and Latin.

The earliest mention of the Manichæans in the Roman or
Greek empire occurs in an edict of Diocletian (see Hänel, Cod.
Gregor. tit. XV.), which is held by some not to be genuine,
and by others is dated A.D. 287, 290, 296, or 308 (so Mason,
The Persec. of Dioclet., p. 275 sq.). Eusebius gives a brief
account (H. E. VII. 31). The main authority, however, for
Greek and Roman writers was the Acta Archelai, which though
not what they pretended to be, namely, an account of a disputation between Mani and Bishop Archelaus of Cascar in
Mesopotamia, yet contain much that is reliable, esp. as to the
doctrine of Mani, and also embrace Manichæan fragments.
The Acts, which for the rest consist of various documents,
originated at the beginning of the fourth century (in Edessa?).
Jerome maintains (De vir. inl. 72) that they were originally
composed in Syria (so also Kessler); but Nöldeke (Ztschr. d.
deutsch. morgenl. Gesellsch. vol. 43, p. 537 ff.) and Rahlfs have
disproved Kessler's arguments (Gött. Gel. Anz., 1889, No. 23).
They have made it very probable that the Acts, while they may
have been based on Syrian sources, were originally written in
Greek. They were soon afterwards translated into Latin. We
only possess this version (Edited by Zacagni, 1698; Routh,
Reliq. S. Vol. V., 1848); of the Greek version small fragments
have been preserved (see on the Acta Archelai the discussions
by Zittwitz in the Zeitschr. f. die histor. Theol., 1873, and the
Dissertation by Oblasinski, Acta disp. Arch. et Manetis, 1874.
In the form in which we now have them, they are a compilation
largely edited on the pattern of the Clementine Homilies). The

Acta were made use of by Cyril of Jerusalem (Catech. VI.),
Epiphanius (Hær. 66) and very many others. All Greek and
Latin students of heresy have put the Manichæans in their
catalogues; but they only rarely give any original information
about them (see Theodoret Hær. fab. I. 26).

Important matter occurs in the decrees of Councils from the
fourth century (see Mansi, Acta Concil., and Hefele, Concilien-
geschichte, Vols. I.—III.), and in the controversial writings of
Titus of Bostra (4th century, in Syriac after a MS. of A.D. 411)
πρὸς Μανιχαίους (edit. by de Lagarde, 1859), and Alexander of
Lycopolis, Λόγος πρὸς τὰς Μανιχαίου δόξας (edit. by Combefis.).
Of Byzantines, John of Damascus (De hæres and Dial.) and
Photius (cod. 179 Biblioth.) deserve special mention; see also
the Manichæan form of oath in Tollii insignia itiner. ital. p.
126 sq., and in Cotelier, P. P. App. Opp. I. p. 543; further,
Rahlfs, l.c. The controversy with the Paulicians and Bogomilians,
who were frequently identified with the Manichæans, renewed
the interest in the latter. In the West the works of Augustine
are the great repository for our knowledge of the Manichæans :—
"Contra epistolam Manichæi, quam vocant fundamenti", "Contra
Faustum Manichæum", "Contra Fortunatum", "Contra Adim-
antum", "Contra Secundinum ", "De actis cum Felice Manichæo",
"De genesi c. Manichæos", "De natura boni", "De duabus anim-
abus", "De utilitate credendi", "De moribus eccl. Cathol. et
de moribus Manichæorum", "De vera religione", "De hæres."
But the more complete the view of Manichæism to be obtained
from these writings, the more cautious we must be in our
generalisations; for the Manichæism of the West undoubtedly
received Christian elements which were wanting in its original
and oriental form.

Mani's Life.

Mani (Μάνης; Manes, Μανιχαῖος, Manichæus—the name has
not yet been explained; it is not even known whether it is of
Persian or Semitic origin) is said, as the Acta Archelai inform
us, to have been originally called "Cubricus". Nothing reliable was ever known as to his life in the Romano-Greek

empire; for the account in the Acta Archelai is wholly biassed
and untrustworthy. Even if criticism succeeded in pointing out
the sources from which it was derived, in discovering the tendencies that were at work, and in thus sifting out portions that
were tenable, yet it could only do so by depending on the
comparatively trustworthy Oriental Mohammedan tradition. We
must therefore examine the latter alone. According to it, Mani
was a Persian of distinguished birth belonging to Mardin. The
date of his birth is uncertain; Kessler holds the statement in
Bîrunî to be reliable, that he was born in anno 527 of the era
of the Babylonian astronomers, *i.e.*, A.D. 215—216. He received a careful education from his father Fâtàk (Πατέκιος) at
Ctesiphon. Since the father afterwards adhered to the confession
of the "Moghtasilah", the Baptists, in southern Babylonia, the
son was also brought up in their religious doctrines and practices. The Baptists (see the Fihrist) were probably not uncon-
nected with the Elkesaites and Hemerobaptists, and were in
any case allied to the Mandæans. It is not improbable that
this Babylonian sect had adopted Christian elements. The boy
accordingly became early acquainted with very different forms
of religion. If even a small proportion of the narratives about
his father rest on truth—the greater number being certainly
only Manichæan legends—he had already introduced his son
into the religious medley, out of which the Manichæan system
arose. Manichæan tradition tells us that Mani received revelations, and took up a critical attitude towards religious instruction, even when a boy. But it is all the less trustworthy, as it
also relates that he was forbidden to ventilate publicly his new
religious knowledge. It was only when he was from 25 to 30
years of age that he began to preach his new religion at the
court of the Persian king, Sapores I.—on the day, it is stated,
of the king's coronation, A.D. 241—242. A Persian tradition
says that he was previously a Christian presbyter, but this, in
any case, is wrong. Mani did not remain long in Persia, but
undertook long journeys for the purpose of spreading his religion,
and he also sent out disciples. According to the Acta Archelai,
his missionary activity extended into the West, into the territory of the Christian Church; but it is certain from Oriental

sources that his work was rather carried on in Transoxania, Western China, and southwards into India. His labours met with success there as well as in Persia. Like Mohammed after him, and the founder of the Elkesaites before him, he proclaimed himself the last and greatest of the prophets, whose revelation of God surpassed all that had been given till then, the latter being allowed only a relative value. He instituted the absolute religion. In the last years of the reign of Sapores I. (c. A.D. 270) Mani returned to the Persian capital, and gained adherents even at the court. Naturally, however, the ruling priestly caste of the Magi, on whom the king was compelled to lean, were hostile to him, and after a few successes Mani was taken prisoner and driven into exile. The successor of Sapores, Hormuz (272—273), seems to have been favourable to him, but Bahrâm I. abandoned him to the fanaticism of the Magi, and had him crucified at the capital, A.D. 276—277. His dead body was skinned; and his adherents were dreadfully persecuted by Bahrâm.

Mani's Writings.

Mani himself composed very many writings and epistles, of which a large proportion were still known to the Mohammedan historians, but which are now all lost. The later heads of the Manichæan Churches also wrote religious tractates, so that the ancient Manichæan literature must have been very extensive. According to the Fihrist, Mani made use of the Persian and Syriac languages; he invented, however, like the Oriental Marcionites before him, an alphabet of his own which the Fihrist has transmitted to us. In this alphabet the sacred works of the Manichæans were afterwards written. The Fihrist enumerates seven principal works by Mani, six in Syriac and one in Persian; as to some of them we possess statements also in Titus of Bostra, Epiphanius, Augustine, and Photius, as well as in the oath-formula and the Acta Archelai. We have (1) The Book of mysteries: see Acta Archelai; it contained discussions with the Christian sects which were spreading in the East, especially the Marcionites and Bardesanians, as well as with

their conception of the Old and New Testaments. (2) The
Book of Giants (demons? probably in connection with Gen. VI.).
(3) The Book of Regulations for the hearers,—apparently identical with the "epistula fundamenti" of Augustine and the
"Book of the Chapters" of Epiphanius and the Acta Archelai.
It was the most extensively circulated and popular of Manichæan works, and was also translated into Greek and Latin—
being a brief summary of the whole fundamentally authoritative
doctrine. (4) The Book Schâhpûrakân. Flügel was unable to
explain this title; according to Kessler, it means "Epistle to
King Sapores". This tractate contained eschatological teaching.
(5) The Book of quickening. It is identified by Kessler with
the "Thesaurus (vitæ)" of the Acta Archelai, Epiphanius, Photius, and Augustine; in that case it was also in use among the
Latin Manichæans. (6) The Book πραγματεία—contents unknown. (7)—In the Persian language; a book whose title is not
stated in the Fihrist, as we have it, but which is probably
identical with the "Holy Gospel" of the Manichæans; see the
Acta Archelai and many witnesses. This was the work set up
by the Manichæans in opposition to the Gospels of the Church.
Besides these main works, Mani wrote a great number of shorter
tractates and letters. The epistolography was then established
by his successors. These Manichæan treatises were also familiar
in the Græco-Roman empire and existed in collections—see the
βιβλίον ἐπιστολῶν in the oath-formula; and an "epistula ad virginem Menoch" in Augustine. Fabricius has collected the Greek
fragments of Manichæan epistles in the Bibliotheca Græca VII. 2,
p. 311 sq. There also existed a Manichæan Book of "memoirs"
and one of "prayers" in the Greek language, as well as many
others (e.g., the "Canticum Amatorium" cited by Augustine),
all of which, however, were destroyed by Christian Bishops in
alliance with the magistracy. A Manichæan Epistle to one
Marcellus has been preserved to us in the Acta Archelai. Zittwitz supposes that this letter was much fuller in its original
form, and that the author of the Acts has borrowed from it
the material .for the speeches which he makes Mani deliver in
the discussion. The same scholar refers the account of Turbo
in the Acts and their historical statements (in section 4) to the

writing of a Turbo of Mesopotamia, a Manichæan renegade and Christian. But on this point it is at least possible to hold a different opinion.

Mani's Doctrine.   The Manichæan System.

Clearly as the main features of the Manichæan doctrine can be presented even at the present day, and certain as it is that Mani himself published a complete system, yet many details are uncertain, being differently described in different places, and it often remains doubtful what the original doctrinal view of the founder was.

The Manichæan system of religion was a consistent and uncompromising dualism, in the form of a fanciful view of nature. No distinction was drawn between the physical and ethical: in this respect the character of the system was thoroughly materialistic; for Mani's identification of the good with light, and the bad with darkness, was not merely figurative. The light was really the only good, and darkness the only bad. Hence it followed, that religious knowledge could be nothing but the knowledge of nature and its elements, and that redemption consisted exclusively in a physical deliverance of the fractions of light from darkness. But under such circumstances, ethics became a doctrine of abstinence from all elements arising from the realm of darkness.

The self-contradictory character of the present world formed for Mani the starting-point of his speculation. But the inconsistency appeared to him to be primarily elemental, and only secondarily ethical, in so far as he regarded the material side of man as an emanation from the bad parts of nature. From the self-contradictory character of the world he inferred two beings, originally wholly separate from each other,—light and darkness. Both were, however, to be thought of after the analogy of a kingdom. The light appeared as the good Primeval Spirit—God, shining in the ten (twelve) virtues of love, faith, fidelity, magnanimity, wisdom, gentleness, knowledge, intelligence, mystery, and insight. It also manifested itself in the heaven and earth of light with their guardians, the

glorious Æons. The darkness, similarly, was a spiritual realm:
more correctly, it was represented in a spiritual, or feminine,
personification; but it had no "God" at its head. It embraced
an "earth of darkness". As the earth of light had five distinguishing features—the gentle breeze, cooling wind, bright
light, cheering fire, and clear water—so also the earth of
darkness had five—fog, fiery heat, burning wind, darkness, and
damp. Satan with his demons was born from the realm of
darkness. From eternity the two realms stood opposed. They
came into contact on one side, but they did not mingle. Then
Satan began to storm, and made an attack on the realm, the
earth, of light. The God of light, with his Syzygos (mate) "the
spirit of his right hand", now generated the Primeval man, and
sent him, equipped with the five pure elements, to fight against
Satan. But Satan proved himself the stronger. Primeval man
was defeated for a moment. Now indeed the God of light
himself marched forth, utterly defeated Satan by the help of
new Æons—the spirit of life, etc.—and delivered the Primeval
man. But a part of the light of the latter had already been
robbed by darkness, the five dark elements had already mingled with the generations of light. The Primeval man could
only descend into the abyss and hinder the increase of the
dark "generations" by cutting off their roots; but the elements
once mixed he could never again separate. The mixed elements
were the elements of the present visible world. This was
fashioned out of them at the command of the God of light;
the formation of the world was itself the first step in the
redemption of the imprisoned portions of light. The world
itself was represented as an ordered chain of different heavens
and different earths, which was borne and supported by the
Æons, the angels of light. In sun and moon, which from their
nature were almost wholly pure, it possessed great reservoirs,
in which the rescued portions of light were stored. In the sun
Primeval man himself dwelt along with the holy spirits, who
pursued the work of redemption; in the moon the Mother of
life was throned. The twelve signs of the zodiac constituted
an artificial machine, a great wheel with buckets which poured
the portions of light delivered from the world into the moon

and sun, the illuminating vessels swimming in space. There they were purified anew, and finally reached God himself in the realm of pure light. The later Manichæans of the West designated the portions of light scattered in the world—in elements and organisms—and waiting for redemption, "Jesus patibilis."

Now it is characteristic of the materialistic and unhuman character of the system, that while the construction of the world is regarded as the work of the good spirits, the creation of man is referred to the princes of darkness. The first man, Adam, was begotten by Satan in conjunction with "sin," "greed" and "lust." But the spirit of darkness conjured into him all the portions of light which he had robbed, in order to make more certain of his power to rule over them. Adam was accordingly a divided being, created in the image of Satan, but bearing the stronger spark of light within him. Eve was associated with him by Satan. She was seductive sensuousness, although even she had a tiny spark of light in her. If the first human beings thus stood under the rule of Satan, yet from the very first the glorious spirits took an interest in them. These sent Æons—e.g., Jesus— down to them, who instructed them as to their nature, and warned Adam especially against the senses. But the first man fell a victim to sexual lust. Cain and Abel, indeed, were not sons of Adam, but of Satan and Eve ; but Seth was the light-possessed offspring of Adam and Eve. Thus arôse mankind, among whose individual members light was very variously distributed. It was always stronger, however, in men than women. Now the demons sought in the course of history to bind men to themselves through sensuality, error, and false religions, which included above all the religion of Moses and the prophets, while the spirits of light continued their process of distillation, in order to obtain the pure light in the world. But they could only deliver men by giving the true Gnosis as to nature and its powers, and by recalling them from the service of darkness and sensuousness. For this purpose prophets, preachers of the true knowledge, were sent into the world. Mani himself appears, in accordance with the example set by Gnostic Jewish Christians, to have held Adam, Noah, and Abraham, and perhaps Zoroaster

and Buddha to have been such prophets. Probably Jesus was
also considered by him to have been a prophet come down
from the world of light; not, however, the historical Jesus, but
a contemporary, seemingly human, Jesus who neither suffered
nor died (Jesus impatibilis). Some Manichæans taught that Primeval
man himself, as Christ, spread the true Gnosis. But in any case
Mani was held, as he claimed, to be the last and greatest prophet, having taken up the work of "Jesus impatibilis," and of Paul,
who is also recognised, and having been the first to bring
complete knowledge. He was the "guide," the "ambassador of
the light," the "Paraclete." Only by his labours and those of
his "imitators, the Elect," was the separation of light from
darkness accomplished. The process by which the unfettered
parts of light finally ascend to the God of light himself are
very fancifully elaborated. He who has not succeeded in becoming
elect in his life-time, has not completely redeemed himself, has
to pass through severe purifications in the future state, until he
also is gathered to the blessedness of the light. A doctrine of
transmigration of souls has, however, been erroneously imputed
to the Manichæans. Bodies fall naturally, like the souls of un-
redeemed men, to the powers of darkness. But those souls,
according at least to the oldest conception, contain no light at
all; a later view, adapted to the Christian, taught that the parts
of light existing in them were really lost. Finally, when the
elements of light are delivered—completely, or as far as possible—
the end of the world takes place. All glorious spirits assemble,
the God of light himself appears, accompanied by the Æons
and the perfectly righteous. The angels who uphold the world
withdraw from their burden, and everything collapses. An
enormous conflagration destroys the world: once more the two
powers are completely severed: high above is the realm of light
restored to its perfect state, low down is the darkness (now
powerless?).

Ethics, Social Constitution and Cultus of the Manichæans.

The only possible ethics based on this doctrine of the world
were dualistic and ascetic. But as it was not only considered

necessary to escape from darkness, but also to cherish, strengthen, and purify the parts of light, the ethics were not merely negative. They aimed not at suicide, but at preservation. Yet in practice they assumed a thoroughly ascetic form. The Manichæan had to abstain above all from sensuous enjoyment. He was to deny himself to it by means of three seals: the *signaculum oris, manus, and sinus* (the seal of the mouth, hand, and breast). The *signaculum oris* forbade any use of unclean food, as well as impure talk; unclean were all animal flesh, wine etc.; vegetable food was permitted, because plants contained more light; but the destruction of plants, even the plucking of fruits or breaking of twigs, was not allowed. The *sign. manus* prevented any occupation with things, in so far as they contained elements of darkness. Finally, the *sign. sinus* forbade especially any satisfaction of sexual desire, and therefore prohibited marriage. Besides, life was regulated by an extremely rigorous list of fasts. Fast-days were selected in obedience to certain astronomical conjunctures. Moreover, men fasted, *i.e.*, held holiday, regularly on Sunday, and generally also on Monday. The number of fast-days amounted almost to a quarter of the year. Times of prayer were appointed just as exactly. Four times a day had the Manichæan to utter prayers; and these were preceded by ablutions. He who prayed turned to the sun or moon, or to the North as the seat of light. Yet the inference that the Manichæans worshipped the sun and moon themselves is wrong. The Fihrist has preserved some Manichæan forms of prayèr. They were directed to the God of light, the whole realm of light, the glorious angels and Mani himself, who is addressed in them as "the great tree in whom is all healing." According to Kessler, these prayers are closely allied to the Mandæan and ancient Babylonian hymns.

An asceticism so minute and strict as that demanded by Manichæism,[1] could only be practised thoroughly by a few. The religion would, therefore, have been compelled to forego an extensive propaganda, had it not conceded a morality of two kinds. A distinction was accordingly drawn within the

---

[1] It also professed imitation of the apostolic life; see Raumer's note on Confess. Aug. VI. 7 (12).

community between the "Electi" (perfecti), the perfect Manichæans, and the Catechumeni (auditores), the secular Manichæans. Only the former submitted to all the demands imposed
by the religion; for the latter the regulations were relaxed.
They required to avoid idolatry, witchcraft, greed, lying,
fornication, etc.; above all, they must kill no living creature—
keeping Mani's ten commandments. They were to renounce
the world as far as possible; but they lived in fact very much
like their fellow-citizens of other faiths. We have here,
accordingly, substantially the same state of matters as in the
Catholic Church, where a twofold morality also prevailed, viz.,
that of the religious orders and of the secular Christians. The
only difference was that the position of the Electi was still
more distinguished than that of the monks. For the Christian
monks never wholly forgot that redemption was a gift of God
through Christ, while the Manichæan Electi were really themselves redeemers; therefore it was the duty of the Auditores to
pay the deepest veneration and render the greatest services to
the Electi. These perfect beings, as they languished away in
their asceticism, were admired and cherished most devotedly.
Analogous is the reverence paid by Catholics to the saints,
and by Neoplatonists to the "philosophers," but the prestige
of the Manichæan Electi surpassed that of both. Foods were
brought to them in abundance; by using them the Electi
delivered the parts of light from the plants. They prayed for
the Auditores, they blessed and interceded for them, thereby
abbreviating the purgatory through which the latter had to
pass after death. And the Electi alone possessed complete
knowledge of religious truths—it was otherwise in Catholicism.

The distinction between Electi and Auditores did not, however, constitute the whole idea of the Manichæan Church; it
possessed a hierarchy also. This fell into three grades, so that
altogether there were five in the religious constitution. In its
fivefold division the social order was conceived to be a copy
of the numbers of the realm of light. At the head stood the
Teachers ("the sons of gentleness" = Mani and his successors);
these were followed by the Administrators (" sons of knowledge "
= the Bishops); then the Elders (" sons of understanding " = the

presbyters); the Electi ("sons of mystery"); and finally the
Auditores ("sons of insight"). The number of Electi was at all
times small. According to Augustine, there were twelve Teachers
and seventy-two Bishops. One of the Teachers appears to have
stood as president at the head of the whole Manichæan Church.
At least Augustine speaks of such an one, and the Fihrist also
knows of a supreme head over all Manichæans. The constitution
accordingly had here also a monarchical head.

The cultus of the Manichæans must have been very simple,
and have consisted essentially of prayers, hymns, and ceremonies
of adoration. This simple divine service promoted the secret spread
of the doctrine. Besides, the Manichæans seem, at least in the
West, to have adhered to the Church's order of festivals. The
Electi celebrated special festivals; but the chief one common to
all was the "Bema" (Βῆμα), the festival of the "doctoral chair,"
in memory of the death of Mani, in the month of March. Believers prostrated themselves before a decorated, but vacant
chair, erected on a pedestal with five steps. Long fasts accompanied the festival. Christian and Mohammedan writers were able
to learn little concerning the mysteries and "sacraments" of the
Manichæans; the Christians therefore raised the charge that
obscene rites and repulsive practices were observed. But it may
be held certain that the later Manichæan mysteries were solem-
nised after the style of Christian Baptism and the Lord's Supper.
They may have been based on old rites and ceremonies instituted
by Mani himself, and descended from natural religion.

The Historical Position of Manichæism.

In the present state of the inquiry it is made out, and the
account given above will also have shown, that Manichæism did
not rise on the soil of Christianity. We would even be better
justified if we were to call Mohammedanism a Christian sect;
for Mohammed approaches the Jewish and Christian religions
incomparably more closely than Mani. Kessler has the credit of
having shown that the ancient Babylonian religion, the original
source of all the Gnosis of Western Asia, was the foundation
of the Manichæan system. The opinion formerly held is accord-

ingly wrong, viz., that Manichæism was a reformation on the ground of Parsiism, a modification of Zoroastrianism under the influence of Christianity. It was rather a religious creation *belonging to the circle of Semitic religions:* it was the Semitic nature-religion lifted out of national limitations, modified by Christian and Persian elements, raised to the level of Gnosis, and transforming human life by strict rules. But when we have perceived this, we have only obtained a very general explanation of the origin of Manichæism. The question rises, through what means and to what extent Mani adopted Persian and Christian elements, and further, in which form the nature-religion of ancient Babylonia was made use of by him.

Now as regards the latter point, it is well known that the Semitic nature-religions had been taken up, centuries before Mani, by isolated enthusiastic or speculative heads, had been philosophically deepened and remodelled into "systems", in support of which missions were conducted by means of mysterious cults. Mani's enterprise was accordingly nothing new, but was rather the last in a long series of similar attempts. Even the earlier ones, from Simon Magus the Samaritan down, had adopted Christian elements to a greater or less extent, and the Christian Gnostic scholastic sects of Syria and Western Asia all pointed back to ancient Semitic nature-religions, which were transformed by them into a philosophy of the world and of life. But in particular the doctrines of the Babylonian sect of Moghtasilah, which were indeed influenced also by Christianity, seem to have afforded Mani material for his religio-philosophical speculation. The religion of this sect was not, however, purely Semitic (see the treatise by Kessler on the Mandæans in the Real-Encyklopædia für prot. Theol. u. Kirche, 2 Ed., Vol. IX., p. 205 ff.; the Mandæans were allied to the Moghtasilah, Brandt, l. c.). From this source sprang the rigid dualism on which Mani's system was based; for the ancient Persian religion was not in principle dualistic, but in its ultimate foundation Monistic, since Ahriman was created by Ormuzd. However, ancient Persian theologoumena were employed by Mani. Even the designation of the antitheses as "light" and "darkness" was hardly independent of Parsiism, and elsewhere in Manichæism there occur

technical terms taken from the Persian religion. Whether Mani's
idea of redemption goes back to the ancient Babylonian religion
or to Zoroastrianism, I do not venture to decide; the idea of
the "Prophet" and the "Primeval man" is at all events Semitic.

It is very difficult to determine how far Mani's acquaintance
with Christianity went, and how much he borrowed from it;
further, through what agencies Christian knowledge reached
him. In any case, in those regions where Manichæism was settled and where it came more closely into contact with Christianity, it was at a later stage influenced by the latter. Western
Manichæans of the fourth and fifth centuries were much more
"Christian" than those of the East. In this respect the system
passed through the same development as Neoplatonism. As
regards Mani himself, it is safest to suppose that he held Judaism as well as Christianity to be entirely false religions. But
if he not only characterised himself as the Paraclete—and it is
probable that he originated this use of the title—but also admitted "Jesus" to so high a role in his system, we can hardly
explain this otherwise than by supposing that he distinguished
between Christianity and Christianity. The religion which eman-
ated from the historical Christ was to him as objectionable as
that Christ himself and as Judaism; *i.e.*, Catholicism was to him
a diabolical religion. But he distinguished the Jesus of darkness from the Jesus of light, who wrought contemporaneously
with the other, This distinction agrees as strikingly with that
of the Gnostic Basilides, as the criticism of the O. T. conducted
by Manichæism with that of the Marcionites; (see even the Acta
Archelai in which Marcion's antitheses are placed in Mani's
lips). Finally, Manichæan doctrines show agreement with those
of the Christian Elkesaites; yet it is possible, nay, probable,
that the latter are to be derived from the common ancient
Semitic source, and therefore they do not come further into
consideration. Mani's historical relation to Christianity will
therefore be as follows: from Catholicism, with which in all
probability he was not very accurately acquainted, Mani borrowed
nothing, rejecting it rather as a devilish error. On the other
hand, he regarded Christianity in the form which it had assumed
in the Basilidian and Marcionite sects (also among the Barde-

sanians?) as a relatively valuable and correct religion. But from them, as also from the Persians, he took hardly anything but names, and perhaps, besides, what criticism he had of the O. T. and Judaism. His lofty estimate of Paul (and his epistles?), as well as his express rejection of the Acts of the Apostles, also point to influences due to Marcionitism. He seems to have recognised and to have interpreted in accordance with his own teaching a part of the historical matter of the Gospel.

Finally, the question further rises whether Buddhistic elements are not to be observed in Manichæism. The majority of later scholars since F. Chr. Baur have answered this question in the affirmative. According to Kessler, Mani used Buddha's teaching, at least for his ethics. There is no doubt that he took long journeys to India, and was familiar with Buddhism. The occurrence of the name of Buddha (Budda) in the legend about Mani and perhaps in his own writings points to the fact that the founder of this religion concerned himself with Buddhism. But what he borrowed from it for his own doctrine must have been very unimportant. On a closer comparison we find that the difference between the two faiths is in all their main doctrines very great, and that the resemblances are almost always merely accidental. This is true even as regards morality and asceticism. There is no point in Manichæism for whose explanation we need have recourse to Buddhism. Under such circumstances any relationship between the two religions remains a bare possibility; nor has the investigation of Geyler raised this possibility to a probability (Das System des Manichäismus und sein Verhältniss zum Buddhismus, Jena 1875).

How are we to explain the fact that Manichæism spread so rapidly and really became a world-religion? The answer has been given that it was because it was the complete Gnosis, the fullest, most consistent, and most artistic system based on the ancient Babylonian religion (so Kessler). This explanation is not sufficient, for no religion makes an impression mainly by its doctrinal system, however complete that may be. But it is also incorrect, for the older Gnostic systems were not more meagre than the Manichæan. What rather gave Manichæism its strength was, above all, *the combination of ancient mythology and a rigid materialistic dualism with an extremely simple, spiritual cultus, and a strict morality;* this was supplemented by the personality of the founder (of which indeed we know little enough). If we compare it with the Semitic nature-religions, it is obvious that it retained their mythologies, transformed into "doctrines," but did away with the whole sensuous cultus, substituting a spiritual worship as well as a strict morality. Thus it was capable of satisfying the new wants of an old world. It offered revelation, redemption, moral virtue, and immortality, spiritual blessings, on the ground of nature-religion. Further, the simple and yet firm constitution calls for attention which Mani himself gave to his institution. The learned and the ignorant, the enthusiast and the man of the world, could here find a welcome, no one had more laid upon him than he could and would bear; moreover, each was attracted and secured by the prospect of reaching a higher stage, while those who were gifted were besides promised that they would require to submit to no authority, but would be led by pure reason to God. As this religion was thus adapted, perhaps beforehand, to individual needs, it was also capable of continuously appropriating what was foreign. Furnished from the first with fragments of different religions, it could increase or diminish its store, without breaking its own elastic structure. But a great capacity for adaptation was quite as necessary to a world-religion, as a divine founder in whom men could see and venerate the supreme revelation of God himself. While Manichæism in fact knew of no redeemer, although it gave Mani this title; while it only recognised a physical and Gnostic process of redemption; yet in Mani it possessed the chief prophet of God.

If we notice, finally, that Manichæism presented a simple, apparently profound, and yet easy, solution of the problem of good and evil, which had become especially burdensome in the second and third centuries, we have named the most important phenomena which explain its rapid extension.

Sketch of the History of Manichæism.

Manichæism first got a firm footing in the East, in Persia, Mesopotamia, and Transoxania. The persecutions which it had to endure did not hinder its extension. The seat of the Manichæan Pope was for centuries in Babylon, and afterwards in Samarcand. Even after Islam had conquered the East, Manichæism held its ground; it even seems to have spread still further owing to the Mohammedan conquest, and it gained secret adherents among the Mohammedans themselves. The doctrine and discipline of the Manichæan Church underwent little change in the East, it especially did not there approach much nearer the Christian religion. But it experienced attempts at reform several times; for, as was natural, its "Auditores" readily became secularised. These attempts also led temporarily to schisms and the formation of sects. At the close of the tenth century, the time when the Fihrist was written, the Manichæans had been already expelled from the cities in Mesopotamia and Persia, and had withdrawn into the villages. But in Turkestan and up to the borders of China, there existed numerous Manichæan communities, nay, even whole tribes which had adopted the religion of Mani. Probably the great Mongolian migrations first put an end to Manichæism in Central Asia. But in India, on the coasts of Malabar, there were Manichæans even in the fifteenth century, side by side with Thomist Christians (see Germann, Die Thomaschristen, 1875). Manichæism first penetrated into the Græco-Roman Empire about A.D. 280, in the time of the Emperor Probus (see Eusebius. Chronicon). If we may hold Diocletian's edict against the Manichæans to be genuine, they already had a firm footing in the West at the beginning of the fourth century; but Eusebius did not know the sect accurately as late as about A.D. 325. It was only after about A.D. 330 that the religion spread rapidly in the Roman Empire. Its adherents were recruited, on the one hand, from the ancient Gnostic sects, especially the Marcionites, Manichæism having, besides, strongly influenced the development of the Marcionite Churches in the fourth century. On the other hand, it gained followers from the great number of the "cultured", who sought for a "rational" and yet to some extent Christian, religion, and who had exalted "free inquiry"— esp. as regards the O. T.—into a battle-flag. Criticism on Catholicism, and polemics, were now the strong point of Manichæism, esp. in the West. It admitted the stumbling-blocks which the O. T.

presented to every thinker, and gave itself out as a Christianity without the O. T. Instead of the subtle Catholic theories about divine predestination and human freedom, and the difficult Theodicy, it offered an extremely simple conception of sin and goodness. It did not preach the doctrine of the incarnation, which was particularly repugnant to those who were passing from the ancient cults to the Universal Religion. In its rejection of this doctrine, it coincided with Neoplatonism. But while the latter, with all its attempts to accommodate itself at various points to Christianity, found no formula that would introduce into its midst the special veneration of Christ, the Western Manichæans succeeded in giving their doctrine a Christian colouring. Of the Manichæan mythology all that became popular was the rigid physical dualism; its barbarous portions were prudently disguised as "mysteries"; nay, they were even frankly disavowed here and there by the adepts. The farther Manichæism pushed into the West, the more Christian and philosophical it became; in Syria it kept itself comparatively pure. It found its most numerous adherents in North Africa, where it had secret followers even among the clergy; this may perhaps be explained by the Semitic origin of a part of the population. Augustine was an "Auditor" for nine years, while Faustus was at the time the most distinguished Manichæan teacher in the West. In his later writings against Manichæism Augustine chiefly discusses the following problems: (1) the relations of knowledge and faith, reason and authority; (2) the nature of good and evil, and the origin of the latter; (3) the existence of free-will, and its relation to divine omnipotence; (4) the relation of evil in the world to the divine government.

The Christian Byzantine and Roman Emperors from Valens onwards issued strict laws against the Manichæans. But at first these bore little fruit. The "Auditores" were difficult to detect, and really gave slight occasion for a persecution. In Rome itself the doctrine had a large following, especially among the scholars and professors, between A.D. 370 and 440, and it made its way among the mass of the people by means of a popular literature, in which even the Apostles played a prominent part ("Apocryphal Acts of the Apostles"). Manichæism also experienced attempts at reform in the West; but we know little about them. Leo the Great, in alliance with the civil power, was the first to adopt active measures against Manichæism. Valentinian III. sentenced its adherents to banishment, Justinian made the penalty death. It seems to have been extinguished in North Africa by the persecution of the Vandals. It really died out nowhere else, either in the Byzantine Empire, or in the West; for it gave an impulse to the formation of new sects which were allied to it in the early part of the Middle Ages. If it has not been proved that the Spanish Priscillians had been already influenced by Manichæism in the fourth century, still it is undoubted that the Paulicians and Bogomilians, as well as the Cathari, are to be traced back to it (and Marcionitism). Thus, if not the system of Mani the Persian, yet Manichæism modified by Christianity accompanied the Catholic Church of the West on into the thirteenth century.

Literature.—Beausobre, Hist. critique de Manichée et du Manichéisme, 2 vols. 1734 sq. Too great prominence is given in this work to the Christian elements in Manichæism. Baur, Das manichäische Religionssystem, 1831. Manichæan speculation is here presented speculatively. Flügel, Mani, 1862; an investigation based on the Fihrist. Kessler, Unters. z. Genesis des manich. Religionssystems, 1876; by the same author, "Mani, Manichäer" in the R.-Encykl. f. protest Theol. u. Kirche, 2 Ed., Vol. IX., p. 223—259; the account given above is based in several of its expositions on this article. Kessler has since published a work, "Mani, Forschungen über die manich. Relig. Ein Beitrag z. vergleichenden Religionsgeschichte des Orients. I. Bd. Voruntersuchungen und Quellen, 1889;" see on this the acute reviews of Rahlfs (Gött Gel. Anz. 1889, No. 23), Nöldeke (Zeitschrift d. deutschen morgenl. Gesellsch. Vol. XLIII., p. 535 ff.) and August Müller (Theol. Lit.-Ztg., 1890, No. 4). The older accounts may be mentioned of Mosheim, Lardner, Walch, and Schröckh, as also the monograph of Trechsel, Ueber Kanon, Kritik und Exegese der Manichäer, 1832, and A. Newmann's Introductory Essay on the Manichæan heresy, 1887.

Date Due

JAN 1 1 '63			
GB	PRINTED IN U. S. A.		